PILGRIMAGE IN THE MIDDLE

CW00343323

READINGS IN MEDIEVAL CIVILIZATIONS AND CULTURES: XVI
series editor: Paul Edward Dutton

PILGRIMAGE IN THE MIDDLE AGES

A READER

edited by

BRETT EDWARD WHALEN

UNIVERSITY OF TORONTO PRESS

www.utphighereducation.com

LIBRARY AND ARCHIVES CANADA CATALOGUING IN PUBLICATION

Pilgrimage in the Middle Ages : a reader / edited by Brett Edward Whalen.
(Readings in medieval civilizations and cultures ; 16) Includes bibliographical references and index.
Issued also in electronic formats.
ISBN 978-1-4426-0199-4

   1. Christian pilgrims and pilgrimages – History – To 1500—Sources.
2. Christian life – History – To 1500 – Sources. 3. Pilgrims and pilgrimages – History – To 1500 – Sources. 4. Travel, Medieval—Sources. I. Whalen, Brett Edward II. Series: Readings in medieval civilizations and cultures ; 16

BX2323.P55 2011   263'.0410902   C2011-905078-1

We welcome comments and suggestions regarding any aspect of our publications – please feel free to contact us at news@utphighereducation.com or visit our Internet site at www.utphighereducation.com.

North America
5201 Dufferin Street
Toronto, Ontario, Canada, M3H 5T8

2250 Military Road
Tonawanda, New York, USA, 14150

ORDERS PHONE: 1-800-565-9523
ORDERS FAX: 1-800-221-9985
ORDERS EMAIL: utpbooks@utpress.utoronto.ca

UK, Ireland, and continental Europe
NBN International
Estover Road, Plymouth, PL6 7PY, UK

TEL: 44 (0) 1752 202301
FAX ORDER LINE: 44 (0) 1752 202333
enquiries@nbninternational.com

The University of Toronto Press acknowledges the financial support for its publishing activities of the Government of Canada through the Book Publishing Industry Development Program (BPIDP).

Book design and composition by George Kirkpatrick.
Printed in Canada

For Alfred J. Andrea,

Who first led me ad fontes

PILGRIMAGE IN THE MIDDLE AGES

CONTENTS

ACKNOWLEDGMENTS

This reader would not have happened without Paul Edward Dutton, who convinced me to tackle the project, encouraging and assisting me in his capacity as series editor. He also read and generously commented upon a complete draft of the entire volume. I would also like to thank for their assistance Matthew Gabrielle, Ahmed El Shamsy, Jaroslav Eolda and Brad Gregory, along with Jon Powell and Michael Bazemore. Whatever shortcomings remain are entirely my own. In addition, my thanks go to the Andrew W. Mellon Foundation and the Medieval and Early Modern Studies (MEMS) program at the University of North Carolina, Chapel Hill, for funding that enabled me to make my own "intellectual pilgrimage" to Jerusalem in the spring of 2010. This volume is dedicated to Alfred J. Andrea, a mentor and friend, who first introduced me to the historian's craft of reading and analyzing primary sources. As always, last but not least, I offer personal thanks to my wife, Malissa, my fellow traveler on this pilgrimage we call life.

INTRODUCTION

The pilgrim – an earthly traveler seeking a sacred destination and, through that journey, an experience of the divine – stands among the most captivating and popular images of the Middle Ages. This Reader offers students an opportunity to take a journey of their own across approximately fifteen centuries of history organized around the theme of pilgrimage, defined in the widest possible sense as any sort of travel, both local and long-distance, made at least in part for the purpose of religious devotion. Although some space is devoted to non-Christian sources, the central focus of this collection remains Christian pilgrimage in medieval Europe. Pilgrimage, of course, does not represent an exclusively Christian, medieval, or European phenomenon. Nevertheless, for scholars and students of the Middle Ages, the topic of devotional travel forms part of a common instructional narrative that runs from the origins and spread of Christianity to the emergence of a relatively homogenous European society, characterized by Christian beliefs, practices, and institutions that endured until the Protestant Reformation of the sixteenth century.

To a certain extent, the topic of medieval Christian pilgrimage involves the historian in the study of places and people. Jerusalem stands among the most famous of such places, part of a land promised by God to Abraham and his descendants (a promise that the earliest Christians appropriated) and sanctified by Christ's blood. Starting in the fourth century, with the conversion of the Roman emperor Constantine to Christianity, a highly visible landscape of churches and other devotional sites emerged to form an unrivaled source of spiritual appeal for Christian believers around the Roman Empire and beyond. From beginning to end, this Reader tracks the centrality of Jerusalem for the development of Christian pilgrimage, part of an ongoing claim by the followers of Christ to the very same "Promised Land" venerated first by Jews and later by Muslims. In this regard, Christian attitudes toward and travel to Jerusalem form one strand in our broader understanding of the historical relationship between Christianity, Judaism, and Islam – a relationship that, where the possession of Jerusalem was concerned, could sometimes lead to the shedding of blood in God's name.

Incomparable in its spiritual appeal, Jerusalem did not represent the only major pilgrimage attraction of the Middle Ages. Sometimes in conjunction with their journey to the Holy Land, Christian pilgrims also sought out the shrines and churches of Constantinople – since the fourth century, the capital of the Roman Empire and the location of numerous sacred relics – and of Rome, the former imperial capital, whose bishops – the popes of Rome – claimed a special place of pastoral authority over Christians everywhere. Over the course of the period covered by this Reader, a number of pilgrimage sites developed into regional or pan-European destinations of devotional travel, including the church of St. James of Compostela in Spain, and Canterbury Cathedral in England. Alongside such notable attractions for the pious (or not so pious) pilgrim, medieval Europe witnessed the growth of innumerable local shrines, accessible by a short journey for those who lived close at hand and by long-distance travelers who made their way along the network of pilgrimage routes that crisscrossed the continent. For many Christians, such humbler pilgrimages meant just as much, if not more, to their faith than did the possibility of longer, more audacious (but more infrequent) journeys to far-off places such as Jerusalem or Constantinople.

As for the people, historians and students will meet pilgrims, men and women who left their homes and routines to seek out God's grace as mediated through their "liminal" experience of travel, an intermediary or transitional time outside the strictures and norms of daily life. For most pilgrims, this physical journey represented a finite circuit to and from their sacred destination, thereby fulfilling a vow taken to perform their pilgrimage. During much of the medieval period, such pilgrims were marked by a special badge and wore distinctive clothes, carrying a staff and scrip (that is, a purse or satchel) that symbolized their status "between worlds." For others, their pious travels did not have a clear goal but consisted of a more open-ended spiritual wandering; for still others, their journey to a particular holy site was intended as a one-way trip, ending when they settled or even died at the place of their choosing. The range of motivations for medieval pilgrims varied widely. For those who went to Jerusalem, for example, their pilgrimages offered a chance to witness the historical locations associated with the life, ministry, death, and resurrection of their savior, Jesus Christ, bringing a concrete reality to the stories they knew from the Bible. Some pilgrims apparently felt a deep-seated mystical connection with Christ during the course of their stay in the holy places. In Rome, pilgrims might carry out ecclesiastical business at the papal court, while visiting the city's unrivaled collection of holy relics associated with the days of the martyrs. At local shrines, pilgrims sought healing miracles for disease, injuries, and other ailments. For still others, their pilgrimages were imposed by church authorities or self-imposed as a form of penance, an arduous journey intended as an act of contrition for their sins and misdeeds. By contrast, some pilgrims apparently undertook their travels to escape trouble at home or for the thrill of seeing new places, rather than for pious motives – at least, this is what critics of pilgrimage sometimes claimed.

One must also consider the people who made pilgrimage possible or more tolerable through their humble acts of logistical support, often difficult to see in the existing sources that focus on the experiences of literate, elite pilgrims: porters, hostel-keepers, sailors, and others who made their living through the provision of basic goods and services to travelers. As pilgrims, kings and queens, noble men and women, abbots and abbesses, bishops and priests often received a hero's welcome as they passed through various communities en route to their destinations, eagerly greeted by prominent locals, given tours of nearby holy sites, and celebrated as distinguished guests for the duration of their stay. Nor should one forget the saints themselves, living and dead, whose presence during their lifetimes and through their physical remains infused otherwise mundane places with the presence of the holy. Without the cult of saints and relics, medieval Christian pilgrimage might not have existed or at the very least would have looked radically different. If we consider pilgrimage as a metaphor for the transitory nature of life itself, as medieval thinkers sometimes did, then we might think of the saints as the ones who helped to alleviate the all too frequent sorrows of the journey, reigning as they did with the Lord while remaining here on Earth in the form of their relics to shower the faithful with their miraculous power and access to the bounty of God's grace.

The general trajectory of this volume is chronological. Chapter One, "The Origins of Christian Pilgrimage," starts with pre-Christian forms of devotional travel and the development of Christian pilgrimage (above all to Jerusalem) through the failure of the western Roman Empire. Chapter Two, "Saints, Travelers, and Sacred Spaces in the Early Medieval West," covers the post-Roman period from the fifth to the tenth centuries, an era that witnessed the formation of Europe's Christian landscape. Chapter Three, "Jerusalem and the Holy Places under Islamic Rule," shifts attention back toward the eastern Mediterranean during and after the Muslim conquest of the "Promised Land" in the seventh century. Chapter Four, "Pilgrimage Before and After the Millennium," covers the late tenth and early eleventh centuries on either side of the year 1000, a period that saw a revitalization of Europe's economic, political, and social fortunes that included – not coincidently – a flourishing of local and long-distance pilgrimage. Chapter Five, "Pilgrimage and Holy War," explores the crusades, a particular and controversial form of medieval devotional travel from the close of the eleventh to the thirteenth centuries. Chapter Six, "Pilgrimage and Medieval Society," presents sources from the twelfth and thirteenth centuries, the so-called High Middle Ages, when pilgrimage to local shrines and famous European destinations such as Rome, Compostela, and Canterbury formed one prominent strand in a thriving and confident medieval culture. Even at this point, however, pilgrimage and other forms of "popular" religious devotion did not lack critics. Chapter Seven, "Pilgrimage and the Wider World," moves the focus of the Reader beyond the bounds of Europe in the twelfth through fourteenth centuries, looking at Christian and non-Christian pilgrimage during an era when Europe, Africa, and Asia had grown closer than ever before in terms of commercial integration and long-distance travelers who ranged from the Mediterranean to China. Finally, Chapter Eight, "Pilgrimage and Piety in the Late Middle Ages," arrives at the close of the medieval period, paradoxically marked by the continued prominence of devotional travel and the emergence of sustained criticism aimed at pilgrimage, the cult of the saints, and the authority of the Roman papacy.

Much like the other volumes in "Readings in Medieval Civilizations and Cultures," this reader offers students a variety of sources and genres to encounter and analyze, including first-person pilgrimage accounts, letters, chronicles and other forms of historical writing, hagiographies (that is, saints' lives and stories about relics), religious polemics, and works of geography and literature. Some of the texts consist of older translations, revised and modernized, while others are taken from more recent publications and some appear here translated into English for the first time. The square brackets throughout the texts represent insertions by the editor or the translators to clarify certain points or offer additional information.

CHAPTER ONE

THE ORIGINS OF CHRISTIAN PILGRIMAGE

Long before the Middle Ages, the inhabitants of the ancient Mediterranean world traveled near and far to places of religious significance. For "pagan" polytheists, sacred sites dotted the landscape, each one connected to a local tradition, cult, or god. For the monotheistic Jews, by contrast, one land in particular – the Hebrew homeland of Israel, centered on the city of Jerusalem – possessed a special divine significance, promised by the one true God to his faithful followers. Emerging from the Jewish religious tradition, the earliest Christians had mixed feelings about Jerusalem and its surroundings. On the one hand, they viewed themselves as the inheritors of God's promises to the Jews, including possession of the land where their messiah, Jesus Christ, had lived, died, returned from the dead, and ascended into heaven. On the other hand, Christians viewed the earthly Jerusalem as insignificant compared with the "heavenly" Jerusalem, God's eternal kingdom. In the fourth century, when the Roman emperor Constantine (r. 306–337) made it official policy to recognize and support the Christian church, attitudes toward the "Promised Land" began to shift. A new sacred landscape emerged in Jerusalem, as Christians built churches and shrines to mark and celebrate sites associated with the Bible and the earliest days of their faith. From around the world in the fourth and fifth centuries, pious believers began to undertake the sometimes arduous journey to Jerusalem for the purposes of prayer and devotion, giving rise to the new and distinctive tradition of Christian pilgrimage.

1. PAUSANIAS'S *GUIDE TO GREECE*

Like other peoples of the classical world, the ancient Greeks and Romans believed that the landscape around them was dotted with shrines, sanctuaries, groves, and other holy places where religious devotees could experience the power of the gods though prayer, visions, healing miracles, and other activities. At the same time, much like modern tourists, visitors could enjoy seeing notable works of art and architecture, while hearing about local myths, legends, and history. In his Guide to Greece, *Pausanias, a learned and well-traveled doctor from Asia Minor, described the almost innumerable sacred sites scattered across the various regions of Greece. Although Pausanias wrote his account in the second century CE, his guide celebrated many buildings, objects, practices, and traditions that predated the Common Era.*

Source: trans. A.R. Shilleto, in *Pausanias' Guide to Greece*, 2 vols. (London: George Bell and Sons, 1900), vol. 1, pp. 143–44; vol. 2, pp. 10–12, 227–28; revised.

Epidaurus

The sacred grove of Asklepius is walled in on all sides, nor do any deaths or births take place in the precincts of the god, just as is the case at the island Delos. They consume the sacrifices in the precincts, whether the one making the sacrifice is a native of Epidaurus or a stranger. The same, I know, happens at Titane. The statue of Asklepius is half the size of that of the Olympian Zeus at Athens, and is made of ivory and gold. The inscription shows that it was made by the Parian Thrasymede, the son of Arignotus. The god sits on a seat holding a staff in one hand, and the other hand he rests on a dragon's head, and a dog is seated at his feet. On the seat are represented the actions of Argive heroes, such as Bellerophon killing the Chimera, and Perseus with the head of Medusa. Beyond the temple is a sleeping-place for suppliants. A round building has been built nearby, well worth seeing, of white stone called the Rotunda. In it there is a painting by Pausias of Cupid throwing away his bow and arrows and taking up a lyre instead. There is also here a painting of "Drunkenness," also by Pausias, drinking out of a glass bowl. You may see in the painting the glass bowl and in it a woman's face reflected. To this day, six pillars stand in the precincts, but in days long past there were more. On these are recorded the names of men and women healed by Asklepius and the complaint from which each suffered, and how they were cured, written in Doric.

Ionia

The Ionians have a most magnificent country for the fruits of the earth and temples such as there are nowhere else, the finest being that of Ephesian Artemis for its size and richness; the next two, dedicated to Apollo, are not quite finished, one at Branchidre in Milesia, and the other at Claros in Colophonia. Two temples in Ionia were burnt down by the Persians, one of Hera in Samos, and one of Athene in Phocrea. They are still wonderful though the fire has damaged them. And you would be delighted with the temple of Hercules at Erythrae, and with the temple of Athene at Priene, the latter for its statue of the goddess, the former for its great antiquity. At Erythrae is a work of art unlike the most ancient of Aginetan or Attic workmanship: its design is perfect Egyptian. It is the wooden raft on which the god sailed from Tyre in Phoenicia, although why we should believe this, the people of Erythrae do not explain. To prove that it came into the Ionian Sea, however, they say it was moored at the promontory called Mid, which is on the mainland about half-way from the harbor of Erythrae to the island of Chios. When this raft was at the promontory, the people of Erythrae and also the Chians had no small trouble in trying to get it on shore. At last a native of Erythrae, Phormio by name, who got his living from the sea by catching fish but had lost his eyesight through some disease, dreamed that the women of Erythrae were to cut off their hair and that the men making a rope out of this hair were to drag the raft ashore. The women who were citizens would not hear of it, but all the women who were slaves of Thracian race, or who being free had yet to earn their own living, allowed their hair to be cut off, and so at last the people of Erythrae got the raft to shore. So Thracian women alone are allowed to enter the temple of Hercules and the rope made of hair is still kept by the people of Erythrae. They also say that the fisherman recovered his sight and saw for the rest of his life. At Erythrae there is also a temple of Athene Polias, and a huge wooden statue of the goddess seated on a throne, in one hand holding a distaff, and in the other a globe. We imagine that it was made by Endous for several reasons, especially looking at the workmanship of the statue inside, and the Graces and Seasons in white marble, which used to stand in the open air. In my time, the people of Smyrna also had a temple of Asklepius between the mountain Coryphe and the sea which is unmixed with any other water.

Besides the temples and the healthiness of the air, Ionia has several other things worthy of record. Near Ephesus is the river Cenchrius, and the fertile Mount Pion, and the well Halitrea. In Milesia is the well of Biblis: they still sing of the love passages of Biblis. In Colophonia is the grove of Apollo, consisting of ash trees, and not far from the grove the river Ales, the coldest river in Ionia. The people of Lebedus have baths which are both wonderful and useful to men. The people of Teos also have baths at the promontory Macria, some natural consisting of sea-water that bursts in at a crevice of the rock, others built at wonderful cost. The people of Clazomenae also have baths. Agamemnon is honored there. There is a grotto called the grotto of Pyrrhus' mother, and they have a tradition about Pyrrhus as a shepherd. The people of Erythrae have also a place called Chalcis, from which the third of their tribes takes its name, where there is a promontory extending to the sea, and some sea baths, which of all the baths in Ionia are most beneficial to men. The people of Smyrna have the most beautiful river Meles and a cave near its springs, where they say Homer wrote his poems. The Chians also have a notable sight in the tomb of Oenopion, about whose deeds they have several legends. The Samians too on the way to the temple of Hera have the tomb of Rhadine and Leontichus, which those are accustomed to visit who are melancholy through love. The wonderful things indeed in Ionia are not far short of those in Greece altogether.

Delphi

The high-road from here to Delphi is very steep and rather difficult even for a well-equipped traveler. Many varying legends are told about Delphi, and still more about the oracle of Apollo. For they say that in the most ancient times it was the oracle of Earth, and that Earth appointed as priestess of her oracle Daphnis, who was one of the Mountain Nymphs.... I have also heard of some shepherds meeting with the oracle, becoming inspired by the vapor, and prophesying through Apollo. The greatest and most widespread fame, however, attaches to Phemonoe, who was the first priestess of Apollo, and the first who recited the oracles in hexameters. Boeo, however, a Phocian woman who composed a hymn for Delphi, says that the oracle was set up to the god by Olen and some others that came from the Hyperboreans, and that Olen was the first who delivered oracles and in hexameters....

They say that the most ancient temple of Apollo was built of laurel, from branches brought from a tree at Tempe so that temple would resemble a hut. The people of Delphi say the next temple was built of the wax and wings of bees, and was sent by Apollo to the Hyperboreans. There is also another tradition that this temple was built by a Delphian whose name was Pteras, and that it got its name from its builder, from whom also a Cretan city by the addition of one letter got called Apteraei. As for the tradition about the fern that grows on mountains, that they made the temple of this while it was still green, I cannot accept this. As to the third temple, that it was of brass is no marvel since Acrisius made a brazen chamber for his daughter, and the

Lacedaemonians have still a temple of Athene Chalciocus, and the Romans have a forum remarkable for its size and magnificence with a brazen roof. So that the temple of Apollo should be brazen is not improbable.... Moreover, I found varying accounts about the destruction of this temple, for some say it was destroyed by a landslide, others by fire. The fourth (built of stone by Trophonius and Agamedes) was burnt down when Erxiclides was Archon at Athens, in the first year of the fifty-eighth Olympiad, when Diognetus of Croton was victor. The temple which still exists was built by the Amphictyones out of the sacred money, and its architect was the Corinthian named Spintharus.

What sort of information does Pausanias's work give to its readers about the places it describes? What evidence does his account provide that pagans identified certain sites as having special religious significance? Imagine a second-century visitor to Greece who had read Pausanias: how might the guide-book have informed his or her experience as a traveler?

2. JOSEPHUS ON THE JEWISH TEMPLE AT JERUSALEM

About a thousand years before the Common Era, the Jewish people had made Jerusalem into a center for their religious services, above all at the temple built by King Solomon. After the Babylonians destroyed the temple in the sixth century BCE, the Jews rebuilt the sacred precinct, which endured until the Romans razed the site during the Jewish rebellion against Rome in the first century CE. The Jewish historian Josephus, one of the rebels who survived the first-century conflict and eventually became a Roman citizen, memorialized these events in his works The Antiquities of the Jews *and* The Jewish War. *In the first two selections, Josephus describes the construction of the First Temple by Solomon, followed by a gathering to celebrate its consecration. In the third selection, he relates how Roman armies sacked the Second Temple in 70 CE. Eventually, after crushing a second revolt by the Jews in 135 CE, the Romans renamed Jerusalem "Aelia Capitolina" and forbade the Jews from entering the city.*

Source: trans. W. Whiston, in *The Life and Works of Josephus* (Philadelphia: John C. Winston Co., 1936), pp. 243–44, 246–47, 822–23; revised.

The Antiquities of the Jews, Book Eight

3.1. Solomon began to build the temple in the fourth year of his reign, on the second month, which the Macedonians call *Artemisius,* and the Hebrews *Jur,*

592 years after the exodus out of Egypt, but 1020 from Abraham's coming out of Mesopotamia into Canaan, and after the Flood 1440. From the time of Adam, the first man who was created, until Solomon built the temple, there had passed in all 3102. Now that year on which the temple began to be built was already the eleventh year of the reign of Hiram, but from the building of Tyre to the building of the temple, there had passed 240 years.

3.2. The king, therefore, laid the foundations of the temple very deep in the ground and the materials were strong stones, such as would resist the force of time. These were to unite themselves with the earth, and become a basis and a sure foundation for that superstructure which was to be erected over it. They were to be so strong, in order to sustain with ease those vast superstructures, and precious ornaments, whose own weight was to be not less than the weight of those other high and heavy buildings which the king designed to be very ornamental and magnificent. They erected its entire body, up to the roof, of white stone. Its height was 60 cubits, and its length the same, and its breadth 20. There was another building erected over it, equal to it in its measures, so that the entire altitude of the temple was 120 cubits. Its front faced the east....

3.9. Solomon made all these things for the honor of God, with great variety, and magnificence, sparing no cost, but using all possible liberality in adorning the temple, and these things he dedicated to the treasures of God. He also placed a partition round about the temple, which (in our tongue) we call *Gison*, but it is called *Thrigcos* by the Greeks, and he raised it up to the height of three cubits. It was for the exclusion of the multitude from coming into the temple, and showing that it was a place that was free and open only for the priests....

4.1. When King Solomon had finished these works, these large and beautiful buildings, and had laid up his donations in the temple, and all this in the interval of seven years, and had given a demonstration of his riches and alacrity therein (insomuch that anyone who saw it would have thought that it must have been an immense time before it could have been finished, and would be surprised that so much should be finished in so short a time, short, I mean, if compared with the greatness of the work), he also wrote to all the rulers and elders of the Hebrews, and ordered all the people to gather themselves together to Jerusalem, both to see the temple which he had built, and to remove the ark of God into it. When this invitation of the whole body of the people to come to Jerusalem was everywhere carried abroad, it was the seventh month before they came together (which month is, by our countrymen, called *Thisri*, but by the Macedonians *Hyperberetaeus*). The feast of Tabernacles happened to fall at the same time, which was kept by the Hebrews as a most holy and most eminent feast. So they carried the ark and the tabernacle which Moses had pitched, and all the vessels that were for ministration to the sacrifices of God, and removed them to the temple.

The king himself, and all the people and the Levites [priests], went before, rendering the ground moist with sacrifices and drink offerings, and the blood of a great number of oblations, and burning an immense quantity of incense – this till the air itself everywhere round about was so full of these odors that it met, in a most agreeable manner, persons at a great distance and was an indication of God's presence, and (as men's opinion was) of his habitation with them in this newly built and consecrated place. They did not grow weary, either of singing hymns, or of dancing, until they came to the temple. In this manner did they carry the ark, but when they should transfer it into the most secret places, the rest of the multitude went away, and only those priests that carried it set it between the two cherubim, which embracing it with their wings (for so they were framed by the artificer), they covered it, as under a tent or cupola. Now the ark contained nothing else but those two tables of stone that preserved the ten commandments, which God had spoken of to Moses on Mount Sinai, and which were engraved upon them, but they set the candlestick, and the table, and the golden altar, in the temple, before the most secret place, in the very same places wherein they stood till that time in the tabernacle. So they offered up the daily sacrifices; but for the brazen altar, Solomon set it before the temple, over against the door, that when the door was opened, it might be exposed to sight, and the sacred solemnities, and the richness of the sacrifices, might be thence seen; and all the rest of the vessels they gathered together, and put them within the temple.

The Jewish War, Book Six

4.5. So Titus retired into the tower of Antonia, and resolved to storm the temple the next day, early in the morning, with his whole army, and to encamp round about the holy house. As for the house, God had for certain long ago doomed it to fire, and now that fatal day was come, according to the revolution of the ages: It was the tenth day of the month *Lous Ab*, upon which it was formerly burnt by the king of Babylon, although these flames took their rise from the Jews themselves, and were occasioned by them. For upon Titus's retiring, the seditious lay still for a little while, and then attacked the Romans again, when those that guarded the holy house fought with those that quenched the fire that was burning in the inner court of the temple. These Romans put the Jews to flight, and proceeded as far as the holy house itself. At which time one of the soldiers, without staying for any orders, and without any concern or dread upon him at so great an undertaking, and being hurried on by a certain divine fury, snatched somewhat out of the materials that were on fire, and being lifted up by another soldier, he set fire to a golden window, through which there was a passage to the rooms that were round about the holy house, on the north side of it. As the flames went upward the Jews made a clamor, such as so mighty an affliction required, and ran together to prevent it. Now they spared not their lives any longer, nor suffered anything to restrain their force, since that holy house was perishing, for whose sake it was that they kept such a guard about it....

4.7. And now, since Caesar was no way able to restrain the enthusiastic fury of the soldiers and the fire proceeded on more and more, he went into the holy place of the temple with his commanders and saw it, with what was in it, which he found to be far superior to what the relations of foreigners contained, and not inferior to what we ourselves boasted of and believed about it. As the flame had not as yet reached to its inward parts, but was still consuming the rooms that were about the holy house, and Titus supposing what the fact was, that the house itself might yet be saved, he came in haste and endeavored to persuade the soldiers to quench the fire and gave order to Liberalius the centurion, and one of those spearmen that were about him, to beat the soldiers that were refractory with their staves, and to restrain them. Yet were their passions too hard for the regard they had for Caesar, and the dread they had of him who forbade them, as was their hatred of the Jews, and a certain vehement inclination to fight them, too hard for them also. Moreover, the hope of plunder induced many to go on, as having this opinion, that all the places within were full of money, and as seeing that all round about it was made of gold. Besides, one of those that went into the place prevented Caesar, when he ran so hastily out to restrain the soldiers, and threw the fire upon the hinges of the gate, in the dark, whereby the flame burst out from within the holy house itself immediately, when the commanders retired, and Caesar with them, and when nobody any longer forbade those that were without to set fire to it. Thus the holy house burnt down without Caesar's approval.

4.8. Now although anyone would justly lament the destruction of such a work as this was, since it was the most admirable of all the works that we have seen or heard of, both for its curious structure and its magnitude, and also for the vast wealth bestowed upon it, as well as for the glorious reputation it had for its holiness, yet might such a one comfort himself with this thought, that it was fate that decreed it so to be, which is inevitable, both as to living creatures and as to works and places also. However, one cannot but wonder at the accuracy of this period thereto relating, for the same month and day were now observed, as I said before, wherein the holy house was burnt formerly by the Babylonians....

Why did King Solomon build the Jewish Temple? What was the importance of the "ark" placed inside the Temple? What role did the priests play in the sacred space of the Temple? What significance did the Temple seem to have for the "common" believers who visited it? According to Josephus, was the destruction of the Temple by the Romans by chance or part of a greater design?

3. THE PROMISED LAND IN CHRISTIAN SCRIPTURE

The Christian Bible, consisting of the "Old Testament" (the Hebrew Bible) and the "New Testament" (the story of Jesus Christ and his earliest followers), reveals a deep-seated ambivalence toward Jerusalem and its surroundings. On the one hand, God had literally promised that region to Abram (Abraham) and his descendants, the "Chosen People" of Israel. When Israel violated God's law, the Lord punished his wayward followers by temporarily turning Jerusalem over to its enemies. For Christians, Jerusalem assumed a special significance as the site of Christ's ministry, death, and resurrection. At the same time, Jerusalem possessed an apocalyptic significance, both as the terrestrial site of tribulations at the end of time, and as a symbol for the coming kingdom of God.

Source: *The Holy Bible*, Douay-Rheims Version; revised.

Book of Genesis

13.1 And Abram went up out of Egypt, he and his wife, and all that he had, and Lot with him into the south. **2** And he was very rich in possession of gold and silver. **3** And he returned by the way that he came, from the south to Bethel, to the place where before he had pitched his tent between Bethel and Hai, **4** in the place of the altar which he had made before. And there he called upon the name of the Lord....

12 Abram lived in the land of Canaan; and Lot dwelled in the towns that were about the Jordan, and lived in Sodom. **13** And the men of Sodom were very wicked, and sinners before the face of the Lord beyond measure. **14** And the Lord said to Abram, after Lot was separated from him: "Lift up your eyes, and look from the place wherein you now are, to the north and to the south, to the east and to the west. **15** All the land which you see, I will give to you and to your seed for ever. **16** And I will make your seed as the dust of the earth: if any man be able to number the dust of the earth, he shall be able to number your seed also. **17** Arise and walk through the length and breadth of the land: for I will give it to you." **18** So Abram removing his tent came and dwelt by the Vale of Mamre, which is in Hebron: and he built there an altar to the Lord.

Book of Isaiah

3.1 For behold the sovereign the Lord of hosts shall take away from Jerusalem, and from Juda the valiant and the strong, the whole strength of bread, and the whole strength of water, **2** the strong man, and the man of war, the judge, and the prophet, and the cunning man, and the ancient, **3** the captain over fifty, and the honorable in countenance, and the counselor, and the architect, and the skillful in eloquent speech. **4** And I will give children to be their princes, and the effeminate shall rule over them. **5** And the people shall rush one upon another, and every man against his neighbor: the child shall rise up against the ancient, and the base against the honorable. **6** For a man shall take hold of his brother, one of the house of his father, saying: "Thou hast a garment, be thou our ruler, and let this ruin be under thy hand." **7** In that day he shall answer, saying: "I am no healer, and in my house there is no bread, nor clothing: make me not ruler of the people." **8** For Jerusalem is ruined and Juda is fallen: because their tongue, and their devices are against the Lord, to provoke the eyes of his majesty. **9** The show of their countenance has answered them: and they have proclaimed abroad their sin as Sodom, and they have not hid it: woe to their souls, for evils are rendered to them.

Gospel of Mark

15.16 The soldiers led him [Jesus] away into the court of the palace, and they called together the whole band. **17** And they clothed him with purple, and platting a crown of thorns, they put it upon him. **18** And they began to salute him: "Hail, king of the Jews." **19** And they struck his head with a reed and they did spit on him. Bowing their knees, they adored him. **20** And after they had mocked him, they took off the purple from him, and put his own garments on him, and they led him out to crucify him....

22 They brought him into the place called Golgotha, which being interpreted is, "The Place of Calvary." **23** And they gave him to drink wine mingled with myrrh, but he took it not. **24** And crucifying him, they divided his garments, casting lots upon them, what every man should take. **25** And it was the third hour, and they crucified him....

37 And Jesus having cried out with a loud voice, gave up the ghost. **38** And the veil of the Temple was rent in two, from the top to the bottom. **39** And the centurion who stood over against him, seeing that crying out in this manner he had given up the ghost, said: "Indeed this man was the son of God." **40** And there were also women looking on afar off, among whom was Mary Magdalene, and Mary the mother of James the less and of Joseph, and Salome, **41** who also when he was in Galilee followed him, and ministered to him, and many other women that came up with him to Jerusalem. **42** And when evening was now come (because it was the Parasceve, that is, the day before the Sabbath), **43** Joseph of Arimathea, a noble counselor, who was also himself looking for the kingdom of God, came and went in boldly to Pilate and begged the body of Jesus. **44** But Pilate wondered that he should be already dead. And sending for the centurion, he asked him if he were already dead. **45** And when he had understood it by the centurion, he gave the body to Joseph. **46** And Joseph buying fine linen, and taking him down, wrapped him up in the fine linen, and laid him in a sepulcher which was hewed out of a rock. And he rolled a stone to the door of the sepulcher. **47** And Mary Magdalene, and Mary the mother of Joseph, beheld where he was laid.

Gospel of Luke

21.1 And looking on, he [Jesus] saw the rich men cast their gifts into the treasury. **2** And he saw also a certain poor widow casting in two brass mites. **3** And he said: "Verily I say to you, that this poor widow has cast in more than they all. **4** For all these have of their abundance cast into the offerings of God, but she of her want, has cast in all the living that she had." **5** And some saying of the temple, that it was adorned with goodly stones and gifts, he said: **6** "These things which you see, the days will come in which there shall not be left a stone upon a stone that shall not be thrown down...."

20 "And when you shall see Jerusalem compassed about with an army, then know that its desolation is at hand. **21** Then let those who are in Judea, flee to the mountains, and those who are in its midst, depart out it, and those who are in the countries, not enter into it. **22** For these are the days of vengeance, that all things may be fulfilled, that are written. **23** But woe to them that are with child, and give suck in those days, for there shall be great distress in the land, and wrath upon this people. **24** And they shall fall by the edge of the sword and shall be led away captives into all nations, and Jerusalem shall be trodden down by the Gentiles till the times of the nations be fulfilled. **25** And there shall be signs in the sun and in the moon and in the stars, and upon the earth distress of nations, by reason of the confusion of the roaring of the sea and of the waves, **26** men withering away for fear, and expectation of what shall come upon the whole world. For the powers of heaven shall be moved. **27** And then they shall see the Son of man coming in a cloud, with great power and majesty...."

Book of Revelation

21.1 And I saw a new heaven and a new earth: For the first heaven and the first earth was gone, and the sea is now no more. **2** And I John saw the holy city, the new Jerusalem, coming down out of heaven from God, prepared as a bride adorned for her husband. **3** And I heard a great voice from the throne, saying: "Behold the tabernacle of God with men, and he will dwell with them." And they shall be his people, and God himself with them shall be their God. **4** And God shall wipe away all tears from their eyes and there shall be no more death, nor mourning, nor crying, nor sorrow, for the former things are passed away. **5** And he that sat on the throne, said: "Behold, I make all things new." And he said to me: "Write, for these words are most faithful and true...."

10 And he took me up in spirit to a great and high mountain, and he showed me the holy city Jerusalem coming down out of heaven from God, **11** having the glory of God, and its light was like to a precious stone, as to the jasper stone, even as crystal. **12** And it had a wall great and high, having twelve gates, and in the gates twelve angels, and names written on them, which are the names of the twelve tribes of the children of Israel. **13** On the east, three gates, and on the north, three gates, and on the south, three gates, and on the west, three gates. **14** And the wall of the city had twelve foundations, and in them, the twelve names of the twelve apostles of the Lamb....

22 And I saw no temple inside. For the Lord God Almighty is its temple and the Lamb. **23** And the city hath no need of the sun, or of the moon, to shine in it, for the glory of God has enlightened it and the Lamb is its lamp. **24** And the nations shall walk in the light of it, and the kings of the earth shall bring their glory and honor into it. **25** And its gates shall not be shut by day, for there shall be no night there. **26** And they shall bring the glory and honor of the nations into it. **27** There shall not enter into it any thing defiled, or that work an abomination or make a lie, but they that are written in the book of life of the Lamb.

In the Book of Genesis, what does God promise to Abram? How does the Book of Isaiah describe Jerusalem: does the prophet seem to be speaking about the actual city of Jerusalem, Jerusalem as a symbol, or both? In the Gospel of Luke, what fate does Jesus Christ predict for Jerusalem and the Jewish Temple? What happens to the Temple in the Gospel of Mark when Jesus dies? What does Jerusalem represent in the Book of Revelation? How might an early Christian reading these parts of the Bible have felt about visiting the earthly city of Jerusalem?

4. EUSEBIUS ON THE CONSTANTINIAN PEACE

In 313 CE, following a brutal crackdown on Christian communities by the Roman emperor Diocletian, the new emperor Constantine and his co-emperor Licinius declared a policy of religious toleration throughout the Roman Empire. Whatever his personal convictions, Constantine soon showed particular favor and support for Christianity, showering gifts, legal privileges, and other benefits upon the catholic (i.e., universal) Christian church and its leadership. In 324, Constantine defeated Licinius, who had renewed the persecution of Christians, and became sole emperor. Among his ongoing acts of patronage, he initiated a lavish program of church building throughout the Roman Empire, including such places as Jerusalem, Rome, and his newly established capital, Constantinople. By doing so, Constantine and his supporters dramatically transformed the religious landscape of Christian devotion and pilgrimage. The following account, written by the emperor's biographer Eusebius of Caesarea, describes these changes and the famous journey of Constantine's mother, Helena, to the holy places of Jerusalem in 328.

Source: trans. John H. Bernard, in *Eusebius' Life of Constantine*, Palestine Pilgrims' Text Society, vol. 1 (London, 1887–97), pp. 3–13; revised.

3.25. After these things the emperor, beloved of God, undertook another memorable work in the province of Palestine. What, then, was this? It seemed to him to be a duty to make conspicuous and an object of veneration to all the most blessed place of the savior's resurrection in Jerusalem. So, right away, he gave orders for the building of a house of prayer, not having hit upon this project without the aid of God, but having been impelled to it in his spirit by the savior himself.

3.26. For ungodly men [pagans], or rather the whole race of demons by their means, set themselves to consign to darkness and oblivion that divine monument of immortality at which the angel who came down from heaven, radiant with light, rolled away the stone for those who were stony in heart and supposed the Living One was yet with the dead, bringing good tidings to the women and removing the stone of unbelief from their understanding, thus convincing them of the life of him whom they sought. This cave of salvation did certain ungodly and impious persons determine to hide from the eyes of men, foolishly imagining that they would in some such way as this conceal the truth. Having expended much labor in bringing in earth from outside, they cover up the whole place; and then having raised this to a certain height, and having paved it with stone, they entirely conceal the divine cave beneath a great mound. Next, as if nothing further were left for them to do, they prepare above ground a dreadful thing, a veritable sepulcher of souls, building to the impure demon, called Aphrodite, a dark shrine of lifeless idols, offering their foul oblations on profane and accursed altars. For in this way only, and in no other fashion, did they suppose that they would accomplish their purpose, even by concealing the cave of salvation by means of these detestable abominations. For the wretched men were not able to understand that it was not possible that he [Christ] who had gained the prize of victory over death should leave his glorious achievement in obscurity, any more than it is possible that the sun which shines over the earth, and runs its accustomed course in the heavens, should escape the notice of the whole race of men. In a far higher degree was that power of salvation, which illumines the souls, and not merely the bodies of men, filling the whole world with its own rays of light.

Be that as it may, the machinations of ungodly and impious men against the truth continued for a long time. No one of the [Roman] governors, of the praetors, or even of the emperors, was found capable of abolishing these daring impieties, save only that one who was dear to God the ruler of all. He [Constantine], being inspired by the divine spirit, could not bear to see the place we have been speaking of concealed through the artifices of adversaries by all kinds of impurity, and consigned to oblivion and neglect, nor did he yield to the malice of those who had brought this about, but calling upon God to help him, he gave orders that the place should be purified, counting it especially fitting that a spot which had been polluted by his enemies should enjoy the mighty working of the All-Good at his hands. As soon as his orders were given, the contrivances of deceit were cast down from on high to the ground, and the dwelling-places of error, images, and demons and all were overthrown and utterly destroyed.

3.27. Nor did his zeal stop here. The emperor further gave directions that the material of that which was destroyed, both wood and stone, should be removed and thrown as far from the spot as possible, which was done in accordance with his command. Only to go thus far, however, did not satisfy him. Again, being inspired with holy zeal, he issued orders that, having dug up the soil to a considerable depth, they should transport to a far-distant spot the actual ground, earth and all, inasmuch as it had been polluted by the defilements of demon-worship.

3.28. This also was accomplished without delay. As one layer after another was laid bare, the place which was beneath the earth appeared. Then, right away, contrary to all expectation, did the venerable and hallowed monument of our savior's resurrection become visible, and the most holy cave received what was an exact emblem of his coming to life. For after its descent into darkness it again came forth into light, and afforded to those who came to see a clear insight into the history of the wonders which had there been wrought, testifying to the resurrection of the savior by deeds more eloquent than any voice could be.

3.29. These things being so done, forthwith the emperor, by the injunction of pious edicts, accompanied by the abundant supply of all things needful, gave orders that a house of prayer worthy of God should be erected round about the cave of salvation on a scale of rich and imperial costliness. This project he had held for some time in view and had foreseen, as if by superior intelligence, what was going to happen. To the governors of the provinces in the east he gave instructions that with liberal and abundant grants they should make the work exceedingly large, great, and costly, but to the bishop who at that time presided over the church in Jerusalem he sent the following letter, in which he set forth the saving doctrine of the faith in clear language, writing in the following manner.

3.30. Constantine, Victor, Maximus Augustus, to Macarius: "So great is the grace of our savior that no power of language seems worthy to describe the present wonder. For that the token of that most holy passion, long ago buried underground, should have remained unknown for so many cycles of years, until it should shine forth to his servants now set free through the removal of him [Licinius, Constantine's former co-emperor and subsequent foe], who was the common enemy of all, truly transcends all marvel. For if all who are reputed wise throughout all the world were to come together to one place and try to say something worthy of this event, they would not be able to match themselves against such a work in the smallest degree, for the nature of this wonder as far transcends all capacity of man's reason as divine things surpass in permanence those which are human. Wherefore this is always my first and only object that as the faithfulness of the truth displays itself daily by fresh wonders, so the souls of us all may become more zealous for the holy law in all sobriety and earnestness with concord. I desire, then, that you should especially be convinced of this (which, indeed, I suppose is plain to everyone), that of all things it is most my care how we may adorn with splendor of buildings that sacred spot which, under divine direction, I relieved as it were from an incumbent load, even from the disgraceful adjunct of an idol: a place holy indeed from the beginning of God's judgment, but which has been made to appear still more holy since it brought to light the assurance of the savior's passion.

3.31. It is therefore fitting that your sagacity do so order and make provision for everything necessary, that not only shall this basilica be the finest in the world, but that the details also shall be such that all the fairest structures in every city may be surpassed by it. Concerning the building and beautifying of the walls, know that my intention has been entrusted to my friend Dracilianus, deputy of the praetorian prefects, and to the governor of the province. For by my piety has it been commanded them that artificers and workmen and all things which they may learn from your sagacity to be necessary for the building shall be furnished by their provision. Concerning the columns and marbles, whatever you shall judge after the plan has been inspected to be most precious and most serviceable, be careful to inform us in writing so that those things of whatever sort, and in whatever quantity, which we learn from your letter to be needful, may be procured from every quarter. For it is just that the place which is more wonderful than the whole world should be worthily decorated.

3.32. As to the roof of the basilica, I wish to know from you whether you think it should have a paneled ceiling or be finished in any other fashion. If it be paneled, it may also be ornamented with gold. It remains for your holiness to make it known to the aforesaid magistrates with all speed how many workmen and artificers, and what expenditure of money, is needful; and you will also be careful to report forthwith to me, not only concerning the marbles and the columns, but also concerning the paneled ceiling if you should judge this the more beautiful. God guard you, beloved brother."

3.33. These things did the emperor write, and his instructions were at once carried into effect. So on the monument of the salvation itself was the new Jerusalem built, over against the one so famous of old, which, after the pollution caused by the murder of the Lord, experienced the last extremity of desolation, and paid the penalty for the crime of its impious inhabitants. Opposite this the emperor reared, with rich and lavish expenditure, the trophy of the savior's victory over death. Perhaps this was that strange and new Jerusalem, proclaimed in the oracles of the prophets, to which long passages prophesying by the aid of the divine spirit make countless allusions in song. And, first of all, he adorned the sacred cave, which was, as it were, the chief part of the whole work, that divine monument at which once an angel, radiant with light, proclaimed to all the good news of regeneration manifested through the savior....

3.41. And having selected other places in the same region which were held in honor on account of two sacred caves, he adorned them also with lavish expenditure; rendering due honor to that cave which had been the scene of the first manifestation of the savior when he submitted to be born in the flesh, and, in the case of the second, magnifying the memory of his ascension into heaven on the mountain-top. To these he gave magnificent honors, immortalizing the memory of his mother, who did such good service to mankind.

3.42. For she, having purposed to pay a fitting return of a pious disposition to God the ruler of all, thought it right to make thank-offerings by means of prayers for her son, now so great an emperor, and for his sons, her own descendents, the Caesars beloved by God. So she came, though advanced in years, with the energy of youth to acquaint herself with this land worthy of all veneration, with exceeding wisdom, and to visit with imperial solicitude the provinces, townships, and people. And when she had bestowed fitting worship on the footprints of the savior, in accordance with the prophetic word which says "Let us worship at the place where his feet have stood," she immediately bequeathed to those who were to come after the fruit of her personal piety.

3.43. And forthwith she dedicated two temples to the God whom she worshipped, one at the cave of the Nativity, and the other on the Mount of the Ascension. For he who was God with us submitted for our sakes to be born under ground, and the place of his birth in the flesh was called by the Hebrews Bethlehem. Wherefore the most pious empress adorned the scene of the labor of the Mother of God with rare monuments, beautifying in every way this sacred cave. Shortly afterward the emperor also honored it with imperial offerings, with treasures of gold and silver, and with embroidered curtains, thus enhancing the artistic design of his mother.

Again the imperial mother erected a stately edifice on the Mount of Olives as a monument of the progress into heaven of the savior of all, raising a sacred church and temple on the mountain ridge at the very summit of the hill. Here, in this cave, true history has it that the savior of all initiated his disciples into sacred mysteries. Here did the empress honor the Great King with offerings and beautiful gifts of all kinds. And so Helena Augusta, the God-beloved mother of a God-beloved prince, dedicated to God her savior, as tokens of her pious disposition, these two venerable and beautiful sacred edifices at the two divine caves, which are indeed worthy of everlasting remembrance, her son affording her the aid of his imperial authority. Not long after the aged lady received her due reward, having passed the whole time of her life up to the very threshold of old age in all good things, showing forth the goodly fruits of the message of salvation in word and deed; and having consequently spent a life of healthy purpose, well ordered and tranquil in body and soul alike, she at length received from God an end worthy of her piety, as well as recompense of good things in the present life....

3.48. Distinguishing with special honor the city [Constantinople] which was called after his own name, he [Constantine] adorned it with many places of worship, very large martyr memorials, and very splendid buildings, some in the suburbs, and others in the city itself, by which he at the same time honored the memory of the martyrs' God. Being altogether inspired with divine wisdom, he determined to purge from all idolatry that city which he had decreed should be called by his own name, so that there should nowhere appear in it statues of the gods of common repute worshipped in the temples, nor altars defiled by pollutions of blood, nor whole burnt offerings, nor demon festivals, nor any other thing customary among the superstitious....

3.51. Such were the emperor's most notable sacred buildings. But having heard that one and the same savior, who had lately appeared on earth, had also long ago afforded a manifestation of his divine presence to pious men in Palestine near the oak of Mamre, he ordered that a house of prayer should by raised there to the God who was seen. To the rulers of the provinces an imperial commission went by letters forwarded to each, bidding them bring to completion what had been proposed, but to us who write this history he sent instruction in the matter, entering more into reasons, an exact copy of which I think it well to insert in this present work, that his pious care may be clearly discerned. Finding fault with practices which he had heard went on at the place in question, he wrote to me in the following terms.

3.52. Constantine, Victor. Maximus Augustus, to Macarius and the Other Bishops of Palestine: "One benefit, and that a very great one, has been conferred on me by that most pious lady, my wife's mother [Eutropia], in that she has informed me by letters of the mad folly of abandoned men, which has hitherto escaped your notice; for thus the error that has been overlooked may obtain at my hands that fitting correction and attention which, if somewhat tardy, is yet necessary. For truly it is a very great impiety that the holy places should be defiled with unhallowed pollutions. What, then, dearest brethren, was that concerning which, though it eluded your sagacity, she of whom I speak could not keep silence because of her reverence for God?

3.53. She says that the place which is called after the oak of Mamre, where we learn that Abraham had his home, is defiled in every possible way by certain superstitious persons; for she declared that idols worthy of utter destruction are being erected beside it, and that an altar stands near, and that impure sacrifices are continually offered. Now, since this seems to our majesty to be both foreign to the spirit of our times and unworthy of the sanctity of the place, we wish to inform your reverences that we have by letter signified to the illustrious Count Acacius our friend that without any delay the idols, as many as may be found in the aforesaid place, are to be committed to the flames, and that the altar is to be completely demolished. We also regard anyone who after this our mandate shall dare to perform any impious act in this place, as worthy of condign punishment. We have given further orders that the place itself shall be adorned with an unpolluted building – a basilica – that it may be made a fit place of assembly for holy men. If anything be done contrary to this injunction, it is fitting that without any delay it be clearly communicated to our clemency by letters from you, in order that we may direct the detected person to undergo the extreme penalty as a transgressor of the law. For you are not ignorant that there first did God the Lord of all appear to Abraham and converse with him; there first did the observance of the holy law receive its beginning; there first did the savior himself with the two angels vouchsafe the manifestation of his presence to Abraham. There he gave promise to Abraham concerning his future, and forthwith fulfilled that promise. There he foretold that he would be the father of very many nations. Since these things are so, it is proper, as it seems to me, that this place should be kept by your care free from all pollution, and should be restored to its primitive sanctity so that nothing should be done there except the performance of fitting service to him who is Almighty God and our savior and Lord of all. This it is fitting that you should care for with due attention, if, indeed (as I am persuaded), your reverence wishes to accomplish my wishes, which are especially concerned with the service of God. God guard you, brethren beloved."

Why did pagans hide the place of Christ's tomb? Why did Constantine take it upon himself to order the restoration of that site? Consider Eusebius's comparison of the earthly Jerusalem after Constantine's building program to the prophesied "new" Jerusalem: what might this comparison imply? How did the visits of Helena and Eutropia contribute to the changing face of the Christian church in the "Promised Land"? Imagine a Christian who traveled to Jerusalem before and after the time of Constantine: what might his or her reaction have been to the changes that he or she saw?

5. THE DISCOVERY OF THE TRUE CROSS

Not long after the death of Emperor Constantine, a tradition developed that his mother Helena had discovered the actual cross from Christ's crucifixion and other relics during her devotional journey to the Holy Land. This legend became immensely popular in both the Western and Eastern churches, helping to make the portion of the True Cross kept at Jerusalem a focal point of subsequent Christian pilgrimage to the city. The account below comes from the Greek historian Socrates Scholasticus during the fifth century.

Source: revised translation by A.C. Zenos, in *A Select Library of the Nicene and Post-Nicene Fathers of the Christian Church*, 2nd series, vol. 2 (New York: The Christian Literature Co., 1890–1901), pp. 21–22; revised.

Helena, the emperor's mother ... being divinely directed by dreams went to Jerusalem. Finding that which was once Jerusalem desolate "as a preserve for autumnal fruits," according to the prophet, she sought carefully the sepulcher of Christ, from which he arose after his burial. After much difficulty, by God's help she discovered it. What the cause of the difficulty was I will explain in a few words. Those who embraced the Christian faith, after the period of his passion, greatly venerated this tomb, but those who hated Christianity, having covered the spot with a mound of earth, erected on it a temple to Venus, and set up her image there, not caring for the memory of the place. This succeeded for a long time and it became known to the emperor's mother. Accordingly she having caused the statue to be thrown down, the earth to be removed, and the ground entirely cleared, found three crosses in the sepulcher: one of these was that blessed cross on which Christ had hung, the other two were those on which the two thieves that were crucified with him had died. With these was also found the tablet of Pilate, on which he had inscribed in various characters, that the Christ who was crucified was king of the Jews.

Since, however, it was doubtful which was the cross they were in search of, the emperor's mother was not a little distressed, but from this trouble the bishop of Jerusalem, Macarius, shortly relieved her. And he solved the doubt by faith, for he sought a sign from God and obtained it. The sign was this: a certain woman of the neighborhood, who had been long afflicted with disease, was now just at the point of death. The bishop therefore arranged it so that each of the crosses should be brought to the dying woman, believing that she would be healed on touching the precious cross. Nor was he disappointed in his expectation: for the two crosses having been applied which were not the Lord's, the woman still continued in a dying state; but when the third, which was the true cross, touched her, she was immediately healed, and recovered her former strength. On this manner then was the genuine cross discovered. The emperor's mother erected over the place of the sepulcher a magnificent church, and named it "New Jerusalem," having built it facing that old and deserted city. There she left a portion of the cross, enclosed in a silver case, as a memorial to those who might wish to see it: the other part she sent to the emperor, who being persuaded that the city would be perfectly secure where that relic should be preserved, privately enclosed it in his own statue, which stands on a large column of porphyry in the forum named after Constantine at Constantinople. I have written this from report indeed, but almost all the inhabitants of Constantinople affirm that it is true.

Moreover the nails with which Christ's hands were fastened to the cross (for his mother having found these also in the sepulcher had sent them) Constantine took and had made into bridle-bits and a helmet, which he used in his military expeditions. The emperor supplied all materials for the construction of the churches, and wrote to Macarius the bishop to expedite these edifices. When the emperor's mother had completed the New Jerusalem, she reared another church not at all inferior, over the cave at Bethlehem where Christ was born according to the flesh: nor did she stop here, but built a third on the mount of his Ascension. So devoutly was she affected in these matters that she would pray in the company of women. Inviting the virgins enrolled in the register of the churches to a meal, serving them herself, she brought the dishes to table. She was also very munificent to the churches and to the poor. Having lived a life of piety, she died when about eighty years old. Her remains were conveyed to New Rome [Constantinople], the capital, and deposited in the imperial sepulcher.

According to Socrates Scholasticus, how did Helena's journey to Jerusalem fit in with her other religious convictions and activities? What significance did her discovery of the True Cross have for her son, the Roman emperor Constantine? Compare this account of Helena's visit to Jerusalem with the one given by Eusebius of Caesarea (doc. 4): what similarities and differences are evident?

6. JULIAN THE APOSTATE AND THE TEMPLE MOUNT

After Constantine, the rulers of the Roman Empire were all Christians, with one notable exception. Although raised as a Christian, Julian the "Apostate," who reigned from 361–363, openly rejected the Christian faith in favor of pagan religious and philosophical traditions. According to later accounts, Julian recognized the importance of Jerusalem as a holy place of Christian veneration and took steps to restore the Temple Mount, site of the First and Second Temples, to the followers of the Jewish religious tradition.

Source: revised translation by A.C. Zenos, in *A Select Library of the Nicene and Post-Nicene Fathers of the Christian Church*, 2nd series, vol. 2 (New York: The Christian Literature Co., 1890–1901), pp. 89–90; revised.

The superstition of the emperor [Julian] became still more apparent in his further attempts to harass the Christians. Being fond of sacrificing, he not only himself delighted in the blood of victims, but considered it an indignity offered to him, if others did not do likewise. Since he found but few persons of this stamp, he sent for the Jews and inquired of them why they abstained from sacrificing, since the law of Moses enjoined it. On their replying that it was not permitted them to do this in any other place than Jerusalem, he immediately ordered them to rebuild Solomon's Temple. Meanwhile he himself proceeded on his expedition against the Persians. The Jews, who had been long desirous of obtaining a favorable opportunity for rearing their temple afresh, in order that they might therein offer sacrifice, applied themselves very vigorously to the work. Conducting themselves with great insolence toward the Christians, they threatened to do them as much mischief as they had themselves suffered from the Romans. After the emperor ordered that the expenses of this structure should be defrayed out of the public treasury, all things were soon provided, so that they were furnished with timber and stone, burnt brick, clay, lime, and all other materials necessary for building. On this occasion Cyril, bishop of Jerusalem, calling to mind the prophecy of Daniel, which Christ also in the holy Gospels has confirmed, predicted in the presence of many persons that the time would very soon come in which "one stone should not be left upon another in that Temple," but that the savior's prophetic declaration should have its full accomplishment.

Such were the bishop's words: and on the night following a mighty earthquake tore up the stones of the old foundations of the Temple and dispersed them all together with the adjacent edifices. This circumstance exceedingly terrified the Jews and the report of it brought many to the spot who resided at a great distance. When therefore a vast multitude was assembled another prodigy took place. Fire came down from heaven and consumed all the builder's tools, so that for one entire day the flames were seen preying upon mallets, irons [used] to smooth and polish stones, saws, hatchets, adzes, in short all the various implements which the workmen had procured as necessary for the undertaking. The fires continued burning among these for a whole day. The Jews indeed were in the greatest possible alarm, and unwillingly confessed that Christ is God, yet they did not do his will, but influenced by inveterate prepossessions they still clung to Judaism. Even a third miracle which afterwards happened failed to lead them to a belief in the truth. For the next night luminous impressions of a cross appeared imprinted on their garments, which at daybreak they in vain attempted to rub or wash out. They were therefore blinded as the apostle says, and cast away the good which they had in their hands. So the Temple, instead of being rebuilt, was at that time wholly overthrown.

Why did the Roman emperor Julian allow the Jews a chance to rebuild the Temple at Jerusalem? How might a fourth-century Christian pilgrim to Jerusalem have reacted if he or she had seen the rebuilding of the Temple? As presented in this account, what does the ultimate failure of the Jews' effort imply about the divine significance of Jerusalem?

7. THE PILGRIMAGE OF ETHERIA

By the second half of the fourth century, a thriving tradition of Christian pilgrimage to the holy places of Jerusalem had begun to emerge. The contemporary account of one such pilgrim, the Spanish abbess Etheria, illustrates the far-reaching appeal of the region's holy places for Christian believers from around the Roman world. Etheria, who described her journey in a letter to her sisters back home in Spain, also visited cities such as Edessa, Tarsus, and Constantinople, thereby participating in a wider devotional landscape of churches, monasteries, shrines, and other sacred sites around the eastern Mediterranean. Her account, written in the first person, allows us a glimpse into the immediacy and emotion of the pilgrimage experience in late antiquity.

Source: revised by S.J. Allen and E. Amt, in *The Crusades: A Reader*, ed. S.J. Allen and E. Amt (Peterborough, ON: Broadview Press, 2003), pp. 3–6, from the translation by M.L. McClure and C.L. Fletoe, *The Pilgrimage of Etheria* (New York: The Macmillan Co., 1919), pp. 32–33, 41–44, 95–96.

Edessa

... Departing [from Bathnae], we arrived at Edessa in the name of Christ our God, and, on our arrival, we straightway repaired to the church and memorial of St-Thomas. There, according to custom, prayers were made and the other things that were customary in the holy places were done; we read also some things concerning Saint Thomas himself. The church there is very great, very beautiful and of new construction, well worthy to be the house of God, and as there was much that I desired to see, it was necessary for me to make a three days' stay there. Thus I saw in that city many memorials, together with holy monks, some dwelling at the memorials, while others had their cells in more secluded spots farther from the city.

Moreover, the holy bishop of the city, a truly devout man, both monk and confessor, received me willingly and said: "As I see, daughter, that for the sake of devotion you have undertaken so great a labor in coming to these places from far-distant lands, if you are willing, we will show you all the places that are pleasant to the sight of Christians." Then, first thanking God, I eagerly asked the bishop that he would deign to do as he said. He thereupon led me first to the palace of King Abgar, where he showed me a great marble statue of him – very much like him, as they said – having a sheen as if made of pearl. From the face of Abgar it seemed that he was a very wise and honorable man. Then the holy bishop said to me: "Behold King Abgar, who before he saw the Lord believed that he was in truth the Son of God." Then we entered the inner part of the palace, and there were fountains full of fish such as I never saw before, of so great size, so bright and of so good a flavor were they. The city has no water at all other than that which comes out of the palace, which is like a great silver river....

Antioch to Tarsus

When I had got back to Antioch, I stayed there for a week, while the things that were necessary for our journey were being prepared. Then, starting from Antioch and journeying through several stations, I came to the province called Cilicia, which has Tarsus for its metropolis. I had already been at Tarsus on my way to Jerusalem, but as the memorial of St-Thecla is at the third station from Tarsus, in Hisauria, it was very pleasant for me to go there, especially as it was so very near at hand.

So, setting out from Tarsus, I came to a certain city on the sea, still in Cilicia, which is called Pompeiopolis. Thence I entered the borders of Hisauria and stayed in a city called Coricus, and on the third day I arrived at a city which is called Seleucia in Hisauria; on my arrival I went to the bishop, a truly holy man, formerly a monk, and in that city I saw a very beautiful church. And as the distance from there to [the church of] St-Thecla, which is situated outside the city on a low hill, was about fifteen hundred paces, I chose rather to go there in order to make the stay that I intended. There is nothing at the holy church in that place except numberless cells of men and of women. I found there a very dear friend of mine, to whose manner of life all in the East bore testimony, a holy deaconess named Marthana, whom I had known at Jerusalem, where she had come for the sake of prayer; she was ruling over the cells of *apotactitae* [holy women] and virgins. And when she had seen me, how can I describe the extent of her joy or of mine? But to return to the matter in hand: there are very many cells on the hill and in the midst of it a great wall which encloses the church containing the very beautiful memorial. The wall was built to guard the church because of the Hisauri, who are very malicious and who frequently commit acts of robbery, to prevent them from making an attempt on the monastery which is established there. When I had arrived in the name of God, prayer was made at the memorial, and the whole of the acts of Saint Thecla having been read, I gave endless thanks to Christ our God, who deigned to fulfill my desires in all things, unworthy and undeserving as I am.

Then, after a stay of two days, when I had seen the holy monks and *apotactitae* who were there, both men and women, and when I had prayed and made my communion, I returned to Tarsus and to my journey. From Tarsus, after a halt of three days, I set out on my journey in the name of God, and arriving on the same day at a station called Mansocrenae, which is under Mount Taurus, I stayed there. On the next day, going along the foot of Mount Taurus, and traveling by the route that was already known to me, through each province that I had traversed on my way out, namely, Cappadocia, Galatia, and Bithynia, I arrived at Chalcedon, where I stayed for the sake of the very famous martyr memorial of St-Euphemia, which was already known to me from a former time.

On the next day, crossing the sea, I arrived at Constantinople, giving thanks to Christ our God who deigned to give me such grace, unworthy and undeserving as I am, for he had deigned to give me not only the will to go, but also the power of walking through the places that I desired, and of returning at last to Constantinople. When I had arrived there, I went through all the churches — that of the apostles and all the martyr-memorials, of which there are very many — and I ceased not to give thanks to Jesus our God, who had thus deigned to bestow his mercy upon me. From which place, ladies, light of my eyes, while I send these [letters] to your affection, I have already decided, in the name of Christ our God, to go to Ephesus in Asia, for the sake of prayer, because of the memorial of the holy and blessed apostle John. And if after this I am yet in the body, and am able to see any other places, I will either tell it to your affection in person, if God deigns to permit me this, or, if I have another project in mind, I will send you news of it in a letter. But do you, ladies, light of my eyes, deign to remember me, whether I am in the body or out of the body.

Jerusalem

... [The anniversaries of the] days when the holy church in Golgotha, which they call the martyrium, was consecrated to God are called "the days of dedication"; the holy church also which is at the Anastasis, that is, in the place where the Lord rose after his Passion [his suffering and death], was consecrated to God on that day. The dedication of these holy churches is therefore celebrated with the highest honor, because the cross of the Lord was found on this same day. And it was so ordained that, when the holy churches above mentioned were first consecrated, that should be the day when the cross of the Lord had been found, in order that the whole celebration should be made together, with all rejoicing, on the self-same day. Moreover, it appears from the Holy Scriptures that this is also the day of dedication, when holy Solomon, having finished the house of God which he had built, stood before the altar of God and prayed, as it is written in the books of the Chronicles.

So when these days of dedication come, they are kept for eight days. And people begin to assemble from all parts many days before, not only monks and *apotactitae* from various provinces, from Mesopotamia and Syria, from Egypt and the Thebaid (where there are very many monks), and from every different place and province – for there is none who does not turn his steps to Jerusalem on that day for such rejoicing and for such high days – but lay people too in like manner, both men and women, with faithful minds, gather together in Jerusalem from every province on those days, for the sake of the holy day. And the bishops, even when they have been few, are present to the number of 40 or 50 in Jerusalem on these days, and with them come many of their clergy. But why should I say more? For he who on these days has not been present at so solemn a feast thinks that he has committed a very great sin, unless some necessity, which keeps a man back from carrying out a good resolution, has hindered him. Now on these days of the dedication the adornment of all the churches is the same as at Easter and at Epiphany; also on each day the procession is made to the several holy places, as at Easter and at Epiphany. For on the first and second days it is to the greater church, which is called the martyrium. On the third day it is to Eleona, that is, the church which is on that mount from which the Lord ascended into heaven after his Passion, and in this church is the cave wherein the Lord used to teach his apostles on the Mount of Olives.

What was Etheria's primary reason for undertaking her pilgrimage? What sort of people did she encounter during her travels, and how did they influence her travels? What evidence does her account provide that local men and women played an active part in shaping the devotional experience of Christian visitors to the Holy Land? As described by Etheria, what was Jerusalem like during the "days of dedication"?

8. JEROME ON THE PILGRIMAGE OF PAULA

In the year 386, the well-known Christian thinker Jerome left Rome for Antioch, where he joined two Roman women, Paula and her daughter Eustochium, before the three of them proceeded to Jerusalem. Eventually, they all settled there. Nineteen years later, Jerome described Paula's experience at the holy places. For Jerome, the landscape of her pilgrimage followed the contours of the Bible, including prophecies that foretold the coming of Christ. In many ways, the text tells us more about Jerome's view of the Promised Land than Paula's actual pilgrimage. Nevertheless, at points, one can still glean some impression of Paula's devotional interaction with the places sanctified by Christ and other figures from Scripture.

Source: trans. W.H. Fremantle, in *A Select Library of the Nicene and Post-Nicene Fathers*, 2nd series, vol. 6 (New York: The Christian Literature Co., 1893), pp. 198–202; revised.

8. I speak not of her journey through Coele-Syria and Phoenicia, for I have no intention of giving you a complete itinerary of her travels. Instead, I will only name such places as are mentioned in the sacred Scriptures. After leaving the Roman colony of Berytus and the ancient city of Zidon, on the shore at Zarephath she entered Elijah's turret and therein adored her Lord and Savior. Next, passing over the sands of Tyre, on which Paul had once knelt, she came to Acco or (as it is now called) Ptolemais, rode over the plains of Megiddo, which had once witnessed the slaying of Josiah, and entered the land of the Philistines. Here she could not fail to admire the ruins of Dor, once a most powerful city, and Strato's Tower, which though at one time insignificant was rebuilt by Herod king of Judea and named Caesarea in honor of Caesar Augustus. Here she saw the house of Cornelius, now turned into a Christian church, and the humble abode of Philip and the chambers of his daughters, the four virgins "who did prophesy."

She arrived next at Antipatris, a small town half in ruins, named by Herod after his father Antipater, and at Lydda (now become Diospolis), a place made famous by Dorcas's resurrection and the restoration of Aeneas's health. Not far from this are Arimathea, the village of Joseph who buried the Lord, and Nob, once a city of priests, but now the tomb in which their slain bodies rest. Joppa too is close by, the port of Jonah's flight, which also – if I may introduce a poetic fable – saw Andromeda bound to the rock. Again resuming her journey, she came to Nicopolis, once called Emmaus, where the Lord became known in the breaking of bread, an action by which he dedicated the house of Cleopas as a church. Starting from there she made her way up lower and higher Bethhoron, cities founded by Solomon, but subsequently destroyed by several devastating wars. She saw on her right Ajalon and Gibeon, where Joshua the son of Nun when fighting against the five kings gave commandments to the sun and moon, and where also he condemned the Gibeonites, who by a crafty stratagem had obtained a pact to be hewers of wood and drawers of water. At Gibeah also, now a complete ruin, she stopped for a little while remembering its sin and the cutting of the concubine into pieces, and how in spite of all this three hundred men of the tribe of Benjamin were saved so that Paul in later days might be called a Benjamite.

9. To make a long story short, leaving on her left the mausoleum of Helena, queen of Adiabene, who in time of famine had sent corn to the Jewish people, Paula entered Jerusalem, Jebus, or Salem, that city of three names which, after it had sunk to ashes and decay, Aelius Hadrianus had restored it once more, naming it Aelia. Although the proconsul of Palestine, who was an intimate friend of her household, sent forward his public officials and gave orders to have his official residence placed at her disposal, she chose a humble cell in preference to it. Moreover, when visiting the holy places,

so great was the passion and the enthusiasm she exhibited for each, that she could never have torn herself away from one had she not been eager to visit the rest. Before the Cross she threw herself down in adoration as though she beheld the Lord hanging upon it. When she entered the tomb which was the scene of the Resurrection, she kissed the stone which the angel had rolled away from the door of the sepulcher. Indeed so ardent was her faith that she even licked with her mouth the very spot on which the Lord's body had lain, like one thirsty for the river which one has longed for. What tears she shed there, what groans she uttered, and what grief she poured forth, all Jerusalem knows, as does the Lord to whom she prayed....

10. After distributing money to the poor and her fellow-servants, so far as her means allowed, she then proceeded to Bethlehem, stopping only on the right side of the road to visit Rachel's tomb.... After this she came to Bethlehem and entered into the cave where the savior was born. Here, she looked upon the inn made sacred by the virgin, and the stall where the ox knew his owner and the ass his master's crib, and where the words of the same prophet had been fulfilled: "Blessed is he that sows beside the waters where the ox and the ass trample the seed under their feet." When she looked upon these things, I say, she protested in my hearing that she could behold with the eyes of faith the infant Lord wrapped in swaddling clothes and crying in the manger, the wise men worshipping him, the star shining overhead, the virgin mother, the attentive foster-father, the shepherds coming by night to see "the word that was come to pass," and thus even then to consecrate those opening phrases of the Gospel-writer John, "In the beginning was the Word," and "the Word was made flesh." She declared that she could see the slaughtered innocents, the raging Herod, Joseph and Mary fleeing into Egypt, and with a mixture of tears and joy she cried: "Hail Bethlehem, house of bread, where that Bread that came down from heaven was born!"

12. After this Paula visited the tomb of Lazarus and beheld the hospitable roof of Mary and Martha, as well as Bethphage, "the town of the priestly jaws." Here the restless foal typical of the Gentiles received the bridle of God and, covered with the garments of the apostles, offered its lowly back for him [Jesus] to sit on. From this she went straight on down the hill to Jericho thinking of the wounded man in the Gospel, of the savagery of the priests and Levites who passed him by, and of the kindness of the Samaritan (that is, the guardian), who placed the half-dead man upon his own beast and brought him down to the inn of the church. She noticed the place called Adomim, or the Place of Blood, so-called because much blood was shed there in the frequent incursions of marauders. She beheld also the sycamore tree of Zacchaeus, by which is signified the good works of repentance whereby

he trod under foot his former sins of bloodshed and rapine, and from which he saw the Most High as from a pinnacle of virtue. She was shown too the spot by the wayside where the blind men sat who, receiving their sight from the Lord, became types of the two peoples [Jews and Gentiles] who should believe in him.....

14. No sooner did Paula come in sight of it [the city of Alexandria] than there came to meet her the reverend and estimable bishop, the confessor Isidore, accompanied by countless crowds of monks, many of whom were of the priestly or of Levitical rank. On seeing these, Paula rejoiced to behold the Lord's glory manifested in them, but protested that she had no claim to be received with such honor. Need I speak of the [monks] Macarii, Arsenius, Serapion, or other pillars of Christ? Was there any [monastic] cell that she did not enter? Or any man at whose feet she did not throw herself? In each of his saints she believed that she saw Christ himself, and whatever she bestowed upon them she rejoiced to feel that she had bestowed it upon the Lord. Her enthusiasm was wonderful and her endurance scarcely credible in a woman. Forgetful of her sex and of her weakness, she even desired to make her abode, together with the girls who accompanied her, among these thousands of monks. As they were all willing to welcome her, she might perhaps have sought and obtained permission to do so, had she not been drawn away by a still greater passion for the holy places. Coming by sea from Pelusium to Maioma on account of the great heat, she returned so rapidly that you would have thought her a bird. Not long afterwards, making up her mind to dwell permanently in holy Bethlehem, she took up her abode for three years in a miserable hostel, until she could build the requisite cells and monastic buildings, to say nothing of a guest house for passing travelers where they might find the welcome which Mary and Joseph had missed. At this point, I conclude my narrative of the journeys that she made accompanied by Eustochium and many other virgins.

What importance did the Bible hold for Paula as she traveled around the holy places? How might her experiences in Bethlehem at the birthplace of Christ be characterized, and what do they imply about early Christian devotion to Jesus? Why did the clergy and monks of Alexandria offer her such an enthusiastic welcome? What did Paula do when she had completed her travels, and what did her actions suggest about her sense of commitment to the holy places?

9. JEROME ON THE CULT OF SAINTS

Not everyone approved of the increasingly popular devotion shown to the saints and their relics at churches and shrines. One priest from southern Gaul (modern France) named Vigilantius wrote a tract criticizing the extravagance that surrounded the saints and their remains, including the burning of candles and stories of their miracles. Vigilantius, who had spent time in Bethlehem with Jerome, also complained that churches sent alms to support Christians at holy places in Jerusalem, rather than using them to assist the poor in their own communities. In 406, Jerome offered a spirited defense of such practices in his treatise Against Vigilantius.

Source: trans. W.H. Fremantle, in *A Select Library of the Nicene and Post-Nicene Fathers*, 2nd series, vol. 6 (New York: The Christian Literature Co., 1893), pp. 418–22; revised.

5. Who in the world, you madman, ever worshipped the martyrs? Who ever thought that man was God? When the people of Lycaonia thought Paul and Barnabas to be Jupiter and Mercury, and would have offered sacrifices to them, did they not rend their clothes and declare they were men? Not that they were not better than Jupiter and Mercury (men who had died long ago), but because, under the mistaken ideas of the Gentiles, the honor due to God was being paid to them. We read the same thing about Peter, who, when Cornelius wished to worship him, raised him by the hand and said, "Stand up, for I also am a man." And you dare to speak about "the mysterious something or other which you carry about in a little vessel and worship." I want to know what it is that you call "something or other." Explain more clearly, giving free reign to your blasphemy, what you mean by the phrase "a bit of powder wrapped up in expensive cloth in a tiny vessel." He is upset to see that it is nothing less than the relics of the martyrs covered with a costly veil, not bound up with rags or hair-cloth or thrown on the trash-heap, so that he, Vigilantius alone, drunk and oblivious may be worshipped.

Are we, therefore, committing sacrilege when we enter the churches of the apostles? Was the emperor Constantius committing sacrilege when he moved the sacred relics of Andrew, Luke, and Timothy to Constantinople? In their presence the demons cry out and those of them possessing Vigilantius confess that they feel the influence of the saints. In the present day, is the emperor Arcadius to be considered sacrilegious, who conveyed the bones of the blessed Samuel from Judea to Thrace after such a long time? Are all the bishops to be considered not only sacrilegious, but judged foolish, because they carried that most worthless thing, dust and ashes, wrapped in silk in a golden vessel? Are the people of all the churches stupid, because they rushed forth to meet the sacred relics and welcomed them with as much joy as if they beheld a living presence in their company, so that a great crowd of people from Palestine to Chalcedon was joined together, sounding the praises of Christ with a single voice? Truly, they were venerating not Christ, but Samuel, who was Christ's priest and prophet. You surmise that there is only a dead body, and therefore commit blasphemy. Read the Gospel – "The God of Abraham, the God of Isaac, the God of Jacob: He is not the God of the dead, but of the living." If they are alive, they are not (as you would have it) kept in honorable confinement....

7. As to the question of candlesticks, however, we do not light them by day, as you vainly accused us of doing, but rather dispel the shadows of the night by their comfort, watching for the dawn so that we do not sleep in the shadows like you. And if some people do these things out of honor for the martyrs, being ignorant and simple-minded laymen, or, certainly, religious women (of whom we can truly say "I allow that they have zeal for God, but not according to knowledge"), what harm is it to you? Once upon a time, even the Apostles complained that the ointment was wasted, but they were rebuked by the voice of the Lord. For Christ did not need the ointment, nor do martyrs need the light of candles, and yet that woman still poured out the ointment in Christ's honor and her heart's devotion was accepted. All those who light these candlesticks have their reward according to their faith, as the Apostle says, "Let every one abound in his own meaning." Do you call men of that sort idolaters? I do not deny that all of us who believe in Christ have passed from the error of idolatry. For we are not born, but reborn as Christians. Because we formerly worshipped idols, does it follow that we ought not now to worship God, in case we seem to pay like honor to him as to the idols? In the former case, respect was paid to idols, and therefore this ought to be abhorred; in the latter, the martyrs are venerated, and this ought to be allowed. Throughout the whole eastern church, where there are no relics of the martyrs, the candles are lighted whenever the Gospel is read, even as dawn is reddening the sky, not of course to scatter the darkness but to show evidence of our joy. Accordingly the virgins in the Gospel always have their lamps lighted and the Apostles are told to have their loins girded and their lamps burning in their hands; we read of John the Baptist "He was the lamp that burns and shines," so that under the figure of a bodily light, that light is represented of which we read in the Psalter, "Thy word is a lamp unto my feet, O Lord, and a light unto my paths."

10. ... He [Vigilantius] argues against the signs and miracles that happen in the churches of the martyrs, and says that they are of service to the unbelieving, not to believers, as if the issue at hand was for whose advantage they occur, not by whose power. Granted that signs belong to the faithless, who, because they do not believe the word and doctrine, are brought to believe

by means of signs. Even our Lord gave signs for the unbelieving, and yet our Lord's signs are not to be impugned because those people were faithless, but ought to be admired even more because they were so powerful that they subdued even the hardest hearts and compelled men to believe. So I will not have you tell me that signs are for the unbelieving; but answer my question – how is it that poor worthless dust and ashes, who knows of what, are associated with this wonderful power of signs and miracles?... Let me give you some advice: go to the churches of the martyrs and some day you will be cleansed. You will find there many people like yourself and will be set on fire, not by the martyrs' candles which offend you, but rather by invisible flames. Then you will confess what you now deny, and will freely proclaim your name – that you who speak in the person of Vigilantius are really either Mercury, greedy of gain, or Nocturnus, who, according to Plautus' "Amphitryon," slept while Jupiter had his adulterous connection for two nights with Alcmena, and thus begat the mighty Hercules, or at all events with Father Bacchus, of drunken fame, with the tankard hanging from his shoulder, with his ruddy face, foaming lips, and wild partying.

13. Something also appears to be troubling you. You are afraid that, if continence, sobriety, and fasting take root among the people of Gaul, your taverns will not pay, and you will be unable to keep up through the night your devilish vigils and drunken revels. What's more, I have learned from those same letters that, in defiance of the authority of Paul, nay rather of Peter, John, and James (who gave the right hand of fellowship to Paul and Barnabas, and commanded them to remember the poor), you forbid any financial support to be sent to Jerusalem for the benefit of the saints. Now, if I reply to this, you will immediately cry out that I am pleading my own cause. You, in truth, showed so much largess to everyone, acting as if you had not come to Jerusalem, and thrown around your own money or that of your patrons we all would have starved. I say what the blessed apostle Paul says in nearly all of his letters, and makes as a rule for the churches of the Gentiles: on the first day of the week, that is, on the Lord's day, contributions should be made by every one which should be sent up to Jerusalem for the relief of the saints, and that either by his disciple, or by those approved of by them, and if it were thought fit, he would himself either send or take what was collected. Also in the Acts of the Apostles, when speaking to the governor Felix, he says, "After many years I went up to Jerusalem to bring alms to my nation and offerings, and to perform my vows, amidst which they found me purified in the temple." Could he not have distributed what he received in some other part of the world, in the newly born churches which he was training in his own faith? He longed, however, to give to the poor of the holy places who,

abandoning their own little possessions for the sake of Christ, turned with their whole heart to the service of the Lord.

According to Jerome, what are Vigilantius's main criticisms of the cult of sacred relics and those who venerated them? How does Jerome respond to his complaints? Why did the faithful send money specifically to Jerusalem, and why does Vigilantius complain about this practice? Imagine that Vigilantius had read about the pilgrimages of Etheria (doc. 7) and Paula (doc. 8): how might he have reacted to news of their pious travels, including their visits to saints' shrines?

10. *THE LIFE OF MELANIA THE YOUNGER*

Around 408 or 409, an aristocratic Christian woman named Melania departed from Rome for Africa with her mother, Albina, and husband, Pinian, also called her "spiritual brother." After some debate, the couple had sworn vows of celibacy and committed themselves to living lives of ascetic poverty, using their worldly wealth to establish and support religious institutions. Seven years later, the three proceeded to Jerusalem, where they would spend the remainder of their lives, aside from journeys to holy places in Egypt, Constantinople, and elsewhere. The account of Melania's life, written by her companion and hagiographer Gerontius, reveals the networks of elite men and women that helped to facilitate devotional travel, even as the barbarian incursions of peoples such as the Visigoths were destabilizing the western Roman Empire.

Source: trans. E. Clark, *The Life of Melania the Younger: Introduction, Translation, and Commentary* (New York: The Edwin Mellen Press, 1984), pp. 41–43, 50–52, 54, 62–65, 68–72.

19. Furthermore, they fearlessly gave away the remainder of their possessions in Rome, as we have said before – possessions that were, so to speak, enough for the whole world. For what city or country did not have a share in their enormously good deeds? If we say Mesopotamia and the rest of Syria, all of Palestine, the regions of Egypt and the Pentapolis, would we say enough? But lest we continue on too long, the entire West and the entire East shared in their numerous good deeds. I myself, of course, when I traveled the road to Constantinople, heard many old men, especially Lord Tigrius, the priest of Constantinople, give thanks to the holy ones. When they acquired several islands, they gave them to holy men. Likewise, they purchased monasteries of monks and virgins and gave them as a gift to those who lived there, furnishing each place with a sufficient amount of gold. They presented their numerous and expensive silk clothes at the altars of churches and monasteries. They

broke up their silver, of which they had a great deal, and made altars and ecclesiastical treasures from it, and many other offerings to God. When they had sold their properties around Rome, Italy, Spain, and Campania, they set sail for Africa. Just then Alaric [the Visigoth] set foot on the property the blessed ones had just sold. Everyone praised the Lord of all things, saying: "Lucky are the ones who anticipated what was to come and sold their possessions before the arrival of the barbarians"....

20. Then they departed from the island [of Sicily] and sailed toward Africa, as we mentioned before. When they arrived there, they immediately sold their property in Numidia, Mauretania, and in Africa itself. Some of the money they sent for the service of the poor and some for ransoming captives. Thus they distributed the money freely and rejoiced in the Lord and were gladdened, for they were fulfilling in action what had been written: "He has given funds; he gave to the poor; his righteousness remains from age to age." When the blessed ones decided to sell all their property, the most saintly and important bishops of Africa, I mean the blessed Augustine [of Hippo], his brother Alypius, and Aurelius of Carthage, advised them, saying: "The money that you now furnish to monasteries will be used up in a short time. If you wish to have memorial forever in heaven and on earth, give both a house and an income to each monastery." Melania and Pinian eagerly accepted the excellent counsel of the holy men and did just as they had been advised by them. Henceforth, advancing toward perfection, they tried to accustom themselves to complete poverty in their living arrangements and in the food they ate....

34. When they had remained in Africa for seven years and had renounced the whole burden of their riches, they at last started out for Jerusalem, for they had a desire to worship at the holy places. They set sail from Africa and headed eastward, arriving at Alexandria, where the most holy bishop Cyril received them in a manner worthy of his holiness. At that time, it just happened that the holy father Nestoros, a man who possessed prophetic gifts, was in the city. This holy man was accustomed to come once a year to the city for the purpose of curing the sick. He also possessed this gift from the Lord, that he could deliver from diverse diseases those who came to him, using oil that had been blessed. As soon as the saintly ones, who were great friends of the holy men, heard about him, they immediately set out to receive spiritual profit. Because of the immense crowd of people who came to him, they got separated from one another. The first to enter with the limitless crowd was Pinian, the most blessed brother of the saint. He was eager to receive the blessing so that he could leave. The holy man, however, looking intently at him with his spiritual eyes, recognizing the beauty of his soul, seized him, and made him stand alongside him. Then Melania, the servant of Christ, also

came in with a great crowd. When Nestoros saw her, he recognized her with his spiritual eyes and made her stand with her brother. Thus when Melania's holy mother came in third, Nestoros stopped her and made her stand with the two. After he had dismissed the whole crowd, he began to tell them first with exhortation and prophetic speech what diverse troubles they had endured in their renunciation. He counseled them like his own children and exhorted them not to lose heart, since the goal of affliction is to have unutterable bliss. He said, "For the sufferings of the present time are not worthy to be compared to the coming glory that is to be revealed to us."

35. Thus being much encouraged and praising God even more, they set sail for Jerusalem and hastened on to their destination. They stayed in the church of the Holy Sepulcher. Since they themselves did not want to distribute with their own hands the gold left to them, they gave it to those who were entrusted with administering charity for the poor. They did not wish for people to see them doing good deeds. They were in such a state of poverty that the holy woman Melania assured us of this: "When we first arrived here, we thought of inscribing ourselves on the church's register and of being fed with the poor from alms." Thus they became extremely poor for our sakes of the Lord, who himself became poor for our sakes and who took the form of a servant. It happened that Melania was sick when we were first in Jerusalem and had nowhere to lie down except in her sackcloth. A certain well-born virgin presented her with a pillow as a gift. When she became healthy again, she spent her time in reading and prayer, sincerely serving the Lord.

36. Thus Melania and her mother lived together by themselves. Melania was not quick to see anyone except the holy and highly reputed bishops, especially those who stood out for their doctrine, so that she might spend the time of their conferences inquiring about the divine word. As we said before, she wrote in notebooks and fasted during the week. Every evening, after the church of the Holy Sepulcher was closed, she remained at the cross until the psalm-singers arrived. Then she departed for her cell and slept for a short while.

37. Because of the barbarian invasion, they could not sell all their property, and hence some of it remained un-purchased. A certain believer whose heart God had awakened was able to sell part of it in the area of Spain where peace prevailed. Having collected a little gold from the sales, he took it to the blessed ones in Jerusalem. Melania seized it as if from the lion's mouth and dedicated it to God, saying to her spiritual brother in the Lord, "Let us go to Egypt to inquire after the holy men," and he, who did not hesitate to perform such works, obeyed her cheerfully, as she was truly a good teacher. When she was about to depart on this spiritual journey, Melania asked her holy mother to have a little cell built for her near the Mount of Olives, with

its interior made from boards, where she might dwell peacefully in the near future. They arrived in Egypt and toured the cells of the holy monks and the very faithful virgins, supplying to each as he had need, as it is written, for they were indeed wise administrators....

40. The blessed ones returned to Jerusalem carrying a full cargo of piety. Having completed the work of our Lord Jesus Christ's service with much eagerness, they both fell ill due to the bad quality of the air. The blessed woman found the little cell of the Mount of Olives already finished through the effort of her saintly mother. There, after the day of Holy Epiphany, she shut herself in, and sat in sackcloth and ashes, seeing nobody, with the exception that on some days she met with her very holy mother and her spiritual brother. Her cousin, the blessed virgin Paula, also came to see her. The holy woman Melania had guided Paula in all the commandments of God, and had brought her back to much humility from great vanity and the Roman way of thinking. She also had as a servant one virgin who often assured us, "At the time of Holy Easter, when the blessed woman emerged from that exceedingly narrow cell, we shook the sack that lay under her and enormous lice fell out." Melania lived in this kind of ascetic regime for fourteen years.... [Over this period of fourteen years, Melania's mother and husband both died; Melania also founded monasteries on the Mount of Olives for both men and women.]

50. Immediately, other battles fell to her, greater than the earlier labors. For when the monastery was finished and she was catching a little breath, straightway letters arrived from her uncle Volusian, ex-prefect of greater Rome, stating that he was going to Constantinople on a mission to the most pious empress Eudoxia, who had been pledged in marriage to our Christ-loving emperor Valentinian. There arose in Melania a desire to see her uncle. She was spurred by grace from above to entertain this desire so that she might save his soul through great effort, for he was still a pagan. She struggled mightily, lest she do something contrary to God's pleasure. She told all the holy men about the matter and exhorted them to pray earnestly that her journey might be in accordance with God's will. And after she entrusted the monasteries to the Lord, she left Jerusalem.

51. From the beginning of her journey, the holy men of every city and country (I mean bishops and clergy) gave her glory and indescribable honor. The God-loving monks and pious virgins, when they had seen her whose illustrious virtues they had heard about for a long time, were separated from her with many tears.

52. I do not consider it without risk to pass over in silence the miracle that God did on her behalf in Tripoli, because, as scripture says, "It is good to hide a king's secret, but the works of God are glorious to reveal." When we arrived there we stayed in the martyrion of St-Leontius, in whose shrine

not a few miracles took place. Since many who were traveling with her did not have the prearranged documents, the official proved to be very difficult about releasing the animals. His name was Messala. The blessed woman was very upset about this; she remained in prayer and kept vigil by the relics of the holy martyr Leontius from evening until the time when the animals had arrived. We left Tripoli and had traveled about seven miles when the aforementioned official came after us, in total confusion, and asked, "Where is the priest?" Since I was inexperienced about traveling, I was afraid lest he had come to retrieve the animals. Getting down, I asked him why he was upset, and he replied, "I am eager to have the honor of meeting the great woman." Then, when he saw her, he fell down and seized her feet amid many tears and said, "I beg your pardon, O servant of Christ, that I, not knowing your great holiness, held back the release of the animals." And Melania replied, "God bless you, child, that you did indeed release them, even if belatedly." He straightway took out the three coins that we had given him as a tip and begged us to take them back from him. Since I was not of a mind to do so, he started to confess to the saint: "All night long, both I and your servant, my wife, were strongly tested by the holy martyr Leontius. Thus we got up immediately and both ran to the martyrion. When we did not find you, she returned, because she was not able to run any further, but I who have overtaken you, beg your holiness to pray for us both, in order that the God of all things may deign to be gracious to us." When we heard this, we accepted the coins, offered a prayer, and let the official go in peace, rejoicing. Since all those traveling along with us were amazed by what had happened, the saint said, "Take courage, for our journey is in accordance with God's will." And when all of us asked her to teach us openly the reason why, the saint answered, "All night I prayed to the holy martyr Leontius that he might show us an auspicious sign for this trip. And behold, though I am unworthy, my request has been fulfilled." Then we joyfully traveled on and were welcome by everyone.

53. When we finally arrived near the Christ-loving city of Constantinople, the saint was anxious, since she was about to enter this sort of an imperial city after so much ascetic discipline and solitude. We came to the martyrion of St-Euphemia in Chalcedon where the Victorious One greatly comforted the saint, providing her with much cheer and encouragement. Then strengthened in the Lord, she·entered Constantinople.... [While at Constantinople, Melania finds her uncle ill and encounters the Devil in the form of a "young black man." She repudiates him but falls ill herself. Eventually, her uncle is baptized and she recovers, remaining at his bedside until he dies.]

56. Melania remained at Constantinople until she had done her time of forty days. She had greatly benefited from all who were there, most

particularly the Christ-loving imperial women. She also edified the most pious emperor Theodosius. And since his wife had a desire to worship at the holy places, Melania begged him to let her go. We departed from there at the end of the month of February. At that time the winter was so fierce that the Galatian and Cappadocian bishops asserted that they had never seen such a winter. And although we were completely covered with snow all day, we made our journey without faltering. We saw neither the ground nor the mountains, nothing except the hostels in which we stayed at night. Melania, who was like [stone made of] adamant, did not let up on her fasting at all. She said, "We ought now to fast more and to give thanks to God, the ruler of everything, because of the great wonders he has accomplished with me." Persevering in her unceasing prayer, she prevented both herself and us from suffering anything disagreeable in that most terrible cold. She showed that the prayer of a just person is a very strong weapon through which even the very elements are moved and overcome. While all the holy men tried to delay us en route, she was not persuaded by any of them to do so, but had one wish, to celebrate Christ's Passion in Jerusalem. This God granted to her, according to the trustworthy promise he spoke through his most holy prophet, "He will do the desire of those who fear him and will hear their prayer."

57. We arrived at the third day of the week before the savior's Passion. Having celebrated Easter in a spiritual manner and the Holy Resurrection in great cheerfulness among her own sisters, she again submitted to the customary rule, taking care of both monasteries. And when she saw how well the psalmody was performed in the church by the God-loving monks, another pious desire came to her: she wanted to have built a small martyrion. Thus she said to my own humble self, "This is the place in which the feet of the Lord stood. Therefore let us build here a holy oratory, so that after my journey from this world to the Lord, an offering on behalf of my soul and those of my masters can also be offered unceasingly in this place." Since every wish and desire of hers satisfied the God of all things, the work was completed in a few days. She again gathered other holy men and established them there.

58. When this had taken place, it was announced that the most pious empress was coming to Jerusalem and had already gotten as far as the city of Antioch. Thus Melania considered within herself what then she might do to glorify God and to benefit human beings. She said, "If I go out to meet her, I fear lest I bring reproach by traveling through the cities in this humble attire. But if I remain here, I must beware that this behavior not be thought arrogant on my part." So finally, having gone over this matter in pious reflection, she set out, saying: "It is fitting that we who have taken on the yoke of Christ, and were strong enough to do so, should carry on our own shoulders such a faithful empress, exulting in the power of the Lord because he has

established such a Christ-loving empress." She then went to meet Eudocia at Sidon, repaying with gratitude the extreme love the empress had showed to her at Constantinople. She stayed in the martyrion of St-Phocas, which is said to have been the dwelling of the faithful Canaanite woman who said in the holy Gospel of the Lord, "Yes, Lord, for even the little dogs eat the crumbs that fall from the table of their masters." Thus the blessed woman was zealous to please the Lord even in the matter of a dwelling, as well as in conversation and every other activity.

When the God-loving empress saw her, she fittingly received her with every honor, as Melania was a true spiritual mother. It was a glory for her to honor the woman who had so purely glorified the heavenly king. The saint, acknowledging her faith and the burden of her journey, exhorted her to proceed still further in good works. The pious empress answered her with this speech, worthy of remembrance: "I am fulfilling a double vow to the Lord, to worship at the holy places and to see my mother, for I have wished to be worthy of your holiness while you still serve the Lord in the flesh." In an excess of spiritual love, the Christ-loving empress was eager to get to the saint's monastery. Having arrived there, she regarded the virgins as if they were her own sisters. And since she had been greatly benefited, the empress desired also to go to the monastery of the men and be blessed. The deposition of the relics in the martyrion newly built by Melania, as we mentioned earlier, was about to occur. The empress requested that the festival take place while she was present.

59. And the enemy of good [the Devil], again envious of such spiritual love, prepared to twist the empress's foot at the deposition of the holy remains, and there resulted from this incident extraordinary trouble. This probably occurred as a contest for the faith of the holy woman. For at the very hour that Melania had escorted Eudocia to the church of the Holy Sepulcher, she had seated herself by the relics of the holy martyrs. Not standing aloof from them, she had prayed earnestly in much sorrow and fasting along with the virgins until the time the empress summoned her and the pain had stopped. When the pain had improved, the blessed woman did not cease fighting against the Devil, who had desired to make such a difficulty in their midst. When Melania had spent a few days with the empress and had benefited her immeasurably, she escorted her as far as Caesarea. They were scarcely able to be separated from one another, for they were strongly bonded together in spiritual love. And when she returned, the saint gave herself anew to ascetic discipline, praying thus up to the end that the pious empress would be returned to her husband in good health, which the God of all things granted to her.

What was Melania's attitude toward her riches and property before and during her pilgrimage? What sort of interaction did she have with the holy man, Nestoros, during her visit to Alexandria? How did Melania spend her time after her arrival at Jerusalem, and what did this imply about her status as a pilgrim? Why did she travel to Constantinople, and how did she conduct herself during this journey? What seems to have been the relationship between Melania and Empress Eudocia during their travels?

11. THE *BREVIARY OF JERUSALEM*

The following guidebook to Jerusalem, known in Latin as the Brevarius de Hierosolyma, *probably dates to around the late fifth or early sixth century. The text, found in a variety of manuscripts, exists in many different versions with varying details. It might have been intended for readers in Western Europe planning to go on pilgrimage, or carried by actual pilgrims – travelers similar to Etheria, Paula, and Melania – as they made their way about the sacred sites and churches of Jerusalem during the later Roman Empire.*

Source: trans. B.E. Whalen, from the *Brevarius de Hierosolyma (forma a)*, in *Itineraria et alia geographica*, Corpus Christianorum Series Latina, vol. 175 (Turnhout: Brepols, 1965), pp. 109–12.

Here begins the brief description about how the city of Jerusalem is built:

1. That city sits on a hill. The basilica of Constantine lies in the middle of the city. At the entrance to the basilica, on the left-hand side, there is a small chamber where the cross of the Lord is placed. From there, you enter into the church of St-Constantine. There is a great apse to the west, where the three crosses were discovered. Also, there is an altar in that same place, made from silver and pure gold, supported by nine columns. Around that apse, there are twelve marble columns set in a circle, marvelous to see, and atop each column there are twelve silver vases, in which Solomon sealed the demons. In the middle of the basilica, there is the lance that was used to strike the Lord. From this, a cross has been made that shines at night with the strength of the sun by day.

2. From there, you enter into Golgotha, where there is a large court. Here the Lord was crucified. All around that hill, there are silver screens; also on that hill, there is found a kind of flint rock. It has silver doors, where the Lord's cross was placed, thoroughly decorated with gold and precious stones, exposed to the open sky above. A great deal of gold and silver adorn the screens. At that spot, there is the platter upon which the head of John the Baptist was carried; there is also the horn that was used to anoint David and

Solomon. In that same place, there is the ring made from amber that Solomon used to seal the demons. Adam was created here; here Abraham brought his son Isaac as a sacrifice at this same spot, where the Lord was crucified.

3. Moving to the west, you enter [the church of] the Holy Resurrection, where the sepulcher of the Lord lies; before it is the stone, a kind of flint. Set over it, there is a rotund church. A roof of gold and silver is set above that sepulcher, and everything around it is gold. Before the sepulcher is the altar where blessed Zacharias was killed, and his blood is dried there. After that, you proceed to the sacristy of the church of St-Constantine, where there is a small chamber that contains the rod, the sponge, and the cup, which the Lord blessed and gave to his disciples to drink, saying: "this is my body and my blood." From there, you go to the basilica, where Jesus found the men buying and selling doves, and drove them outside.

4. From there, you go to the massive basilica of Holy Zion, where there is the column upon which the Lord Jesus was scourged. There is a mark where he grasped it, impressed into it just like in wax. From there, you enter into the sacristy, containing the stone that was used to stone Saint Stephen to death. In the middle of the basilica is the crown of thorns, which the Lord received. The upper-room is also there, where the Lord instructed his disciples when they shared supper. Also there is the rod encased inside a column of silver.

5. From there, you go to the house of Caiphas, where Saint Peter made his denial. There is a large basilica of St-Peter on the spot. From there, you go to the house of Pilate, where he handed the Lord over to the Jews for scourging. There is a large basilica there, and a small chamber, where they stripped him bare and scourged him. It is called [the church of] Holy Wisdom.

6. From there, you go to the temple built by Solomon, of which nothing to remains but a crypt. From there, you go to that pinnacle, upon which Satan placed the Lord. As you descend to Siloam, there is the pit where they placed blessed Jeremiah....

What seems to have been the main purpose of the Breviary? *Imagine a pilgrim who visited Jerusalem in the sixth century: how might he or she have used this text? Compare the* Breviary *with Jerome's account of Paula's pilgrimage (doc. 8): are there similarities evident between them?*

12. LIFE AS PILGRIMAGE: AUGUSTINE'S *CONFESSIONS*

Even as pilgrims flocked to the holy places of Jerusalem, Christian thinkers never lost sight of their belief that the earthly Jerusalem formed but an imperfect reflection of the heavenly Jerusalem. For the famous theologian Augustine of Hippo (354–430), the idea of pilgrimage offered a metaphor for human existence here in this world – a transitory journey toward the eternal kingdom of God. In the first selection below from his Confessions, Augustine meditates upon the death of his mother and father, Monica and Patricius; in the remaining two selections, he speculates about his own relationship with God. In all three selections, Augustine employs the notion of pilgrimage to illustrate the fleeting nature of existence in the here and now.

Source: trans. V.J. Bourke, in *Saint Augustine: Confessions*, Fathers of the Church, vol. 21 (Washington, DC: Catholic University Press, 1953), pp. 261–62, 267–68, 384–85; revised.

Book Nine

13.37. May she be in peace, therefore, along with her husband, before and after whom she was married to no other, whom she obeyed, bearing fruit for you [God] with patience so that she might also win him for you. Inspire, O my Lord, my God, inspire your servants, my brothers, your children, my masters, those whom I serve with my heart and my voice and my pen, so that, whoever reads these words may remember at your altar your servant Monica and Patricius her former spouse, through whose flesh you did bring me into this life, in a way that remains inscrutable to me. Let them remember with holy feeling my parents in this transitory light and my brothers under you, O Father, in our Catholic Mother [the church], and also my fellow citizens in the eternal Jerusalem, for which the pilgrimage of your people sighs from beginning to end. In this way, her last request of me will be granted to her more fruitfully in the prayers of many through my confessions, more so than through my own prayers.

Book Ten

4.6. This is the fruit of my confessions, that I should confess not what kind of man I was, but what kind I am, not only before you in hidden rejoicing with trembling, and in hidden grief with hope, but even to the ears of believers among the sons of men, the companions of my joy and the colleagues of my mortality, my fellow citizens and pilgrims in my company, those who have gone before and those who go after, and those who share my company on the way. These are your servants, my brothers, whom you did desire as your sons, my masters, whom you did command me to serve, provided I wish to live with you and from you. This word of yours would amount to little, if it gave me instructions by word only and did not first lead the way by deed. I serve these men by words and deeds, doing so "under your wings," with every great peril, except for the fact that my soul is protected under your wings and my weakness is known to you. I am very little, but my Father lives forever and my protector is sufficient for me, for it is he himself who gave me life and kept me safe. For he is the same being who is with me even before I am with you. So, I will reveal myself to such men, the kind whom you have commanded me to serve – showing not what I was, but what I now am and what I am still, although "I do not even judge myself." Thus, then, may I be heard.

Book Twelve

16.23. Now, I want to talk a little before you, O my God, with those who concede that all these things are true, about which your truth is not silent within my mind. As for those who deny them, let them blather as much as they want and become agitated on their own. I will try to persuade them to quiet down and to hold the way open to themselves for your word. Now, if they refuse me and push me away, I beg you, O my God, "be not silent to me." Do you speak truthfully within my heart, for only you speak in that manner. I shall leave those people outside, blowing on the dust and stirring up the earth into their own eyes, and I shall go into my own little room [the heart] and sing love songs to you, groaning unutterable groanings during my pilgrimage, recalling in my heart the Jerusalem to which my heart has been uplifted, Jerusalem my homeland, Jerusalem my mother, and you ruling over it, enlightening it, its father, protector, spouse, its chaste and strong delight, the undivided joy and all its indescribable goods – all at once together, for it is the one highest and true good! Nor shall I be turned aside, until you gather all that I am from this dispersion and deformity in the peace of that place, that dearest mother, where are the first fruits of my spirit, from which these certitudes come to me, conforming and confirming me for eternity, O my God, my mercy!

What does Jerusalem represent for Augustine? How does he speak with God about his own life, his family, and others during the "pilgrimage" of this earthly existence? Compare Augustine's vision of Jerusalem to the Book of Revelation (doc. 3): what similarities are between them? Imagine a friend of Augustine's who set out on pilgrimage to the actual city of Jerusalem: what advice might Augustine have given to him or her?

CHAPTER TWO

SAINTS, TRAVELERS, AND SACRED SPACES
IN THE EARLY MEDIEVAL WEST

During the later fourth and fifth centuries, Western Europe experienced a series of profound political, social, and economic transformations caused by the prolonged collapse of Roman imperial power and its replacement by various "barbarian" kingdoms. It was not until the eighth and early ninth centuries that the Carolingian dynasty restored an appreciable level of unity and cohesion to the regions formerly ruled by Rome and beyond. In this age after the Roman Empire, bishops, monks, and other members of the clergy emerged as prominent sources of authority, helping to create a new sacred landscape of churches and saints' shrines. In many ways, it is more accurate to describe this early medieval "Church" as a Christian community of local churches, ranging from Italy to Ireland, each possessing its own traditions and holy sites. While long-distance travel suffered due to the political dislocation caused by the disintegration of the Roman Empire, pious believers flocked to nearby shrines, seeking the healing power and other miracles of the saints, whose earthly remains channeled God's grace to his followers. Even in this localized world, moreover, pilgrims made the sometimes long journey to Rome, which claimed a special status as the head of Christendom, due in part to the belief that Christ's chief apostle Saint Peter had founded the Roman church and been martyred in the city. His remains, along with those of Saint Paul and other martyrs, became an important focal point for veneration by Christian believers, making Rome a pilgrimage destination of unrivaled significance in Western Europe.

13. THE CHURCHES OF ROME

In addition to massive building projects in Jerusalem and Constantinople, Emperor Constantine's conversion enabled the construction of new churches in Rome, the ancient capital of the Roman Empire. One popular legend maintained that Constantine had actually received baptism from the bishop of Rome, Sylvester, who thereby cured him of leprosy. Starting in the fourth century, the Roman popes contributed to the enrichment of the city's churches, enlarging and endowing them with considerable gifts. Although written centuries later, the selections below from the Book of the Popes *describe some of these early transformations in the city's religious landscape, including one of Rome's main attractions: the remains of the apostles, Peter and Paul.*

Source: trans. L.R. Loomis, in *The Book of Popes (Liber pontificalis)*, Records of Civilization: Sources and Studies, vol. 1 (New York: Columbia University Press, 1916), pp. 41–44, 47–48, 50, 53–54, 57–58, 105–6, 115, 120–22; revised.

34. Sylvester, born a Roman, son of Rufinus, occupied the see 23 years, 10 months, and 11 days. He was bishop in the time of Constantine and Volusian, from 1 February until 1 January in the consulship of Constantius and Volusianus. He was an exile on Mount Syraptin, driven by the persecution of Constantine. Afterward, he returned and gloriously baptized Constantine Augustus, whom the Lord cured of leprosy through baptism, and from whose persecution he had fled when he was in exile. He built a church in the city of Rome, in the garden of one of his priests named Equitius, and he appointed it as a parish church of Rome near the baths of Domitian. Even to this day, it is called the church of Equitius. There also he offered the following gifts: a silver paten, weighing 20 lbs., a gift of Constantine Augustus; he also gave 2 silver beakers, weighing each 10 lbs.; a golden chalice, weighing 2 lbs.; 5 chalices for service, weighing each 2 lbs.; 2 silver pitchers, weighing each 10 lbs.; 1 silver paten, overlaid with gold, for the chrism, weighing 5 lbs.; 10 chandeliers, weighing each 8 lbs.; 20 bronze lamps, weighing each 10 lbs.; the Valerian manor in the Sabine region, which yields 80 solidi; the Statian manor in the Sabine region, which yields 55 solidi; the manor of Duae Casae in the Sabine region, which yields 40 solidi; the Percilian manor in the Sabine region, which yields 20 solidi; the Corbian manor in the Sabine region,, which yields 60 solidi; a house in the city with a bath in the Sicinine district, which yields 85 solidi; a garden within the city of Rome in the district of Ad Duo Amantes, yielding 15 solidi; and a house in the district of Orfea within the city, which yields 58 and ⅓ solidi....

In his time, Constantine Augustus built the following churches and adorned them: The Constantinian basilica [the Lateran Palace], where he offered the following gifts: a ciborium of hammered silver, which features on its front the Savior seated upon a chair, in height 5 feet, weighing 120 lbs.; and also the 12 apostles, who weigh each 90 lbs. and are 5 feet in height and wear crowns of purest silver; on the back, looking toward the apse, are featured the Savior seated upon a throne in height 5 feet, of purest silver, weighing 140 lbs., and 4 angels of silver, which weigh each 105 lbs. and 5 feet in height, having jewels from Alabanda in their eyes and carrying spears. The ciborium itself weighs 2025 lbs. of wrought silver, with a vaulted ceiling of purest gold. A lamp of purest gold hangs beneath the ciborium, with 50 dolphins of purest gold, weighing each 50 lbs., and chains that weigh 25 lbs.... the holy font where Constantine Augustus was baptized by the same bishop Sylvester [is made] of porphyry, overlaid with purest silver on every side within and without, above and as far as the water, weighing 3009 lbs. In the center of the font is a porphyry column, which bears a golden basin of purest gold, weighing 52 lbs., where there is a flame, burning 200 lbs. of balsam during the Easter season. The wick is made of asbestos. At the edge of the font in the baptistery there is a golden lamb pouring water, weighing 30 lbs.; to the right of the lamb, the Savior of purest silver, 5 feet in height, weighing 170 lbs., and to the left of the lamb, John the Baptist, of silver, 5 feet in height, holding an inscribed scroll that bears these words: "Behold the Lamb of God, behold, who takes away the sins of the world," weighing 125 lbs....

At the same time, at the request of Bishop Sylvester, Constantine Augustus built the basilica of blessed Peter the apostle, in the [former] shrine of Apollo, and laid there the coffin with the body of the holy Peter. The coffin itself he enclosed on all sides with bronze, which is unchangeable: at the head 5 feet, at the bottom 5 feet, at the right side 5 feet, at the left side 5 feet, underneath 5 feet, and overhead 5 feet. Thus he enclosed the body of blessed Peter the apostle and laid it away. Above, he set porphyry columns for adornment and other spiral columns which he brought from Greece. He made also a vaulted roof in the basilica, gleaming with polished gold, and over the body of the blessed Peter, above the bronze which enclosed it, he set a cross of purest gold, weighing 150 lbs., an appropriate size for the place, and upon it were inscribed these words: "Constantine Augustus and Helena Augustus this house shining with like royal splendor a court surrounds," inscribed in clear, enameled letters upon the cross.... At the same time, at the bidding of Bishop Sylvester, Constantine Augustus built a basilica of blessed Paul the apostle and laid the body away there in bronze and enclosed it, as he had done with the body of blessed Peter. To this basilica he offered the following gifts: near Tarsus, in Cicilia, the island of Cordionon, yielding 800 solidi. As he had done in the basilica of blessed Peter the apostle, so he also ordained all the consecrated vessels of gold and silver and bronze to be set there for the basilica of blessed Paul the apostle. Moreover he placed a golden cross over the tomb of blessed Paul the apostle, weighing 150 lbs.... At the same time Constantine Augustus constructed a basilica in the Sessorian palace, where also he placed and enclosed in gold and jewels some wood of the holy cross of our Lord Jesus Christ, and he dedicated the church under the name by which it is called even to this day, Jerusalem....

49. Simplicius, born a Tiburtine, son of Castinus, occupied the see 15 years, 1 month, and 7 days. He dedicated the basilica of the holy Stephen on the Celian Hill in the city of Rome and the basilica of the blessed apostle Andrew near the basilica of the holy Mary and another basilica of the holy Stephen near the basilica of the holy Lawrence, and another basilica of the blessed martyr Bibiana within the city of Rome beside the Licinian palace where her body rests. He appointed [holy] weeks for blessed Peter the apostle and for blessed Paul the apostle, and for blessed Lawrence, the martyr, when priests should be in attendance to administer baptism and penance to those who sought them, throughout the third district for the blessed Lawrence, the first district for the blessed Paul, the sixth and seventh districts for the blessed Peter....

53. Symmachus, born a Sardinian, son of Fortunatus, occupied the see 15 years, 7 months, and 27 days ... he adorned with marbles the basilica of blessed Peter. The fountain of blessed Peter with the square portico around it he beautified with marble work and with lambs and crosses and palms of mosaic. Likewise he widened the steps before the doors of the basilica of Saint Peter, the apostle, and he made other steps of wood on the right and on the left. Also he built palaces in the same place on the right and on the left. Also, below the steps into the atrium, outside in the square, he set another fountain and an accommodation for human necessity. In addition, he built other steps for ascent into the church of blessed Andrew and set up a fountain. He built the basilica of the holy martyr Agatha on the Via Aurelia on the estate Lardarium; he raised it from the ground up and offered there 2 silver coffers. At that time he built the basilica of Saint Pancratius, where he set a silver coffer, weighing 15 lbs.; he also built a bath in the same place.

In the church of blessed Paul the apostle, he also rebuilt the apse of the basilica that was falling into ruin, and embellished it with a picture behind the saint's tomb; he made a vaulting and a transept, and over the saint's tomb he erected a silver image of the savior and the 12 apostles that weighed 120 lbs. Before the doors of the basilica he built steps into the atrium and a fountain, and behind the apse he brought down water and built a bath from the foundation. Within the city of Rome he built the basilica of Saints Sylvester and Martin from its foundation, near the baths of Trajan and there also he set a silver ciborium above the altar, which weighed 120 lbs.... In addition, he enlarged the basilica of the archangel Michael, building steps and bringing down water. He also erected from the ground up an oratory of Saints Cosmas and Damian beside [the church of] Saint Mary. On the Via Trivana, twenty-seven miles from the city of Rome, he dedicated a basilica to blessed Peter on the estate Pacinianum at the request of Albinus and Glaphyra, the illustrious praetorian prefects, who raised it from the ground up at their own expense. Also, near [the churches of] blessed Peter and blessed Paul the apostles, and Saint Lawrence the martyr, he erected lodging houses for the poor.

How did the conversion of Constantine transform the Christian landscape of Rome? What evidence does this text provide that the bodily remains of the saints were critical for the establishment of holy sites in the city? Why does the author pay so much attention to the riches lavished upon local churches by the bishops of Rome? What signs were there that the holy sites of the city were attracting larger crowds of people than before?

14. DEVOTION IN ITALY: PAULINUS OF NOLA'S *LETTERS*

By the turn of the fifth century, Rome and its surroundings had become home to a thriving scene of religious devotion, both for local residents and travelers from more distant lands. In his correspondence, Paulinus of Nola (354–431), who lived much of his life not far from the city, captured a sense of Rome's growing importance as a site of worship. At the same time, his letters display some ambivalence toward Rome, a place where the rich and powerful met to carry out worldly business. Included below are Paulinus's description of Saint Peter's basilica during a funeral held by his friend Pammachius for his deceased wife, and his account of the pilgrim Melania the Elder during her return to Italy from Jerusalem. Melania the Elder, grandmother to Melania the Younger (doc. 10), brought with her relics from Jerusalem, including a fragment of the True Cross, demonstrating how pilgrims could literally bring a piece of the Eastern biblical landscape back to their Western homes.

Source: trans. P.G. Walsh, in *Letters of St. Paulinus of Nola*, 2 vols., Ancient Christian Writers 35 (New York: Newman Press, 1966), vol. 1, pp. 127–31, 161–62; vol. 2, pp. 105–6, 112–17, 125–27, 144–46.

Letter 13 to Pammachius (396)

11. I intend to pass now to the proclamation of your deeds, to the mention of your deeds, to the mention of your religious acts springing from your holy

tears. You discharged what was due to both parts of your wife; you shed tears for her body and lavished alms for her soul. As a son of light really aware of truth, you shed tears where you knew there was death, but performed good works where you believe there is life. So upon the empty you bestow empty things, but on the living, living things.

In the basilica of the apostle you gathered together a crowd of poor people, the patrons of our souls, those from the whole of Rome deserving of alms. I myself feast on the splendid scene of this great work of yours. For I seem to behold all those pious swarms of the wretched populace, the nurslings of God's affection, thronging in great lines deep into the huge basilica of the renowned Peter, through that venerable colonnade smiling afar with azure front, so that all the precincts are thronged – inside the basilica, before the gates of the atrium, and on the whole level area before the gates of the atrium, and on the whole level area before the steps. I see the gathering being divided amongst separate tables, and all the people being filled with abundance of food, so that before their eyes there appears the plenty bestowed by the Gospel's blessing and the picture of those crowds whom Christ, the true bread and the fish of living water, filled with five loaves and two fishes.... For by divine provision a hidden hand served a visible feast, pouring out bodily nourishment with spiritual abundance; from a source of bread and flesh which cannot be named it brought physical repletion and spiritual refreshment to peoples hungering for faith, inspiring hope in the races still unfed. With hidden increase it swelled the foodstuffs, supplied abundance of what was to be consumed, and proffered extra fragments to the diners, so that the food grew bigger in the hands or mouths of those who ate it. They experienced abundance of food, but they did not see the masticated food return from their mouths, nor did they see it being lifted as it approached their teeth.

13. It is still pleasant even now to linger in visualizing and praising this great work, for we are praising not the acts of a man but those of God performed through a man. How joyful to God and to his holy angels was the show you put on from your abundant store, as the saying is, a holy and not profane exhibitor! With what pleasure did you delight the apostle himself when you packed the whole of his basilica with dense crowds of the needy! They stood where, under its lofty roof, the huge basilica extends far beneath the central ceiling, and glittering afar from the apostle's tomb arrests the eyes and delights the hearts of those who enter; or where under the same imposing roof it extends sideways with twin colonnades on each side; or where the gleaming atrium merges with the projecting entrance, in which a cupola roofed with solid bronze adorns and shades a fountain spouting forth water to tend our hands and faces, and encloses the jets of water with four columns

which lend it a mystical appearance. Such adornment is proper to the entrance of a church, so that the performance of the mystery of the salvation within may be marked by a worthy construction without. For the one faith of the Gospel sustains with its fourfold support the temple of our body; and since the grace by which we are reborn flows from that Gospel, and Christ by whom we live is revealed in it, it is sure that "a fountain of water springing up unto life eternal" is born there in us on the four columns of life. It waters us within and engenders heart inside us, but only if we can say, or deserve to feel, that we have "our heart burning within us in the way," enflamed by Christ as he walks along with us.

14. What a happy sight, then, you have afforded to God to the angels of peace, and to all the spirits of the saints! First of all, you showed your veneration for Peter, whose faith and memory you have celebrated with such repeated offerings of your wealth; for you first offered to God pure libations as a sacred sacrifice, with the most welcome commemoration of the apostle himself. Then with appropriate generosity, with pure heart and lowly spirit, you offered a most acceptable sacrifice to Christ, "in whose tabernacle you have offered up a sacrifice of true jubilation," by refreshing and feeding those who with many blessings "offered to God the sacrifice of praise." With what happy din did our city then resound, when you poured forth the entrails of your mercy by feeding and clothing the poor! You transformed the pallid bodies of the needy, watered the dry throats of the thirsty, clothed the trembling limbs of the shivering, and brought them from their prison so that their countenances were ready for God's blessing.

But as you cherished those bodies in need, your good works redounded to your advantage, for you have nurtured your spirit with God's reward and refreshed the soul of your blessed wife. For Christ's hand poured over her the gifts you expended on the poor, as at the blink of an eye that earthly food was transformed into heavenly nourishment. All the money which you cheerfully gave and untiringly allotted, pouring it from your laden hand into the twin palms of the recipients, was immediately deposited in the bosom of the rejoicing Lord by angels who interrupted it in flight, and it was restored to you to be counted that your reward and revenue might be thirtyfold. To your reward were added not merely riches, but also graces of blessings; for that cry and prayer of the poor, by which through your gift they blessed God, were accounted to your justice. For the voices of the poor are readily directed to the ear of God; as Scripture says: "The prayer of the poor men pierces the clouds."

Letter 17 to Severus (ca 399)

1. ... For almost two years you have kept me in suspense, torturing me with the daily hope of seeing you. First I lived through the summer after our courier's return to you, until winter closed in, believing that every day was to dawn on your arrival here. And since no information came about your being delayed, I consoled myself with the reflection that you had not sent anyone because you were going to arrive yourself, however late in the day. Meanwhile this summer, too, was slipping away as I still flattered myself with this hope or belief. I set out for Rome for the revered feast of the apostles, promising myself that I would meet you there during that obligatory but joyful commemoration. Your absence greatly diminished the pleasure of that anticipated hope, but did not extinguish it since I received your letter through the servant of my most dear friend and brother Sabinus. To begin with, I was surprised at his clothes and boots, which were most unlike a monk's; and his face was as ruddy as his cloak, for his cheeks betrayed no fine-drawn spirituality. But finally I ascertained that the courier was not of our number. This I discovered when his master asked me to write to you an answering letter. I also found that Sabinus and yourself are close relatives, so though he was a friend before, I embrace him now with redoubled affection.

2. I had no opportunity, however, of replying from Rome. I had only ten days to see the city, and saw nothing. The mornings I spent in prayerful vows, the reason for my visit, at the sacred tombs of the apostles and martyrs. Then, though I returned to my lodging, I was detained by countless meetings, some caused by friendship and some by duty. Since our gatherings scarcely broke and gave me relaxation in the evening, I had to postpone my duty to you through lack of free time. Then after I returned home an unpleasant bodily illness caused further delay by severely afflicting me for many days. But he [Christ] who is our life and resurrection visited my lowliness with good, and after his "chastening had chastised me, he did not deliver me over to death. For many are the scourges of a sinner, but mercy shall encompass them that hope in the Lord." So I have been scourged as a sinner, but freed as one hoping in the mercy of him who "heals the broken of heart and binds up their bruises."

Letter 29 to Severus (ca 400)

5. I cannot worthily repay you in words or deeds, but with the sole quality in which I equal you, that love which is my sole endowment, I have sent you a tunic. Kindly accept it (for I have worn it) as a shirt obtained from

the foulness of a dunghill; for it suits your blameless life, being woven from soft lambs-wool which soothes the skin with its touch. But let me mention an additional value and grace which it possesses, so that it may be approved as more worthy of your use. It is a pledge to me of the blessing of the holy Melania, famous amongst the holy women of God. So the tunic seemed more worthily yours, for your faith has greater affinity with her than has my blood. Yet I confess that though I earmarked it for you at the very moment I received it, I disregarded this intention to the extent of wearing it first. I knew that by thus wronging you I would visit you more effectively than if I honored you with the tunic all new and unworn. I also wished to snatch a prior blessing from the garment which was now yours, so that I might boast that I shared your clothing; for I was putting on the shirt which with God's kindness you will wear, as if you had already worn it.

6. But the Lord conferred a further grace as a result of your gifts and letter. Our brother Victor arrived here about the very time when I welcomed that holy lady who was returning from Jerusalem after twenty-five years. What a woman she is, if one can call so virile a Christian a woman! What am I to do now? Fear of being unbearably tedious forbids me to add more to the volumes written about her; yet the worth of her person, or rather God's grace in her seems to demand that I should not exclude with hasty omission a mention of this great soul. Just as voyagers, seeing some notable spot on the shore, so as not to pass by [that place], briefly draw in their sails, or lift their oars, and linger to feast their eyes in gazing, so I must alter the course of my words to tell you about her for a moment. In this way I may be seen to make some return for that book of yours, so splendid in its matter and style, if I describe the woman who is a soldier of Christ with the virtues of [Saint] Martin, though she is of the weaker sex. She is a noble woman who has made herself nobler than her consular grandfathers by her contempt for mere bodily nobility....

10. Melania had many struggles, too, with the hate-filled dragon [the Devil] during her training for this service, because the envy of the spiteful enemy did not allow her to depart without difficulty and in peace. The devil attempted, through the utmost pressure of her noble relatives, whom he equipped to detain her, to block her design and prevent her from going. But she was lent strength superior to the power of the tempters. She gladly threw off the bonds of human love with the ropes of the ship, as all wept. She joined unwearied battle with the waves of the sea, so that she could conquer these as well as the billows of the world, and sailed away. Abandoning worldly life and her own country, she chose to bestow her spiritual gift at Jerusalem, and to dwell there in pilgrimage from her body. She became an exile from her fellow citizens, but a citizen amongst the saints. With wisdom and sanctity

she chose to be a servant in this world of thrall so as to be able to reign in the world of freedom....

12. I shall now hasten over her other achievements and days, and in imitation of her journey I shall embark on the crossing on which she made her return, so that I may conclude my words more speedily by recounting her arrival here. In this event, I witnessed the great grace of God. She put in at Naples, which lies a short distance away from the town of Nola where I live. There she was met in welcome by her children and grandchildren, and then she hastened to Nola to enjoy my humble hospitality. She came to me here surrounded by a solicitous retinue of her very wealthy dear ones. In that journey of mother and children I beheld the glory of the Lord. She sat on a tiny thin horse, worth less than any ass; and they attended her on the journey, their trappings emphasizing the extraordinary contrast. For they had all the pomp of this world with which honored and wealthy senators could be invested. The Appian Way groaned and gleamed with swaying coaches, decorated horses, ladies' carriages all gilded, and numerous smaller vehicles. Yet the grace of Christian humility outshone such vain brilliance. The rich marveled at this poor saint while our poverty mocked them. I beheld the world in a turmoil fit for God's eyes, crimson silk and gilded trappings playing servant to old black rags. I blessed the Lord who exalts the humble, lends them wisdom, and fills them with good things, while the rich he sends empty away....

13. ... Up until now the daughter of Sion has possessed her, and longs for her; but now the daughter of Babylon possesses and admires her. For even now Rome herself in the greater number of her population is the daughter of Sion rather than Babylon. So Rome admires Melania, as she dwells in the shadow of humility and the light of truth, as she offers incentives to faith among the rich and the consolations of poverty among the poor. Yet now that she is among the crowds of Rome, she yearns for her silence and obscurity at Jerusalem, and cries: "Woe is me that my sojourning is prolonged!" Has my journey been postponed that I might now "dwell with the inhabitants of Cedar" (for I have discovered that "Cedar" in Hebrew means darkness)? So I think she is to be felicitated on the virtues I have mentioned, provided that she is fearful about her present abode, and as long as so outstanding a soul bestows more on Rome than she draws from it. She must "sit on the rivers of Babylon yet remember Sion." She must keep the instrument of her body above all the ambushes and attractions of hostile Babylon, secure in the steady course of her committed life, which we may call the willows always thriving on true moisture. So she may flourish unceasingly, and with enduring constancy of faith and the grace of virtue, "her leaf will not fall off." Just as on the journey of this life she is a model, so at its end her praise will be sung.

Letter 31 to Severus (ca 402)

1. In telling me of your other activities and desires, our brother Victor has reported to me that you desire for our basilica, which you have built in the village of Primuliancum on bigger lines than your previous one, some blessed object from the sacred relics of the saints, with which to adorn your family church in a manner worthy of your faith and service. The Lord is my witness that if I had even the smallest measure of sacred ashes over and above what we shall find necessary for the dedication of the basilica soon to be completed here in the Lord's name, I should have sent it to you, my loving brother. Because I did not possess such a gift in abundance and because Victor said that he had a great hope of a similar favor from the holy Silvia who had promised him some of the relics of many Eastern martyrs, I have found instead a fragment of a sliver of the wood of the holy Cross to send you as a worthy gift. This will enhance both the consecration of your basilica and your holy collection of sacred ashes.

This goodly gift was brought to me from Jerusalem by the blessed Melania, a gift from the holy bishop John there; my fellow servant Therasia has sent it especially to our venerable sister Bassula. Though presented to one of you, it belongs to you both, for you are both animated by a single vocation, and the faith which brings you together "into a perfect man," empties you of your sex. So from your loving brethren, who long to associate with you in every good, receive this gift which is great in small compass. In this almost indivisible particle of a small sliver, take up the protection of your immediate safety, and the guarantee of your eternal salvation. Let not your faith shrink because the eyes of the body behold the evidence so small; let it look with the inner eye on the whole power of the cross in this tiny segment. Once you think that you behold the wood on which our salvation, the Lord of majesty, was hanged with nails while the world trembled, you, too, must tremble, but you must also rejoice.

Let us remember that "the rocks were rent" when this cross was seen; so let us imitate the rocks at least, and rend our hearts with fear of God. Let us recall that "the veil of the temple was" also "rent" by this same mystery of the cross. We must realize that the rending of this veil was revealed to us that, hearing the voice of the Lord and the mystery of his boundless love, we may refrain from hardening our hearts, and may surrender ourselves from things of the flesh and rend in two the veil of unbelief. So, when we have uncovered the surface of our hearts, we may behold the mysteries of the saving gifts of God.

2. But I do not also bid you to imitate the arrangement by which I have enclosed this relic, which imparts a great blessing, in a golden casing.

Rather in this adornment I have imitated your faith. I sent your own ex-
emplar clothed with gold, for I know that you have within you, like gold
tried in fire, faith in the cross, by which we enter the kingdom of heaven.
As scripture says, if we suffice with him we shall also reign with him. So
this is not given to strengthen your faith, because you believed before you
saw, but because of the merit of your faith, which you received by hearing
the word and now prove in action. This is why I have sent you this gift
of wood bearing salvation in the Lord, so that you might both physically
possess the cross which you hold in spirit and carry with the strength of
your vocation....

*How was the funeral of Pammachius's wife transformed into a spiritual experience for
the worshippers gathered in the church of Saint Peter? When Paulinus visited Rome,
what did he spend his time doing? How did the citizens of Rome greet Melania the
Elder when she returned from her pilgrimage to Jerusalem? Based on Paulinus's description of her arrival, what connections did he see between pilgrimage and the rejection
of worldly wealth? Why did Melania have mixed feelings about returning to Rome?
Why did Paulinus think that portions of the True Cross were such important relics?*

15. GREGORY OF TOURS ON SHRINES AND MIRACLES IN MEROVINGIAN GAUL

In his History of the Franks, *Bishop Gregory of Tours, who died around 594,
painted a colorful portrait of the barbarian kingdom of Merovingian Gaul after the
collapse of Roman imperial power in the West. In this work and others, Gregory paid
particular attention to the lives of saints, who dominated the spiritual and ecclesiastical
landscape of the Merovingian kingdom. In the selections below, he reveals the devotional travel of often humble Christians to seek the healing power of the saints, both
living and dead, at churches, shrines, and monasteries.*

Source: trans. O.M. Dalton, in *The History of the Franks by Gregory of Tours* (Oxford: Clarendon
Press, 1927), pp. 58–59, 119, 175–76, 238–42, 465–68; revised.

2.14. In the city of Tours, when Eustochius died in the seventeenth year of
his episcopate, Perpetuus was consecrated as the fifth [bishop] in succession
from Saint Martin. Now when he saw the continual wonders wrought at
the tomb of the saint, and observed the small size of the chapel erected over
him, he judged it unworthy of such miracles. He caused it to be removed and
built on the spot the great basilica which has endured until our day, standing
550 paces from the city. It is 160 feet long by 60 broad, and its height to the

ceiling is 42 feet. It has 32 windows in the sanctuary and 20 in the nave with 41 columns. In the whole structure there are 52 windows, 120 columns, and 8 doors, 3 in the sanctuary, 5 in the nave. The great festival of the church has a threefold significance: It is at once a feast of the dedication [of the church], of the transfer of the saint's body [into the church], and of his consecration as bishop. This festival you shall keep on the fourth day of July; the day of the saint's burial you shall find to fall on the eleventh of November. They who keep these celebrations in faith shall deserve the protection of the holy bishop both in this world and the next. As the ceiling of the earlier chapel was fashioned with delicate workmanship, Perpetuus deemed it unseemly that such work should perish, so he built another basilica in honor of the blessed apostles Peter and Paul, and in it he fixed the ceiling. He built many other churches, which are still standing today in the name of Christ.

2.15. At this time, the church of St-Symphorian, the martyr of Autun, was also built by the priest Eufronius, who himself afterwards became bishop of this city. He was the one who, in his great devotion, sent the marble which covers the holy sepulcher of Saint Martin.

2.16. After the death of Bishop Rusticus, the holy Namatius became in these days eighth bishop of Clermont. By his own efforts he built the church which still exists, and is deemed the older of those within the town walls. It is 150 feet long, 60 feet broad, that is across the nave, and 50 feet high to the ceiling: it ends in a rounded apse, and has on either side walls of skilled construction; the whole building is disposed in the form of a cross. It has 42 windows: 70 columns, and 8 doors. There, one feels the dread of God and the great brightness of his glory, and indeed, there often the devout are aware of a most sweet odor just like spices wafted to them. The walls of the sanctuary are adorned with a lining of many kinds of marble. After the building was completed in the twelfth year, the blessed bishop sent priests to the city of Bologna in Italy to bring him relics of Saints Vitalis and Agricola, crucified, as is known by all men, for the name of Christ our Lord.

2.17. The wife of Namatius built the church of the holy Stephen without the walls. As she wished it to be adorned with paintings, she used to hold a book upon her knees, in which she read the story of deeds done of old time, and pointed out to the painters what subjects should be represented on the walls. One day, it happened as she was sitting reading in the church that a certain poor man came in to pray. When he saw her clad in black, for she was advanced in years, he deemed her one of the needy. Producing a piece of bread, he put it in her lap, and went his way. She did not despise the gift of the poor man, who did not perceive her quality, but took it and thanked him and put it aside, afterwards preferring it to her costlier food and receiving a blessing from it every day until it was all consumed....

4.5. When, as I have described above, the blessed Quintianus had passed from this world, the holy man Gall, with the king's support, was appointed in his place. In his time there raged the pestilence known as the plague of the groin in various regions, but especially in the province of Arles, yet the holy Gall trembled not so much on his own account as for his flock. By day and night, he beseeched the Lord that he might not live to see his people devastated, and behold! There appeared to him an angel of the Lord, whose hair and raiment were as white as snow. And the angel said to him: "You do well, bishop, thus to entreat the Lord on behalf of your people: your prayer is heard and behold, you and your people shall be freed from this malady, for while you live, no man in this region shall perish of this plague. Fear not therefore now, but when eight years are gone by, then fear." On this account, it was clear that after that lapse of time he should depart from the world. He awoke and giving God thanks for such action, in that he had deigned to comfort him by a messenger from above, he instituted those Rogations [prayers] in which all went on foot at mid-Lent to the tomb of the blessed Julian martyr, a distance of about 360 *stadia*. Then suddenly, as men looked, signs appeared on the walls of the houses and churches, which writing was called *Tau* by the people. But while, as I have elsewhere related, that plague that consumed other regions, through the intercession of Saint Gall it did not reach Clermont. I hold it no small grace that this shepherd by his merit was not left to see his sheep devoured, for the Lord preserved them....

5.6. In the above-mentioned year, which is the year when Sigibert died and Childebert his son began to reign, many miracles were made manifest at the tomb of Saint Martin, recorded by me in the books which I have tried to compose about these matters. And though mine is an unrefined speech, yet I could not leave unrelated things which either I myself witnessed, or heard from the lips of the faithful. I will only recount that which befell the thoughtless, who after experience of the celestial power had recourse to earthly remedies, for that power is displayed no less in the punishment given out to the foolish than in the grace given to those who are made whole.

Leunast, archdeacon of Bourges, lost his sight through cataract. He went first from one doctor to another, but in the smallest degree did he recover his vision. Then he came to the church of St-Martin. Abiding there for the space of two or three months, and fasting continually, he prayed that he might once more possess the light of his eyes. And when the feast of Martin came round, his eyes were made clear and he began to see. But on his return home he consulted a Jew, who applied cupping-glasses to his shoulders, the action which was to strengthen his sight. But as soon as the blood was drawn off, he relapsed into his former blindness. Thereupon he came back to the holy shrine, but though he again made a long sojourn, he could not now recover his vision. In my belief it was denied him by reason of his sin, according to the oracle of the Lord: "For whosoever has, to him shall be given, and he shall have more abundance: but whosoever has not, from him shall be taken away even that which he has." And this also: "Behold, you are made whole: sin no more, lest a worse thing befall you." For this man would have remained whole if he had not brought in a Jew after he had felt the miraculous power of God. It is such men as these that the apostle admonishes and condemns, saying: "Be not unequally yoked together with unbelievers: for what fellowship has righteousness with unrighteousness? And what communion has light with darkness? And what concord had Christ with Belial [the Devil]? Or what part has he that believes with an infidel? And what agreement has the temple of God with idols? For you are the temple of the living God. Wherefore, come out from among them, and be separate, says the Lord." Thus, let this example teach every Christian that when he has received the medicine from on high, he should not seek after worldly arts....

6.6. There was at this time near the town of Nice a man named Hospicius, a recluse and great ascetic, who wore iron chains wound close about the bare skin and over them a hair shirt. He would eat nothing but dry bread with a few dates. During Lent he nourished himself on the roots of the Egyptian herbs which the hermits eat, brought to him by merchants. He first drank the water in which they were cooked, then ate the roots themselves. Great miracles the Lord deigned to perform by his means. For upon a time the Holy Spirit revealed to him the coming of the Lombards into Gaul, which he foretold after this manner: "The Lombards," he said, "will enter Gaul, and lay waste seven cities because their wickedness is waxed great in the sight of the Lord. For there is none that understands, none that seeks the Lord, none that do good to appease the wrath of God. The entire people is without faith, given to perjuries, prone to thefts, swift to shed men's blood. From such, the fruit of justice does not grow in any way. They do not pay tithes, they do not feed the poor, they do not clothe the naked, they do not take in the stranger, nor do they give him meat according to his need. For this cause, this blow comes upon them. Now, therefore, I say to you: Gather together all your substance within your walls, that it be not pillaged by the Lombards, and fortify yourselves in the strongest places that you have." At these words all were amazed, and, bidding him farewell, returned, greatly marveling, to their own homes. And to the monks he said: "Remove yourselves also from this place, and take all your possessions with you, for behold! The people which I have foretold draw nigh."

Then they said: "We will not leave you, most holy father." But he answered: "Fear not for me. They shall vex me, but they shall not harm me to the death." And when they were gone that people came, laying waste all things within reach, and arrived at the place where the holy man of God lived in his solitude. And he showed himself to them through a window of his tower. Then they went about the tower, but could not find an entrance whereby they might come in to him. So two of them climbed up and uncovered the roof, and saw him girded with chains, and wearing a hair shirt; and they said: "This is a malefactor who has slain a man. For this cause, he is held in these bonds." And they called to them an interpreter and inquired of him what evil he had wrought that he was thus gravely punished. He himself confessed to them that he had wrought manslaughter and was guilty of every crime. Then one drew a sword to strike him on the head, but his right arm was suspended in the act to strike and turned stiff, so that he could not draw it back. Then he loosed his hold on the sword, and let it fall to the ground. At sight of this his comrades raised a shout heaven high, beseeching the holy man of his mercy to tell them what they ought to do. He made the sign of our salvation over the arm and made it whole again. And the man was converted on the spot, and received the tonsure, and is now held the most faithful of the monks. Two dukes who listened to the words of Hospicius returned in safety to their country, but those of the Lombards who scorned his injunction perished miserably in that land of Provence. Many of them were possessed by demons, and cried aloud: "O holy and most blessed, wherefore do you torment us and burn us thus?" But he laid his hands upon them and healed them.

A little while after this, there was an inhabitant of Angers who through exceeding fever had lost his speech and hearing. On his recovery from the fever, he remained deaf and dumb. Now a deacon was being sent from that district to Rome to bring back relics of the blessed apostles and other saints who protect that city. When the parents of the sick man heard this, they asked him of his goodness to take their son with him on his journey, having faith that if he could only visit the tombs of the most blessed apostles he should at once find healing. The two set forth, and came to the place where the blessed Hospicius dwelled. The deacon, having saluted and embraced him, set forth the causes of their journey, told how he was on his way to Rome, and besought him to commend them to any of the clergy who were among his friends. But while they stayed with him the saint felt the power of miracle present within him through the spirit of the Lord, and he said to the deacon: "I beg you, bring the sick man into my sight, who is your companion on the journey." The other man, losing no time, went swiftly to their lodging and found the sick man in a high fever, who, by a sign of the head, let him know that there was a ringing sound in his ears. He took him and brought him to the holy man of God, who grasped his hair with one hand and drew his head into the window. There, holding the sick man's tongue with his left hand, he took consecrated oil and poured it into his mouth and on the top of his head, saying: "In the name of my Lord Jesus Christ, let your ears be unsealed, and your mouth opened by that same power which cast out the evil spirit from him that was deaf and dumb." With these words he asked of him his name. He answered: "I am called so-and-so." And when the deacon saw it he said: "I give you thanks without end, Christ Jesus, who deigns it worthy to reveal such wonders by the hand of your servant. I was seeking Peter, I was seeking Paul and Lawrence, and the other martyrs who have glorified Rome through their blood, and behold! I have found them all here. Here I have discovered them all." But as he said this, marveling and with many tears, the man of God, eschewing all thought of vainglory, said to him: "Hold to your peace, most beloved brother, for it is not I who do these things, but he who created the world out of nothing. Putting on our mortal nature, he made the blind to see, the deaf to hear, and the dumb to speak. He restores to lepers their skin as it was before, and grants to all the sick remedy abounding." Then the deacon bade him farewell, rejoicing, and departed with his companions.

When they were gone, a certain man named Dominicus, blind from his birth, came to put to proof this miraculous power. This man had stayed in the monastery for two or three months, constant in prayer and fasting, when at length the man of God summoned him and said: "Do you desire to recover your sight?" "It was ever my wish," answered the other, "to know things unknown to me. For I am ignorant what thing light may be. This only I know, that it is praised by all men. As for me, from the beginning of my life until now, I have not had grace to look thereon." Then the saint, making the sign of the holy cross over his eyes with consecrated oil, said to him: "In the name of Jesus Christ our redeemer, let your eyes be opened." And forthwith they were opened, and there he was, marveling and beholding the wonderful works of God that he saw for the first time in this world. Afterwards, a woman was brought to him who, as she herself proclaimed, was possessed of three devils. And when he had blessed her with his holy touch, and set the cross upon her brow with the sacred oil, the devils were driven forth, and she departed healed. By his benediction he made whole another girl vexed by an unclean spirit.

But when the day of his death now drew near, he called to him the prior of the monastery and said: "Bring a crowbar, and break through the wall, and send messengers to the bishop of the city, that he may come and bury me. For on the third day from now I shall pass from the world, and enter into my appointed rest which the Lord hath promised me." Thereupon the prior of the monastery sent to the bishop of the city of Nice to give him this news. Now a certain Crescens came to the window, and beholding

Hospicius bound with chains and covered with worms, said to him: "O my lord, how are you able to endure such grievous torments?' The other replied: "He gives me comfort for whose name I suffer these things. And I tell you that now I am released from these chains, and go into my rest." And when the third day came, he put from him the chains with which he was bound, and prostrated himself in prayer. And when he had prayed with tears for a long time, he laid himself down upon a bench, with his feet stretched out and his hands raised towards heaven, and rendering thanks to God, gave up the ghost. And straightway all the worms which had gnawed his holy limbs vanished. Then the bishop Austadius came and with utmost care committed the hallowed body to the earth. All these things I learned from the lips of the man who, as I have related, was deaf and dumb and healed by the saint. The same man told me much more of his miracles; but I was prevented from speaking of them because I heard that his life had already been written by many writers....

10.10. I must now speak of the miracles and death of the abbot Aredius, who in this year quitted this earth and at the summons of the Lord passed to heaven. He was a native of Limoges and of free birth, born from parents of no mean station. In his youth, he was sent to King Theudebert, and became one of the noble youths attached to the royal household. At that time, Bishop Nicetus was at Trier, a man of eminent holiness who enjoyed great fame among the people both for the admirable eloquence of his preaching and for his good works and miracles. Noticing the boy in the palace, and seeing in his face I know not what quality that seemed divine, he commanded him to follow him. So Aredius left the royal palace and followed after him. Going to the bishop's cell, they talked together of things relating to God. The youth then asked the holy bishop to correct, to teach, to influence him, and to instruct him in the knowledge of the holy scriptures. Thereafter he dwelled with the bishop, consumed with ardent zeal for this study, and received the tonsure [entered the monastic life]. One day, while the clergy were chanting psalm in the church, a dove descended from the ceiling, and lightly fluttering round him, perched upon his head, providing a sign, I believe, that already he was filled with the grace of the Holy Spirit. He sought to drive the bird away, not without confusion, but after circling round a little while, it settled once more upon his head or on his shoulder. Not only in the church, but even when he went into the bishop's cell, it kept him company continually. This happened for several days, to the wonder of the bishop.

Afterwards this man of God, filled, as I have said, with the divine spirit, returned to his own country, his father and brother being dead, to console his mother Pelagia, who had none of her kindred to look to but this son alone. His time was now all devoted to fasting and prayers, and he besought her to be responsible for all the care of his house, whether in respect of the discipline of the servants, or the cultivation of the fields, or the tilling of the vineyards so that there might be no interruption of his prayers. He claimed but one thing for himself, the privilege of superintending the erection of churches. What need to say more? He built churches of God in honor of the saints, sought and obtained their relics, made tonsured monks from those of his own household, and founded a monastery in which not only the [monastic] rule of Cassian was observed, but also the rules of Basil and other abbots who instituted the monastic life. His holy mother provided for every monk his food and raiment. But this heavy toil was not enough to hinder her from singing the praises of God. Even when she was engaged on any work, she was ever constant in offering prayer to the Lord, as it were, a fragrance of incense finding favor in his sight. In the meantime, the sick began streaming from all sides to the holy Aredius, and he restored them to health by the laying on of hands with the sign of the cross. Were I to attempt to make several descriptions of them, I should never be able to go through their number or record their names. This one thing I know, that whoever went to him sick returned from him whole. I will only set down some few facts concerning his greater miracles.

He was once making a journey with his mother on his way to the church of St-Julian the Martyr. They came at evening time to a certain place which was very dry and sterile for want of running water. His mother then said to him: "My son, we have no water. How therefore can we abide here this night?" But he prostrated himself in prayer, and for a long while poured forth supplication to the Lord. Then, rising up, he fixed a stick which he carried in the ground, and after making it revolve two or three times, he drew it out with great content, and soon so great a flow of water flowed that they not only first drank of it themselves, but afterwards were able to water their beasts. A very short time ago he was on a journey, when a rain-cloud rapidly came up. As soon as he saw it he bowed his head a little over the horse which he rode, and stretched forth his hand towards the Lord. And when his prayer was over, behold! The cloud was divided into two parts, and all round them rain came down in torrents, but upon themselves there fell hardly a drop. A citizen of Tours, Wistrimund, surnamed Tatto, suffered from violent tooth ache, which caused a swelling of the jaws. He complained about it to the holy man, who laid his hand upon the place, whereupon right away the pain was driven away and never afterwards revived to cause further trouble. It was the patient himself who told me the story. As for the miracles which the Lord wrought by his hands through the power of the blessed martyr Julian, and of the blessed confessor Martin, I have recorded most of them in my Books of Miracles, as he himself has related them.

After these and many other miracles performed by Christ's aid, he came to Tours when the feast of Saint Martin was over, and after a short sojourn told us that he should not be kept much longer in this world, and that his time of death was surely near. He told me farewell and departed, giving thanks to God that it had been granted him to kiss the tomb of the holy bishop before he passed away. Upon his return to his cell, he made his will and set all his affairs in order, and made the holy Martin and the holy Hilary his heirs. He then began to fall ill and was attacked by dysentery. On the sixth day of his sickness, a woman, often vexed by an unclean spirit, from which the holy man had not been able to deliver her, bound her hands behind her back and began crying aloud, saying: "Run, O citizens! Leap for joy, O people! Go forth to meet the martyrs and confessors who are now come together for the passing of the blessed Aredius. Behold, here is Julian come from Brioude, Privatus from Mende. Here are Martin from Tours and Martial from Aredius's own city. Here too are Saturninus from Toulouse, Denis from Paris, and many another now in heaven to whom you pray as confessors and martyrs of God." When she thus cried aloud at nightfall, her master put her in bonds, but it was impossible to hold her. She burst the bonds and rushed to the monastery, uttering these same cries. Soon afterwards the holy man gave up the ghost, not without true testimony that he had been taken of angels. During his funeral, when the grave closed upon him, he delivered the woman from the evil of the infesting demon, together with another woman vexed by a yet more evil spirit. And I believe it to have been by God's will that he should not heal these women in his lifetime, in order that his praises might be glorified by this miracle. And after they had been celebrated, a certain dumb woman with a wide gaping mouth came to his tomb and kissed it, after which she received the gift of speech.

What sorts of miracles did the saints of Merovingian Gaul perform in life and death? Who built the churches and shrines that housed their remains? During Gregory's account of the miracles of Hospicius, why did a pilgrimage to Rome become unnecessary for the deacon and deaf man from Angers? How did the life, travels, and death of saints such as Aredius contribute to the development of a new devotional landscape in early medieval Gaul?

16. PILGRIMS AS WANDERERS: *THE VOYAGE OF SAINT BRENDAN*

In the Irish monastic tradition, a distinctive notion of pilgrimage developed as an ascetic journey and self-imposed exile, rather than a delimited devotional journey from one point to another. The popular Latin legend of Saint Brendan, which dates in its present form from around the late eighth or early ninth century, captured that vision of pious wandering. In this fantastical tale, the Irish monk and his companions spend years at sea searching for the elusive Promised Land of the Saints, surrendering themselves to God's will as they sail year after year to visit (and visit again) various islands in the vast ocean to the west of Ireland.

Source: trans. John J. O'Meara, in *The Voyage of Saint Brendan: Journey to the Promised Land* (Atlantic Highlands, NJ: Humanities Press, 1976), pp. 7–14, 18–19, 37–39, 67–70.

2. Saint Brendan, therefore, when fourteen brothers out of his whole community had been chosen, shut himself up in one oratory with them and spoke to them, saying: "From you who are dear to me and share the good fight with me I look for advice and help, for my heart and all my thoughts are fixed on one determination. I have resolved in my heart if it is God's will – and only if it is – to go in search of the Promised Land of the Saints of which father Barrind spoke. How does this seem to you? What advice would you give?" They, however, having learned of the holy father's will, say, as it were with one mouth: "Abbot, your will is ours. Have we not left our parents behind? Have we not spurned our inheritance and given our bodies into your hands? So we are prepared to go along with you to death or life. Only one thing let us ask for, the will of God."...

4. Having received the blessing of the holy father [Edna] and of all the monks that were with him, he [Brendan] set out for a distant part of his native region where his parents were living. But he did not wish to see them. He pitched his tent at the edge of a mountain stretching far out into the ocean, in a place called Brendan's Seat, at a point where there was entry for one boat. Saint Brendan and those with him got iron tools and constructed a light boat ribbed with wood and with a wooden frame, as is usual in those parts. They covered it with ox-hides tanned with the bark of oak and smeared all the joints of the hides on the outside with fat. They carried into the boat hides for the makings of two other boats, supplies for forty days, fat for preparing hides to cover the boat and other things needed for human life. They also placed a mast in the middle of the boat and a sail and the other requirements for steering a boat. Then Saint Brendan ordered his brothers in the name of the Father, Son, and Holy Spirit to enter the boat.

5. While Saint Brendan remained alone on the shore and blessed the landing place, three brothers from his own monastery came up, following after
him. They fell immediately at the feet of the holy father, saying: "Father,
leave us free to go with you wherever you are going; otherwise we shall die
on this spot from hunger and thirst. For we have decided to be pilgrims for
the days of our life that remain." When the man of God saw their trouble,
he ordered them to enter the boat, saying: "Your will be done, my sons."
And he added: "I know why you have come. One of you has done something
meritorious, for God has prepared a suitable place for him. But for you others
he will prepare a hideous judgment."

6. Saint Brendan then embarked, the sail was spread, and they began to
steer westwards into the summer solstice. They had a favorable wind and,
apart from holding the sail, had no need to navigate. After fifteen days the
wind dropped. They set themselves to the oars until their strength failed.
Saint Brendan quickly began to comfort them, saying: "Brothers, do not fear.
God is our helper, sailor, and helmsman, and he guides us. Ship all the oars
and the rudder. Just leave the sail spread and God will do as he wishes with
his servants and their ship." They always had their food, however, at evening
time. When they got a wind, they did not know from what direction it came
or in what direction the boat was going....

When they had circled the island for three days, on the third day about
three o'clock they found an opening where one boat might enter. Saint Brendan stood up immediately and blessed the entry. It was a cutting with rock of
remarkable height on either side, straight up like a wall. When they had all
disembarked and stood outside on land, Saint Brendan forbade them to take
any equipment out of the boat. As they were walking along the cliffs of the
sea, a dog ran across them on a path and came to the feet of Saint Brendan
as dogs usually come to heel at the feet of their masters. Saint Brendan said
to his brothers: "Has not God sent us a good messenger? Follow him." Saint
Brendan and his brothers followed the dog into a town. On entering the
town they caught sight of a great hall, furnished with beds and chairs, and
water for washing their feet. When they had sat down Saint Brendan gave
an order to his companions, saying: "Beware, brothers, lest Satan lead you
into temptation. For I can see him persuading one of the three brothers, who
came from our monastery to follow after me, to commit a bad theft. Pray for
his soul. For his body has been given into the power of Satan." The house
where they were staying had hanging vessels of different kinds of metal fixed
around its walls along with bridles and the horns encased in silver.

Then Saint Brendan spoke to the one who usually placed bread before
the brothers: "Bring the meal that God has sent us." This man stood up

immediately, found a table made ready and linen and a loaf for each of marvelous whiteness and fish. When all were brought before him, Saint Brendan blessed the meal and said to his brothers: "Give praise to the God of heaven who gives food to all flesh." The brothers sat back, therefore, and glorified God. In the same way they found as much drink as they wanted. When supper was over and the office of compline said, he spoke: "Rest now. There is a well-dressed bed for each of you. You need to rest, for your limbs are tired from too much toil." When the brothers had fallen asleep, Saint Brendan saw the devil at work, namely an Ethiopian child holding a bridle in his hand and making fun with the brother already mentioned to his face. Saint Brendan got up immediately and began to pray, thus spending the whole night until day. In the morning when the brothers had hurried to the divine office and later had gone to the boat, they saw a table laid out just like the day before. And so for three days and three nights God prepared a meal for his servants.

7. After that Saint Brendan with his companions set out again, saying to the brothers: "Make sure that none of you takes anything belonging to this island with him." But they all replied: "God forbid, father, that our journey should be desecrated by any theft." Then Saint Brendan said: "Look, our brother whom I referred to a few days ago has a silver bridle in his bosom given to him last night by the devil." When the brother in question heard this, he threw the bridle out of his bosom and fell before the feet of the man of God, saying: "I have sinned, father. Forgive me. Pray for my soul, that it may not perish." Immediately all prostrated themselves on the ground, praying to the Lord for the brother's soul. As they rose from the ground and the holy father raised up the brother, they saw a small Ethiopian jump out of his bosom, wailing with a loud voice, and saying: "Why, man of God, do you expel me from my dwelling, where I have lived now for seven years, and make me depart from my inheritance?" Saint Brendan replied to this voice: "I order you in the name of the Lord Jesus Christ not to injure any man to the day of Judgment." Turning again to the brother, the man of God said: "Receive the body and blood of the Lord, for your soul will now leave your body. Here you will be buried. But your brother here, who came from our monastery with you, has his burial place in Hell." And so when the Eucharist had been received, the soul of the brother left his body, and before the eyes of the brothers was received by the angels of light. His body, however, was buried on the spot by the holy father....

10. When they approached the other island, the boat began to ground before they could reach its landing-place. Saint Brendan ordered the brothers to disembark from the boat into the sea, which they did. They held the boat

on both sides with ropes until they came to the landing-place. The island was stony and without grass. There were a few pieces of driftwood on it, but no sand on its shore. While the brothers spent the night outside in prayers and vigils, the man of God remained sitting inside the boat. For he knew the kind of island it was, but did not want to tell them, lest they be terrified.

When morning came he ordered each of the priests to sing his Mass, which they did. While Saint Brendan was himself singing his Mass in the boat, the brothers began to carry the raw meat out of the boat to preserve it with salt, and also the flesh which they had brought from the other island. When they had done this they put a pot over a fire. When, however, they were plying the fire with wood and the pot began to boil, the island began to be in motion like a wave. The brothers rushed to the boat, crying out for protection to the holy father. He drew each one of them into the boat by his hand. Having left everything they had had on the island behind, they began to sail. Then the island moved out to sea. The lighted fire could be seen over two miles away. Saint Brendan told the brothers what it really was, saying: "Brothers, are you surprised at what this island has done?" They said: "We are very surprised and indeed terror-stricken." He said to them: "My sons, do not be afraid. God revealed to me during the night in a vision the secret of this affair. Where we were was not an island, but a fish – the foremost of all that swim in the ocean. He is always trying to bring his tail to meet his head, but he cannot because of his length. His name is Jasconius."...

15. ... As they came near the landing-place they had chosen on that is-land [the Island of Birds], all the birds chanted, as if with one voice, saying: "Salvation belongs to our God who sits upon the throne, and to the Lamb!" And again: "The Lord God has given us light. Appoint a holy day, with festal branches up to the horn of the altar." Thus they chanted and beat their wings for a long time – for about half an hour – until the holy father and his holy companions and the contents of the boat were landed and the holy father had taken his place in his tent. When he had celebrated there with his community the feasts of Easter, the steward came to them, as he had told them beforehand, on Sunday the octave of Easter, bringing with him all the food needed for human life.

When they sat down at the table, the same bird again sat down on the prow of the boat, stretching her wings and making a noise like the sound of a great organ. The man of God then realized that she wished to convey a message to him. The bird said: "God has ordained for you four points of call for four periods of the year until the seven years of your pilgrimage are over, namely, on Maundy Thursday with your steward who is present every year; Easter you will celebrate on the back of the whale; the Easter feasts until the octave of Pentecost with us; Christmas you will celebrate with the community of Ailbe. Then after seven years and great and varied trials you will find the Promised Land of the Saints that you seek. There you will live for forty days, and afterwards God will bring you back to the land of your birth."

When the holy father heard this, he prostrated himself on the ground with his brothers, giving thanks and praise to his creator. When the venerable elder had finished this, the bird returned to her own place. When they had finished eating, the steward said: "With God's help I shall return to you with your provisions on the feast of the coming of the Holy Spirit upon the Apostles." Having received the blessings of the holy father and all that were with him, he returned to his own place. The venerable father remained there the number of days indicated. When the feast days were over, Saint Brendan ordered his brothers to prepare to sail and fill the vessels from the well. They brought the boat to the sea, while the steward came with his own boat laden with food for the brothers. When he had placed all in the boat of the holy man, he embraced them all and then returned where he had come from....

28. Saint Brendan and those who were with him sailed to the island of the steward, who was with them, and there they took on board provision for forty days. Their voyage was for forty days toward the east. The steward went to the front of the boat and showed them the way. When the forty days were up, as evening drew on, a great fog enveloped them, so that one of them could hardly see another. The steward, however, said to Saint Brendan: "Do you know what fog this is?" Saint Brendan replied: "What?" Then the other said: "That fog encircles the island for which you have been searching for seven years."

After the space of an hour a mighty light shone all around them again and the boat rested on the shore. On disembarking from the boat they saw a wide land full of trees bearing fruit as in autumn time. When they had gone in a circle around that land, night had still not come on them. They took what fruit they wanted and drank from the wells and so for the space of forty days they reconnoitered the whole land and could not find the end of it. But one day they came upon a great river flowing through the middle of the island. Then Saint Brendan said to his brothers: "We cannot cross this river and we do not know the size of this land." They had been considering these thoughts within themselves when a youth met them and embraced them with great joy and, calling them each by his name, said: "Happy are they that live in your house. They shall praise you from generation to generation." When he had said this, he spoke to Saint Brendan: "There before you lies the land which you have sought for a long time. You could not find it immediately because God wanted to show you his varied secrets in the great ocean. Return, then, to the land of your birth, bringing with you some of the fruit of this land and as many of the precious stones as your boat can carry. The final day of your pilgrimage draws near so that you may sleep with your fathers. After the passage of many times this land will become known to your successors, when persecution of the Christians shall have come. The river that you see divides this land. Just as this land appears to you ripe with fruit, so shall it remain always without any shadow of night. For its light is Christ."

Saint Brendan with his brothers, having taken samples of the fruit of the land and of all its varieties of precious stones, took his leave of the blessed steward and the youth. He then embarked in his boat and began to sail through the middle of the fog. When they had passed through it, they came to the island called the Island of Delights. They availed themselves of three days' hospitality there and then, receiving a blessing, Saint Brendan returned home directly....

29. The brothers received him with thanksgiving, glorifying God who was unwilling that they should be deprived of seeing so lovable a father by whose absence they were for so long orphaned. Then the blessed man, commending them for their love, told them everything that he remembered happening on his journey and the great and marvelous wonders God deigned to show him. Finally he mentioned also the speed of his approaching death – emphasizing its certainty – according to the prophecy of the youth in the Promised Land of the Saints. The outcome proved this to be correct. For when he had made all arrangements for after his death, and a short time had intervened, fortified by the divine sacraments, he migrated from among the hands of his disciples in glory to the Lord, to whom is honor and glory from generation to generation. Amen.

How and why did Brendan set out on his journey? How did his commitment to monastic living and pilgrimage complement each other? What sort of people and beasts did he and his companions encounter? How did their "pilgrimage" draw them closer to God?

17. PENANCE AND PILGRIMAGE

For early Christians, penance was a form of satisfaction made to God for one's sins. It could consist of prayer, fasting, and other forms of self-denial. Penance could also take the form of undertaking a pilgrimage, either to a certain destination and back, or wandering in exile from one's homeland. The selections below are taken from a number of early medieval "penitential manuals," a form of handbook that originated in the monastic tradition of the Irish church but later spread throughout Europe. Such manuals listed a variety of sins and assigned certain forms of appropriate penance for them, including pilgrimage. The penitentials also make it clear that Christians had an obligation to support pilgrims and the needy.

Sources: Penitential of Saint Columbus, Old Irish Penitential, Three Irish Canons, Synod of the Grove of Victory, Penitential of Finnian, trans. L. Bieler, in *The Irish Penitentials*, Scriptores Latini Hiberniae (Dublin: Dublin Institute for Advanced Studies, 1963), pp. 69, 85–87, 199, 183, 267; Penitential of Silense, trans. B.E. Whalen, from *Paenitentialia Hispaniae*, ed. Francis Bezler, Corpus Christianorum: Series Latina, vol. 156A/2 (Turnhout: Brepols, 1998), p. 33; Penitentials of Sangallense and Merseburg, trans. B.E. Whalen, from *Paenitentialia minora Franciae et Italiae saeculi VIII-IX*, ed. Raymund Kottje, Corpus Christianorum: Series Latina, vol. 156 (Turnhout: Brepols, 1994), pp. 8, 139, 161.

Penitential of Saint Columbus (Version B)

Diversity of offenses causes diversity of penances. For doctors of the body also compound their medicines in diverse kinds; thus they heal wounds in one manner, sickness in another, eye diseases in another, bruises in another, burns in another.

So also should spiritual doctors treat with diverse kinds of cures the wounds of souls, their sickness, offenses, pains, ailments, and infirmities. But since this gift belongs to few, namely to know to a nicety all these things, to treat them, to restore what is weak to a complete state of health, let us set out even a few prescriptions according to the traditions of our elders, and according to our own partial understanding, for we prophesy in part and we know in part. First we must enact concerning capital sins, which are punished even by the sanction of the law.

1. If any cleric had committed murder and killed his neighbor, let him do penance for ten years in exile; after these, let him be restored to his native land, if he has performed his penance well on bread and water, being approved by the testimonial of the bishop or priest with whom he did penance and to whose care he was entrusted, on condition that he make satisfaction to the relatives of the slain, taking the place of son, and saying: "Whatever you wish I will do for you." But if he does not make satisfaction to his relatives, let him never be restored to his native land, but like Cain let him be a wanderer and fugitive upon the earth.

The Old Irish Penitential, Chapter Three

7. Anyone who plunders an altar or shrine, or steals a Gospel-book, seven years' penance. If it be a bell, or crozier, or service-set, it is forty years on bread and water....

9. Anyone who takes a reward to kill a man or to bear false witness or

to bring a false suit or to give a false judgment, does three and a half years' penance.

10. Anyone who persists in avarice to the end of his life must go on a pilgrimage or must distribute the value of seven *cumals* to the poor and needy for his soul's sake.

Three Irish Canons

1. If anyone in any way breaks into the place of keeping of the chrismal of any saint, or a place of keeping for staves or cymbals, or takes away anything by robbery, or in any way injures a man, he shall make sevenfold restitution and remain through five years in hard penance in exile abroad. And if his penance is commendable, let him afterwards come to his own country; but if not, let him remain permanently in exile.

2. If anyone breaks into the place of keeping of a Gospel book or removes anything by robbery, he shall make sevenfold restitution, on account of the sevenfold graces of Christ and on account of the seven ecclesiastical ranks; but he shall also remain through seven years in hard penance in exile. But if he does not do penance he is to be excommunicated from the whole Catholic church and from communion of all Christians, and burial in holy ground is not to be accorded to him.

Synod of the Grove of Victory

1. He who commits theft once shall do penance for one year; more than once, for two years.

2. He who slays his brother not with malice aforethought, if from sudden anger, shall do penance for three years.

3. Likewise shall an adulterer do penance for three years....

6. He who defiles his mother, three years with perpetual pilgrimage.

Penitential of Finnian

30. He who despoils monasteries, falsely saying that he is collecting money for the redemption of captives, shall do penance for one year with bread and water, and all that he has gathered he shall give to the poor, and for two years he shall do penance without wine and meat.

31. But if he does not repent he is to be excommunicated and be anathema to all Christians; he shall be driven from the bounds of his country and beaten with rods until he is converted – if he has compunction.

32. We prescribe and urge contributing for the redemption of captives. By the teaching of the church, money is to be spent fruitfully on the poor and needy.

33. We are also obliged to serve the churches of the saints and, within our means, have pity on all those who are in need; pilgrims are to be received into our houses, as the Lord has commanded; the infirm are to be visited; those who are in chains are to be ministered to; and all commandments of Christ are to be performed, from the least unto the greatest.

Penitential of Silense

171. Let clergy who marry be banished in exile until the end of their days; let their wives and sons be sold as slaves and sent into foreign lands.

Penitential of Sangallense

1. If a bishop or priest commits murder, let him lose his rank and do twelve years' penance wandering in exile.

Penitential of Merseberg

43. Whoever fornicates with his father's widow or his uncle's widow, or with his sibling or his cousin, or if a father "uncovers the nakedness" of his son or fornicates with his step-daughter, let him do ten years' penance as a pilgrim, with two of those years on bread and water; if he is not able to go on pilgrimage, let him give twelve *solidi* for one year. If he is a layman, let him be beaten and, if he is in a position to do so [meaning he owns a slave], let him give a man his freedom....

126. It is not right to surrender the tithe [a tenth of one's income owed to the church] except for the needy and pilgrims, nor should priests be compelled to give up the tithe.

What sorts of sins merited a period of exile from one's community or time of wandering as penance? What evidence do you see that members of the clergy and the laity (that is, non-clergy) were held to different standards in terms of sin and penance? Why do you think that pilgrimage and exile were considered appropriate forms of penance?

18. SAINT BONIFACE ON PILGRIMAGE: ADVICE AND CRITICISM

Saint Boniface, born in Wessex, England, around the year 675, became a priest at about the age of thirty. Sometimes called the "apostle to the Germans," he is best known for his missionary activities among the "heathen" peoples of that region. Over the course of his career, he received support from the rulers of the Franks and the Roman papacy for his efforts to spread the Christian faith. In his letters, Boniface, one of the most influential holy figures of his day, offered his carefully measured opinion about the merits of pilgrimage to Rome and excoriated some questionable "pagan" practices that could be found in the heart of the city, right by the church of Saint Peter.

Source: trans. E. Emerton, in *The Letters of Saint Boniface*, Records of Civilization: Sources and Studies, vol. 31 (New York: Columbia University Press, 1940), pp. 56–57, 81–82, 86–87, 140–41.

Letter 19

To the beloved lady, Abbess Bugga, sister and dearest of all women in Christ, Boniface, a humble and unworthy bishop, wishes eternal salvation in Christ. I desire you to know, dearest sister, that in the matter about which you wrote asking advice of me, unworthy though I am, I dare neither forbid your pilgrimage on my own responsibility nor rashly persuade you to it. I will only say how the matter appears to me. If, for the sake of rest and divine contemplation, you have laid aside the care for the servants and maids of God and for the monastic life which you once had, how could you now subject yourself with labor and wearing anxiety to the words and wishes of men of this world? It would seem to me better, if you can in no wise have freedom and quiet mind at home on account of worldly men, that you should obtain freedom of contemplation by means of a pilgrimage, if you so desire and are able, as our sister Wietburga did. She has written me that she has found at the shrine of St-Peter the kind of quiet life which she had long sought in vain. With regard to your wishes, she sent me word, since I had written to her about you, that you would do better to wait until the rebellious assaults and threats of the Saracens [Muslims] who have recently appeared about Rome should have subsided. God willing, she will then send you an invitation. To me also this seems the best plan. Make ready what you will need for the journey, wait for word from her, and then act as God's grace shall command.... Farewell in Christ.

Letter 40

To our best beloved Lord [Pope] Zacharias, the apostolic man wearing the insignia of the supreme pontificate, Boniface, a servant of the servants of God.... Some of the ignorant common people, Alemanians, Bavarians, and Franks, hearing that many of the offenses prohibited by us are practiced in the city of Rome imagine that they are allowed by the priests there and reproach us for causing them to incur blame in their own lives. They say that on the first day of January year after year, in the city of Rome and in the neighborhood of Saint Peter's church by day or night, they have seen bands of singers parading the streets in pagan fashion, shouting and chanting sacrilegious songs and loading tables with food day and night, while no one in his own house is willing to lend his neighbors fire or tools or any other convenience. They also say that they have seen there women wearing amulets and bracelets of heathen fashion on their arms and legs, offering them for sale to willing buyers. All these things, seen by evil-minded and ignorant people, are a cause of reproach to us and a hindrance to our preaching and teaching. It is of such things that the apostle [Paul] says reprovingly: "You observe days and times; I fear I have labored with you in vain." And Saint Augustine [of Hippo] said:

> He who believes in such evil things, as incantations or diviners or soothsayers, or amulets, or any kind of prophecies, even though he fast or pray, or run to church continually, and though he give alms generously, or torment his body with all kind of tortures, it shall profit him nothing so long as he does not abandon these sacrilegious rites.

If your paternity would prohibit these heathen practices at Rome, it would bring rewards to you and great advantage to us in our teaching.... May God's hand protect your holiness and may you have health and length of days in Christ.

Letter 41

Zacharias, servant of the servants of God, to his very reverend and holy brother and fellow bishop, Boniface.... In regard to the New Year celebrations, auguries, amulets, incantations, and other practices which you say are observed after heathen fashion at the church of St-Peter the apostle or in the city of Rome, we hold them to be wrong and pernicious for us and for all Christians, according to God's word: "Neither shall you use enchantment,

nor observe times." And again scripture says: "Surely there is no enchantment against Jacob, neither is there any divination against Israel." So we
think we should be on our guard and not pay any attention to auguries and
divinations, for we have been taught that all such things were repudiated by
the fathers. And because they were cropping up again, we have abolished
them all from the day when divine favor ordered us, unworthy as we are,
to act in place of the apostle. In the same way we desire you to teach the
people subject to you and so to lead them in the way of eternal life. All these
practices were prohibited loyally and faithfully by a decree of our predecessor
and teacher, Gregory of sacred memory, and also many others which, at the
instigation of the devil, were cropping up in the sheepfold of Christ. We
hasten to follow his example for the salvation of that people.... May God
keep you in safety, most reverend and holy father.

Letter 62

To his brother and fellow bishop, Cuthbert, raised to the dignity of the
archepiscopate and joined to him by the bond of spiritual kinship, Boniface,
legate for Germany of the catholic and apostolic church of Rome, sends
greetings of intimate love in Christ.... Finally, I will not conceal from your
Grace that all the servants of God here who are especially versed in scripture
and strong in fear of God are agreed it would be well and favorable for the
honor and purity of your church, and provide a certain shield against vice,
if your synod and your princes would forbid matrons and veiled women to
make these frequent journeys back and forth to Rome. A great part of them
perish and few keep their virtue. There are very few towns in Lombardy
and Frankland or Gaul where there is not a courtesan or a harlot of English
stock. It is a scandal and a disgrace to your whole church.... May God's hand
preserve you safe, reverend and beloved brother, against all adversity, to make
intercession for us.

*How did Boniface react to Abbess Bugga's desire to visit Rome? What did he find
upsetting about the "heathen" practices being carried out in the city? Why did he think
it was inappropriate for women to undertake the journey to Rome?*

19. CHARLEMAGNE AND THE CHURCHES OF ROME

Starting in the mid-eighth century, a new ruling dynasty, the Carolingians, assumed power over the barbarian kingdom of the Franks. Their legitimacy rested, in part, upon the close connection they had established with the bishops of Rome. Under the authority of King Charles the Great (r. 768–814), or Charlemagne, the Franks vastly expanded their kingdom, including the conquest of the Lombard kingdom of Italy in 774. During this campaign, Charles took the opportunity to act much like any other pious traveler, visiting the churches and holy sites of Rome to pray and to celebrate Easter. Of course, as seen below in excerpts from the Book of Popes, *Charles was not just any other pilgrim: his visit to Rome further cemented the spiritual and political relationship between the Carolingians and the Roman papacy. During another visit to Rome, on Christmas Day 800, Pope Leo III crowned Charles emperor of the Romans in the church of Saint Peter, marking the formal beginning of the Carolingian Empire.*

Source: trans. P.D. King, in *Charlemagne: Translated Sources*, ed. P.D. King (Lancaster: P.D. King, 1987), pp. 193–96, 199–200.

Life of Pope Hadrian I

35. After he had spent six months at Pavia besieging the [Lombard] city, the king of the Franks, feeling a strong desire to hasten to the thresholds of the apostles and mindful too that the most sacred feast of Easter was imminent, then marched swiftly through Tuscany here to Rome, bringing with him various bishops, abbots and judges – that is, dukes and counts – and large numbers of troops. He came so rapidly that he presented himself at the apostolic thresholds on Holy Saturday. On hearing of his arrival, the most blessed pope Hadrian, thrown into great bewilderment and consternation because the king of the Franks had arrived so unexpectedly, sent all the judges out to meet him some thirty miles from this city of Rome ... and there they greeted him, with the standard. When the king had approached to about the first milestone from the city of Rome, he sent out all the regional militia regiments, with their commanders, and also the schoolboys, all carrying palm and olive branches: and these, all singing acclamations and praises to him, greeted the king of the Franks with the strains of those same acclamatory praises. And his holiness, sending reverend crosses – that is, banners – to be borne towards him, caused him to be received with immense honor, as is customary for the reception of an exarch or patrician.

37. But directly the God-instituted and most gracious Charles, great king of the Franks and patrician of the Romans, caught sight of those most sacred

crosses and banners coming towards him, he dismounted from the horse on which he was riding and was at pains to hurry forward to St-Peter's with his judges on foot. For the gracious pontiff, having risen at daybreak on that same holy Saturday and hastened to St-Peter's with all the clergy and people of Rome to receive the king of the Franks, was awaiting him with his clergy on the steps of the apostolic church.

38. When the most excellent and most gracious king Charles arrived, he kissed each single step of the same most sacred church of St-Peter in turn and in this way called to the pontiff where he stood in the porch at the top of the steps, by the church-doors. After they had greeted each other and exchanged embraces, that most Christian king Charles took the pontiff's right hand: and thus they entered the reverend church of St-Peter, prince of the apostles, with all the clergy and all the religious servants of God singing praise to God and to his excellence and acclaiming with swelled voices: "Blessed is he that comes in the name of the Lord" and so forth. And then the king of the Franks, together with all the bishops, abbots and judges and all the Franks who had come with him, approached the shrine of St-Peter with the pontiff, and there they prostrated themselves on the floor and offered their prayers to our almighty God and to the said prince of the apostles, glorifying the power of God forasmuch as he had commanded, by virtue of the intercessory prayers of that same prince of the apostles, that they be granted such a victory.

39. When the praying was at an end, however, the king of the Franks implored the gracious pontiff with all his strength to grant him permission to enter Rome, that he might fulfill his vows of prayer in some of God's churches. And the most holy pope and the most excellent king of the Franks, accompanied by the judges of the Romans and the Franks, went down together to the body of Saint Peter and protected themselves by a reciprocal oath; and immediately thereafter the king of the Franks, with his judges and people, entered Rome with the pontiff. Together, on that same Holy Saturday, they went to the church of the Savior at the Lateran, where the most excellent king and all his men remained throughout the celebration of the sacrament of sacred and holy baptism by the thrice most blessed pontiff. Afterwards the most gracious king retraced his steps to St-Peter's.

40. At dawn on the following day, however, the radiant Holy Sunday of that most sacred Easter feast, the most holy prelate sent all the judges and all those serving in the militia to the king and they greeted him with great honor. With all the Franks who had accompanied him Charles hastened to the church of the Holy Mother of God ad Praesepe [At the Manger] where the solemnities of the mass were celebrated for him, and then they proceeded with the pontiff to the Lateran palace, where they banqueted together at the apostolic table. Likewise on the next day, Monday, the distinguished father

and illustrious pontiff celebrated the solemnities of the mass in the church of St-Peter, as was customary, and had acclamations offered to almighty God and to the aforementioned Charles, most excellent king of the Franks and patrician of the Romans. On the Tuesday it was in the church of St-Paul the apostle, in accordance with custom, that he said mass for the king.

41. On the Wednesday, however, the afore-named pontiff came out to the church of the blessed apostle Peter with his judges, both clerical and military, and joined the king for mutual discussions. Steadfastly he implored and admonished him, zealously and with fatherly fondness he exhorted him, to fulfill in every particular that promise which his father of holy memory, the late king Pippin, and he himself, the most eminent Charles, together with his brother Carloman and all the judges of the Franks, had made to Saint Peter and his vicar of holy memory, the lord pope Stephen II, on the occasion of the latter's journey to Francia, concerning the grant of various cities and territories of the province of Italy and their handing over in their entirety to Saint Peter and all his vicars, to be held in perpetuity.

42. Charles had this promise, which was made in Francia at the place called Quierzy, read out to him, and all its contents found full favor with him and his judges. Of his own accord, with noble and willing heart, that aforesaid most eminent and truly most Christian Charles, king of the Franks, ordered another promise of donation to be drawn up on the model of the earlier one by Itherius, his religious and most sagacious chaplain and notary, where he granted the same cities and territories to Saint Peter and promised that these would be handed over in their entirety to the aforementioned pontiff according to the designated boundary as this is shown to be constituted in the same donation, namely, from the gulf of Spezia, with the island of Corsica, to Sarzana, thence to the Cisa pass (Berceto, that is), on to Parma, then to Reggio, and from there to Mantua and Monselice, and also the entire exarchate of the Ravennans, as it was in olden times, and the provinces of Venetia and Istria as well as the whole of the duchies of Spoleto and Benevento.

43. After this donation had been drawn up, that most Christian king of the Franks confirmed it by his own hand and had all the bishops, abbots, dukes, and counts add their names to it. Then, placing it first upon the altar of the blessed Peter and afterwards within, in his holy shrine, the king of the Franks and his judges handed it over to Saint Peter and his most holy vicar, Pope Hadrian, promising under awesome oath that they would maintain everything contained in the same donation. However, the most Christian king of the Franks had the said Itherius draw up a copy of that same donation and with his own hands deposited this within, on the body of Saint Peter, beneath the gospels which lie there to be kissed, as the most secure of sureties and for the eternal remembrance of his name and that of the kingdom of the

Franks. And further copies of the donation, made by the archivist of this our holy Roman church, were taken away with him by his excellence.

Life of Pope Leo III

17. After the most serene king had kept him [Pope Leo] with him for some time in great honor, those aforesaid wicked men and sons of the devil, having perpetrated dreadful and wicked arson against the possessions and property of the blessed apostle Peter, heard of this and, God opposing them, caused false charges to be laid against the most holy pontiff and sent after him to the king. It was quite impossible for them to prove such unspeakable allegations because these were the product of their own plots and iniquities and wish to humble the holy church.

18. But while the pontiff was staying with the aforesaid most clement and great king in great and becoming honor, archbishops, bishops and other priests came to that place from all quarters and, after consultation with the same most pious great king and all the Franks of distinction, sent him forth with the immense honor that was appropriate to be returned in honor, God going before, to Rome and his apostolic see. And through one city after another, each receiving him as if he were the apostle himself, they escorted him to Rome.

19. The Romans, for their immense joy at recovering their pastor, all massed together on the vigil of the blessed apostle Andrew – the chiefs and all the rest of the clergy, the nobles, senate and all the soldiers, the whole Roman people, with nuns and deaconesses, most noble matrons and all the women – together with all the colonies of the visiting schoolmen, namely, Franks, Frisians, Saxons and Lombards, and, receiving him at the Milvian bridge with crosses, banners and holy psalms, conducted him into the church of St-Peter the apostle, where he celebrated the solemnities of the mass and all partook together in faith of the body and blood of our Lord Jesus Christ.

20. And on the following day [30 November], when the birthday of the blessed apostle Andrew was being celebrated according to ancient custom, he entered amid the crowds, to immense rejoicing and delight, and then [went to] the Lateran palace. And some days later the most faithful representatives who had come with him in the pontifical retinue – namely, the most reverent archbishops Hildebald and Arno, the most reverent and most holy bishops Cunipert, Bernard, Atto, and Jesse, the bishop-elect Erflaic and the most glorious counts Helmgaud, Rodgar, and Germar – took their seats in the chamber of the lord pope Leo and for a week and more interrogated those most abominable evil-doers, Paschal, Campulus and their followers, as to what evil they had suffered from their pontiff. And they had nothing which

they could say against him. Then the representative of the great king arrested them and sent them to Francia....

23. After this, when the birthday of our Lord Jesus Christ arrived, everyone again congregated in the aforesaid basilica of the blessed apostle Peter. Then, with his own hands, the venerable and gracious prelate crowned him [Charles] with a most precious crown. By the will of God and the blessed Peter, holder of the keys of the heavenly kingdom, all the faithful Romans, recognizing the magnitude of his protection and affection for the holy Roman church and its vicar, exclaimed as one at the top of their voices: "To Charles, most pious Augustus, crowned by God, great and pacific emperor, life and victory!" Three times was this proclaimed, with the invocation of many saints, before the sacred shrine of the blessed apostle Peter; and he was constituted emperor of the Romans by all.

How did Charlemagne spend his time while visiting Rome? Were his reasons for coming to the city mostly political or religious? How did the sacred sites of the city provide a public "stage" for negotiations between the Frankish ruler and the popes? Imagine a minor lord who accompanied Charlemagne on his journeys to Rome: How might he describe the churches of the city in a letter sent back to his friends and family?

20. REGULATING PILGRIMAGE IN THE CAROLINGIAN EMPIRE

As part of the effort to govern their far-flung "Christian Empire," the Carolingians issued a number of different law codes or "capitularies" during the late eighth and ninth centuries. Among many other concerns, these legal proclamations (sometimes drawn from earlier acts of church legislation) attempted to regulate local pilgrimage and devotion, along with other kinds of religious activities that involved travel and veneration at the shrines of the saints.

Source: trans. P.D. King, in *Charlemagne: Translated Sources*, ed. P.D. King (Lancaster: P.D. King, 1987), pp. 213, 217–18, 220, 222, 229, 235, 239.

General Admonition (789)

42. To bishops: Further, in the same [council of Africa], that false names of martyrs and uncertain shrines of saints are not to be venerated.

75. To all: This too seems to us becoming and worthy of respect, that strangers, pilgrims, and the poor should have hostels established by monks and canons in various places, for the Lord himself will say on the great day

of reward: "I was a stranger and you took me in," and the apostle, praising hospitality, said: "Through this some have pleased God, that they have given hospitality to angels."

79. In part to priests, in part to all: Further, that those swindlers and tramps who roam around this land as vagabonds, subject to no law whatsoever, are not to be allowed to wander and to practice frauds upon people. Nor are those who, naked and in chains, declare that they go wandering around as a result of a penance which has been imposed upon them. It seems better, if they have committed some unusual and capital sin, that they should remain, working and serving and carrying out such penance as may have been canonically imposed upon them, in one place.

Double Edict of Commission, Aachen (789)

2. Concerning anchorites [hermit monks]: It is better that they be encouraged to remain in a monastic community than that their will should tempt them to wander elsewhere.

32. Concerning the poor who lie on the highways and at crossroads: That they are to come to church and make their confessions.

Capitulary of Frankfurt (794)

42. That no new saints are to be venerated or invoked and no shrines for them to be put up along the roads; but those alone are to be venerated in church, who have been chosen on the basis of their passions or lives.

Programmatic Capitulary, Aachen (802)

5. That no one is to presume to defraud, rob, or otherwise harm God's holy churches or widows or orphans or pilgrims; for the lord emperor has himself been appointed their protector and defender, after the Lord and his saints.

27. And we command that no one in our whole realm is to dare to deny hospitality, whether to rich or to poor or to pilgrims, that is, that no one is to deny a roof, a fire, and water to pilgrims traversing the land on God's behalf or to any person making a journey for love of God and the salvation of his soul. And if someone wishes to bestow some further benefit on these, let him know that he will have the best of rewards for himself from God, since he himself said: "And whoever shall have received one little child because of me has received me," and elsewhere, "I was a stranger and you took me in."

What evidence do the capitularies provide that Carolingian authorities were concerned about the safety of religious travelers? Why did the capitularies try to regulate the creation of new saints and shrines? Why were these laws concerned about the travel of "vagabond" monks and "the poor," and what might this imply about Carolingian society as a whole?

21. THE TRANSLATION AND MIRACLES OF SAINTS MARCELLINUS AND PETER

During the ninth century, the cult of relics achieved an unprecedented prominence in the Carolingian world, due in part to the Carolingians' insistence that every church altar contain some portion of a saint's remains. In addition, Frankish rulers mandated that oaths be sworn over holy relics. To meet the growing demand for such relics, members of the clergy increasingly sought to "translate" or transfer saintly remains from one site to another. In some cases, pious travelers would even carry out acts of "holy theft," furtively removing the saints from their long-standing resting place to a new and apparently more deserving home. Rome, in particular, offered a rich trove of such sacred treasures. Such relics, in turn, could form centers of local devotion to the saints in their new "homes," attracting pilgrims from surrounding regions. The account below of one such act of pious thievery, involving the relics of fourth-century martyrs Marcellinus and Peter, was written around 830 by Einhard, best known as Charlemagne's close associate and biographer.

Source: trans. P.E. Dutton, *Charlemagne's Courtier: The Complete Einhard*, ed. P.E. Dutton (Peterborough, ON: Broadview Press, 1998), pp. 69–78, 92–98.

Preface

Einhard, a sinner, [sends greetings] to the true worshippers and genuine lovers of the true God, of our Lord Jesus Christ, and of his saints. Those who have set down in writing and recorded the lives and deeds of the just [the saved] and of people living according to divine commands, seem to me to have wanted to accomplish nothing but to inspire by means of examples of this sort the spirits of all people to emend their evil ways and to sing the praises of God's omnipotence. These [writers] did this, not only because they lacked envy, but because they were completely full of charity, which seeks the improvement of all. Since their praiseworthy intention was so obviously to accomplish nothing other than those [goals] I described, I do not see why their [plan] should not be imitated by many other [writers]. Therefore, since I am aware that the books I have written, with what skill I could, concerning the translation of the bodies of the blessed martyrs of Christ, Marcellinus and Peter, and concerning the signs and miracles the Lord wished to bring about through them for the salvation of believers, were composed with the same wish and purpose [in mind], I have decided to disseminate these books and to offer them to the lovers of God to read. For I suppose that this book will not only seem deep and meaningful to the faithful, but I also assume that I will have worked productively and usefully if I am able to move the spirit of [even] one person reading these things to rise up in praise of its creator.

1.1 When I was resident at the palace and occupied with the business of the world, I used to give much thought to the retirement I hoped one day to enjoy. Due to the generosity of Louis [the Pious, Charlemagne's son], the ruler whom I then served, I [had] obtained a certain remote piece of property that was well out of most people's way. This estate is in Germany in the forest that lies halfway between the Neckar and Main rivers, which in these days is called Odenwald by both its inhabitants and those living nearby. I had constructed there, as far as my resources would allow, not only permanent houses and dwellings, but also a well built church that was suitable for holding divine services. Then I became very concerned, wondering in whose name and honor – to which saint or martyr – that church should be dedicated.

After I had passed quite some time unsure what to do, it [so] happened that a certain deacon of the Roman church by the name of Deusdona came to the palace to appeal to the king for help in some pressing problems of his own. He remained there for some time and, when he had finished the business for which he had come, he was preparing to return to Rome. One day, to show courtesy to the traveler, I invited him to share a meager meal with us. Then, after we had spoken of many things over dinner, we came to a point in our conversation where the translation of the body of the blessed Sebastian was mentioned. [We also spoke] of the neglected tombs of the martyrs, for there are many of those in Rome. When the conversation came to the [question of the] dedication of my new church, I began to inquire how I might arrange to obtain some particle of the genuine relics of the saints buried in Rome. At first, in fact, he hesitated, and stated that he did not know how it could be done. Then, when he saw that I was both distressed and intrigued by this business, he promised that he would respond to my inquiry on another day.

After that I invited him [to my place] again and he [then] produced a document from his purse and handed it to me. He asked me to read it thoroughly when I was alone and to be sure to tell him whether I liked what it said. I took the document and, as requested, read it carefully when I was alone. It said that he possessed many saints' relics at home and that he wished to give them to me, if [only] I could help him return to Rome. He knew that I had two mules [and said that], if I gave one to him and sent along one of my faithful men to receive the relics from him and bring them back to me, he would immediately send those [relics] to me. The plan he suggested was very appealing to me, and I hastily decided to check out the truth of his uncertain claim.

As a result, after giving him the animal he requested and even adding [some] money for his daily expenses, I ordered my notary, Ratleig, who had made a vow to travel to Rome to pray, to accompany him. Therefore, they set out from the palace at Aachen, where the emperor [Louis] was then holding court, and traveled to Soissons. There they spoke with Hilduin, the abbot of the monastery of St-Medard, because the deacon [Deusdona had] promised him that he could arrange for the body of the holy martyr Tiburtius to come into his possession. Seduced by these promises, [Hilduin] sent a certain priest, a cunning man by the name of Hunus, with them and ordered him to bring him back the body of the martyr [Tiburtius] once he had received it from [Deusdona]. And so having started out on their journey, they made their way as quickly as they could toward Rome.

1.2. After they had entered Italy, however, it happened that my notary's servant, whose name was Reginbald, was seized by a tertian fever [malaria]. His sickness led to a serious delay in their progress, since during those times when he was gripped by bouts of fever they could not continue their journey, for their number was small and they did not want to be separated from each other. Although their journey had been considerably delayed because of this trouble, they nevertheless tried to hurry as fast as they could. Three days before they reached [Rome], the feverish man had a vision in which a man in a deacon's clothes appeared to him and asked him why his master was rushing to Rome. When [Reginbald] revealed to him, as much as he knew, about the deacon's promises to send saints' relics to me and about what he had promised Abbot Hilduin, [the figure] said: "[Events] will not turn out as you think [they will], but quite differently, and yet the goal of your mission will [still] be achieved. For that deacon, who asked you to come to Rome, will bring about few or none of the things he promised you. For that reason, I want you to come with me and to pay careful attention to the things I am about to reveal and describe to you."

Then grasping him by the hand, which is how it seemed to him, he made him ascend with him to the peak of an extremely high mountain. When they stood on the summit together, he said: "Turn to the east and look down upon the landscape before your eyes!" When he had done that and had seen the landscape [the figure] had mentioned, he saw buildings of immense size rising up there like some great city. When he was asked if he knew what that was, he answered that he did not. Then [the figure] said, "That is Rome you see." He also added: "Direct your gaze to the more distant parts of the city and see if any church is visible to you there." And when he had said that, [Reginbald] did [in fact] see a certain church, and [his guide] said: "Go and tell Ratleig that in the church you just saw is hidden the very thing that he should carry to his lord. Let him strive to acquire it as soon as possible and then return to his lord." When he said that none of his companions would believe an account of this sort, [his guide] answered, saying: "You know that everyone making this journey with you is aware that you have struggled with a tertian fever for many days [now] and that you have not yet been released from it." He said: "It is just as you say." His [guide] said, "For that reason, I wish [to provide] a sign to you and to those to whom you will recount what I have said, for from this [very] hour you will be so cured, by the mercy of God, from the fever that has gripped you until now, that it will no longer bother you on this journey." [Reginbald] awoke at these words, and made sure to recount everything he thought he had seen and heard to Ratleig. When Ratleig had revealed these things to the priest traveling with him, it seemed [prudent] to both of them to accept [as true] the experience of the dream if [Reginbald regained] his health as promised. On that very day, according to the usual nature of the fever he was suffering from, the one who had seen the dream should have become feverish [again]. But [the dream] was shown to have been a true revelation rather than a vain illusion, since he perceived no sign of the usual fever in his body on that day or on the ones that followed. Thus, they came to believe in the vision and [now] had no faith in the promises of the deacon [Deusdona].

1.3. When they arrived in Rome, they took up residence near the church of the blessed Apostle Peter that is called [St-Peter] in Chains, in the house of the very deacon with whom they had come. They stayed with him for some time, waiting for him to fulfill his promises. But that man, like those not able to carry out their promises, concealed his inability by procrastinating. Finally, they spoke to him and asked him why he wished to deceive them like that. At the same time they asked him not to detain them any longer by trickery or by delaying their return home with false hopes. When he had heard them out, and realized that he could now no longer take advantage of them with cunning of this sort, he first let my notary know that he could not [at present] obtain the relics I had been promised, because his brother, to whom he had entrusted his house and all his possessions while he was away, had left for Benevento on business and he had no idea when he would return. He had given him those relics to watch over, along with his other moveable property, but he was entirely unable to determine what he had done with them, since he had not found them in the house. Hence he did [not] see what he could do, since there remained nothing on his part that he could hope for.

After he said that to my notary, [Ratleig] complained that he had been deceived and badly treated by him. I do not know with what empty and meaningless words [Deusdona] spoke to Hilduin's priest, [but] he sent him away filled with little hope. The very next day, when he saw how sad they were, he urged them all to come with him to the saints' cemeteries, for it seemed to him that something could be discovered there that would satisfy their desires, and that there was no need for them to go home empty-handed. Since this plan appealed to them, they wanted to begin what he had urged them to do as soon as possible, [but] in his usual manner he neglected the matter and threw those men, whose spirits had been high a short while before, into such a state of despair by this postponement, that they gave up on [Deusdona] and resolved to return home, even though their business had not been accomplished.

1.4. But my notary, recalling the dream his servant had seen, began to press his partner [the priest Hunus] to go [with him] to the cemeteries without their host. [Deusdona had] promised that he wanted to take them there to see those [cemeteries]. Thus, after they had found and hired a guide to the [holy] places, they first traveled three miles outside the city to the church of the blessed martyr Tiburtius on the Via Labicana. There they investigated the tomb of the martyr with as much care as they could, and cautiously inspected whether it could be opened in such a way that others would not detect [it]. Then they descended into the crypt connected to the same church, in which the bodies of the blessed martyrs of Christ, Marcellinus and Peter, were entombed. After they had also examined the condition of this monument, they departed. They thought that they could hide their activity from their host, but it turned out otherwise than they supposed. Word of their activity quickly reached him, though they were unsure how. Since [Deusdona] was worried that they might achieve their goal without him, he was determined to thwart their plan and so rushed to them. He spoke to them seductively and advised them that, since he had a complete and detailed knowledge of those holy places, they should visit them together and, if God chose to answer their prayers, they would do [together and] as agreed upon by all whatever they thought they needed to do. They gave in to his plan and together set a time for carrying out [this business].

Then, after a fast of three days, they traveled by night to that place without any Roman citizens noticing them. Once in the church of St-Tiburtius, they first tried to open the altar under which it was believed his holy body was located. But the strenuous nature of the job they had started foiled their plan, for the monument was constructed of extremely hard marble and easily resisted the bare hands of those trying to open it. Therefore, they abandoned the tomb of that martyr and descended to the tomb of the blessed Marcellinus and Peter. There, once they had called on our Lord Jesus Christ [for help] and had adored the holy martyrs, they were able to lift the tombstone from its place covering the top of the sepulcher. Once it had been lifted off, they saw the most sacred body of Saint Marcellinus set in the upper part of that sepulcher and a marble tablet placed near his head. It contained an inscription clearly indicating which martyr's limbs lay there. They lifted up the body, treating it, as was proper, with the greatest reverence. After they had wrapped it in a clean linen shroud, they handed it over to the deacon [Deusdona] to carry and hold for them. Then they put the tombstone back into place, so that no trace of the body's removal would remain, and they returned to their dwelling place in Rome. The deacon, however, asserted that he could and would keep the body of the most holy martyr, which he had received, in that house where he lived, [which was located] near the church of the blessed apostle Peter that is called [St-Peter] in Chains. He entrusted it to the care of his own brother Luniso. [Deusdona] thought that this [relic] would satisfy my notary [and so] began to urge him to return to his own country, now that he had obtained the body of the blessed Marcellinus.

1.5. But [Ratleig] was contemplating and considering something very different. For, as he told me later, it seemed wrong to him to return home with only the body of the blessed Marcellinus. [Indeed] it would almost be a crime for the body of the blessed martyr Peter, who had been his companion in death and who had for more than five hundred years rested with him in the same sepulcher, to remain there after his [friend] had left. Once this thought had occurred to him, his mind labored under such great anxiety and torment that he could neither eat nor sleep with any pleasure until the martyrs' bodies were joined together again on the trip they were about to make far from home, just as they had been joined together in death and in their tomb. He was in great doubt, however, about how this [reunification of the relics] could be achieved. For he realized that he could not find any Roman to help him in this affair, nor in fact was there [a Roman] to whom he dared reveal his secret thoughts. While wrestling with this worry in his heart, he happened to meet a foreign monk by the name of Basil who two years before had traveled from Constantinople to Rome. He resided in Rome with four of his students on the Palatine hill in a house occupied by other Greek [monks]. [Ratleig] went to him and revealed the [nature of the] anxiety troubling him. Then, encouraged by [the monk's] advice and confident of his prayers, he discovered such strength in his own heart that he was determined to attempt the deed as soon as he could, despite the danger to himself. He sent for his partner, Hilduin's priest, and suggested to him that they should return in secret to the church of the blessed Tiburtius, just as they had before, and try once again to open the tomb in which the body of the martyr was thought to be buried. This plan pleased [them] and [so], in the company of the servants they had brought with them [to Rome], they set out secretly at night. Their host had no idea where they were going. After this band had come to that place and prayed for success in their mission before the doors of the church, they entered. The group [then] split up. The priest stayed with some of them to search for the body of the blessed Tiburtius in his church. Ratleig [descended] with the rest into the crypt connected to the church and approached the body of the blessed Peter. They opened the sepulcher with no trouble and [Ratleig] removed the sacred limbs of the holy martyr without any resistance and carefully placed the recovered [bones] on the silk cushion he had prepared for this purpose. [After further adventures, and acquiring even more relics, Ratleig departs from Rome and begins the journey home.]

1.8. When, however, he had gone by that place known as the Head of Lake [Villeneuve in Switzerland], he reached the point where the way leading into Francia splits into two. He took the path to the right and came via the territory of the Alemannians to Solothurn, a town of the Burgundians. There he encountered the people I [Einhard] had sent from Maastricht to meet him after word of his return had reached me. For when the letter of my notary was brought to me by my steward's servant, the one I mentioned before, I was at the monastery of St-Bavo on the Scheldt River. After reading that letter I learned about the approach of the saints and I immediately ordered a member of my household to go to Maastricht to collect priests, other clergymen, and also laymen there, and then to hasten to meet the oncoming saints at the first possible place. With no delay, he and the group he brought with him met up in a few days with those who were carrying the saints at the place I mentioned above [Solothurn]. They joined forces at once and were accompanied from that point on by an ever increasing crowd of chanting people. Soon they came, to the great joy of everyone, to the city of Argentoratus, which is now called Strasbourg. From there they sailed down the Rhine until they came to a place called Portus [the port at Sandhofen] where they disembarked on the eastern shore of the river, and, after a trip lasting five days and with a great crowd of people reveling in the praise of God they came to that place called Michelstadt. It lies in the German forest known today as Odenwald and is located about six leagues from the Main River. In that place they found the church I had recently built, but had still not dedicated, and they carried those sacred ashes into it and deposited them as though they were destined to stay there forever. [After a series of signs and visions from the saints, under Einhard's supervision, the relics were transferred to Seligenstadt.]

Preface to Book Three

I am about to write of the remarkable things and miracles that those most blessed martyrs of Christ, Marcellinus and Peter, brought about in various places after their most sacred bodies had been transported from Rome into Francia. Rather [I should say] that it is through their holy merits and pious prayers that God himself, our Lord Jesus Christ, the king of martyrs, deigned to bring about these [miraculous] cures for people. I think it is necessary to mention in this brief preface that most of the things I have decided to record were brought to my attention by the accounts of others. But I was entirely convinced to trust these accounts, because of the things I myself had seen and knew personally. Thus I was able to believe without the slightest doubt that these events, which were reported to me by those who said that they themselves had witnessed them, were true, even though I might, up until then, have had little or no [personal] knowledge of the individuals from whom I had heard these things.

Still, it seems [best to me] to record first of all those [miracles and cures] I myself saw and that happened in the place [Seligenstadt] to which those most blessed martyrs had said their sacred ashes should be translated. After that those [miracles] that occurred in the palace at Aachen under the very eyes of the courtiers should be recalled. Then I thought I should record those things that were reported to have happened in various places to which, at the request of religious men and by my permission, the sacred relics were carried. If I stick to this plan in my account, none of the various signs and miracles that came to the attention of my smallness should be left out. But now that the preface is complete, let me set forth the miracles themselves, for they need to be described.

3.1. As already set out above [in the previous books], the sacred bodies of the blessed martyrs were brought to the great joy of the faithful to that place in which they now rest. They had themselves ordered [this translation] and we had complied. After a mass had been solemnly celebrated in a field, the relics were carried in the hands of priests, for a large number of them had gathered there at that time, into the church. The bier on which the [relics] were carried was set down near the altar. Another service had just begun there, when suddenly a young man, who was suffering from kidney failure and so was bent over and supporting himself on crutches, burst forth from the middle of the crowd of people standing around. He wanted to bow down in adoration and [so] fell forward onto his knees, but [this happened] in a remarkable way, for it was as though someone had pulled him away or, rather, pulled him back, so that he fell on his back and lay there like someone sleeping for a very long time. Then, as if he were waking up, he lifted himself into a sitting position and, a little while later, got up with no one's help. He stood in the middle of the crowd surrounding him and praised the mercy of God and gave thanks along with the others for the restoration of his health. He told me, when I asked, that he had come there [to Seligenstadt] from the Portian district with other poor people and pilgrims, and that his name was Daniel.

3.2. At almost the same hour and, indeed, at the exact same moment, if I may put it so, at which [Daniel], about whom I was just speaking, regained his health within the church before the altar by means of the power of Christ and the intercession of the martyrs, a certain woman who was paralyzed and almost entirely without the use of her limbs was lying outside the doors of the church. She called upon the holy martyrs to help her. Very soon, before all those who were present, her stomach began to heave as if she were about to be sick, and then she began to vomit a great quantity of phlegm and bile. After that, she drank a small amount of cold water and asked to be lifted up from the spot where she was lying. Leaning on her crutch she entered the church. After she had prayed to the martyrs and had recovered the power of her limbs, she returned home on foot.

3.3. At about the same time a man by the name of Willibert, who owned a house not far from the church in which the bodies of the blessed martyrs now lie [in Seligenstadt], approached the bier with others who had also gathered to venerate the saints. He presented forty silver coins as a gift [to the saints]. When I asked him who he was and what he hoped to get for himself from offering this sort of gift, he replied that he had been overcome by intense fatigue a few days earlier and had sunk so low that everyone who saw him thought he was near death. He was urged to bequeath all his property right away for the salvation of his soul, and so he did. But when the bequest of all his things had been decided and to which holy places his property should be given, [he said that] one of his servants had complained loudly that they had handled things very badly and carelessly, since none of his property had been conferred upon the saints who had recently arrived from Rome. Then he had asked those standing nearby if they knew whether any of his possessions remained that could be sent to the martyrs. In fact [the martyrs] were still in Michelstadt at that time and it had not yet been revealed by any signs that they should leave that place. [He said] that someone had then informed him that only a single pig remained from all his [former] possessions and that it had not [yet] been decided to which [holy place] it should be given. It pleased him a great deal [to learn that] and he ordered them to sell the pig and send the money, after his death, [to purchase] candles for the martyrs. As soon as he had finished giving [this command], he claims, he felt so suddenly cured that he was immediately free of all pain and even had a desire to eat [again]. After he had eaten, he felt strong so soon that the very next day he was easily able to go about managing and accomplishing all the work that his affairs demanded. After those [events] the pig was sold for the estimated price [40 silver coins], which he presented to the blessed martyrs to honor his vow.

3.4. I have decided that the other remarkable things and miracles that the Lord brought about in order to cure people should be described as they occur to my memory, since I see nothing of significance to report in the order in which they are set out. What must be considered more [significant] in the description of these miracles is what happened and why something happened rather than when it happened.

After the relics of the blessed martyrs had been solemnly installed in that church, it happened one day that a mass was in progress, since according to standard ecclesiastical practice the sacred rites of the mass were celebrated daily [there]. I had taken my place in the upper parts of the same church and was looking down upon the people gathered below in the lower parts [of the church]. I saw a half-naked cleric who had come with others to the same service. He was standing in the middle of the crowd when suddenly he collapsed so hard that he lay for a very long time on the floor as though he were dead. When some of the people standing nearby attempted to raise the man, who was breathing heavily, into a standing position, such a great flow of blood poured from his mouth and nostrils that the entire front of his body from his chest and stomach right down to the clothes covering his groin was drenched with this overflow [of blood]. He revived after he took some water and, with his strength restored, he spoke clearly. A little while later I questioned him. He informed me that he had neither been able to hear anything nor to speak from infancy right up until the present. He said that his native land was Britain and that he himself was English. In order to see his mother, who was undertaking a pilgrimage to Rome, he had hastily started upon this journey. In this way, he and other pilgrims who wanted to travel together to Rome had come to that place. But, when his companions departed, he had remained behind. He had been cured on the seventh day after coming there. When I asked him his name, he responded that he was completely ignorant of it, because he had never heard his name spoken while he was deaf.

3.5. A few days later, when we had solemnly gathered together in the church for the evening service, a deaf and mute girl from the region of Bourges was at long last brought there and made to stand with the others in that church. Her father and brother had taken her to many shrines of the saints in search of a cure. Suddenly, as if overcome by madness, she slammed together as hard as she could the tablets by whose noise she used to seek alms and threw [them] with a fury into the [crowd of] people assembled in front of her. Then she ran to the church's left wall and leaped three or more feet into the air, as if she was about to climb it. Then she fell down flat on her back. After she lay there for a little while more like someone dead than someone sleeping and was almost entirely covered with blood that was pouring from her mouth and nostrils, people standing nearby picked her up and carried her into the middle of the church. After she had lain there for a short time, she sat up like someone who had just awakened from a deep sleep. Then she extended her hands to the people beside her and pleaded [with them] with nods [of her head] to lift her onto her feet. Once she had been lifted up, she was led to the altar. When she saw that Ratleig was standing there near the altar with other clerics and that he was looking at her, she at once blurted out these words:

"You are Ratleig," she said. "You are known by this name and you are the servant of these saints." When he asked her how she knew this and who had told her his name, she said: "Those saints of yours, who lie here, approached me while I lay there like someone sleeping and they thrust their fingers into my ears and said to me: 'When you arise and approach the altar, you should know that the young cleric you will see standing before you looking at you is named Ratleig and that he is our servant. For he was the very one who carried our bodies to this place.'" That was the case, of course, since [Ratleig] was the man, as I recorded in the first book, whom I had sent to Rome to receive the relics of the saints from a certain deacon and to carry them to me. Indeed, it was in this way and in my presence that the spirit of sickness was driven out by the power of the blessed martyrs and this girl regained her complete health. Her father and brother, who had led her there, declared that she had been deaf and mute since birth.

3.6. Although I myself did not see the miracle I am about to describe, I am able to believe the account of those who told it to me no less than if I had seen it with my own eyes. Thus, without any hesitation or doubt, I have decided to present it not as if I had [just] heard it, but rather as if I myself had actually seen it.

Some merchants from the city of Mainz, who were in the habit of purchasing grain in the upper parts of Germany and transporting it by the river Main to their city, brought to the church of the blessed martyrs a blind man, an Aquitanian by the name of Alberic. They had taken him on board their boat, as he himself had requested, in order to win God's favor. After he had disembarked [at Seligenstadt] and was admitted as a guest in the house of the church's guardian, he stayed there for seven days or more. Besides being blind, which seemed natural to him since he lacked eyes, he suffered from a horrible and vile disease of his entire body. For all his limbs shook so violently that he was entirely incapable of passing food to his mouth with his own hands.

One day, in the morning, when [Alberic] had fallen asleep while lying in his lodgings, he saw in his sleep a man approach him. He urged him to get up at once and hurry to the church. He said that the time had arrived, when, through the power of the saints, he was sure to be released from his wretched suffering. After he awoke and was led to the church, he sat upon a stone in front of the [church] doors. At that very moment a divine service was being solemnly celebrated within the church. After the prayers that come before the sacred reading of the Gospel were finished, the Gospel itself was read out. Scarcely two verses of the reading had been completed, when, all of a sudden, it was as if [Alberic] was struck by a blow and trembling he screamed out loud, saying: "Help me, Saint Marcellinus!" Although everyone in the church was greatly alarmed by the commotion and clamor, most, because of their respect for the reading of the Gospel, stayed where they were, but many rushed over to see what the noise was all about. As they declared later on, they found [Alberic] in that place where he had been sitting, but now he was lying stretched out flat on his back and his chin and chest were covered with blood that was pouring from his nostrils. After they had lifted him onto his feet and he had taken a little cold water, he came around. He said that it had seemed to him, at the point at which he cried out, that someone had punched him in the neck, and so he had begged for the help of the blessed martyr. Still all agree that this blow was so beneficial to him that from that moment on no further evidence of that vile shaking was seen in his body.

After that he remained for almost two years in the same place [Seligen-stadt], and, as he himself declared, there was no night in that two-year period in which he did not see the very martyrs who had cured him in his dreams. He also learned many things from them that he was ordered to tell others. I now see that many of the things that he then predicted would happen are coming true.

3.7. A few days later we saw another man suffering from a similar disease who was cured in the same church in the same way by the merits of those same saints. For on a certain night when I was sitting in the church to celebrate the morning service and to listen to the reading of the divine law [the Bible], a man in clerical habit entered [the church]. With his limbs trembling and leaning on a crutch, he [could only] control his faltering steps with difficulty. While he was leaning up against a wall in order to pray, he let forth a loud scream and fell in a sudden collapse onto his face. After a short delay, he rose up cured of the disease that had held him. I sought [to learn] from him if anything had appeared to him at the moment when he was cured other than what all of us could see. He said that not long before he had entered the church he had gone to pray at the old church [in Seligenstadt], which lay a short distance to the west of the new church [built between 830 and 836] where the martyrs were then resting. But since he had come upon it when it was locked up, he had prayed outside its doors. After that, when he had arisen [from praying] and had begun to move toward the [new] church, he had seen a cleric with venerable white hair, dressed in a white robe, preceding him to the place he himself wished to go. He said that he followed him as far as the church door. When both of them had arrived there, the [figure] in front moved to the side and stood against the left doorpost, as if he wanted the man he had just been in front of to enter first. When he was reluctant [to enter], [the figure] ordered him with a nod of his head to enter before he did. After he had entered and kneeled down to pray, [the white-haired figure] stood behind his back and hit him on the neck with his fist, knocking him down. [The figure] then immediately vanished. But, no one except the man who was cured was able to see him.

3.8. At almost the same time, when I had arisen one night and gone to church, I discovered a boy lying in the narthex before the [inner] doors of the church. He was so miserably deformed that his knees were touching his chin. He asked one of the men following us to carry him into the church. Moved by pity, [that fellow] lifted him up and arranged for him to lie down near the choir in the church. Drowsiness immediately overcame the boy and he fell asleep where he was lying. He did not wake up completely until he was entirely cured of that wretched tightening [of his limbs] because of the intercession of the saints. Then he awoke on his own, got up from the place into which he had been carried by someone else, and approached the altar to give thanks to God. When it was light outside and I was able to talk to him, he said that he had been summoned and warned three times before the church bell had sounded by a cleric he did not know to let nothing stand in the way of him going to church for the morning service. He had just done that and afterwards, as I myself saw, he had received a complete cure of his body while he slept in the church. [This boy] seemed to be around fifteen years old.

3.9. I also saw another person cured in the same place in a similar way at about the same time. He was not a boy, as this one had been, but a very old and decrepit man who had been afflicted with a similar disease. One night when we had come to the door of the church to celebrate the morning service, we found him in the doorway. He was holding himself up on two canes while struggling forward on his knees. His extremely slow pace delayed our entrance [into the church]. While we were stuck behind him and waited for his slow advance, such a powerful fragrance of the most alluring kind poured forth from the church and filled our noses that it exceeded in its effect all artificial combinations of spices and thymes. Finally he entered [the church] and, before our eyes, lay down near the choir as if he was about to go to sleep. We too entered the church and took our places, and sang along with the others the psalms that were being sung in a solemn fashion. But when the first reading had begun, we heard that old man moan and beg for help as though he were being attacked. A little later we saw him lift himself into a sitting position and right after that he took up the crutches he had used to walk, and then stood up on his feet. In fact, I myself saw these things, but he told me that it had seemed to him as if two men had grabbed hold of him while he lay there. One had seized him by his shoulders and arms, the other by his knees and feet. It seemed as if by pulling him that they had stretched out his tendons, which had been very tight. He said that, aside from the problem with his tightened tendons, he had also been deaf, but when he had lifted himself into a sitting position it was as if an extremely powerful punch had landed on the top of his head. At the same moment he had heard someone's voice commanding him to hear from that point on. The old man declared that he had been cured in this way. He said that he had come from the land of the Swiss which is now called Aarau and that he was of German stock.

How did Einhard arrange for the acquisition of sacred remains from Rome? How did his representative Ratleig actually manage to obtain relics of Marcellinus and Peter? How did the relics create a new center of devotion for local and regional pilgrims around Seligenstadt? What kind of miracles did the saints perform there?

22. CRITICIZING THE CULT OF SAINTS: CLAUDIUS OF TURIN'S COMPLAINT

Not everyone in the Carolingian world was as enthusiastic about devotion to the saints and their relics as Einhard (doc. 21). Bishop Claudius of Turin, formerly active at the court of Charlemagne's son, Louis the Pious, criticized many such common devotional practices of his day. In the selection below, Claudius responds to charges made against him by Abbot Theodemir of Psalmody (near Nîmes), who accused him, among other things, of questioning the power of the saints and the effectiveness of penitential pilgrimages to Rome.

Source: trans. A. Cabaniss, in *Early Medieval Theology*, ed. G.E. McCraken and A. Cabaniss, *The Library of Christian Classics*, vol. 9 (Philadelphia: Westminster Press, 1957), pp. 241–48.

Your letter of chatter and dullness, together with the essay subjoined to it, I have received from the hands of the bumpkin who brought it to me. You declare that you have been troubled because a rumor about me has spread from Italy throughout all the regions of Gaul even to the frontiers of Spain, as though I were announcing a new sect in opposition to the standard of catholic faith – an intolerable lie. It is not surprising, however, that they have spoken against me, those notorious members of the Devil who proclaimed our head himself [Christ] to be a diabolical seducer. It is not I who teach a sect, I who really hold the unity and preach the truth. On the contrary, as much as I have been able, I have suppressed, crushed, fought, and assaulted sects, schisms, superstitions, and heresies, and, as much as I am still able, I do not cease to do battle against them, relying wholeheartedly on the help of God. For which reason, of course, it came to pass that as soon as I was constrained to assume the burden of pastoral duty and to come to Italy to the city of Turin, sent there by our pious prince Louis, the son of the Lord's holy catholic church, I found all the churches filled, in defiance of the precept of truth, with those sluttish abominations – images. Since everyone was worshipping them, I undertook singlehanded to destroy them. Everyone thereupon opened his mouth to curse me, and had not God come to my aid, they would no doubt have swallowed me alive.

Since it is clearly enjoined that no representation should be made of anything in heaven, on earth, or under the earth, the commandment is to be understood, not only of likenesses of other gods, but also of heavenly creatures, and of those things which human conceit contrives in honor of the creator. To adore is to praise, revere, ask, entreat, implore, invoke, offer prayer. But to worship is to direct respect, be submissive, celebrate, venerate, love, esteem highly. Those against whom we have undertaken to defend God's church say, "We do not suppose that there is anything divine in the image which we adore. We adore it only to honor him whose likeness it is." To whom we reply that if those who have abandoned the cult of demons now venerate the images of saints, they have not deserted their idols but have merely changed the name. For if you portray or depict on a wall representations of Peter and Paul, of Jupiter, Saturn, or Mercury, the latter representations are not gods and the former are not apostles, and neither the latter nor the former are men, although the word is used for that purpose. Nonetheless the selfsame error always persists both then and now. Surely if men may be venerated, it is the living rather than the dead who should be so esteemed, that is, where God's likeness is present, not where there is the likeness of cattle or (even worse) of stone or wood, all of which lack life, feeling, and reason. But if the works of God's hands must not be adored and worshipped, one should ponder carefully how much less are the works of men's hands to be adored and worshipped or held in honor of those whose likenesses they are. For if the image which one adores is not God, then in vain should it be venerated for honor of the saints who in vain arrogate to themselves divine dignities.

Above all, therefore, it should be perceived that not only he who worships visible figures and images, but also he who worships any creature, heavenly or earthly, spiritual or corporeal, in place of God's name, and who looks for the salvation of his soul from them (that salvation which is the prerogative of God alone), that it is he of whom the apostle speaks, "They worshipped and served the creature rather than the Creator." Why do you humiliate yourselves and bow down to false images? Why do you bend your body like a captive before foolish likenesses and earthly structures? God made you upright, and although other animals face downward toward the earth, there is for you an upward posture and a countenance erect to heaven and to God. Look thither, lift your eyes thither, seek God in the heights, so that you can avoid those things which are below. Exalt your wavering heart to heavenly heights....

If you say that I forbid men to go to Rome for the sake of penance, you lie. I neither approve nor disapprove that journey, since I know that it does not injure, nor benefit, nor profit, nor harm anyone. If you believe that to go to Rome is to do penance, I ask you why you have lost so many souls in so much time, souls whom you have restrained in your monastery, or whom for the sake of penance you have received into your monastery and have not sent to Rome, but whom you have rather made to serve you. You say that you have a band of 140 monks who came to you for the sake of penance, surrendering themselves to the monastery. You have not permitted one of them to go to Rome. If these things are so (as you say, "To go to Rome is to do penance"), what will you do about this statement of the Lord: "Whoever causes one of these little ones who believe in me to stumble, it is expedient for him that a millstone be hung around his neck and that he be drowned in the deep, rather than cause one of these little ones who believe in me to stumble"? There is no greater scandal than to hinder a man from taking the road by which he can come to eternal joy.

We know, indeed, that the evangelist's account of the Lord Savior's words are not understood, where he says to the blessed apostle Peter: "You are Peter, and on this rock I will build my church, and I will give you the keys of the kingdom of heaven." Because of these words of the Lord, the ignorant race of men, all spiritual understanding having been disregarded, wishes to go to Rome to secure eternal life. He who understands the keys of the kingdom in the manner stated above does not require the intercession of blessed Peter in a particular location, for if we consider carefully the proper meaning of the Lord's words, we find that he did not say to him, "Whatever you shall loose in heaven shall be loosed on earth and whatever you shall bind in heaven shall be bound on earth." One must know hereby that that ministry has been granted to bishops of the church just so long as they are pilgrims here in this mortal body. But when they have paid the debt of death, others who succeed in their place gain the same judicial authority, as it is written, "Instead of your fathers, sons are born to you; you will appoint them princes over all the earth."

Return, O you blind, to the true light that enlightens every man who comes into this world, because the light shines in darkness, and the darkness does not envelop it. By not looking at that light you are in the darkness. You walk in darkness and you do not know whither you are going, because the darkness has blinded your eyes. Hear this also and be wise, you fools among the people, you who were formerly stupid, who seek the apostle's intercession by going to Rome; hear what the same oft-mentioned most blessed Augustine [of Hippo] utters against you. In *On the Trinity*, book eight, he says, among other things, "Come with me and let us consider why we should love the apostle. Is it because of the human form, which we hold to be quite ordinary, that we believe him to have been a man? By no means. Besides, does not he whom we love still live although that man no longer exists? His soul is indeed separated from the body, but we believe that even now there still lives what we love in him." Whoever is faithful ought to believe in God when he makes a promise, and by how much the more when he makes an oath. Why is it necessary to say, "O that Noah, Daniel, and Job were present here"? Even if there were so much holiness, so much righteousness, so much merit, they, as great as they were, will not absolve son or daughter. He therefore says these things that no one may rely on the merit or intercession of the saints, for one cannot be saved unless he possess the same faith, righteousness, and truth which they possessed and by which they were pleasing to God.

On what grounds does Claudius object to the veneration of the saints? How does he respond to Theodemir's accusation that he doubted the virtue of visits to Rome as a form of penance? What does Claudius think about such devotional pilgrimage to Rome (and presumably, elsewhere)? Compare Claudius's views to those of Vigilantius in the fifth century, as presented by Saint Jerome (doc. 9): are the two men's positions similar or different?

23. THE "SARACEN" SACK OF SAINT PETER'S BASILICA

In 846, Muslim raiders from northern Africa attacked Ostia and sailed up the Tiber to menace Rome itself. Although they did not enter the city, they plundered its outskirts, including the churches of Saint Paul and Saint Peter, stealing the altar from Saint Peter's sacred precincts. The selection below from the Book of Popes *describes the reaction of the Romans under Pope Leo IV (r. 847–852) to this raid that had struck at one of the most important pilgrimage sites in medieval Europe.*

Source: trans. B.E. Whalen, from *Le Liber Pontificalis*, ed. L. Duchesne, Bibliothèque des écoles françaises d'Athènes et de Rome, vol. 2 (Paris: E. de Boccard, 1955), pp. 106–7, 113–14.

Life of Pope Leo IV

In his time, the churches of the blessed princes Peter and Paul were thoroughly plundered by the Saracens. Due to this calamity, or rather misery, the strength of the Romans was exhausted and worn out. After this happened, an assembly of all the Romans judged that it was impossible to escape the peril of their doom on account of two reasons or dangers: namely, the sudden death of the [previous] pope [Sergius II], and also the destruction wrought in the holy churches and throughout the lands of the Romans. When all of the Roman nobles with equal devotion and common counsel deliberated about the future pope, that he be someone God-fearing, able to govern and rule over such a sacred and inviolable place, right away rumor of the most blessed pontiff [Leo] spread justly and immediately through the entire city, disclosed by everyone. For the dead pope who only just then had been carried away to his awaiting tomb, when behold, among those [present], everyone from the least to the greatest cried out with one voice, in unison all at once, that the venerable priest Leo would be their next pope, and that they wished to have no other bishop over them, unless it was he, about whom there was so much excitement and open discussion. Then everyone, as described above, went with joy and the rapture of great devotion to the church where he was residing, [the church] of the Four Crowns, and dragged him forth from there unwillingly and reluctantly; they led him to the Lateran palace with hymns and special praises. Keeping with ancient custom, everyone kissed his feet. It is not possible for anyone to narrate briefly the unanimity and concord present when he was elected pope.

Either for the remembrance or fearful lesson of posterity, it seems not inappropriate or wrong-headed to note in these present passages what divine power did to those Saracens, who had committed such a wicked crime in the time of his election, by the interceding prayers of the saints and assent of the apostles. After they committed their iniquity and crime of plundering, all of those men who wished to return to Africa, from where they had come, were drowned in accordance with God's will (as we learned from a certain report) by the force of the winds and storms in the vast wilderness of the sea. So the prayers of the apostles were worthy to bring about newly that ancient miracle of the Egyptians [who drowned in the Red Sea]....

After he [Leo] had carried out and completed those works [the repair of various churches around Rome], each of which we described above and celebrated by name, immediately that same shepherd and noble father, although he showed worthy care and concern for the improvement of all the churches of God and proved himself to be committed to every good work, sighing deeply from the depths of his heart, looked daily before all others to the most sacred altar of the blessed prince of apostles Peter violated, reduced to shame, and defiled by the perfidious Saracens (who are contrary to God). He wept and grieved, as we were just saying, because on this account the Christian people who journeyed from everywhere to the most sacred threshold of the aforesaid prince of apostles for the sake of prayer or spiritual grace were not able to fulfill their vows like they did before. Strengthened by the aid and counsel of almighty God and fortified by virtue, he most honorably and decently decorated with gold and silver sidings not only the sacred tomb, but the entire front of the altar, so that the work dedicated in that place might show itself more clearly in the light before all present. On this account, he totally encircled the noble front of that venerable altar, newly decorated with sidings of the finest gold along with gems, as numerous as they were rich and totally precious, bringing it to such a state and condition that it was better than before. On those gold sidings, as described before, not only did a representation of our redeemer shine forth, but likewise there radiated and shone forth on those aforesaid sidings the faces of Peter, Paul, and also Andrew, and the sign of the sacred and life-giving cross and the venerable resurrection. Among them, for future memory or record, the persons of the most holy pope Leo IV and also his spiritual son emperor Lothar [I], dear to God and venerated throughout the ages, were depicted.

Why did the Muslim raid on Rome cause such anxiety among the citizens of Rome? After reading about Charlemagne's previous visits to Rome (doc. 19), why might the Carolingians have been concerned about the plundering of Saint Peter's basilica? What evidence does this text provide that the attack on the church of Saint Peter represented a problem not just for the Romans and Carolingians, but for Christians everywhere?

CHAPTER THREE

JERUSALEM AND THE HOLY PLACES UNDER ISLAMIC RULE

In the mid-seventh century, the followers of a new monotheistic religion, Islam, emerged from the Arabian peninsula and conquered vast portions of the eastern Roman (that is, Byzantine) Empire. Among other territories, Muslim warriors subdued Jerusalem and its surroundings, opening another chapter in the history of the city's holy sites. The prophet of the Islamic tradition, Muhammad, had received a final series of divine revelations from God or "Allah" (eventually compiled in the Qur'an), but much of his message would have sounded familiar to Jewish and Christian contemporaries, including his belief that Muslims were the true inheritors of the Lord's promises to Abraham, Moses, Jesus, and other prophetic figures. Pilgrimage formed an important component of the new Islamic faith: if they were able, every believer was expected to make the Hajj, a pious journey to Muhammad's native city of Mecca, at least once in his or her lifetime. In addition, Muslim believers quickly demonstrated their own connections with Jerusalem, developing a tradition of Islamic devotional travel to its holy sites (in some cases, the same ones venerated by Jews and Christians). After the initial conquest by the Muslims, Christian pilgrims from Europe resumed their visitations to the sacred city under Islamic rule, facing new challenges during the often arduous journey to the Promised Land.

24. A CHRISTIAN REACTION TO THE ISLAMIC CAPTURE OF JERUSALEM

For seventh-century Christians, the Muslim seizure of Jerusalem seemed to represent another turning point in God's plan for history. According to the anonymous Syrian author of the "Edessene Apocalyptic Fragment," the conquests of the Muslims (the "Children of Ishmael" or "Children of Hagar") set the stage for the coming of the end times. First, a Byzantine ruler would defeat the Muslims, ushering in an era of universal peace before the coming of Antichrist, the final battle between good and evil, and the Last Judgment. Jerusalem stood at the center of the apocalyptic stage.

Source: trans. S. Bock, in *The Seventh Century in the West-Syrian Chronicles*, Translated Texts for Historians, vol. 15 (Liverpool: Liverpool University Press, 1993), pp. 244–50.

... [As a result of the Islamic invasion] the East will be laid waste by the sword and by many wars, for nation will stand against nation, and kingdom against kingdom. Their own sword will fall among them. Armenia will be laid waste, and part of the territory of the Byzantines will be laid waste, [including] many cities. When of the said [number of years], a week and a half, that is, ten and a half years, are left to the Children of Hagar, their oppression will increase: they will take everything made of gold, silver, bronze, and iron, and their clothes, and all their habitation from the [...] of the dead, until the living will pass by the dead and exclaim: "Happy are you who have not remained alive at this time." And seven women will seize hold of a man and say to him [...], as it is written in the good news of the Gospel: "A man will flee from his wife and his children, and a wife from her husband" as a result of oppression, distress, and famine. The rains will be withheld, spring water will fail, the fruits of the trees and all the bounty of the land will be scarce at that time, as a result of the unbelief of the Children of Ishmael.

When the said number of years, that week and a half has passed, at the end of 694 years, then the king of the Greeks [the Byzantine emperor] will come forth, having a sign in the city of Rome [concerning] the nails which were in the hands of our Lord Jesus Christ and in the hands of the thief: they were mixed together and no one knew those of our Lord from the others. Then they cast them into the fire all together and forged a bit or bridle, which they suspended in a church. When a horse that has never been ridden and never even been fitted with a bridle puts its head into that bridle of its own accord, then the Romans will know that the kingdom of Christians has come: they will "take the kingdom of the whole earth from the Children of Hagar, etc." Subsequently the king of the Greeks will hand over the kingdom of God, as is written. Now the bridle is still there today.

Then the king of the Greeks shall go forth from the west, and his son from the south, whereupon the Children of Ishmael will flee. They will resemble Babylon, but the king of the Greeks will catch up with them in Babylon, and they will flee thence to the town of Mecca, where their kingdom shall come to an end; and the king of the Greeks will rule the entire earth. Bounty shall return to the earth, the fruits of the trees, the rains, and water shall be plentiful, and so will the fish in the seas and rivers. There will be well-being and peace in the whole of creation and among all nations and peoples. Then once again the living will pass by a dead person and say, "You would have been fortunate if you had been alive today in this kingdom."

The kingdom of the Greeks will endure for 208 years. Subsequently sin will increase in the world once again, and there will be fornication openly, like beasts, without cover, in the streets and meeting places, as formerly; the earth will be polluted by sin.

Then the gates of Armenia will be opened, and the descendants of Gog and Magog shall issue forth. When King Alexander [the Great] saw these people eating the reptiles of the earth and all sorts of polluted things, including human flesh, eating the dead and every kind of unclean thing, performing magic rites and all kinds of evil deeds, he gathered them together, took them to the interior of these mountains, and confined them there. He then besought God that the mountains should come together, which came to pass, leaving a gateway [only] 20 cubits wide between the mountains. This gateway he closed up with the stones called "magnetic," of a substance which clings to iron, extinguishes fire, and resists all enchantment.

At the end of times these gates will be opened, and they will come out and pollute the earth. They will take a son from the womb of his mother, kill him and give him back to his mother to cook; and if she does not eat him, they will kill her. They will eat mice and all sorts of unclean reptiles. God's mercy shall be far removed from the inhabitants of the earth; people shall live to see all sorts of evils, famines, drought, cold frost, and widespread oppression, such that people bury themselves in the ground, while they are still alive. Had not God shortened those days, no flesh would have survived.

Some people say they will reign for two years and eight months from the time they issue forth to the time when they perish. When they go around the whole creation and rile over the whole world, God will have compassion on his servants; he will gather them to that land where the Children of Ishmael perished, that is, to Mecca. Then God will bid the angels to stone them with hailstones, so that not one of them survives: they shall all perish. During their lifetime [fairness in] weights and measures will be obsolete. Their faces are ugly, and everyone who sees them will abhor and fear them. The stature of each one of them is an arm's length.

At that time the Son of Perdition, who is named "False Messiah," shall emerge. He will seize the world by fraud and deceit, without the use of the sword. His sin will be even greater than Satan's. This is what Jacob Israel said to his children, "Gather around and I will show you what shall happen to you at the end of days." He was hinting to them at the time; and what our Lord hinted will be fulfilled, namely that Satan would be united with this false Christ. He will perform signs, open ones but useless – just as the divinity was united with the humanity and performed signs and wonders. He will utter false and distant rumors, he will raise the dead through falsehood and magic; likewise he shall heal the paralyzed and the blind.

His birth will take place in the region of Tyre and Sidon, but he will live in Capernaum. For this reason our Lord said, "Woe unto you, Chorazin, woe to you Bethsaida, and you, Capernaum: how long will you be exalted? You shall be brought down to Sheol." He will gain control of the whole world without a fight. He will say that he is the Christ. He will move from one place to another, his band with him – many thousands of demons will be with him, tens of thousands, demons without number. He will put an end to liturgical offerings and altars. The first to follow him out into error are crowds of Jews, who will say, "He is the Christ." Brides will abandon their husbands and go after him, and he will reign over the whole earth; however he will not enter the city of Edessa, for God has blessed and protected her. Nor will he enter these four monasteries which will endure as the first ones in the world.

Finally he will enter Jerusalem and the sanctuary, as the Gospel says, "When you see an abomination in the holy place." This refers to wickedness, sin and fornication, for the false Christ is the abomination and when he enters Jerusalem, Enoch and Elijah shall come out of the Land of the Living; they will take their stand, fighting and cursing him. When he sees them, he will melt away like salt in contact with water. He will be judged first of all, before humanity, along with the demons who had entered him.

Then the king of the Greeks will come to Jerusalem, climb Golgotha, where our savior was crucified, and in his hand will be the cross of our Lord. Now this king of the Greeks shall be descended from Kushyat, daughter of Kushyat, of the kings of Kush; they are also called Nubians. As he goes up with the Cross in his hands, the crown which descended from heaven upon the head of King Jovian of old will pass over the top of our Lord's cross and he will raise up the cross and crown towards heaven. And Gabriel the archangel will descend and, taking the cross and the crown, will raise them up to heaven. Then the king will die, along with every human being on earth and all the wild animals and cattle: nothing will remain.

As for the light which God created for the children of Adam, the sinner, that light was created for them alone: God, whose honor be revered, had no need of light, or of anything else. The stars will fall like leaves, and the earth shall revert to its original chaos and confusion.

Once all created things have come to an end, all of a sudden, as in a twinkling of an eye, a horn and a trumpet shall give out a sound: then good and bad will be gathered together, for there is a single resurrection for human beings and for everyone. Pangs shall smite the earth, like those of a woman who is on the very point of giving birth. Adam shall come forth, and all his children. No human being shall remain behind who will not rise at that moment. Then light will shine out from the east, more intense than the light of the sun and our Lord Jesus Christ shall come, like lightning and fulfill everything that the prophet David has spoken: "A mighty sound shall issue from the East and be heard in heaven."

The light shall distinguish between the good and bad, for they [the good] shall see light the like of which never existed before for them to see. The resurrection is the same for all, but the reward will not be the same. There shall be no greater torment for sinners than when they do not see that light. Then the moment of reckoning and of judgment shall come. Judgment is the separation of the sinners from the wicked. Languages and dialects will cease. The good and the wicked alike will go up to the judgment. The good will ascend to heaven, while the bad will remain on earth — this is the Gehenna of the wicked. Thus Lord Ephream the teacher said, "The fire inside a person comes from himself and acts like a hot fever: Gehenna is within them." Thus the good ascend to heaven and to the kingdom; the reward will not be the same for all, but everyone will be rewarded at that time in accordance with what he has done.

How does this text portray the "Sons of Hagar" (the Muslims)? What does it suggest about their possession of the holy places? What would happen when the final "king of the Greeks" came to Jerusalem, and what did this imply about the significance of that city in God's plan for history? Does it seem likely that Jerusalem's association with apocalyptic events would have encouraged or discouraged religious travelers to the city?

25. THE NIGHT JOURNEY OF MUHAMMAD

According to one tradition about the "apostle" or "messenger" of God, Muhammad himself made a celestial visitation to Jerusalem with the archangel Gabriel, further cementing the connection between pious Muslims and the holy city. The description below of this "night journey" comes from the eighth-century biography of the prophet Muhammad by Muhummad ibn Ishaq, who relied upon oral accounts passed down from the prophet's earliest followers.

Source: trans. A. Guillaume, in *The Life of Muhammad: A Translation of Ishaq's Sirat Rasul Allah* (Oxford: Oxford University Press, 1955), pp. 181–87.

Then the apostle was carried by night from the mosque at Mecca to the Masjid-al Aqsa, which is the temple of Aelia [in Jerusalem].... The matter of the place of the journey and what is said about it is a searching test and a matter of God's power and authority, wherein is a lesson for the intelligent; and guidance and mercy and strengthening to those who believe. It was certainly an act of God by which he took him [Muhammad] by night in what way he pleased to show him his signs which he willed him to see so that he witnessed his mighty sovereignty and power by which he does what he wills to do.

According to what I have heard Abdullah ibn Masud used to say: Buraq, the animal whose every stride carried it as far as its eye could reach on which the prophets before him used to ride was brought to the apostle and he was mounted on it. His companion [the archangel Gabriel] went with him to see the wonders between heaven and earth, until he came to Jerusalem's temple. There he found Abraham the friend of God, Moses, and Jesus assembled with a company of prophets, and he prayed with them. Then he was brought three vessels containing milk, wine, and water respectively. The apostle said: "I heard a voice saying when these were offered to me: If he takes the water he will be drowned and his people also; if he takes the wine he will go astray and his people also; and if he takes the milk he will be rightly guided and his people also. So I took the vessel containing milk and drank it. Gabriel said to me, you have been rightly guided and so will your people be, Muhammad."...

In his story, al-Hasan said: The apostle and Gabriel went their way until they arrived at the temple at Jerusalem. There he found Abraham, Moses, and Jesus among a company of the prophets. The apostle acted as their imam [leader] in prayer. Then he was brought two vessels, one containing wine and the other milk. The apostle took the milk and drank it, leaving the wine. Gabriel said: "You have been rightly guided to the way of nature and so will your people be. Wine is forbidden to you." Then the apostle returned to Mecca and in the morning he told [the members of the] Quraysh [tribe] what had happened. Most of them said, "By God, this is a plain absurdity! A caravan takes a month to go to Syria and a month to return and can Muhammad do the return journey in one night?" Many Muslims gave up their faith; some went to Abu Bakr and said, "What do you think of your friend now, Abu Bakr? He alleges that he went to Jerusalem last night and prayed there and came back to Mecca." He replied that they were lying about the apostle; but they said that he was in the mosque at that very moment telling the people about it. Abu Bakr said, "If he says so, then it is true. And what is so surprising in that? He tells me that communications from God from heaven to earth come to him in an hour of a day or night and I believe him, and that is more extraordinary than that at which you boggle!" He then went to the apostle and asked him if these reports were true, and when he said they were, he asked him to describe Jerusalem to him.... Whenever he [Muhammad] described a part of it, he [Abu Bakr] said: "That's true. I testify that you are the apostle of God," until he had completed the description, and then the apostle said, "And you, Abu Bakr, are the *Siddiq* [Witness to the Truth]." This was the occasion on which he got this honorific.

According to this tradition, what happened to the prophet Muhammad during his visit to Jerusalem? What does this story suggest about the significance of Jerusalem for Muslim believers? How might the story of Muhammad's "night journey" have made a Muslim pilgrim during the eighth or ninth century feel about a pilgrimage to Jerusalem? Were there any reasons why some Muslims might have disapproved of this tradition linking Muhammad to Jerusalem?

26. THE PILGRIMAGE OF ARCULF

After some initial disruption, Christian pilgrimage to Jerusalem continued after the Islamic conquest of the city. One such pilgrim from Merovingian Gaul, named Arculf, visited the holy places around the year 670. During his return journey, he was shipwrecked in Scotland. While staying at the monastery of Iona, Arculf described Jerusalem and its surroundings to an Irish monk named Adamnan. The resulting work, On the Holy Places, became highly popular due in part to its enthusiastic reception by the eighth-century English monk and historian Bede.

Source: trans. J.R. Macpherson, in *The Pilgrimage of Arculfus in the Holy Land*, Palestine Pilgrims' Text Society, vol. 3 (London, 1895), pp. 1–15; revised.

1.1. In the name of the Father, the Son, and the Holy Spirit, I am about to write a book concerning the holy places. The saintly bishop Arculf, a man of Gaul by birth, told me, Adamnan, all the things that are written below; he was well acquainted with many far distant lands, a truthful and right worthy witness, who dwelt in the city of Jerusalem for a space of nine months and examined the holy places by daily visits. I sedulously asked him to tell me his experiences, which at first I wrote down on tablets as he dictated in a faithful and unimpeachable narrative, and now briefly inscribe upon parchment.

As to the situation of Jerusalem, we shall now write a few of the details that the saintly Arculf dictated to me, Adamnan.... On the fifteenth day of the month of September every year, an almost countless multitude of various nations is in the habit of gathering from all sides at Jerusalem for the purposes of commerce by mutual sale and purchase. For this reason, there is a need for the crowds of various peoples to stay in that welcoming city for some days, while the very great number of their camels and horses and asses, not to speak of mules and oxen for their varied baggage, strews the streets of the city here and there with the abominations of their excrements. The resulting smell brings no ordinary nuisance to the citizens and even makes walking difficult. Wonderful to say, one night after the above-mentioned day of departure with the crowds' various beasts of burden, an immense abundance of rain falls from the clouds on that city, washing all the abominable messes from the streets and cleansing it from the filthiness. For the very situation of Jerusalem, beginning from the northern brow of Mount Sion, has been so disposed by its founder, God, on a lofty declivity, sloping down to the lower ground of the northern and eastern walls so that the overabundance of rain cannot settle at all in the streets, like stagnant water, but rushes down like rivers from the higher to the lower ground. Furthermore, this inundation of the waters of heaven, flowing through the eastern gates and bearing with it all the filthy abominations, enters the Valley of Josaphat and swells the torrent of Cedron. After baptizing Jerusalem, this over-abundance of rain always ceases. Therefore we must carefully note in what honor this chosen and glorious city is held in the sight of the eternal Lord, who does not permit it to remain any longer filthy, but because of the honor of his only begotten [Jesus Christ] cleanses it so quickly, since it has within the circuit of its walls the honored sites of his sacred cross and resurrection. In that renowned place where once the Temple had been magnificently constructed, however, placed in the neighborhood of the wall from the east, the Saracens now frequent a four-sided house of prayer that they have built crudely, constructing it by raising boards and great beams on some remains of ruins. This house [of worship] can, it is said, hold three thousand men at once. Arculf, when we asked him about the dwellings of that city, answered: "I remember that I both saw and visited many buildings of that city, and that I very often observed a good many great houses of stone through the whole of the large city, surrounded by walls, formed with marvelous skill." All these we must now pass over, I think, with the exception of the structure of those buildings which have been marvelously built in the holy places, those namely of the cross and the resurrection. As to these we asked Arculf very carefully, especially with regard to the sepulcher of the Lord and the church constructed over it, the form of which Arculf himself depicted for me on a tablet covered with wax.

1.2. Certainly this very great church, the whole of which is of stone, was formed of marvelous roundness in every part, rising up from the foundations in three walls, which have one roof at a lofty elevation, having a broad pathway between each wall and the next. There are also three altars in three cleverly formed places of the middle wall. This round and very large church, with the above-mentioned altars, looking one to the south, another to the north, a third towards the west, is supported by twelve stone columns of marvelous size. It has twice four gates, that is four entrances, through three firmly built walls which break upon the pathways in a straight line, of which four means of exit look to the north-east (which is also called the "cecias" wind), while the other four look to the south-east.

1.3. In the middle of the interior of this round house is a round cabin cut out in one and the same rock, in which three times three men can pray standing. From the head of a man of ordinary stature as he stands, up to the arch of that small house, a foot and a half is measured upwards. The entrance of this little cabin looks to the east, and the whole outside is covered with choice marble, while its highest point is adorned with gold and supports a golden cross of considerable size. In the northern part of this cabin is the sepulcher of the Lord, cut out in the same rock in the inside, but the pavement of the cabin is lower than the place of the sepulcher, for from its pavement up to the edge of the side of the sepulcher one reckons a measure of about three palms. So Arculf, who used often to visit the sepulcher of the Lord and measured it most accurately, told me.

Here we must refer to the difference of names between the tomb and the sepulcher, for that round cabin (which we have often mentioned) the Gospel-writers called by another name, the tomb. They speak of the stone rolled to its mouth, and rolled back from its mouth, when the Lord rose. That place in the cabin is properly called the sepulcher, which is in the northern side of the tomb, in which the body of the Lord, when buried, rested, rolled in the linen cloths. Arculf measured its length with his own hand and found it to be seven feet. Now this sepulcher is not (as some think) double, having a projection left from the solid rock, parting and separating the two legs and the two thighs, but is wholly single, affording a bed capable of holding a man lying on his back from his head even to his soles. It is in the manner of a cave, having its opening at the side, and opposite the south part of the sepulchral chamber. The low roof is artificially wrought above it. In the sepulcher there are a further 12 lamps according to the number of the twelve apostles, always burning day and night, four of which are placed down below in the lowest part of the sepulchral bed, while the other 8 are placed higher above its edge on the right hand. They shine brightly, being nourished with oil.

It seems that this also should be noted, that the mausoleum or sepulcher of the Savior (that is, the often-mentioned cabin) may rightly be called a grotto or cave, concerning which (that is to say, concerning our Lord Jesus Christ being in it) the prophet prophesied: "He shall dwell in a most lofty cave of a moist strong rock." And a little after, to gladden the apostles, there is inserted about the resurrection of the Lord: "Ye shall see the King with glory." Accordingly, the frontispiece shows the form of the above-named church with the round little cabin placed above its center, in the northern side of which is the sepulcher of the Lord, and also the forms of the other three churches about which we shall speak below....

1.4. But among these things, it seems that one ought to talk briefly about the stone, mentioned above, which was rolled to the mouth of the Lord's tomb, after the burial of the crucified Lord slain by many men. Arculf relates that it was broken and divided into two parts, the smaller of which, rough hewn with tools, is seen placed as a square altar in the round church (described above) before the mouth of that often-mentioned cabin, that is, the Lord's tomb; while the larger part of that stone, equally hewn around, stands fixed in the eastern part of that church as another four-sided altar under linen cloths. As to the colors of that rock, in which that often-mentioned chapel was hollowed out by the tools of hewers (which has, in its northern side, the sepulcher of the Lord cut out of one and the same rock in which is also the tomb, that is, the cabin), when questioned by me, Arculf said: "That cabin of the Lord's tomb is in no way ornamented on the inside, and shows even to this day over all its surface the traces of the tools, which the hewers or excavators used in their work. The color of that rock both of the tomb and of the sepulcher is not one, but two colors seem to have been intermingled, namely red and white, so that rock appears two-colored." As to these points, however, I think I have said enough....

1.6. Another very large church, looking eastwards, has been built on that place which, in Hebrew, is called Golgotha. High up inside, a great circular chandelier of brass with lamps is hung by ropes, below which has been set up a great cross of silver, fixed in the same spot where once stood fixed the wooden cross, on which suffered the Savior of the human race. In the same church a cave has been cut out in the rock below the site of the cross of the

Lord, where sacrifice is offered on an altar for the souls of certain specially
honored persons whose bodies are meanwhile placed lying in a court before
the gate of that church of Golgotha, until the holy mysteries on their behalf
are finished.

1.7. This four-sided church, built on the site of Calvary, is adjoined on
the east by the neighboring stone basilica, constructed with great reverence
by King [Emperor] Constantine that is also called the Martyrium. It is built
(as is said) on that spot where the cross of the Lord, which had been hidden
away under the earth, was found with the other two crosses of the robbers,
after a period of two hundred and thirty-three years by the permission of the
Lord himself....

1.9. Between that basilica of Golgotha and the Martyrium there is a recess
in which the cup of the Lord, which he blessed and gave with his own hand
to the apostles in the supper on the day before he suffered, as he and they sat
at supper with one another; the cup is [made of] silver, holding the measure
of a French quart, and has two little handles placed on it, one on each side. In
this cup also is the sponge which those who were crucifying the Lord filled
with vinegar and, putting it on hyssop, offered it to his mouth. From the
same cup, as is said, the Lord drank after his resurrection, as he sat at supper
with the apostles. The saintly Arculf saw it and touched it with his own hand,
and kissed it through the opening of the perforated cover of the case within
which it is concealed. Indeed, the whole people of the city resort greatly to
this cup with immense veneration....

1.11. As to the sacred napkin that was placed on the face of the Lord in
the sepulcher, we learn from the tale of the sainted Arculf, who inspected
it with his own eyes. The whole people of Jerusalem bear witness to the
truth of the story we now write. For on the testimony of several faithful
citizens of Jerusalem, the sainted Arculf learned this statement which they
very often repeated to him as he listened attentively. A certain trustworthy
believing Jew, immediately after the resurrection of the Lord, stole from his
sepulcher the sacred linen cloth and hid it in his house for many days. By
the favor of the Lord himself, however, it was found after the lapse of many
years, and was brought to the notice of the whole people about three years
before [this statement was made by Arculf]. When at the point of death,
that happy, faithful thief sent for his two sons and, showing them the Lord's
napkin, which he had at first stolen secretly, he offered it to them, saying:
"My boys, the choice is now given to you. Therefore let each of you say
which he rather wishes to chose, so that I may know without a doubt to
which of you, according to his own choice, I shall bequeath all the substance
I have, and to which only this sacred napkin of the Lord." On hearing this,
the one who wished to obtain all his sire's wealth, received it from his father,

according to a promise made to him under the will. Marvelous to say, from that day all his riches and all his patrimony, on account of which he sold the Lord's napkin, began to decrease, and all that he had was lost by various misfortunes and came to nothing. While the other blessed son of the above-named blessed thief, who chose the Lord's napkin in preference to all his patrimony, from the day when he received it from the hand of his dying sire, became, by the gift of God, more and more rich in earthly substance, and was by no means deprived of heavenly treasure. And thus this napkin of the Lord was faithfully handed down as an heirloom by the successive heirs of this triply blessed man to their believing sons in regular succession, even to the fifth generation. After many years passed, however, believing heirs of that kindred failed, after the fifth generation, and the sacred linen cloth came into the hands of unbelieving Jews, who, while unworthy of such an office, yet embraced it honorably and, by the gift of divine bounty, were greatly enriched with all kinds of riches. When an accurate story about the Lord's napkin spread among the people, however, the believing Jews began to contend bravely with the unbelieving Jews about the sacred linen cloth. The strife that arose divided the common people of Jerusalem into two parties, the faithful believers and faithless unbelievers.

At this point, both parties appealed to Mavias, the king of the Saracens, to adjudicate between them. He said to the unbelieving Jews, who were persistently retaining the Lord's napkin: "Give the sacred linen cloth which you have into my hand." In obedience to the king's command, they bring it from its casket and place it in his bosom. Receiving it with great reverence, the king ordered a great fire to be made in the square before all the people, and while it was burning fiercely, he rose, and going up to the fire, addressed both contending parties in a loud voice: "Now let Christ, the savior of the world, who suffered for the human race, upon whose head this napkin, which I now hold in my bosom, and as to which you are now contending, was placed in the sepulcher, judge between you by the flame of fire, so that you may know to which of these two contending hosts this great gift may most worthily be entrusted." Saying this, he threw the sacred napkin of the Lord into the flames, but the fire could in no way touch it, for, rising whole and untouched from the fire, it began to fly on high, like a bird with outspread wings, and looking down from a great height on the two contending parties, placed opposite one another as if they were two armies in battle array, it flew round in mid-air for some moments. Then, slowly descending, under the guidance of God, it inclined toward the party of Christians, who meanwhile prayed earnestly to Christ, the judge, and finally it settled in their bosom. Raising their hands to heaven and bending the knee with great gladness, they give thanks to God and receive the Lord's napkin with great honor, a gift to be venerated as sent to them from heaven. They render praises in their hymns to Christ, who gave it, and they cover it up in another linen cloth and put it away in a casket of the church. Our brother Arculf saw it one day taken out of the casket, and amid the multitudes of the people that kissed it, he himself kissed it in an assembly of the church; it measures about eight feet in length. As to it, I have said enough....

2.26. Damascus, according to the account of Arculf, who stayed some days in it, is a great royal city, situated in a wide plain, surrounded by an ample circuit of walls, and further fortified by frequent towers. Without the walls there are a large number of olive groves round about; while four great rivers flow through it, bringing great joy to the city. The king of the Saracens has seized the government, and reigns in that city, and a large church has been built there in honor of Saint John the Baptist. There has also been built in that same city a church [mosque] of unbelieving Saracens which they frequent.

3.1. Arculf, who has been mentioned so often, on his return from Alexandria stayed for some days in the island of Crete, and sailed from there to Constantinople, where he spent some months. Beyond a doubt, this city is the metropolis of the Roman Empire. It is surrounded by the waves of the sea except on the north; the sea breaking out from the great sea [the Mediterranean] for forty miles, while from the wall of Constantinople it still further stretches sixty miles up to the mouth of the river Danube. This imperial city is surrounded by no small circuit of walls, twelve miles in length. It is a promontory by the sea-side, having (like Alexandria or Carthage) walls built along the sea coast, additionally strengthened by frequent towers, after the fashion of Tyre. Within the city walls it has numerous houses, very many of which are of marvelous size. These are made of stone, and are built after the fashion of the dwelling-houses of Rome.

3.2. As to its foundation the citizens relate this tradition, which they have received from their ancestors. The emperor Constantine, gathering together an infinite multitude of men and collecting from all sides infinite supplies, so that all other cities were almost stripped bare, began to build a city to bear his name on the Asian side (that is, in Cilicia, across the sea that separates Asia from Europe in these districts). But one night, while the innumerable forces of workmen were sleeping in their tents over the vast length of the camp, all the different kinds of tools used by the artificers of the different works were suddenly removed, no one knew how. At dawn, many of the workmen, troubled and downcast, brought before the emperor Constantine himself a complaint as to the sudden hidden removal of the tools. The king consequently inquired of them: "Did you hear of other things being abstracted from the camp?" "Nothing," they say, "but all the work-tools." Then next the king commands them: "Go quickly to the sea coasts of the neighboring districts on both sides [of the straits] and search them carefully, and if you chance to find your tools in any place in the country, watch over them there meanwhile, and do not bring them back here, but let some of you return to me, so that I may have accurate information as to the finding of the tools."

On hearing this, the workmen follow out the king's directions, and going away did as he ordered, searching the boundaries of the territories next to the sea on both sides. And behold, on the European side, across the sea, they found the tools gathered together in a heap in one place between two seas. On making the discovery, some of them are sent back to the king, and on their arrival they announce the finding of the tools in such a place. On learning this, the king immediately orders trumpeters to pass through the camp, blowing their trumpets and ordering the force to move its camp, saying: "Let us remove from this place to build a city on the spot divinely pointed out to us." At the same time he had ships made ready, and crossed over with his whole force to the spot where the tools were found, as he knew that the place thus shown to him by their removal was that designed by God for the purpose. There he at once founded a city, which is called Constantinople, the name being compounded of his own name and the Greek word for city, so that the founder's name is retained in the former part of the compound. Let this description of the situation and the foundation of that royal city suffice.

3.3. We must not be silent, however, as to that most celebrated round church [of the Apostles] in that city, built of stone and of marvelous size. According to the account of the saintly Arculf, who visited it for some time, it rises from the bottom of its foundations in three walls, being built in triple form to a great height, and it is finished in a very round simple crowning vault of great beauty. This is supported on great arches, with a wide space between each of the above-mentioned walls, suited and convenient either for dwelling or for praying to God in. In the northern part of the interior of the house is shown a very large and very beautiful ambry, in which is kept a wooden chest, which is similarly covered over with wooden work. In this is shut up that wooden cross of salvation on which our Savior hung for the salvation of the human race. This notable chest, as the saintly Arculf relates, is raised with its treasure of such preciousness upon a golden altar, on three consecutive days after the lapse of a year. This altar also is in the same round church, being two cubits long and one broad. On three successive days only throughout the year is the Lord's cross raised and placed on the altar (that is, on the day of the Lord's supper), when the emperor and the armies enter the church and, approaching the altar, after that sacred chest has been opened, kiss the cross of salvation. First of all the emperor of the world kisses it with bent face, then one going up after another in the order of rank or age, all kiss the cross with honor. Then on the next day, that is, on the sixth day of the week before Easter, the queen, the matrons, and all the women of the people, approach it in the above-mentioned order and kiss it with all reverence. On the third day, that is, on [the day of] the Easter Sabbath, the bishop and all the clergy after him approach in order, with fear and trembling and all honor, kissing the cross of victory, which is placed in its chest. When these sacred and joyful kissings of the sacred cross are finished, that venerable chest is closed, and with its honored treasure is borne back to its ambry.

This also should be carefully noted, that there are not two but three short pieces of wood in the cross, that is, the cross-beam and the long one which is cut and divided into two equal parts. From these threefold venerated beams when the chest is opened, there arises an odor of a wonderful fragrance, as if all sorts of flowers had been collected in it, wonderfully full of sweetness, satiating and gladdening all in the open space before the inner walls of that church, who stand still as they enter at that moment. From the knots of those threefold-beams, a sweet-smelling liquid distills, like pressed-out oil, which causes all men of whatever race, who have assembled and enter the church, to perceive the above-mentioned fragrance of so great sweetness. This liquid is such that if even a little drop of it be laid on the sick, they easily recover their health, whatever be the trouble or disease they have been afflicted with. But as to these let this suffice.

Why does Adamnan describe the burial site of Jesus Christ in such detail for his read-ers? What does the story of the Lord's napkin imply about the relationship of Jews and Christians to Jerusalem, including its holy sites and relics? What role do the Muslims play in this text? What does Arculf's story about the foundation of Constantinople suggest about the origins and importance of that city for Christians? Does this pilgrim-age account provide any sense of what Arculf thought or experienced internally during his travels?

27. THE *HODOEPORICON* OF SAINT WILLIBALD

For some Christians, their pilgrimage to Jerusalem formed only one chapter in their life-long accomplishments. The Hodoeporicon *(or "Guidebook") of Saint Willibald, written by an anonymous nun from the Abbey of Heidenheim, traced the eighth-century life of that holy man from his childhood in England through his decade-long pilgrimage and eventual arrival in the missionary territory of Germany, where he became bishop of Eichstadt. For the author of this posthumous account, who spoke personally with Willibald before he died in 785, the saint's travels to Rome, Jerusalem, Constantinople, and other sacred sites provided a showcase for his immense sanctity and importance. Beyond the typical descriptions of Willibald's piety, one can also glimpse some of the historical dangers posed by the arduous road to Palestine in the early Middle Ages, including Willibald's imprisonment by the "Saracens" as a spy.*

Source: trans. W.R. Brownlow, in *The Hodoeporicon of Saint Willibald*, Palestine Pilgrims' Text Society, vol. 3 (London, 1895), pp. 5–9, 12–15, 19–21, 22–23, 27–32; revised.

6. And then ... he began to ponder upon how he could realize this idea: that he should strive to despise and renounce all the perishing things of earthly property, along with his country, his parents and kindred, and attempt to seek another land by a pilgrimage, and to explore the unknown regions of foreign places....

7. Afterwards that youth ... opened the secrets of his heart to his father according to the flesh, and begged him, with earnest prayers, to give his advice and consent to the desire of his will. He asked him not only for permission to go, but also that he might accompany him ... he so allured him [his father] by the sweet promises of the renowned threshold of Peter, prince of apostles. Now his father, at first, when he asked him, declined the journey, excusing himself on account of his wife, and the youth and frailty of his growing children, and answered that it would be dishonorable and cruel to deprive them of his protection, leaving them to strangers. Then that warlike soldier of Christ repeated his solemn exhortations and the persistence of his prayers ... so that at last, by the aid of almighty God, the will of the petitioner and exhorter prevailed. His father and his brother Wunebald promised that they would start on the course that he had desired and encouraged them to run.

8. After this, therefore ... his father and unmarried brother [Wunebald] commenced their predestined and chosen journey [with Willibald]. At a suitable time in the summer they were ready and prepared. Taking with them the means of livelihood, with a band of friends accompanying them, they came to the appointed place, which was known by the ancient name of Hamel-Muth, near to that port which is called Hamwih [modern Southport] ... then, having crossed the sea ... they safely came in sight of dry land. At once they gave thanks and disembarked, and pitched their tents there on the banks of the river which is named the Seine, near the city which is called Rouen, where there was a market. After resting there some days, they began to proceed and made their petitions in prayer at many shrines of the saints that were conveniently situated for them. By degrees proceeding from place to place, they came over into the Gorthonic land. Going on, they came to the city which is called Lucca. Before that point, Willibald and Wunebald had conducted their father with them in their company on the journey. But he was all at once attacked with a sudden failure of bodily strength, such that,

after a short time, the day of his end was at hand. As the disease increased upon him, his worn out and cold bodily limbs wasted away and thus he breathed out his life's last breath. Those two brothers, his sons, then took the lifeless body of their father and with the affection of filial devotion wrapped it in beautiful clothes, burying it at [the church of] St-Frigidian, in the city of Lucca. There rests their father's body.

Without delay they went on steadily through the vast lands of Italy, through the depths of the valleys, the steep heights of the mountains, the level plains, and at the difficult passes of the Alps they climbed on foot and directed their steps on high ... and by the aid of a kind God, and the support of their saints with the whole company of their fellow-countrymen and the whole band of their comrades, they all escaped the violence and cunning of armed men, arriving at the illustrious and renowned threshold of Peter, the prince of apostles. There they sought his protection and rendered unbounded thanks to almighty God ... that they had been counted worthy to approach the famous church of St-Peter.

10. Afterwards, that illustrious lover of the cross of Christ ... sighed after a longer and more unknown pilgrimage than that on which he now seemed to stand still. Then that vigorous one, after taking counsel and obtaining permission from his friends and countrymen, begged that they would follow him with the aid of their supplications, so that through all the course of the journey, by the protection of their prayers, he might be enabled to reach and gaze upon the walls of the delightful and longed-for city of Jerusalem. When the Easter solemnities of our Lord were over, the lively warrior arose with his two companions and began to set out....

12. Sailing from Cyprus, they came into the territory of the Saracens to the city of Tharratae near the sea. From there, they went on foot about 9 or 12 miles to the village which is called Arche. Here there was a bishop of the Greek people, and they performed the litany according their own rite. Going on from there, they walked to a city which is called Emesa, 12 miles distance. There is a large church, which Saint Helena built in honor of Saint John the Baptist. His head, which is now in Syria, was there for a long time. At this point, there was with Willibald seven of his fellow-countrymen, and he made the eighth. All at once those Saracens, hearing that strangers and unknown men had arrived there, took them and held them in captivity, for they knew not of what people they were, but thought them to be spies. They led them as prisoners to a certain wealthy old man that he might see and know from where they came. That old man questioned them as to from where they came and on what errand they were employed. Then they replied and related to him from the beginning the whole reason for their journey. That old man answered and said: "I have often seen men coming from those

parts of the earth, countrymen of these; they have no evil designs, but wish to fulfill their law." Then they went from him, and came to the palace in order to ask their way to pass on to Jerusalem. When they arrived, however, that governor said at once that they were spies, and commanded them to be cast into prison until they could learn from the king how their case stood — what he would have done in their case. While they were in prison they had immediate experience of the wonderful dispensation of God almighty, who kindly deigns to protect his own everywhere, in the midst of spears and instruments of war, among barbarians and warriors, in prisons and bands of rebels, to shield them and keep them safe. For a man was there, a merchant, who wished to redeem them, and deliver them out of prison by way of alms and for the redemption of his own soul, so that they might go free according to their own will. When he could not achieve this, he sent them instead dinner and supper every day. On Wednesday and Saturday he sent his own son to the prison, and he conducted them to the bath, and brought them back again. On Sunday he took them to church through the market, that they might see the things that were for sale: whatever they were pleased with, at his own expense he purchased for them, anything that they desired. The citizens of the neighboring towns, filled with curiosity, used to come in crowds to that place to gaze upon them, for they were young and handsome, and well equipped with fine cloths.

After this, while they were still in prison, a man came from Spain and conversed with them in the prison, diligently inquiring of them who they were, and from where they came. They told him everything about their journey in order. This Spanish man had a brother in the king's palace, who was the chamberlain of the king of the Saracens. When that governor who had put them in prison came to the palace, the Spaniard, who had talked with them in prison, and the ship's captain, whose vessel had brought them from Cyprus, together presented themselves before the king of the Saracens, whose name was Mirmumni. When some words had passed about their case, that Spanish man informed his brother of all that they had told him in the prison and begged him to make it known to the king, pleading their cause. When all these three came before the king, relating everything in order and making known to him their case, the king asked them from where they came. They said: "From the western shores, where the sun sets, the men have come, and we know not any land beyond them, and there is nothing but water." The king answered and said to them: "Why should we punish them? They have committed no offense against us. Give them liberty, and let them depart." Other men who were detained in prison had to pay a three months' assessment, but this was remitted in their case....

18. From there [the monastery of St-Eustochius] they came to Jerusalem, to that place where the holy cross of our Lord was found. There is now a church in that spot which was called the place of Calvary. This was formerly outside Jerusalem, but Helena, when she found the cross, arranged that place so as to be within the city of Jerusalem. There now stand three crosses of wood outside on the eastern wing of the church, by the wall, in memory of the holy cross of our Lord, and of the others who were crucified with him. These are not now within the church, but stand without, outside the church under the eaves of the roof. Along there is that garden, in which was the sepulcher of our Savior. That sepulcher was cut out in the rock, and that rock stands above ground, and is square at the bottom and tapers up towards the top. There stands now on the summit of that sepulcher a cross. There had now been constructed over it a wonderful house, and on the eastern side of that rock of the sepulcher a door has been made, through which men enter into the sepulcher to pray. There is a bed inside, on which the body of our Lord was laid. And there stands in the bed fifteen golden bowls, with oil burning day and night. That bed in which the body of our Lord was laid is situated on the north side within the rock of the sepulcher, and is on the right side of a man when he goes into the sepulcher to pray. And there in front of the door of the sepulcher lies the great stone, squared after the likeness of the former stone which the angels rolled back from the door of the sepulcher.

19. Our bishop [Willibald] arrived there on the feast of Saint Martin. And as soon as he got there, he began to sicken and lay ill until a week before the nativity of the Lord. Then, when he was somewhat recovered, and had got the better of his illness, he got up and went to that church which is called holy Sion. It stands in the middle of Jerusalem. There he prayed, and from that place went into Solomon's porch. There is the pool, and there lay the infirm people, waiting for the moving of the water, when the angel came, and then he who first went down into it was healed; and there our Lord said to the paralytic, "Arise, take up thy bed and walk."

20. Likewise, he also said, that before the gate of the city there stood a high column, and on top of the column stands a cross, for a sign and a memorial of the place where the Jews wished to carry away the body of the holy Mary. When the eleven apostles took up the body of holy Mary, they carried it to Jerusalem, and as soon as they came to the gate of the city, the Jews wished to seize it. Immediately those men put forth their arms toward the bier and tried to take it, but their arms were held, and they stuck to the bier, and were unable to move until by the grace of God and the prayers of the apostles they were loosed again. Then they left them. Holy Mary departed out of the world in that place in the midst of Jerusalem, which is

called holy Sion. Now the eleven apostles carried her (as I said before) and then angels came and took her from the hands of the apostles, and carried her into paradise.

22. From Jerusalem they went to the place where the angel appeared to the shepherds, saying "I announce to you great joy." From there they came to Bethlehem, where our Lord was born, seven miles from Jerusalem. The place where Christ was born was once a cave underground, and is now a square chamber out of the rock, and the surrounding earth has been dug out and thrown away. And there above it a church has now been erected. Over where our Lord was born now stands an altar; and another smaller altar has been made, so that when they wish to celebrate mass inside the cave, they take that smaller altar and carry it inside during the time that mass is being celebrated, and then carry it out again. That church where our Lord was born is a glorious house, built in the form of a cross....

27. ... Before this, Bishop Willibald, when he was in Jerusalem, bought himself some balsam and filled a calabash [a gourd] with it. He took a cane, which was hollow, and had a bottom. He filled that with oil, and put it inside the calabash, and cut that cane even with the calabash so that the edges of both seemed alike even, and so he closed the mouth of the calabash. When they came to the city of Tyre, those inhabitants of the city took them, bound them, and examined all their baggage, in order to find out if they had anything they would at once have punished and made martyrs of them. When they examined everything, however, they found nothing except the calabash that Willibald had, and they opened and smelled what was inside. When they smelled the oil, because it was in the cane above, they did not find the balsam, which was inside the calabash under the oil, and so they let them go....

29. They were for many days waiting for the ship while it was being made ready. Afterwards they were sailing the whole winter, from the feast of Saint Andrew the apostle until one week before Easter. Then they arrived at the city of Constantinople, where rest three saints (Andrew, and Timothy, and Luke the Evangelist) at one altar. And John, he of the Golden Mouth, rests there before the altar, where he stood as a priest and offered Mass; there is his tomb. Our bishop was there for two years, and had a cell inside the church, so that every day he could gaze upon the place where the saints rested. From there he went to the city of Nicaea, where formerly the emperor Constantine held the council [of Nicaea in 325]. There were at the council three hundred and eighteen bishops, all of whom held the synod. The church there is similar to that church on Mount Olivet, where our Lord ascended into heaven. In that church are the pictures of the bishops who were at the council. Willibald went there from Constantinople, so that he might see how the church had been constructed, and he returned by water to Constantinople.

30–31. After two years, they sailed from Constantinople with the envoys of the pope and the emperor to the island of Sicily, to the city of Syracuse.... It was seven years since Willibald began to travel from Rome, and it was ten years in all since he came over from his own country. When the venerable man Willibald and Tidbert, who had traveled with him through all these places, came to St-Benedict [the monastery of Monte Cassino], they found there only a few monks and an abbot named Petronax. At once, with great self-control and natural aptitude for the rules, he joined the happy community of the brethren. Admonished in turn by their diligent instructions, he taught them in turn by his interactions with him, not only by words, but by the beauty of his behavior, and set before them rightly the spirit of their monastic life, in such a manner as to call out and draw to himself the love and respect of all.... Thus passed an interval of ten years, and that venerable man Willibald endeavored in every particular that he could to observe Saint Benedict's sacred rule of life. He led not only himself, but others with him by preceding them in venerated paths of religious life....

33. After these events a priest came from Spain to St-Benedict's, who stayed there, and then asked permission of the Abbot Petronax to go on to Rome. As soon as he had obtained leave, he begged Willibald to go with him and conduct him to St-Peter's ... when they came to Rome, they entered into the basilica of St-Peter, and craved the patronage of the heavenly keeper of the keys, and commended themselves to the pious protection of his prayers. When the holy pontiff of the apostolic see, Gregory III, learned that the venerable man Willibald was there, he commanded him to come to him. When he came ... he at once prostrated himself with his face to the earth and saluted him. Immediately, that kind overseer of the people began to inquire into the order of his journey.... At once the vigorous servant of Christ made known to the glorious ruler of the peoples the course of his journey.

Why might Willibald have desired the company of his father and brother on his pilgrimage? Why did his father hesitate to go, and how did Willibald convince him otherwise? How would you describe Willibald and his companions' captivity by the "Saracens" in Syria, and how did they manage to gain their freedom? What does their treatment as prisoners suggest about the status of Christian pilgrims in Muslim territories? Why was Willibald forced to smuggle some balsam with him during his return trip? How long did he stay in Constantinople and Monte Cassino? What does the pace of his travels imply about his motivations for undertaking such a journey?

28. CHARLEMAGNE'S LEGENDARY JOURNEY TO THE EAST

According to popular legend, the Frankish ruler Charlemagne undertook his own pious journey to Jerusalem and Constantinople in the ninth century, meeting with both Muslim and Eastern Christian rulers. Following this apocryphal tradition, Charlemagne returned from his travels bearing numerous sacred relics from the East. The account below of his pilgrimage was written in the late tenth century by Benedict of St-Andrew at Monte Sorratte, an Italian monastery that claimed to possess relics of the apostle Andrew given to it by the returning Carolingian emperor.

Source: trans. M. Gabrielle, from *Benedicti Sancti Andreae monachi chronicon*, ed. G.H. Pertz, Monumenta Germaniae Historica: Scriptores, vol. 3 (Hannover, 1839), pp. 708–11.

The most brave king directed that the fleet of Norman ships be built, and he commanded that from every port and river, ships throughout the northern rivers of Gaul and Germany be armed and sent from their posts. And he commanded the fleet to sail through the Adriatic and assemble in the province of Benevento. Then he ordered them to gather there from all of Italy, from Benevento to the ends of Aquileia, the communities of Ravenna, Rimini, Ancona, and the entire coast of the Adriatic right up to Brindisi. And the whole fleet from the straits of Messina – Liguria, Corsica, Sardinia, Pisa, Civitavecchia, Rome, and everywhere up to Apulia – gathered at Brindisi as many ships as he could find up to that moment. The truly most serene king, having received the blessing of Pope Leo [III], climbed to [the monastery of] the holy archangel [at Monte Gargano], adoring and beseeching God that he guide his journey in peace.

The trip began. He arrived at Monte Gargano and offered many gifts there. Passing through the boundaries of Naples, Charles arrived from lower Calabria at Brindisi. The fleet stretched for one thousand miles and more. He ordered bridges to be built over the waters, and commanded the multitude – all the Franks, Saxons, Bavarians, Aquitainians, Gascons, Hungarians, Avars, Alamans, and Lombards, whose number could not be grasped – to go out before him. All the peoples of the Greek lands were troubled that their power counted for nothing. [Those on the pilgrimage] praised and prayed to God, who showed the right path to Charles, the servant of Peter, prince of the apostles. When he heard this, the king of the Persians, Harun [al-Rashid], who held all the East except India, made such friendship and concord, that he with friendship freely appointed the prince to rule over the whole world, judging that only Charles was worthy of this honor. Then Charles came to the most sacred sepulcher and place of resurrection of our Lord and savior

Jesus Christ, and he gave that sacred place bejeweled golden apparel and a golden banner of amazing size. He not only adorned the holy place, but King Harun also begged that the manger and sepulcher of our Lord be conceded into Charles' power. How many garments, and spices, and other great works of the East did [Harun] give to Charles! Turning then, the most prudent king went with King Harun to Alexandria. Thus the Franks and sons of Hagar [the Muslims] rejoiced as if they were brothers. King Harun was sent away in peace by Charles the Great and turned towards his home.

The most pious and brave king came to the city of Constantinople. Nikephorus, Michael, and Leo [the Byzantine rulers], fearing that Charles would take away their imperial authority, were very suspicious. The king, aware of their fear, made a pact and most firm treaty with them, so that there remained nothing between them to cause scandal. For the power of the Franks was always suspected by the Romans and Greeks. Whence there is a proverb among the Greeks: "ΤΟΝ ΦΡΑΝΚΟΝ ΦΙΑΟΝ ΕΧΙΓ, ΙΤΟΝΑ ΟΥΚ ΕΧΙΓ," which, in Latin, means: "Franks are unfit friends." Soon afterwards the emperor [Charles] returned to Italy with many gifts and riches and a small piece of the body of the holy apostle Andrew that he received from the emperors at Constantinople. He came to Rome and established an immense gift for blessed Peter. Setting the city in order, Charles gave everything, including all Pentapolis and Ravenna up to the borders of Tuscany, into the apostle's power. He gave thanks to God and the prince of the apostles and accepted the apostolic blessing, and was pronounced "Augustus" by all the Roman people. Together with the same Pope, they arrived at the monastery of St-Sylvester on Monte Sorratte. Then he, with the pope, approached the monastery of St-Andrew on the summit, where the emperor asked the pope that he deposit by consecration the small relics of the body of the holy apostle Andrew in this monastery. Where the relic is located in this monastery's venerable church is unknown to us. Then victorious, crowned, and triumphant, the king returned to Francia.

How does this legend of Charlemagne's journey to the East portray the Frankish ruler? Did Benedict of St-Andrew seem more interested in Charlemagne's religious reasons for traveling to Jerusalem and Constantinople or in his political motivations? How does his account portray Charles's relations with Islamic and Byzantine rulers during his journey? Compare the closing part of this source with the account of Charlemagne's visit to Rome in the Book of Popes *(doc. 19): are any similarities evident?*

29. THE MONK BERNARD'S JOURNEY TO JERUSALEM

Although the journey of Charlemagne to the East was legendary (doc. 28), during the Carolingian era actual Christian travelers from Europe continued to visit the holy places of Jerusalem for devotional purposes. One such Frankish pilgrim, a monk named Bernard, traveled to Cairo and Jerusalem in 867. He started his journey overseas in southern Italy, departing from the city of Bari, which was then under Islamic rule. This account of his journey might have been intended as a source of instruction for other monks wishing to make a similar visitation to the Promised Land.

Source: trans. P.E. Dutton, in *Carolingian Civilization: A Reader*, 2nd ed., ed. P.E. Dutton (Peterborough, ON: Broadview Press, 2004), pp. 472–79.

Here starts the account of the journey of three monks, namely of Bernard and his companions, and of the holy places [they visited] and of Babylon [Old Cairo]. [It contains] a description of the places that the wise Bernard saw when he went to Jerusalem and returned, and of Jerusalem itself and the places around it. We learned of these things in the nine hundred and seventieth year of the incarnation of our Lord Jesus Christ.

1. Wishing in the name of the Lord to see the places of the holy ones which are in Jerusalem, I, Bernard, joined together in affectionate esteem with two monks. One's name was Theudemund [and he came] from the monastery of the St-Vincent of Benevento [San Vincenzo al Volturno]; the other, a Spaniard, was named Stephen. Thus we approached Nicholas [I], the pope, in Rome [and] obtained with his blessing and also his help the desired permission to proceed [with our journey].

2. From there we traveled to Monte Gargano [near modern day Fóggia] in which is [found] the church of St-Michael under solid stone [a cave] upon which there are acorn-bearing oak trees. The archangel himself is said to have dedicated that [shrine], whose entrance is from the north and can admit sixty people in it [at a time]. Inside on the east [wall] there is an image of that angel; to the south there is an altar upon which the Mass is offered and no other offering except that is placed there. However, in front of the altar a certain vessel is suspended in which offerings are dropped. [That vessel] also has other altars near it. The abbot of that place is called Benignatus, who rules over many monks.

3. Leaving Monte Gargano, after [traveling] 150 miles we came to the city of the Saracens called Bari, which for a long time was subject to the Beneventans. This city situated on the sea is protected by two very broad walls on the south,

but juts out exposed to the sea on the north. And so here we sought out the ruler [the emir] of that city, [who] was named Sawdan, [and] we arranged the entire business of sailing by obtaining two letters. The text of these [two] letters for the ruler of Alexandria and also [the ruler] of Babylon [Old Cairo] set out a description of our appearance [for purposes of identification] and journey. For those rulers are under the rule of the caliph who lives in Baghdad and Axinarri [Samarra], which lie beyond Jerusalem, and he rules all the Saracens.

4. Departing from Bari, we walked south for 90 miles until [we came] to the port of the city Táranto where we found six ships, in which there were 9000 Christian Beneventans held captive. In two ships which left first for Africa there were 3000 captives; the next two departing ships similarly carried away 3000 to Tripoli.

5. Entering the two remaining ships, on which there was also the same number of captives, we were taken to the port of Alexandria [after] sailing for 30 days. We wished to proceed onto the shore, [but] were stopped by the captain who was [in command] of more than 60 sailors. We paid him six gold coins to give us the opportunity to leave.

6. Once we left [the boat], we traveled to the ruler of Alexandria, to whom we showed the letter which Sawdan gave us, [but] it did us no good, although he stated that he was familiar with everything in that letter. At his request each one of us on his own behalf paid him 13 denarii and he drew up a letter for us [to give] to the ruler of Babylon. Such is the custom of that people that only [that currency] which can be weighed is taken [as payment] at its weight and not in some other way. [Thus] six solidi and six denarii for us make three solidi and three denarii for them. This Alexandria lies on the sea; in it Saint Mark proclaim[ed] the Gospel and carried out his episcopal office. Outside the eastern gate of this city is the monastery of St-Mark, in which there are monks beside the church in which he [his body] formerly rested. But Venetians coming by boat secretly removed his body from its guardians and transported him to their island. Outside the western gate is a monastery which is dedicated to the Forty Saints where monks also reside. On the north is the port of that city; on the south there enters the Gheon or Nile, which waters Egypt and runs through the middle of the city, entering the [Mediterranean] sea at that port.

7. Embarking upon a ship we sailed south for six days and came to the city of Babylon of Egypt where Pharaoh, the king, once reigned, under whom Joseph built seven granaries which still stand. While we were going forth into Babylon, the guards of the city led us to the ruler, who is called Adelacham [Ibn Kakan], a Saracen, and he inquired of us the full nature of our journey and from which rulers we had letters. For that reason we showed him the letters from Sawdan and from the ruler of Alexandria. But that did

not help us [and] we were sent to prison by him until, after six days had passed [and] with the help of God, a plan took shape. Each of us on his own behalf paid 13 denarii, just as [I described] above. He also gave us a letter [so that] whoever saw it thereafter in whatever city or place would not dare to compel anything from us. For he [Ibn Kakan] was the second [most powerful person] in the empire of the caliph. But after we entered the cities named below we were not allowed to leave before receiving a charter or the impression of a seal, which we obtained for either one or two denarii. In this city the lord patriarch is Michael and by the grace of God he sets the order for all the bishops, monks, and Christians over all Egypt. Those Christians, however, live under such a law among the pagans [Muslims] that on their own behalf each one pays a tribute each year to that ruler [Ibn Kakan] so that he might live securely and freely. He exacts a tribute of either three, two, or one gold aureus or from a lower class person one of 12 denarii. Nevertheless, if it is the case that either a resident or foreign Christian can not pay those 13 denarii, he is cast into prison until either by the mercy of God he is freed by his angel or he is redeemed by other good Christians.

8. With those maintaining themselves in this way, we returned back by way of the river Gheon for three days and we came to the city of Sitinuth. From Sitinuth we proceeded to Maalla; from Maalla we passed over to Damietta, which has the sea on the north, but the Nile river on all [other] sides with the exception of a little land. From there we sailed to the city of Tanis in which there are very pious Christians committed to providing great hospitality. This city, however, has no land without churches and the plain of Zoan is found there. In it in the likeness of three walls lie the bodies of those who were slaughtered in the time of Moses.

9. From Tanis we came to the city of Ferama [Tel el Farma] where there is a church in honor of the blessed Mary at the place to which, after the angel's warning, Joseph fled with the boy and mother. In this city there is a multitude of camels which foreigners rent for a price from the inhabitants of that area to carry loads for them through the desert, which is a journey of six days. The entrance to the desert begins at this city and it is fittingly called a desert since it supports neither grass nor produce from any seed with the exception of palm trees. Rather all is as white as Champagne is when it snows. In the middle of the journey there are two hospices, one called Albara [el Warráda], the other called Albachara [el Bakkara]. In them the business of procuring the things necessary to those making [such] a journey is conducted by Christians and pagans [Muslims]. Between [those two hospices] the earth produces nothing, except what was stated [palm trees]. After Albachara the land is soon found to be fertile until the city of Gaza, which was the city of Samson; it is extremely rich in all things.

10. From there we came to Alariza [el Arisch]. From Alariza we entered Ramla near which is the monastery of the martyr, Saint George, where [the saint's body] rests. From Ramla we hurried on to the fortress of Emmaus. From Emmaus we passed on to the holy city of Jerusalem and were received in the hospice of the most glorious emperor Charles where all who come to that place for the sake of devotion [and who] speak the Roman tongue are welcome. Beside this [hospice] lies a church in honor of Saint Mary which possesses, from the devotion of the emperor [Charlemagne], an extremely fine library along with twelve buildings, fields, vines, and a garden in the valley of Jehoshaphat. [Situated] before that hospice is a market for [the use of] which each one conducting business there pays two gold coins per year to the one who oversees that [market].

11. Within that city [of Jerusalem], with other churches left aside [here], four churches stand out [and] share common walls with each other. One, which lies to the east, contains Mount Calvary and the place where the cross of the Lord was found and it is called the basilica of Constantine. Another [lies] to the south; a third to the west, in the middle of which is the sepulcher of the Lord which has nine columns around it, between which stand walls made of the finest stones. Four of the nine columns are before the face of that monument; with their walls they enclose the [tomb]stone placed before the sepulcher, which the angel rolled back and upon which he sat after the resurrection of the Lord was brought about. It is not necessary to say more about this sepulcher, since Bede in his history says enough about it. This, however, should be said: that on the holy sabbath that is the vigil of Easter the morning service begins in this church and after that service is completed the Kyrie eleison is sung until, when the angel comes, the light in the lamps that hang above the sepulcher is set aflame. From it the patriarch supplies [flame] to the bishops and the rest of the people in order that each might light [a candle] for himself at his own place [in the church]. This patriarch is called Theodosius, who on account of the merit of his devotion was seized by Christians from his own monastery, which lies 15 miles from Jerusalem. And he was established as the patriarch over all Christians who are in the Promised Land. Between these four churches is a park [paradise] without a roof whose walls shine with gold; the floor is arranged with the most precious stone, having in its middle a border of four chains which come from the four churches. The middle of the world is said to be in that spot.

12. Moreover, there is in that city another church to the south on Mount Sion which is called [the church] of St-Simeon where the Lord washed the feet of his disciples. In that church hangs the Lord's crown of thorns and [also] in it one of the dead is reported to be Saint Mary. Near it toward the east is a church in honor of Saint Stephen in that place where he was brought

to be stoned. In a straight [line] to the east is the church in honor of Saint Peter in the place where he denied the Lord. To the north is the Temple of Solomon [now] containing the synagogue of the Saracens [a mosque]. To the south are the iron gates through which the angel of the Lord led Peter forth from prison which afterwards were not open.

13. Departing from Jerusalem, we descended into the valley of Jehoshaphat, which is a mile from the city, and contains the villa of Gethsemani with the place of the birth of Saint Mary. In that place there is a very large church in her honor. Also in the villa itself is the round church of St-Mary where her sepulcher is [located]; it does not have a roof above it, [but] suffers little rain. There is also a church on the spot where the Lord was betrayed; it has the four round tables of that feast [the final supper]. In the valley of Jehoshaphat there is also a church in honor of Saint Leontius where, it is said, the Lord will come to judge.

14. From there we proceeded to the Mount of Olives on whose slope is displayed the place of the Lord's prayer to [God] the father. Also on the side of the same mountain is displayed the place where the Pharisees brought forth to the Lord the woman caught in adultery; it has a church in honor of Saint John in which is preserved in marble the writing which the Lord wrote on the ground.

15. At the peak, however, of that Mount [of Olives], a mile from the valley of Jehoshaphat, is the place of the Lord's ascension to [God] the father. It possesses a roofless round church in the middle of which, that is on the spot of the Lord's ascension, is contained an altar in the open air at which the solemnities of the Mass are celebrated.

16. From there we passed over to Bethany, which is to the south, at a distance of a mile from the Mount of Olives. On the way down from that mountain there is a monastery whose church displays the sepulcher of Lazarus. Near it there is a pond on the north, where by Lord's order the revived Lazarus washed himself. It is said that afterwards he had continued as the bishop of Ephesus for forty years. Also on the way down from the Mount of Olives to the western sea a marble slab is displayed from which the Lord mounted the foal of an ass. Among these [sights] to the south in the valley of Jehoshaphat is the pool of Siloam.

17. Besides [those sights], when we went out of Jerusalem, we crossed over to Bethlehem where the Lord was born, which was six miles [away]. A field was shown to us in which Habakuk was working when the angel of the Lord ordered him to carry lunch to Daniel in Babylon, which is to the south, where Nebuchadnezzar ruled [and] which serpents and beasts now inhabit. Bethlehem has a great church in honor of Saint Mary in the middle of which is a crypt under solid stone [a cave]. The entrance to it lies to the south, but

its exit [lies] to the east. In it on the west [side] of that crypt is displayed the manger of the Lord. However, the place where the Lord [first] cried out is to the east and has an altar at which Mass is celebrated. Near this church to the south is the church of the Blessed Innocents, the martyrs. Next, one mile from Bethlehem, is the monastery of the Holy Shepherds to whom the angel appeared at the Lord's nativity.

18. At last, thirty miles from Jerusalem is the [river] Jordan to the east, beside which is the monastery of St-John the Baptist. In those places there also stand many [other] monasteries.

19. There is, among these [sights] to the western part of the city of Jerusalem at [a distance of] one mile, the church of St-Mamilla. In it are [to be found] the many bodies of the martyrs who were killed by the Saracens. They were carefully buried there by that [saint].

20. Thus, returning from the holy city of Jerusalem we came to the sea. Entering onto the sea [on a ship], we sailed for 60 days with the greatest difficulty, [as we] lacked a good wind. At last, leaving the sea we came to the Golden Mountain [Monte Olevano near Salerno] where there is a crypt [a cave] possessing seven altars [and] also having above it a sizeable forest. No one can enter into that crypt because of its darkness without torches. Valentinus was the lord abbot in that same place [when we passed there].

21. Traveling from the Golden Mountain [Monte Olevano] we came to Rome. Within that city on the eastern part, in the place which is called the Lateran, there is a church well built in honor of Saint John the Baptist, which is the permanent abode of the apostolic [bishops]. Besides, in that same place each night the keys of the universal city are brought to the apostolic [bishop]. But on the western part [of the city of Rome] is the church of St-Peter, prince of the apostles, in which he himself rests in his body. In size there is no comparable church in the whole world to [St-Peter's]. It also contains an array of decorations. In that city also rest the countless bodies of saints.

22. In this city we separated from each other. But I afterwards traveled to Mont St-Michel, which is a place situated on a mountain that extends in the sea for two leagues. On the summit of that mountain is a church in honor of Saint Michael and the sea flows around that mountain twice daily, that is in the morning and at night, and no person can approach the mountain until the sea recedes. However, on the feast of Saint Michael [16 October] the sea is connected in flowing around the mountain, but stands in the likeness of walls on the right and left. And on that solemn day all, [that is] whoever comes for [the purpose of] prayer, can approach the mountain at any hour, which however cannot be done on other days. The abbot there is the Breton Phinimontius.

23. At last I [will] tell you how Christians keep God's law in Jerusalem or in Egypt. The Christians, however, and pagans [Muslims] have such a

peace placed between them there that if I, who exhibits great poverty, was making a journey [there] and on that journey my camel or donkey was to die and I left there all my possessions without a guard and I went to another city nearby, when I returned I would find all my possessions safe and sound. Such is the peace there! But if they find a person in transit either during the day or at night in a city or on the sea or on some journey without some document [a license to travel] or the seal of some king or that land's ruler, he is immediately ordered to be shut up in a prison until the day arrives when he can furnish a reason as to whether [or not] he is a spy or some such thing.

25. Finally [let me say that] in the valley of Gethsemani we saw squared marble stones of such refinement that on them one could catch sight of all the things a person might possibly wish to see as if on a mirror.

How did Bernard secure passage from Bari to Egypt? What seems to have been his general attitude toward the "pagans" (Muslims)? Compare the story of his imprisonment with that of Saint Willibald (doc. 27): what seems more important, the similarities or differences? How did Bernard manage to gain his freedom and continue his travels? How would you describe his interest in the local Christians that he meets during his pilgrimage to Jerusalem? As presented in this account, how important were proper funds and travel documents for Christian pilgrims in Islamic territories?

30. MUKADDASI'S *DESCRIPTION OF SYRIA*

The Muslim conquest of Jerusalem dramatically changed the urban landscape of the sacred city, leading to the construction of spectacular mosques (Islamic houses of worship). One of the most important, the Dome of the Rock, was constructed on the grounds of the Temple Mount, visibly demonstrating Islam's claim to the holy places. Shams ad Dín Abu'Abd Allah Muhammad, better known as Mukaddasi (the "Jerusalemite"), was born in Jerusalem in 946. Highly educated, successful at commerce, and a pilgrim himself to Mecca, Mukaddasi developed a particular interest in geography. In 985, he completed a book devoted to the topic that included a description of Jerusalem along with some observations about the city's special importance for Muslim believers.

Source: trans. Guy le Strange, in *Description of Syria, including Palestine, by Mukaddasi*, Palestine Pilgrims' Text Society, vol. 3 (London, 1895), pp. 34–37, 41–46; modernized.

Jerusalem: Bait al-Mukkadas [the Holy City], also known as Îliyâ and Al Balât. Among provincial towns none is larger than Jerusalem, and many capitals are in fact smaller, as, for instance, Istkhr and Qa-in and al-Firma. Neither the cold nor the heat is excessive here, and snow falls but rarely.

The qadi [an Islamic judge and religious leader] Abu-'l Qasim, son of the qadi of the two holy cities, inquired of me once concerning the climate of Jerusalem. I answered: "It is just right – neither very hot nor very cold." He said in reply: "Just as is that of paradise." The buildings of the Holy City are of stones, and you will find nowhere finer or more solid constructions. In no place will you meet with a more chaste people. Provisions are most excellent here, the markets are clean, the mosque is one of the largest, and nowhere are the holy places more numerous. The grapes are enormous, and there are no quinces to equal those of the Holy City. In Jerusalem are all manner of learned men and doctors, and for this reason the hearts of men of intelligence yearn towards her. All year round, never are her streets empty of strangers.

Now one day at Busrah [Basra] I was seated in the assembly of the chief qadi Abu Yahya ibn Bahram, and the conversation turned on the city of Cairo. Then one said, speaking to me, "And can any city be more illustrious?" I replied, "Why yes, my own native town." Said he, "But is any more pleasant than Cairo?" I answered, "Yes again, my native town." It was said, "Ah, but Cairo is the more excellent; and the more beautiful; and the more productive of good things, and the more spacious." Still, to each and all I replied, "Not so! It is my native town." Then the company was astonished, and they said to me, "Thou art a man of erudition, but you are claiming now more than can be accorded to you, in our belief."...

So I answered them and spoke: "Now, as to my saying that Jerusalem is the most illustrious of cities, why is she not the one that unites the advantages of this world to those of the next? He who is of the sons of this world and yet is ardent in the matters of the next, may with advantage seek her markets; while he who would be of the next world, though his soul clings to the good things of this, he too, may find these here! As to Jerusalem being the pleasantest of places in the way of climate, why the cold there does not injure and the heat is not noxious. And as to her being the finest city, why, has any seen elsewhere buildings finer, or cleaner, or a mosque that is more beautiful? And as for the Holy City being the most productive of all places in good things, why Allah – may He be exalted – had gathered together here all the fruits of the lowlands, and of the plains, and of the hill country, even all of those of the most opposite kinds; such as the orange and the almond, the date and the nut, the fig and the banana, besides milk in plenty, and honey and sugar. And as to the excellence of the city! Why, is not this to be the plain of marshalling on the day of judgment; where the gathering together and the appointment will take place? Indeed, Mecca and Medina have their superiority by reason of the Qa'ba and the Prophet – the blessing of Allah be upon him and his family – but truthfully, on the day of judgment, they will both come to Jerusalem, and the excellences of both of them all will there be united. As to

Jerusalem being the most spacious of cities, why, since all created things are to assemble there, what place on the earth can be more extensive than this?" And the company was pleased with my words, agreeing to the truth of them.

Still Jerusalem has some disadvantages. Thus, it is reported as found written in the Torah, that "Jerusalem is as a golden basin filled with scorpions." Thus you will not find baths more filthy than those of the Holy City; nor in any town are provisions dearer. Learned men are few, and the Christians numerous, and the same are unmannerly in the public places. In the hostelries taxes are heavy on all that is sold, for there are guards at every gate, and no one is able to sell anything at a profit, unless he is satisfied with only little gain. In this city the oppressed have no succor; the meek are molested, and the rich envied. Men of law remain unvisited, and erudite men have no renown; also the schools are unattended, for there are no lectures. Everywhere the Christians and the Jews have the upper hand, and the mosque is void of either congregation or assembly of learned men....

... The Masjid al-Aksa [the Further Mosque] lies at the south-eastern corner of the Holy City. The stones of its foundations [of its outer wall], which were laid by David, are ten ells, or a little less in length. They are chiseled, finely faced, and jointed, and of hardest material. On these the caliph Abd al-Makil subsequently built, using smaller but well-shaped stones, and battlements are added above. This mosque is even more beautiful than that of Damascus, for during the building of it they had for a rival and as a comparison the great church belonging to the Christians at Jerusalem, and they built this to be even more magnificent than that other. But in the days of the Abbasids occurred the earthquakes which threw down most of the main building; all, in fact, except that portion round the Mihrab. Now when the caliph of that day obtained news of this, he inquired and learned that the sum at that time in the treasury would in no wise suffice to restore the mosque. So he wrote to the governors of the provinces and to the other commanders, that each should undertake the building of a colonnade. The order was carried out, and the edifice rose firmer and more substantial than ever it had been in former times. The more ancient portion remained, even like a beauty spot, in the midst of the new; and it extends as far as the limits of the marble columns, for, beyond where the columns are of concrete, the later part commences....

The court is paved in all parts; in its center there rises a platform, like that in the mosque at al-Medina, to which, from all four sides, ascend broad flights of steps. On this platform stand four domes. Of these, the Dome of the Chain, the Dome of the Ascension, and the Dome of the Prophet are of small size, and their domes are covered with sheet lead, and are supported on marble pillars, being without walls. In the center of the platform is the

Dome of the Rock, which rises above an octagonal building having four gates, one opposite to each of the flights of steps leading up from the court. These four are, the Kiblah [or Southern] gate, the gate of Israfîl [to the East], the gate of As Sur [or of the Trumpet, to the north], and [the Women's gate], Bab an Nisa, which last opens toward the west. All these are adorned with gold, and closing each of them is a beautiful door of cedar-wood finely worked in pattern. These last were sent by command of the mother of the caliph al-Muktadir Billah. At each of the gates is a balustrade of marble and cedar-wood, with brass-work without; and in the railing, likewise, are gates, but these are unornamented. Within the building are three concentric colonnades, with columns of the most beautiful marble, polished, that can be seen, and above is a low vaulting. Within these again is the central hall over the Rock; the hall is circular, not octagonal, and is surrounded by columns of polished marble supporting round arches. Built above these, and rising high into the air, is the drum in which are large openings; and over the drum is the Dome. The Dome, from the floor up to the pinnacle, which rises into the air, is in height a hundred ells, and from afar off, you may perceive on the summit of the Dome its beautiful pinnacle, the size of which is a fathom and a span. The Dome, externally, is completely covered with brass plates, gilt, while the building itself, its floor and its walls, and the drum, both within and without, is ornamented with marble and mosaics, after the manner that we have already described when speaking of the mosque of Damascus.... At the dawn, when the light of the sun first strikes on the cupola, and the drum catches the rays; then is this edifice a marvelous sight to behold, and one such that in all Islam I have never see its equal; neither have I heard tell of anything built in pagan times that could rival in grace this Dome of the Rock.

What are the reasons for Mukaddasi's claim that Jerusalem is the best place in the world? What criticism does he offer of the city? What does he believe to be some of its most important holy sites? What seems to have been the role of various caliphs (Islamic rulers) in creating and supporting Muslim places of worship?

31. *DIARY OF A JOURNEY THROUGH SYRIA AND PALESTINE*

During the mid-eleventh century, the Fatimid caliphs of Cairo ruled over the three major pilgrimage sites of the Islamic tradition: Mecca, Medina, and Jerusalem, which together attracted pious Muslims from around the world. One such traveler from modern-day Afghanistan, Nâsir-i-Khusrau, set out on a devotional journey to those holy cities in 1046. Jerusalem was the first major stop on his pilgrimage. He describes a thriving scene of Islamic pilgrimage to the sacred sites of the city and its surroundings. He also provides us with a Muslim perspective on Christian pilgrimage and other religious practices that continued to take place under Islamic rule.

Source: trans. Guy le Strange, in *Diary of a Journey through Syria and Palestine*, Palestine Pilgrims' Text Society, vol. 4 (London, 1895), pp. 23–25, 40–41, 46–48, 52–57, 59–61; modernized.

From Tripoli, which is by the seashore, to the Holy City [Jerusalem] is fifty-six leagues; and from Balkh to the Holy City, eight hundred and seventy-six leagues. It was the 5th of Ramadan, of the year 438 [5 March 1047], that I came to the Holy City; and the full space of a solar year had elapsed since I set out from home, having all that time never ceased to travel onward, for in no place had I yet sojourned to enjoy repose. Now, the men of Syria, and of the neighboring parts, call the Holy City [Bait al-Mukaddas] by the name of Kuds [the Holy]; and the people of these provinces, if they are unable to make the pilgrimage [to Mecca], will go up at the appointed season to Jerusalem, and there perform their rites, and upon the feast day slay the sacrifice, as is customary to do [at Mecca on the same day]. There are years when as many as 20,000 people will be present at Jerusalem during the first days of the [pilgrimage] month of Dhu-l Hijjah; for they bring their children also with them in order to celebrate their circumcision.

From all the countries of the Greeks, too, and from other lands, the Christians and the Jews come up to Jerusalem in great numbers in order to make their visitations of the church [of the Resurrection] and the Synagogue that is there; and this great church at Jerusalem we shall describe further on in its proper place.

The country and the villages round the Holy City are situated upon the hillsides; the land is well cultivated, and they grow corn, olives, and figs; there are also many kinds of trees here. In all the country round there is no [spring] water for irrigation, and yet the produce is very abundant, and the prices are moderate. Many of the chief men harvest as much as 50,000 *manns* weight [about 16,800 gallons] of olive-oil. It is kept in tanks and in pits, and they export thereof to other countries. It is said that drought never visits the soil of Syria. I heard from a certain person, on whose word I can rely, that the Prophet – peace be upon him, and the benediction of Allah! – was seen in a dream by a saintly man, who addressed him, saying: "O Prophet of God, give me assurance forever of my daily bread," and the Prophet – peace be upon him! – replied: "In truth, it shall be warranted unto thee, even by the bread and oil of Syria."

I now propose to make a description of the Holy City. Jerusalem is a city set on a hill, and there is no water therein, except what falls in rain. The villages round have springs of water, but the Holy City has no springs. The city is enclosed by strong walls of stone, mortared, and trees, for it is all built on the rock. Jerusalem is a very great city, and, at the time of my visit, there were in it twenty thousand men. It has high, well-built, and clean bazaars. All the streets are paved with slabs of stone; and where ever there was a hill or a high place, they have cut it down and made it level, so that as soon as the rain falls the whole place is washed clean. There are in the city numerous artificers, and each craft has a separate bazaar. The mosque lies at the [south] east quarter of the city, whereby the eastern city wall forms also the wall of the mosque [court]. When you have passed out of the mosque, there lies before you a great level plain, called the Sahirah, which, it is said, will be the place of the resurrection, where all mankind shall be gathered together. For this reason men from all parts of the world come hither to make their sojourn in the Holy City till death overtakes them, in order that when the day fixed by God – be He praised and exalted! – shall arrive, they may thus be ready and present at the appointed place. O God! In that day vouchsafe to your servants both your pardon and your protection! Amen, O Lord of both worlds!

... Wherever, in the city itself or in the suburbs, the level is below that in the *haram* [sanctuary or forbidden space] area, they have made gateways, like tunnels, cut through, that lead up onto the court [of the Noble Sanctuary]. One such as these is called Bâb an Nabî [or the Gate of the Prophet] – peace and blessing be upon him! – which opens towards the Kiblah point, that is, towards the south. [The passage-way of this gate] is ten ells broad, and the height varies by reason of the steps; in one place it is five ells high, and in others the roof of the passage-way is 20 ells above you. Over this passage-way had been erected the main building of the [Aksa] mosque, for the masonry is so solidly laid that they have been able to raise the enormous building that is seen here, without any damage arising to what is below. They have made use of stones of such a size, that the mind cannot conceive how, by human power, they were carried up and set in place. It is said, however, that the building was accomplished by Solomon, the son of David – peace be upon him! The Prophet – peace and blessing be upon him – on the night of his ascent into heaven, passed into the Noble Sanctuary through this passage-way, for the gateway opens on the road from Mecca....

The great Dome [of the Rock], which rises above the twelve piers standing round the rock, can be seen from the distance of a league away, rising like the summit of a mountain. From the base of the dome to its pinnacle measures 30 cubits, and this rises above the [octagonal] walls that are 20 ells high – for the dome is supported on the pillars that are like in height to the outer walls – and the whole building rises on a platform that itself is twelve ells high, so that from the level of the Court of the Noble Sanctuary to the summit of the dome measures a total of 62 ells. The roofing and the ceiling of this edifice are in woodwork that is set above the piers, and the pillars, and the walls, after a fashion not to be seen elsewhere. The rock itself arises out of the floor to the height of a man, and a balustrade of marble goes round about it in order that none may lay his hand thereon. The rock inclines on the side that is towards the kiblah [or south], and there is an appearance as though a person had walked heavily on the stone when it was soft like clay, whereby the imprint of his toes had remained thereon. There are on the rock seven such footmarks, and I heard it stated that Abraham – peace be upon him! – was once here with Isaac – upon him be peace – when he was a boy, and that he walked over this place, and that the footmarks were his.

In the house of the Dome of the Rock men are always congregated, pilgrims and worshippers. The place is laid with fine carpets of silk and other stuffs. In the middle of the dome, and over the rock, there hangs from a silver chain a silver lamp; and there are in other parts of the building great numbers of silver lamps, on each of which is inscribed its weight. These lamps are all the gift of the [Fatimite caliph, who is] sultan of Egypt, and according to the calculations I made, there must be here silver utensils of various kinds of the weight of a 1000 *manns* [or about a ton and a half]. I saw there a huge wax taper that was seven cubits high, and three spans in diameter. It was [white] like the camphor of Zibaj, and [the wax] was mixed with ambergris. They told me that the sultan of Egypt sent hither every year a great number of tapers, and among the rest, the large one just described, on which the name of the sultan was written in golden letters.

… Now, it was my intention to go down from the Holy City and make my visitation [at Hebron] to [the tomb of] Abraham, the friend of the merciful – peace and benediction be upon him! – and on Wednesday, the first day of the month of Dhu-l Ka'adah, of the year of the Flight 438 [29 April 1047], I set out. From the Holy City to Hebron is six leagues, and the road runs towards the south. Along the way are many villages with gardens and cultivated fields. Such trees as need little water, as, for example, the vine and the fig, the olive and the sumach, grow here abundantly, and of their own accord. A couple of leagues from the Holy City is a place where there are four villages; and there is here a spring of water with numerous gardens and orchards, and it is called Faradis [or the Paradises], on account of the beauty of the spot. At the distance of a league from the Holy City is a place belonging to the Christians, which they hold in greatest veneration, and there are always numerous pilgrims of their people who come hither to perform their visitation. The place is called Bait al-Lahn [Bethlehem]. The Christians hold a festival here, and many will come for it all the way from Rûm [the

Byzantine Empire]. That day I myself left the Holy City, and I passed the night at Bethlehem.

The people of Syria, and the inhabitants of the Holy City, call the Sanctuary [or Mash-had at Hebron] of Khalil [the 'Friend' of Allah] – his blessing be upon him! – and they never make use of the real name of the village, which name is Matlun. This Sanctuary has belonging to it very many villages that provide revenues for pious purposes. At one of these villages is a spring, where water flows out from under a stone, but in no great abundance; and it is conducted by a channel, cut in the ground, to a place outside the town [of Hebron], where they have constructed a covered tank for collecting the water, so that none may run to waste, and that the people of the town, and the pilgrims, may be able to supply their wants. The Sanctuary stands on the southern border of the town, and extends towards the south-east. The Sanctuary is enclosed by four walls, built of squared masonry, and in its upper part [the area] measures 80 cubits long by 40 cubits across. The height of the [exterior] walls is two cubits. The mihrab [or niche] and the maksûrah [or enclosed space for Friday prayers] stand in the width of the building [at the south end]. In the maksûrah are many fine mihrabs. There are two tombs occupying the maksûrah, laid so that their heads lie towards the kiblah [point, south]. Both these tombs are covered by cenotaphs, built of squared stones as high as a man. That lying on the right hand [to the west] is the grave of Isaac, son of Abraham; and that on the left [or to the east] is the grave of his wife [Rebecca] – peace be upon them! Between the two graves many measure the space of ten cubits. In this part of the Sanctuary the floor and the walls are adorned with precious carpets and Maghribi matting that is more costly even than brocade stuff. I saw here a piece of matting, serving as a prayer rug, which they told me the amir juyush [or captain-general], in the service of the sultan of Egypt, had sent to that place, and they said that at Cairo this prayer rug had been bought for thirty gold Maghribî dînârs. Now, the same quantity of Rumi [or Byzantine] brocade would not have cost so much, and the equal of this mat I never saw elsewhere.

Leaving the maksûrah, you find in the court of the sanctuary two buildings. Facing the kiblah, the one lying on the right hand [or to the west], contains the Tomb of Abraham, the friend of Allah – His blessing be upon him! This building is of such a size that inside it is another building which you cannot enter, but which has in it four windows, through which the pilgrims, who stand about it, may look and view the tomb that is within. The walls and the floor of this chamber are covered with brocade stuffs, and the cenotaph is made of stone, measuring three ells [in length], with many silver lamps and lanterns hung above it. The other edifice, lying on the left hand as you face the kiblah [or the eastern side], has within it the tomb of Sarah, the wife of Abraham – peace be upon him! Between the two edifices is the passage-way that leads to both, and this is like a hall, and here also are suspended numerous lamps and lanterns.

After passing by these two edifices, you come to two other sepulchral chambers lying close to another, that to the right [or on the west side] containing the tomb of the prophet Jacob – peace be upon him! – and to the left [or east side] the tomb of his wife [Leah]. Beyond this again are the other buildings, where Abraham – the blessing of Allah be upon him! – was accustomed to dispense his hospitality; but within the sanctuary there are these six tombs only. Outside the four walls [of the Sanctuary] the ground slopes away, here on the [west] side is the sepulcher of Joseph, the son of Jacob – peace be upon them both! – over whose gravestone they have built a dome.

On this side, where the ground is level – that is, beyond the sepulcher of Joseph and the sanctuary – lies a great cemetery, whither they bring the dead from many parts to be buried. On the flat roof of the maksûrah, in the [Hebron] Sanctuary, they have built cells for the reception of the pilgrims who come hither; and their revenues for this charity are considerable, being derived from villages and houses in the Holy City.... The pilgrims and voyagers and other guests [of the sanctuary] are given bread and olives. There are very many mills here, worked by oxen and mules, that all day long grind the flour; and, further, there are slave-girls who, during the whole day, are baking the bread. The loaves they make here are each of them of a *mann* weight [about three pounds], and to every person who arrives they give daily a loaf of bread, and a dish of lentils cooked in olive-oil, also some raisins. This practice has been in usage since the days of [Abraham] the friend of the merciful – peace be upon him! – down to the present hour; and there are some days when as many as five hundred pilgrims arrive, to each of whom this hospitality is offered....

In the Holy City [of Jerusalem], the Christians possess a church which they call Bai'at-al-Kumamah [the church of the Resurrection], and they hold it in great veneration. Every year great multitudes of people from Rûm [the Byzantine Empire] come to this place to perform their visitation; and the emperor of Byzantium himself even comes here, but in secret, so that no one should recognize him.... [The Egyptian sultan] Hâkim at one time ordered the church [of the Resurrection] to be given over to plunder, which was so done, and it was laid to ruin. Some time it remained thus; but afterwards the emperor of Byzantium sent ambassadors with presents and promises of service, and concluded a treaty in which he stipulated for permission to defray the expenses of rebuilding the church, and this was ultimately accomplished.

At the present day the church is a most spacious building, and is capable of containing eight thousand persons. The edifice is built, with the utmost skill, of colored marble, with ornamentation and sculptures. Inside, the church is everywhere adorned with Byzantine brocade, worked in gold and pictures. And they have portrayed Jesus – peace be upon him! – who at times is showed riding upon an ass. There are also pictures representing other of the prophets, as, for instance, Abraham, and Ishmael, and Isaac, and Jacob with his sons – peace be upon them all! These pictures they have overlaid with a varnish of the oil of sandaracha [or red juniper]; for the face of each portrait they have made a plate of thin glass, which is set on there, and is perfectly transparent. This dispenses with the need of a curtain, and prevents any dust or dirt from settling on the painting, for the glass is cleaned daily by the servants [of the church]. Besides this [church of the Resurrection] there are many others [in Jerusalem], all very skillfully built, but to describe them all would take too long. In the church [of the Resurrection] there is a picture divided into two parts, representing heaven and hell. One part shows the people of paradise in paradise, while the other shows the people of hell in hell, with all that there is inside; and assuredly there is nowhere else in the world a picture such as this. There are seated in the church great numbers of priests and monks who read the Gospel and say prayers, for both by day and by night they are occupied after this manner.

What aspects of Jerusalem interested Nâsir-i-Khusrau? What evidence does his account provide that he witnessed Jewish and Christian pilgrims at their own holy sites? What seems to have been his attitude toward them? Why was he interested in Hebron and the tomb of the patriarchs?

CHAPTER FOUR

PILGRIMAGE BEFORE AND AFTER THE MILLENNIUM

Following the internal disintegration of the Carolingian order, accompanied by a fresh wave of external pressures from Viking, Magyar, and Muslim raiders, the peoples of Western Europe experienced another round of disruption and localism in politics, society, and religious life. According to the reports of monks and other churchmen, by the late tenth century, violence had become a way of life for petty lords, who dominated the surrounding land from the numerous castles constructed during this period. Starting around this same time, however, one sees a new vibrancy in the European country-side, towns, and even cities, the humble beginnings of an agricultural and commercial revolution that would dramatically transform the material and cultural circumstances of medieval Europe. In the eleventh century, an outburst of monumental church-building helped to create a new visual landscape of sacred art and architecture, revitalizing saints' shrines and other attractions for pious Christian pilgrims, including churchmen and peasants, and sometimes the very same "predatory" lords who terrorized them. The heightened religious sentiments of the period also contributed to a resurgence of interest in making pilgrimages to Jerusalem, whether voluntary or imposed as penance. Although there is little evidence that Christians around the year 1000 experienced widespread terror over the end of the world, the dawn of the new millennium and the rapidly changing world around them did seem to suggest that a new era of history had begun, perhaps heralding the coming of the apocalypse or a marvelous era of promise and renewal for God's church on earth. At home and abroad, pilgrimage revealed this dynamic awakening of Christian Europe at the dawn of the High Middle Ages.

32. POPULAR DEVOTION AND
THE PEACE OF GOD

Before and after the year 1000, bishops and abbots, apparently with the support of the general populace, responded to the endemic violence of their age with a series of initiatives that modern historians call the "Peace of God," an attempt to limit the legitimate space for warfare, along with offering protections for the poor and for church property. To display their own sources of power and authority, monks and clerics centered their calls for peace around the relics of the saints, attracting crowds of pious believers – one visible sign of the new religious sentiments or forms of devotion that were spreading around Europe at the turn of the millennium. The selections below are from two contemporary sources: Letaldus of Micy, On the Bearing of Saint Junianus' Body to the Council of Charroux; *and Rodulfus Glaber,* The Five Books of Histories.

Sources: Letaldus of Micy, trans. T. Head, in *The Peace of God: Social Violence and Religious Response in France around the Year 1000*, ed. T. Head and R. Landes (Ithaca, NY: Cornell University Press, 1992), pp. 328–29; Rodulfus Glaber, trans. J. France, in *The Five Books of the Histories* (Oxford: Clarendon Press, 1989), pp. 195, 197.

Letaldus of Micy

Brother Letaldus gives salutations to lord father Constantine and to the other brothers of the monastery of Nouaille. The angel Gabriel was once sent by the Lord to alleviate the labors of Tobias. The angel not only delivered him from toil but also gave him the support of the kindness of divine piety. Then he returned to him by whom he had been sent, going forth from whom does not make one absent. Gabriel first taught those who had benefited from heavenly kindness and addressed them, saying, "It is good to hide the secret of a king, but gloriously to reveal the works of God." Therefore it is fitting that we reveal and confess the works of Christ which are allowed to happen in our times through his most glorious confessor Junianus, both for the praise and glory of the saint's name and for the edification of those who will hear the story. All people should learn these things, for such works as were done in the days of our fathers and are still done for us now do not happen on account of our own merits but through the kindness of piety and the intervention of those fathers who are provided as intercessors for us. They provide something for us to copy in the important correction of our own lives.

We therefore approach the task of writing this work which we have promised, not trusting in the help of men, but supported by the aid of divine largess, which comes from him who said, "Open your mouth wide and I will fill it." Reverend fathers and brothers, you have begged us with your prayers and you have enjoined me by your charitable command. Do not allow our rustic speech to be displeasing to you, if only so that truth alone may bring forth the whole narrative, as it was told by you. At that time sinners were rising up like stalks of wheat. Evil people wasted the vineyard of the Lord just as briars and thorns choke the harvest of the land. Therefore it pleased bishops, abbots, and other religious men that a council be held at which the taking of booty would be prohibited and the property of the saints, which had been unjustly stolen, would be restored. Other evils that fouled the fair countenance of the holy church of God were also struck down by the sharp points of anathemas. I think that this council was held at the monastery of Charroux [in 989] and that a great crowd of many people gathered there from the Poitou, the Limousin, and neighboring regions. Many bodies of saints were also brought there. The cause of religion was strengthened by their presence, and the impudence of evil people was beaten back. That council – convoked, as it was thought, by divine will – was adorned by frequent miracles through the presence of these saints. Along with these various relics of the saints honored by God, the remains of the glorious father Junianus were brought with proper honor.

Several things occurred when the relics of the holy father Junianus were brought forth from their monastic enclosure. Not far from the monastery [of Nouaille], those who carried the bundle containing the saint stopped and put down their holy burden. After the most holy relics departed, the faithful in their devotion erected a cross in order to memorialize and record the fact that the relics of the holy father had rested there. From that time to this, whosoever suffers from a fever and goes there is returned to their former health through the invocation of the name of Christ and the intercession of this same father Junianus. When the party came to the little village called Ruffiacus, they sought out the manse house and passed the night there in a vigil singing hymns and praise to God. The next day they resumed their journey. At the place where the relics had rested, faithful Christians erected a sort of fence from twigs, so that the place where the holy body had lain might remain safe from the approach of men and animals. Many days later a wild bull came by and wantonly struck that same fence with his horns and side, when suddenly he retreated from the fence, fell down, and died. In that same place a little pool was created by placing a gutter tile to allow run-off water to be stored up. Because of the reverence for the holy relics, this pool served as an invitation for many people to wash. Among these there was a woman who suffered from elephantiasis. When she washed herself with that water, she was returned to her former health.

Rodulfus Glaber, Book Four

5.14. At the millennium of the Lord's Passion, which followed these years of famine and disaster, by divine mercy and goodness the violent rainstorms ended; the happy face of the sky began to shine and to blow with gentle breezes and by gentle serenity to proclaim the magnanimity of the Creator. The whole surface of the earth was benignly verdant, portending ample produce which altogether banished want. It was then that the bishops and abbots and other devout men of Aquitaine first summoned great councils of the whole people, to which were borne the bodies of many saints and innumerable caskets of holy relics. The movement spread to Arles and Lyons, then across all Burgundy into the furthest corners of the French realm. Throughout the dioceses it was decreed that in fixed places the bishops and magnates of the entire country should convene councils for reestablishing peace and consolidating the holy faith. When the people heard this, great, middling, and poor, they came rejoicing and ready, one and all, to obey the commands of the clergy no less than if they had been given by a voice from heaven speaking to men on earth. For all were still cowed by the recent carnage, and feared lest they might not obtain future abundance and plenty.

5.15. A roll divided into headings was drawn up, giving a list of all that was prohibited, and a record of what men had, by sworn undertaking, decided to offer to almighty God. The most important of these was that the peace should be preserved inviolate so that all men, lay and religious, whatever threats had hung over them before, could now go about their business without fear and unarmed. The robber and the man who seized another's domains were to suffer the whole rigor of the law, either by a heavy fine or corporal punishment. The holy places of all churches were to be held in such honor and reverence that if someone guilty of any crime fled there he would get off unharmed, unless he had violated the peace oath, in which case he could be seized before the altar and made to suffer the established penalty. All clerics, monks, and nuns also were to be given reverence, such that those traveling with them were not to be harmed by anyone.

5.16. Much was decided at these councils which we wish to relate at length. One matter worth remembering is that all agreed, by a perpetual edict, that men, except when gravely ill, should always abstain from wine on the sixth day of the week, and from flesh on the seventh, unless an important feast happened to fall on one of these days. If, for any reason, a man had slightly to relax this prohibition, he was to feed three poor men. Many sick people were cured at these gatherings of holy men. Lest any doubt this, let it be recorded that as the bent legs and arms were straightened and returned to their normal state, skin was broken, flesh was torn, and blood ran freely. These cases provided credence for others when doubts might have been conceived. Such enthusiasm was generated that the bishops raised their croziers to the heavens, and all cried out with one voice to God, their hands extended: "Peace! Peace! Peace!" This was the sign of their perpetual covenant with God. It was understood that after five years all should repeat this wonderful celebration in order to confirm the peace. In that same year there was such a plentiful abundance of corn and wine and other foods that the like could not be hoped to be attained in the following five years. All food was cheap except meat and rare spices: truly it was like the great Mosaic jubilee of ancient times. For the following three years food was no less plentiful.

What happened at the place where Junianus' relics rested en route to Charroux? Why, according to Letaldus and Rodulfus, did churchmen summon councils to declare peace in their lands? What role did the saints and their relics play at these councils? What sort of people attended these gatherings, and how did they react to the presence of the saints? How might the Peace of God movement have created new opportunities for pilgrimage?

33. THE MIRACLES OF SAINT FOY

Situated on one of the popular pilgrimage routes that connected northern Europe to devotional destinations such as Rome and Saint James of Compostela, the French abbey church of St-Foy (or Faith) at Conques emerged as a popular destination in the late tenth and eleventh centuries. The relics of Foy, a young girl martyred in the late third or early fourth century under the Roman emperor Diocletian, brought the monks of Conques considerable revenues, prestige, and influence at a time when even pilgrims could be targets of coercion and violence. The selections below are from The Book of Sainte Foy, *written by Bernard of Angers, who traveled to Conques for the first time in 1013, attracted by the stories he had heard of the miracles occurring there.*

Source: trans. P. Sheingorn, *The Book of Sainte Foy* (Philadelphia: University of Pennsylvania Press, 1995), pp. 39–51, 68–69, 83–87, 145–46, 173.

The beginning of the book of miracles of holy and most blessed Foy, virgin and martyr, related by Bernard, a teacher, master at the school of Angers.

A letter to the holiest and most learned of men, Fulbert, bishop of Chartres, Bernard, the least of teachers, sends a gift of supreme blessedness: during the time when I was at Chartres, where I had the benefit of your sound conversation, I often visited the little church of the martyr Saint Foy located outside the walls of the city, either to write or to pray there. I also remember that many times when we had gathered for discussion we happened onto the subject of Saint Foy and her miracles, which took place constantly with the help of Christ omnipotent in the monastery at Conques where her sacrosanct body is reverently venerated. Partly because it seemed to be the common people who promulgated these miracles and partly because they were regarded as new and unusual, we put no faith in them and rejected them as so much worthless fiction. Nevertheless, what was true through God's will could not be suppressed and belief in its truth was already spreading through all Europe.

Little by little a plan took root in my heart, and although I kept it secret I couldn't forget it; it was a plan to go to the holy martyr's dwelling-place to fulfill my desire to learn about her. Finally the matter returned to my mind so forcefully that I marked down in a little notebook the time and day by which I vowed to go there, so that I wouldn't forget. Meanwhile I had a reason for moving to the city of Angers, for the bishop of that city had implored me to come. For almost three years I wasted time there that should have been used for study on behalf of stupid good-for-nothings – I may as well admit the truth – and the date by which I had vowed to visit Conques passed by. I thought that I was waiting for a good opportunity, but since I was increasingly involved in various duties, I was actually deceived by false hope. I was just like a fish caught in a net – the more I tried to become disentangled, the more entangled I was by increasingly serious problems. Finally, however, lest I should seem to be using the excuse of adversity as a pretext for idleness – although I was becoming more and more aware that these hidden and almost inescapable snares had been prepared for me with diabolical trickery and, in short, that through the skill of the Enemy [the Devil] I was being discouraged from planning to implement my good intentions – all at once I put off the business at hand and with God's guidance I succeeded in reaching my goal, the mausoleum of the glorious martyr.

Since the time of my arrival here I have begun to inquire diligently about Saint Foy's miracles. Such a great number of miracles have poured forth from various narrators that if my mind had not been burningly eager to hear them my brain would have been overwhelmed with weariness. But I myself have been fortunate enough to see the very man whose eyes were violently plucked out by the roots and afterward restored to their natural state, intact and whole. And I can see him even as I write this. Since he himself asserts that this really happened and the whole province attests to it, I know that it is true. Therefore I think that his story ought to be introduced first as the basis for reading the rest of the miracles, and not just my interpretation of his meaning, but word for word as I heard it from his lips; not abbreviated, but in a narrative long enough to satisfy my readers. To his story I have decided to append only a very few miracles so that I can return home quickly. As to the other miracles that remain, I have noted down the more beautiful ones swiftly and with the greatest brevity, but only those that are not older than our own time, and whose eyewitnesses told me not an invented tale but the clearest truth. I am resolved, with God as my guide, to carry these notes back home with me. When I have leisure time for more careful work, I shall make a fuller text for the future reader out of this material.

Therefore, most learned of mortals, when you have received these miracles, correct only the way in which they are written. For, although I am unlearned and ignorant in the art of composition, nevertheless I was not gullible when I listened and I did not easily believe what I heard. But it may seem to you that my foul pen is unequal to the material and has sullied it. If so, you will not offend me by adopting such a noble and glorious theme as your own; you will embellish with a noble and glorious style, since all agree that you stand alone at the pinnacle of wisdom. For if the truth in these stories has been corrupted by my bad style, readers will turn away in disgust and this best of subjects will have been debased. To write up such excellent material myself, thereby degrading those wise scholars who could have done it better, would have been the height of wickedness and presumption if the very fact that I have made the material widely available does not protect me from the charge of harmful boldness. Let me state the case more clearly: it is better that miracles from heaven be committed to writing now, while they are recent and cannot be doubted, no matter what the style, by a scholar however unlearned save in knowing the truth, than to leave this material waiting for the unlikely possibility that a writer who would convey their message with indifference might appear from some unknown part of the world. Therefore I do not judge myself to be so culpable if I strive to the best of my ability to record the works of divine grace on behalf of humankind, when the very scarcity of writers strongly insists that I do it.

And, future readers, I warn you not to be thrown into confusion by the way this work is organized and not to look for a chronological sequence of events. The urgent necessity of returning to Angers did not permit me to complete my investigations in Conques, so I have limited myself to those miracles whose omission would do harm to the results. Therefore here in the writing of this book about Saint Foy's miracles, which I begin to put together with God as my fellow-worker, the miracles will be grouped not in chronological sequence but by the similarity of their subject matter. I have very diligently investigated to determine the inviolable truth of these miracles. Because there is nothing truer, I implore you to bring faith wholeheartedly to my narration so that later you will not regret that you disparaged a holy martyr. Better yet, if the unusual novelty of the miraculous content disturbs you, I prostrate myself on the ground to beg this of your brotherhood: that after my return you also come here, not so much to pray as to gain knowledge through experience. For through lack of experience you might prematurely judge something false whose truth, once you have seen it for yourselves, you will proclaim thereafter.

1.1. Up to the present time in the district of Rouergue where the most blessed virgin Foy rests, in the neighborhood of the village of Conques, there dwells, still alive, a priest named Gerald. This priest had a blood relative who was also, according to the sacrament of confirmation administered by the bishop, his godson. His name was Guibert; he was Gerald's household servant and vigorously managed his business affairs. Once Guibert had made his way to Conques for the feast day, and after the nighttime activity of the vigil was completed according to custom, on the next day, that is on the feast day itself, he was returning by the same road on which he had gone. Then he had the bad fortune to meet his master, who was aroused by a secret hatred against him that was motivated by jealousy. When the priest saw Guibert close at hand in a pilgrim's garb, his initial approach was peaceful:

"Look at you, Guibert, you've been made a *romeus*, I see," for that is what they call pilgrims of the saints in that country. And Guibert answered, "That's right, master, I'm returning from Saint Foy's feast." Then Gerald, pretending to be friendly, inquired about some other matters and gave Guibert permission to depart. But although he went on himself a little way, the priest – as treasonous as a Jew (if it is right that a man is called "priest" who corrupts the priesthood with sacrilege) – turned back and ordered Guibert to wait for him for a little while. Coming after Guibert, Gerald ordered his men to hold him and they soon boxed him in on both sides.

When Guibert saw what was happening he began to tremble with great fear, and he asked of what crime he was being accused. The treacherous man gave this menacing answer: "You have done a wicked thing to me, and you are preparing to do worse; that's why I'll be satisfied with nothing less than your very own eyes as punishment." But he did not describe the kind of crime more clearly and pretended that this was out of a sense of decency. For surely it is disgraceful for priests to render judgment based on their own jealousy. In fact the cause of this trouble had arisen from the suspicion of debauchery with a woman. Guibert was quite confident that he could offer an explanation for anything for which he was blamed, so he said, "Look, master, if you would accuse me openly of any crime of which you suspect me, I am prepared to defend myself according to law. I don't think anything can be found for which I deserve to incur your anger and that of your followers."

Gerald replied, "You might as well stop defending yourself with useless double-talk, for all is lost already. I have pronounced the sentence – you lose your eyes." Guibert saw that Gerald was determined to be his executioner and that the inexorable hour of his destruction was at hand. He perceived that no room was left for any pleading but, even though he despaired of his safety at that moment, he cried out, "Master, I beg you, spare me, if not because of my innocence, at least for the love of God and Saint Foy – it's for love of her that I'm wearing a pilgrim's sacred garment at this very moment."

But this fierce monster, who thought highly neither of God nor of his saint, gnashed his teeth, roared with savage fury, and spewed out the blasphemous poison he had held in for a long time in the form of these sacrilegious words: "Neither God nor Saint Foy will free you today, and you won't succeed in escaping from my hands unpunished by calling on them. And don't think there's a chance that I'll view you as reputable and protected from attack out of respect for pilgrim's clothing, when you have been so wickedly unjust to me!"

Then he ordered that Guibert be thrown down headlong and that the eyes of this innocent man be torn out violently. He couldn't persuade any of his men to commit such a crime (they were only three and I pass over their names because of my distaste for barbaric language), but he at least succeeded with his order that they hold Guibert down. Then Gerald suddenly slid off his horse and, with the very fingers with which he usually touched the sacrosanct body of Christ, he violently tore out the eyes of his own godson and tossed them carelessly to the ground. But divine power was not absent, for it does not leave unheard those who importune heaven's care; it is always present near those invoking it in truth and renders a favorable judgment for those suffering injury. Those who were there were fortunate enough to see that a snow-white dove appeared instantly (or, as the perpetrator of the crime tells it, it was a magpie). The magpie or dove at that very hour took up from the ground the wretch's eyes, which were covered with fresh blood. The bird flew above the mountaintops and appeared to descend to Conques with its burden.

Don't be amazed that God entrusted the rescue of Guibert's eyes in the wilderness to a winged magpie, for in time past he used ravens to send food to Elijah in the desert. Or perhaps, in accordance with divine will, an ambiguously marked bird came, which could be clearly recognized neither as a magpie nor as a dove. But the men who saw the bird didn't see any ambiguity. The others in fact perceived a dove clothed in white, but Gerald asserted that he had seen none other than a magpie adorned with black and white. Just as God will seem terrifying to the wicked but gentle to the just, it could also have happened that the form had seemed to be white to those innocent men who groaned inwardly at the sight of the crime, while to the criminal it had seemed to be of mixed colors.

Nevertheless, when the sacrilegious Gerald saw the bird he was led to repentance and began to weep profusely. One of his companions told him this weeping was in vain and too late. Then Gerald departed, and from that time forward the scoundrel didn't undertake the celebration of the holy mass, either because of the crime he had perpetrated or, as seems more likely, because he neglected it altogether in favor of secular business.

But Gerald's mother was moved by strong feeling for the innocent, wounded man. She took Guibert into her house and very kindly supplied everything he needed until his health was restored. His living in her house at that time was scarcely at the behest of his master but rather was to avoid his ferocity, for Gerald had continued to be stirred up against Guibert by the same gossip that had originally pierced his heart with the wound of false jealousy. At last Guibert regained his health and during that year sought his living with his skill as a jongleur. He received such a profit from it that – as he is in the habit of saying – he didn't care to have his eyes thereafter because both the lust for wealth and the enjoyment of income delighted him so much.

And in this way a year unfolded and the day of the feast was at hand.

On the day before the vigil, while Guibert lay in a deep sleep, a little girl of indescribable grace seemed to stand near him. Her appearance was angelic and quite serene, and her countenance was a dazzling white, besprinkled drop by drop with a rosy blush. The lively expression on her wondrous face exceeded all human charm. Her size, in truth, was what it is said to have been at the time of her passion [martyrdom], that is, she had the stature of a young girl, not yet advanced in age. Her clothing was very flowing and interwoven with the most elegant gold throughout, and delicate, colored embroidery encircled it. Her long sleeves, which hung down to her feet, had been delicately gathered into very tiny pleats on account of their fullness. And the band entwined in a circle about her head gleamed with two pairs of translucent, glossy white pearls. Indeed the form of the little body seemed to me to signify nothing other than what is said regarding the time of her passion, that is, just as I already indicated, that she was young. However, the character of her face and her marvelous style of dress – insofar as it was possible for Guibert to discern them – were, I think, not without a reason, for these things carry in themselves a very clear portent. If we are able to accept her clothes exceeding the measure of her person as the armor or protection of abounding faith, then the golden radiance of her clothing figures overtly the illumination of spiritual grace. Why the delicacy of the embroidery or the pleating of the sleeves if they do not reveal that she was clothed in divine wisdom? And, rightly, on the principal part of the body, that is, on the head, four gems were seen, through which we are able to observe clearly the quadrivium of the cardinal virtues: prudence, justice, fortitude, and temperance. Saint Foy, because she had understanding of these and perfection in them, and because she was deeply inspired by the Holy Spirit, also cultivated most perfectly in her heart the remaining virtues that are derived from these. She pleased the almighty in every way and therefore was not unacquainted with the highest good. To holy martyrdom, to Christ, she offered herself as a sacrifice, a voluntary and pure holocaust.

As to her face, I mentioned it first in my description because I learned of it first from my informant. Nevertheless I place it last in my exposition, because in her face I see a figure of the aim and pinnacle of her whole life, for I perceive that the whiteness of her face signifies charity. As a matter of fact, it is appropriate that through whiteness, which conquers other colors by its own radiance, charity, the most perfect of virtues, is understood. I mentioned the whiteness of her face before describing her blush (which implies martyrdom), as did my informant, not inappropriately, because there is no way to attain to the grace of martyrdom without the preeminence of charity. Foy, God's dearest and most beloved, held to this virtue invincibly; since for love of it she eagerly sought out the untimely bitterness of death.

But soon – I return to my subject – this same most blessed Foy, leaning on the bedpost and slowly and sweetly reaching out her hand toward the right cheek of the sleeper, spoke: "Are you sleeping, Guibert?"

"Who are you who calls me?"

"I am Saint Foy."

"What is the reason, my lady, that you come to me?"

"None other but to see you."

Guibert thanked her, and Saint Foy asked him in turn:

"Do you recognize me?"

But he identified her as if he had already seen her and seemed to answer in this way:

"Indeed I see you clearly, my lady, and I recognize you perfectly well."

"Tell me also how you are situated," she said, "and how your affairs prosper."

"Most satisfactorily, my lady. Fortune advances my affairs and all things, thanks to God, go prosperously for me."

"And what do you mean 'prosperously,'" she said, "when you do not see the light of heaven?"

For, just as people sometimes perceive themselves differently in dreams from the way they actually are, Guibert thought he could see. This last question reminded him of his missing eyes:

"And how," he asked, "could I see? I am the wretch who lost his eyes to the violence of an unjust master when I was returning from your feast day a year ago."

"The man who condemned you to bodily harm without cause," she said, "has greatly offended God and seriously provoked the anger of the highest Creator. But if tomorrow, the vigil of my martyrdom, you go to Conques, purchase two candles, and place one in front of the altar of the holy savior and the other in front of the altar where the clay of my body is enshrined, you will have a proper reason to rejoice because your eyes will be wholly restored. I raised an immense outcry on account of the injury inflicted on you, and with it I swayed the goodness of the heavenly judge to mercy. I importuned God for your health with the diligent presence of my prayer so long, until he returned a favorable and sympathetic outcome to my pleas."

After she had given Guibert these instructions she began to insist repeatedly that he should set out and that he should proceed energetically and swiftly. Since he was unsure about finding the money for the wax necessary to his healing, she instructed him more firmly and advised him in this way:

"1000 people whom you have never seen," she said, "are going to give you alms. But so that you may complete the present business more easily, before that, go speedily at today's dawn to the church of this parish" (doubtless this was near the place where he had lost his eyes; it has been called Spariacus since ancient times) "and hear mass. You will find a man there who will give you six deniers."

But while Guibert was expressing to her the gratitude she deserved for the kindness of her consolation, this divine power returned to heaven. Now awake, Guibert immediately sought out the parish church and recounted the whole vision in sequence to all who were present. They thought it was absurd nonsense, but Guibert didn't give up. He kept canvassing those crowded around him, one by one, asking them to pledge twelve deniers. Finally a man named Hugh came forward and put into Guibert's open money-pouch a donation of six sols and one obol, which just exceeded the amount mentioned in the vision. Then Guibert remembered the divine vision and became more certain that its promise would be fulfilled. What more do I need to say? He went to Conques, he related the vision to the monastic officials, he bought the candles, he placed them in front of the altars, and he kept the vigil near the most holy martyr's golden image.

At about midnight it seemed to Guibert that he saw two light-filled globes like berries, scarcely larger than the fruit of the laurel tree, which were sent from above and driven deeply into the sockets of his excised eyes. The force of the impact disturbed his brain and in a state of bewilderment he fell asleep. But when they were singing the praises of matins he was awakened by the choir and the loud voices of those chanting the psalms, and it seemed to him that he could make out the shadowy forms of shining lamps and people moving about. But because of the pain in his head he had almost forgotten who he was. Since he could hardly believe the truth, he thought he was dreaming. Finally the dullness that had taken over his brain gradually disappeared, and he began to make out the shapes of things more clearly. Scarcely returned to full consciousness, he recalled his vision, and reaching up with his hands he touched the windows of his reborn light with their perfectly restored pupils. Immediately he summoned witnesses and proclaimed the immeasurable greatness of Christ with boundless praise. Therefore there was unutterable joy, unimaginable gladness, incredible bewilderment. They didn't know what to think, especially those who had known Guibert before – should they understand such an unheard-of miracle as the fancy of a dream or as a true event?

In the midst of all this something happened that was amusing and richly deserving of laughter, for, since Guibert was a very simple and unsophisticated man, unnecessary and fearful anxiety crept into his heart. He was afraid that by chance the man who had once wrenched out his eyes had attended the liturgical celebration (which, as usual, was public), and that, if he should encounter the priest, then Gerald, relying on his greater force, would once more destroy the renewed glory of his eyes. Because of this fear and because the confused racket of the crowd reacting to the miracle made it possible, he slipped away secretly. The bewilderment of it all had taken such possession of him that he wasn't yet fully certain about the gift of regained sight. In the press of the crowd converging on the church, now in clear daylight, he bumped against a donkey standing in the way. When he had looked at it, he scolded severely: "Hey there, whoever you are, you fool, get your donkey out of the way or people will stumble over it." This was when he fully accepted the truth of what had happened. Then Guibert fled swiftly to a warrior he knew, whose castle was located on a high cliff. Nature had fortified it on all sides so that it seemed inaccessible to every kind of siege machine. This stronghold was not more than 16 miles from Conques. Guibert took refuge there because of the protection of its impregnable walls, and only with difficulty and with many a prayer was he extracted by the monks. He returned only when he was assured of complete security. Because of the unusual miracle, a great many people from both near and far flocked to see him, vying with one another in their haste. As they left they demonstrated their joy by conferring on him many pious donations. And, as I said, this is what Saint Foy told him when she appeared to him in the vision, "1000 people whom you have never seen are going to give you alms." As is customary in the scriptures, she used a definite number to indicate an indefinite one. In order to provide easier access to the miracle and to give Guibert a more established place to live, Abbot Arladus of blessed memory, with the unanimous consent of the brothers, put him in charge of selling wax, a large amount of which was sold there due to the bountiful hand of God. From these sales he received much profit and he began – for it is in the nature of humankind – to grow arrogant. He found a likeminded and unchaste woman, and immediately he forgot the greatness of the miracle done for him. But then, so that he shouldn't go unpunished for profaning the miracle, suddenly the holy virgin's avenging displeasure was at hand. She blinded him in one eye, but did not utterly destroy it. Then she led him back to the cure of repentance and healed him for the second time with renewed sight. But when he slipped back again and again into his habitual hog wallowing, divine vengeance soon followed: he lost the sight of one eye and repenting, recovered. For every time this happened, I would have been able to write a little chapter of miracles, if I hadn't avoided a taste for redundancy. But finally, because he had fallen into the same behavior without interruption, Guibert lost the service of the other eye. Then, in order to repent of his faults more completely, he shaved his beard, had his head tonsured, and, seeking to become a monk, gave himself over to the order. Although he did this as an ignorant and unlettered person, nevertheless it pleased divine mercy so much that he was fortunate enough to regain his eyesight. But even after so many chastising scourges Guibert was still unable to restrain his lust. It is reported that he sank into the same mire, although no bodily punishment followed. Now he is an old man, impoverished and held in contempt because of his shameless activity. He lives on the common dole provided by the brothers and is content with very little, very often just with an evening meal. He rejoices merely in easing his hunger, safe from the trouble of all his folly.

I bear witness to divine providence that in writing this text I have kept to the truth as I received it from Guibert himself. It is free of any deceitful lies, and I haven't added more than is proper to render it suitable. Moreover I don't imagine that I would be able to escape unpunished if I thought that Saint Foy herself – beloved and perpetual friend of God – would rejoice at praise from a lying pen, when it is undisputed that she underwent the grievous sentence of martyrdom on behalf of the truth which is Christ. Finally, it is well known that many whose authority is generally accepted were content to skillfully describe marvelous events much previous to their time, when the source was only one oral informant who wasn't even present when the thing happened. Then why should I allow something that happens in my own time to go unrecorded in the accounts of history when I even see it myself with my eyes, and Auvergne, the Rouergue, the Toulousain, and all the rest of the people offer their unshakeable witness to it? I must consider my duty as a teacher, especially when, as I said before, the very indifference of writers – which is the reason that such an insignificant little man as myself presumes such perilous and difficult material – vehemently compels me. For if even a rare literary scholar is found anywhere in this country, he either disdains to write down material like this for his own reasons or he does not appreciate the nature of the material and disregards it entirely. Or it could be because of slothful laziness or ignorance in composition. And even supposing that there were a great many people who took pride in the expression of their skill, those who assert that they are highly skilled reveal themselves, by the very act of self-praise, to be the least competent.

Therefore I have resolved rather to be blamed for daring too much than to incur the guilt of negligence. I will devote myself to putting in writing only recent and true events, which, if they were left to be written by those who come later, could never be considered free of doubt, and truth would thereby be injured. And so that there should be no uncertainty about believing this story, when Guibert was deprived of his eyes God in his mercy did not heal him immediately but, as mentioned above, he left Guibert blind for a whole year. He called the attention of a good many inhabitants of the province to the blind man through Guibert's skill as a jongleur, and, after all of the people were aware of his blindness, then God healed him. This miracle is in no way inferior to the one told in the Gospel about the man born blind, and in fact it is much more marvelous by far, since truth herself, who is Christ, promised that his followers would certainly do greater things than he, for he said: "He who believes in me shall also do the works that I do, and greater than these, because I go to the Father."...

1.9. Since the Lord favored me by letting me see something that had a divine cause, as people say in the celebrated monastery at Conques, I will describe it here in the middle of my work. Among the flood of pilgrims who had poured into Conques from various regions, one woman, a widow, kept vigil through the night to pray that her blind daughter would be healed. While the daughter was keeping the night's watch in prayer with her mother, during the first vigil of the night the eyesight she had lost was wholly restored through the power of Saint Foy. The monks who watched over the relics and some of the monks who were taking their turn officiating at night, according to the custom there, saw what had happened. At once they all began to run swiftly to my lodgings. And because they knew that I longed to witness a new miracle, they exhausted one another in their eagerness to report it to me.

"Look! For you, fortunate Bernard, a miracle, a miracle from Saint Foy!" they said. "This is what you have been praying for, what you wished would be shown to you before your departure. You thought it wasn't fair that, when you came so far intending to write miracles, you weren't seeing any yourself." For I had explained the reason for my pilgrimage to the monks when I arrived. They received me with proper hospitality and provided everything I needed to carry out my vow, even assigning me excellent servants who obeyed my orders as long as I was there. I quickly leapt out of my bed, for I had already lain down, and in my joy I hurried out at what, I confess, was not a decorous pace. I entered the monastery, and I saw that the girl could see and could make out the lights of candles. And she even noticed my hand, in which I offered a denier [coin] to that impoverished girl. When she saw it, she received it with thanks.

It is not in my power to describe how many and what kind of miracles happened there continually in regard to various infirmities through divine compassion. A little while before my arrival, eleven people who were gravely afflicted with a variety of ills were completely restored to health in only one night. If I heeded all the miracles worked there daily for the sick, I would have gathered a huge library. I have concentrated on the miracles that were worked to take revenge on evil-doers or on those that are in some way new and unusual, and have greatly abridged them in order to bring out a small but precious volume. But there may be some that I will hear later that need to be included. If so, I shall add them to my second book....

1.18. A noble woman who heard of the renown of Saint Foy's miracles decided to go to Conques. After she had gone a short distance on her journey, she recalled that Saint Foy had a habit of appearing to pilgrims in dreams and asking for their rings. So she turned back, drew her own ring from her finger, and entrusted it for safekeeping to the chambermaid whom she had summoned. "Hold this," she said, "and keep it safe until I return, for Saint Foy may snatch it away from me if I take it from Conques." Now, of course, she thought she was being clever – as if to think that any kind of precaution would be able to deflect the foreknowledge of God, who foresees all things before they happen! What more is there to say? The woman went to Conques, she said the prayers she had promised to say there, and she returned home in peace. On the following night, a maidenly shape appeared to her while she was sleeping. When asked, she said she was Saint Foy and, without pausing, warned with imperious authority that the ring had best be given to her. When the woman denied that she had a ring, Saint Foy reminded her that she was the very woman who, when leaving for Conques, had entrusted her ring to a chambermaid in order to avoid giving it to Saint Foy. When morning came and the woman awoke she decided that the divine vision had only been a fantasy, a meaningless dream. But how much longer will I delay the end of my story? Immediately the woman began to burn with such a fiery fever through her whole body that she could scarcely rest for even an hour. After three days of fever she realized what was happening, remembered her offense, and confessed that she had slighted Saint Foy. While she was ordering that a horse be saddled so that she could make a return journey, the excessive surge of fever abated. And so the woman set out healthy and returned rejoicing, counting it not a small gain to exchange a ring for her health.

1.19. The Lord had already deigned to work so many miracles of this kind through Saint Foy that no one could have preserved all of them, and there isn't enough time for anyone to write out those that have been preserved. Nonetheless, I want to add a few miracles from those that I noted down as they were told to me, because I don't want to appear too taciturn by remaining silent, or too annoying by being too wordy. I know the proverb from before our time that says everything uncommon is precious. And this is why, in comparison to all the remaining miracles, I write the uncommon miracles, because they are precious. Therefore Christ will pardon me for knowingly omitting a great many miracles.

Arsinde was the wife of William, count of Toulouse, brother of the Pons who had later been treacherously killed by Artaud, his own stepson. She owned golden bracelets, which should really be called armlets, since they reached up to the elbow. They were embellished with marvelous craftsmanship and with precious gems. Once when Arsinde was lying alone on her own fine couch she had a dream in which she saw what appeared to be the form of a very beautiful girl passing right in front of her. Because Arsinde admired the girl for her very great elegance, she addressed her with a question: "Tell me, lady, what are you?" Saint Foy answered the humbly inquiring voice: "I am Saint Foy, woman, don't doubt it." At that moment Saint Foy made the inquisitive woman familiar with the business on which she had come: "Give me your golden bracelets. Go to Conques and place them above the altar of Saint Savior. This is the reason I have sought out your presence."

But the prudent woman wouldn't allow such a great gift to leave her hands without some advantage for herself, so she said: "Oh holy mistress, if through your intercession God grants that I conceive a male child I will carry out your command with pleasure." Saint Foy answered her: "The omnipotent Creator will do this quite easily for his own handmaiden, if you do not refuse what I ask." On the next day Arsinde, who was motivated by the saint's reply, conducted an eager and thorough search to determine in what district the village called Conques was located, for only rarely had news of the miracles at Conques passed beyond its own borders. When Arsinde had learned this from those who knew, she performed the duty of a pilgrim herself. She carried the golden bracelets to Conques with the highest devotion and offered them to God and his saint. And there the worthy woman spent some days of the Lord's resurrection honorably and adorned the ceremonies with her gift. Then she returned home. As the divine vision had promised, she conceived and bore a son. And she became pregnant again and gave birth to another. Afterward the gold of the bracelets was used in the work of the altar frontal.

1.20. It delights me to disclose another occasion on which Saint Foy wrested a golden ring away from a woman. Although her husband had forbidden it, this woman had come to Saint Foy out of her great devotion. When she had left the monastery and returned to the guesthouse she met with such sudden pains, for she was near childbirth, that she seemed about to die. The wretched woman didn't know what to do. She had no hope of giving birth at the right time, and if she gave birth prematurely she wouldn't dare to return to her husband. In her great sorrow and anxiety she began to appeal to Saint Foy with repeated cries, imploring the saint to be well-disposed toward her. But in the end, when the pains did not ease, she was carried back into the monastery by faithful porters and there she drew her ring from her finger and offered it to God and his saint on behalf of her health. The intervention of the merciful martyr, so powerful and efficacious, relieved her pain immediately. And so she walked out of the church on her own feet in that very hour, as merry and healthy as she had been a short time before. She went back to the guesthouse and, before she could be prevented by the birth that was at hand, she returned joyfully to her home.

1.21. A young man named William, a native of Auvergne, was worried about a distressing situation and filled with unbearable anxiety, so he vowed to Saint Foy his best ring, which was set with a brilliant green jasper. Things turned out for him better than he had hoped in the matter, and everything else was prospering as well, so William went to Conques because he was concerned to fulfill the vow he owed. But when he had approached the sacred majesty, William brought out and presented three coins, for he calculated that he should be able to redeem the promised gift with one that was larger even though it was different. When he was already about six miles from Conques on his return journey, William suddenly felt drowsy, so he stretched out on the ground and fell asleep for a little while. He soon awakened, but he didn't see his ring, which until now he had worn on his finger. Then he searched his companions thoroughly and very closely but he didn't find it anywhere, and he looked in his own clothing and found nothing. He even proceeded to untie his belt once more, thinking that by chance it might have slipped through an inner fold of his clothing, and there was nothing. What, then, should he do? Downcast and filled with confusion he turned his mount back toward Conques. He returned very quickly to the saint and prostrated himself at the foot of her image. There, in a tearful voice, he complained bitterly about the loss of his ring in this way:

"O Saint Foy, why have you taken my ring from me? Give it back to me, I implore you, and be satisfied with the ring as a gift. I will give it to you and won't think it lost, but rather safe. I have sinned, I confess, I have sinned before God and before you, but, Lady, do not look to my transgression but to the customary compassion of your kindness. Do not cast me, a sinner, into sadness, but forgive and make a gift return with joy." While William was constantly repeating these and other similar pleas, he looked to the side.

Marvelous to report! but believable to the faithful, he saw his ring lying on the pavement. Immediately he snatched it up and returned it to the holy virgin, rejoicing greatly, and those who were standing there marveled at the sight, for they saw Saint Foy's power even in trifling matters....

3.2. At about the same time an unheard-of miracle happened, one that demands reverence from all mortals. If we didn't believe that nothing is impossible for God, this miracle would seem entirely incredible. Pilgrims were coming to the holy martyr's monastery church from the province that was called in former times Interclusana. They were going in great numbers along the fixed route through a marketplace called Saban, which is about two miles from the city of Albi. In this place a river flows in the narrow channel it has carved and descends into a gorge in a series of steep falls. Churning in great turmoil, it plunges over the falls in a manner terrifying to onlookers. From these great falls the water leaps back up, forming a huge cloud of vapor that is carried on the winds. These falls are so filled with noise, with roaring, with so much mist, that they are believed by all to be more of an infernal Gehenna than anything else. People say that Saint Salvius, bishop of Albi, once cast down into this great chasm the malignant spirits that he had driven out of the city, and that the foul mistiness that fills the gorge from the bottom to the top is due to their presence. The gorge is inaccessible not only to the feet but even to the human gaze. Nevertheless, travelers cross the river where it is gripped between steep cliffs that constrict it into a narrow torrent. They cross above the falls on a little wickerwork bridge placed over the river; trembling with acute fear, they hurry across swiftly.

After they had completed their prayers at Saint Foy's abbey church, the pilgrims from Interclusana arrived at this river. While all the rest were crossing over the gorge safely, one of the donkeys bringing up the rear caught its foot up the haunch between the lattices of the bridge and lay reclining on the wickerwork in great danger. As its master approached to help the donkey, it pulled its foot out of the hole with powerful force, struck its master in the chest with its hooves, and knocked him down headlong into the destruction of the falls. The swirling mass of water, a large whirlpool, swallowed him up and kept him immersed for an hour. All were stunned by this, both his companions and the merchants who conducted business in the marketplace there. In a packed crowd they took up positions on both banks of the river and with a great many abuses they blamed Christ's holy martyr Foy, from whose abbey church the pilgrim had been returning. They pushed forward to gain a position from which they would be able to see the limbs of his lacerated body drifting on top of the water. Far beyond the gorge the river spreads out into a wide stream and slides through its bed with gentle waters. While people were standing on both sides of its banks in numbers beyond measure, one man directed his glance towards the frothing water and caught sight of the crown of a head which looked like a little bird swimming. And he soon pointed out the sight to the others with his finger. Carried along by the current, the pilgrim was soon brought near to the shore and grabbed hold of a pole that someone held out to him. And so, still very much alive and suffering no injury from his great headlong fall, he escaped the danger of death. His right arm had been entwined in the strap of the satchel he was carrying, so he did not suffer its loss, for God preserved it. When they saw this, all drenched the shores with tears of joy and praised the magnificence of God. They proclaimed Saint Foy's omnipotent power with splendid declarations of praise. They spoke truly when they maintained that the pilgrim had been plucked out of death's abyss by her sustaining right hand....

3.24. Yet another miracle remains, and I have decided to end this book by recording it. In Albigeois there is a castle called Thuriès. As Christmas neared, a fighting man from that castle named Regimbald was coming to Saint Foy's abbey church. But Regimbald's journey was interrupted by a grievous circumstance: he was taken captive by a priest named Hadimar, who hated him, and confined in chains. Regimbald gave his pledge that he would return to captivity and traveled on to the holy martyr's basilica. There, prostrate on the ground, he made known to her all the bitterness in his heart and the harm he would suffer in captivity. With steadfast prayers he demanded that she come to his assistance. After the feast of Christmas had been celebrated, Regimbald gave himself up to captivity and returned to his chains. But he who "lifts up those who are cast down" and "looses those who are fettered" struck Hadimar from the soles of his feet to the top of his head with a wretched malady so that Regimbald would be freed from the bonds of his chains. Hadimar's sores ran with a discharge so foul that his whole household found it intolerable.

Hadimar freed his captive, who had fulfilled his pledge by returning to him. Then, because he could not walk on the stony path, Hadimar went on horseback to the holy virgin's church. When he arrived there, with sincere groans he confessed his guilt to the holy martyr and to all the monks. Then he began to beat himself severely, to expiate the crime to which he had confessed. After he had humbly completed vows and prayers, Hadimar returned home. God's compassion had cured him, so that after a modest interval his swelling disappeared completely. Wholly recovered, he purchased provisions for a journey and set out for Jerusalem. God granted him a successful pilgrimage and on his return he came to the holy virgin's abbey church. He faithfully pledged himself to her and to all the monks and from then on he honored his pledge by visiting there frequently.

Why did Bernard of Angers decide to record Foy's miracles? What did he experience when he first arrived at Conques? What sort of people sought Foy's help? What does the fate of Guibert or the pilgrim who fell into the falls imply about Foy's treatment of those who came to seek her miraculous intercession? What happened to the pilgrims who tried to avoid giving their rings to Saint Foy? What evidence does this account offer that the monks who maintained Foy's cult and her pilgrims lived in a particularly violent world?

34. A PENITENT PILGRIM IN IRONS

Although the practice of binding pilgrims in bands of iron or chains as a form of penance was not new around the turn of the eleventh century, the increased traffic of pilgrims during this period included more instances of that particular kind of devotional traveler. The account below of an English woman named Godelinda, bound by two iron bands about her left arm, was written at the shrine of Saint Mansuetus in Toul by an anonymous monk in 1009.

Source: trans. B.E. Whalen, from *Miracula s. Mansueti*, in *Acta Sanctorum*, vol. 41 (Paris: Apud Victorem Palme, 1863–), pp. 651–52.

From the lands across the sea [England], there came a certain woman named Godelinda, whose parents were both English. She wore bonds of iron on her left arm, not because she was possessed by a demon, but rather on account of her spilling of paternal blood. How this came to pass, we plan to explain right away. She had a father of noble birth, and a mother who was not inferior in her own birth, blessed by the dignity of their ancestry and surrounded by the offspring of their sons. Death carried off the father, who, not unmindful of his children, called upon their mother; with his dying words, but of clear mind, he begged her to watch over the flock of their children with maternal affection. Soon after her husband died, it became clear that all of his words had fallen on deaf ears. Taking her children's home, surrendering their paternal right, she again joined herself [in marriage] to an ill-fated spouse. The new husband tried to destroy her children, expelling them from their rightful places just like strangers, except for the woman (whom we spoke of earlier), since her feminine sex protected the young lady from being cast out of her proper lodgings. Finally, one of them, a cleric, who could not withstand this injury any further, raised his hand against his step-father in parricide. The aforementioned sister offered to join him, moved grievously to fraternal misery. Thereupon, a nightly assault was prepared, unknown to anyone except for her brother. When her brother hastened to rush in, she opened the entrance to the castle for him. Behold, when the stepson with his companions forcefully invaded the house where the stepfather was sleeping, the entrance was immediately flooded [by them] and anyone in their way was cut down by those rushing in. Meanwhile, the stepfather awoke and rose from his deathbed: both [the daughter and the son] proceeded to the doorway of the bedroom; he [the father] was struck by horror seeing them in the doorway. When the cleric saw his enemy approaching, plucking up his courage combined with his inner-rage, with the weight of his entire body behind him, he thrust out his spear with an unspeakable force. The father, quick on his feet, avoided the thrust and tried to flee; but the woman standing behind him wrapped her arms around his chest. Soon, wounded by the son, he [the father] breathed out his last, pouring forth his blood.

Bound on the inside by this crime, the aforementioned cleric was enchained on the outside by his bishop with penitential irons, the entire trunk of his body wrapped up tight with metal bonds. What's more, the sister, who had consented to this wicked evil, received two irons on her left arm, so that she might render satisfaction for her unheard of evil deed by this lamentable penalty. Then, together, they set out for Jerusalem. En route, the brother surrendered his earthly life. Giving thought to her situation, weakened by her long squalor, she turned her direction toward our sanctuary. Why linger on this matter with too many words? She committed herself to our father, Mansuetus. Immediately, beseeching his mercy with whole-hearted effort, she continued for several days with unstoppable prayer, but Mansuetus opposed her crime with invisible arms. At last, the strength of the iron dissolved, as corrosion broke the bonds so that her arm under the bondage of the two-fold chains was partly freed, since her spirit was entirely held at the tomb as a means of expiation. The other bond, however, did not fall off, so that it might be clearly shown that the saint, who already had partially blotted out her crime, partially delayed blotting it out entirely. Yet she, immediately taking up the pilgrim's staff, set out to seek the merits of Saint Oldericus, looking to go with devout mind to his shrine, where his body resplendently rests at Vosages. With her came a lay brother named Rodulf, who had come with her out of the goodness of his heart, although he was in no way implicated in the contagion of her crime. Therefore, when she had reached the forests of Vosages, at the threshold of St-Deodatus, a unique healing power offered itself to her, namely, the appearance of a young Mansuetus in a dream, who instructed her with a command for her own good that she should return [to his shrine]. Nevertheless, spurning this vision and setting out on the start of her journey, she acted wantonly and proceeded instead to the city of Strasbourg.

Therefore, the saint, making a more attentive return visit to her in her sleep, informed her that she would labor under increasing dangers if she tried to head any further down the prohibited path. Hearing the litany of his words, disobedient Godelinda, filled with guile, set out on the quickest road to persist in what she was doing. Following the saint's words, a great trouble came to pass: the fraudulence of thieves fell violently upon her, as did the considerable bother of shivering, frigid cold, mixed with the misery of extreme heat and a lack of provisions. To conclude this short summary of her torments, she violated Lent by eating cheese and other tidbits. Thus, relenting, the terrified woman turned back from the audacious path that the noble Mansuetus had forbidden her. The terrified woman, compelled by her bitter sufferings, returned and persevered with her watchful vows, imploring the saint by name with deep breaths and sighs; as the brothers carried out the evening vigils for the Lord, she offered constant tears with a single heart until at last she groaned aloud to the highest, and bellowed with a deplorable cry: "O," she said, "Saint Mansuetus, why do you cause this misery? Why do you allow this pilgrim to be semi-chained? Surely, if I might say so, you are giving men the opportunity to see the shame of your imperfection? In the future, departing from you, I will suffer a slow death, poor me! I will be proven as a stranger to longed-for salvation!"

She said these grievous things on both knees and, wailing, stepped away from the altar; she desired, as accustomed, to go to the sleeping-quarters. Suddenly, the iron leapt off, cracking, so that the sound of it struck the ears of the church's custodians. Immediately, she fell to the ground, breathless and at once struck mute, lying there as if all the blood had left her, her neck bent and her head face-up. The janitor of the church found her, looking to all the world as if she were lifeless; therefore, he went to inform the father of the monastery by making gestures (since he was under a vow of silence). He rushed there, concerned, and with prying fingers tried to lift up the iron, which he was scarcely able to cast aside with all of his efforts. After about the space of an hour, she felt the return of her spirit in her breast and sensed that her expiation was entirely complete, feeling her arm freed from the iron. Asking permission from her liberator, she joyfully returned home. The aforesaid bonds – the first of which tumbled off on the kalends of January, and the other on the 13th kalends of June in the year of our Lord 1009, when lord Berthold was bishop of the church of Toul in the 7th indiction – lie at the feet of [an effigy of] our crucified Lord.

Based on Godelinda's crime, how serious a form of penance was the binding of pilgrims in irons? How might onlookers have reacted when they saw such a pilgrim? How did

Godelinda manage to free herself partially from her bonds? What happened when she left the shrine of Mansuetus and refused to follow his directions? How was she ultimately freed from the remainder of her iron bonds? Does this account suggest that saints, according to medieval belief, could be jealous and obstinate, as well as protective figures?

35. THE DESTRUCTION OF THE HOLY SEPULCHER

Around 1009 or 1010, the Fatimid caliph of Cairo, al-Hākim, ordered the church of the Holy Sepulcher in Jerusalem to be destroyed. This action formed part of his broader policy of intolerance toward non-Muslims, including both Christians and Jews. When news of this event reached Western Europe, chroniclers such as Rodulfus Glaber and Adhémar of Chabannes presented this attack on one of the holiest pilgrimage sites of Christendom as part of a conspiracy between the Jews and the Muslims, intended to destroy the most holy places of Christendom.

Sources: Rodulfus Glaber, trans. J. France, in *The Five Books of the Histories* (Oxford: Clarendon Press, 1989), pp. 133, 135, 137; Adhémar of Chabannes, trans. B.E. Whalen, from *Chronicon Ademari Cabannensis*, ed. P. Bourgain, Corpus Christianorum: Continuatio Mediaevalis, vol. 129 (Turnhout: Brepols, 1999), pp. 166–67.

Rodulfus Glaber, Book Four

7.24. In the same ninth year after the millennium, the church at Jerusalem, which contained the sepulcher of our Lord and savior, was destroyed at the command of the prince of Cairo. This is known to have begun in the way I am about to describe. Because of the fame of this monument, great multitudes of the faithful from all over the world were drawn to Jerusalem. Therefore, the devil, driven by envy, sought to pour out the venom of his malice upon the practitioners of the true faith by using his accustomed instruments, the Jews. There were a great many of that race in Orléans, the royal city of Gaul, and they are notorious for being even more arrogant, envious, and insolent than the rest of their brethren. They conceived a dastardly plot: they bribed one Robert, a fugitive serf from the house of Moutiers-Sainte-Marie, who was no more than a vagabond masquerading as a pilgrim. With infinite precaution they sent him to the prince of Cairo with letters written in the Hebrew alphabet; the parchment strips were hidden inside the iron of his staff lest he should be robbed. The fellow set off and delivered these letters, which were full of evil and lies: they alleged that if he did not quickly destroy the venerable church of the Christians, then they would soon occupy his whole realm, depriving him of all his power.

When the prince heard this he was transported with rage, and he sent some of his servants to Jerusalem to destroy the church. Once there they did as he commanded, but when they tried to shatter the block of stone about the sepulcher with iron hammers, they failed. Then they also destroyed the church of the holy martyr George at Ramla, although previously his power had always terrified the Saracens, for it is said that he often struck blind those who invaded his church in search of plunder. A little while after the temple had been destroyed it became quite clear that the wickedness of the Jews had brought about this great disaster. Once they knew this all the Christians throughout the whole world decided unanimously to drive the Jews from their lands and cities. They became the objects of universal hatred; they were driven from the cities, some were put to the sword, others were drowned in rivers, and many found other deaths; some even took their own lives in diverse ways. So it was that after this very proper vengeance had been taken, very few of them were to be found in the Roman world. Then the bishops proclaimed that no Christian could have any kind of dealing with them. They exempted from this section those who wished to convert to the grace of baptism and renounce all Jewish customs and ways. Many of these only did this through fear of death, out of love of this present life rather than aspiration after eternal joy. For all those who had thus falsely demanded to be made Christians soon shamelessly returned to their former state.

7.25. After all this the bearer of the letters, filled with false confidence, returned to his native soil. He began carefully to see if he could find anyone of the Jewish race that was implicated in his evil deeds. Finding only a few living in terror in the city of Orléans, he again began to share their lot as a friend. It so happened that a pilgrim who had been of his company on the journey across the sea and who knew all about the reasons for his voyage came to that city. When he saw that Robert was again cultivating excessively the friendship of Jews, he denounced the wretch in the sight of all as the bearer of such evil, and revealed why he was in possession of Jewish wealth. After he had been arrested and severely beaten, he confessed to his criminal act of tale-bearing; then the royal officers, in the sight of all the people, bore him away to a place outside the city where he was thrown into the flames and perished. The dispersed and wandering Jews who had survived this affliction remained hidden in distant and secret places until five years after the destruction of the Temple, when a few began to reappear in the cities. For it was proper, although ultimately to their confusion, that some of them should survive for the future to serve as witnesses of their own perfidy, or testimony to the blood of Christ which they had shed. That is why, we believe, thanks to the disposition of divine providence, the fury of the Christian people against them was for a moment cooled. In that same year, by divine clemency, the mother of that prince, the emir of Cairo, a truly Christian woman called Maria, began with well-dressed square stones to rebuild the temple of Christ, which had been destroyed by the command of her son. Her husband, the father of the fellow we have been writing about here, was like another Nicodemus, for it is said that he was secretly a Christian. Then an incredible multitude of men from all over the world came exultantly to Jerusalem bearing countless gifts for the restoration of the house of God.

Adhémar of Chabannes

3.47. In that same year, the sepulcher of the Lord at Jerusalem was overturned by the Jews and Saracens, on the third kalends of October, 1000, and 10 years from his incarnation. For the Jews in the West and the Saracens in Spain had sent letters to the East, railing against the Christians and claiming that an army of Franks was coming to fight against the eastern Saracens. Then Nabuchodnosor of Babylon [Caliph al-Hakim of Cairo], whom they call emir, moved to anger by the urging of the pagans, unleashed a considerable persecution against the Christians, issuing a law that any Christians living under his power who refused to become Saracens should either be killed or have their property seized. So it happened that many Christians were converted to the Saracens' law and nobody was worthy enough to die for Christ, except for the patriarch of Jerusalem, tortured in various ways and killed, and two young cousins in Egypt, who had their heads cut off (and who openly displayed many miracles). The church of St-George, which no Saracen had ever been able to violate up until that point, was destroyed at that time along with many other churches of the saints; due to our sins, the church of the Lord's sepulcher was razed to the ground. Yet they were by no means able to fracture a stone of the monument, even when they set a great fire: it remained strong and solid like iron.

When they attempted to destroy the church at Bethlehem, where Christ was born, a radiant light suddenly shone forth upon them, and the great crowd of pagans fell to the ground and died. In a similar manner, the church of the mother of God [Saint Mary] remained intact. Also, around 10,000 armed Saracens issued forth against the monastery of Mount Sinai, where more than 50 monks lived under the authority of their abbot and had their own bishop there, in order to kill the monks and destroy their dwelling places along with their churches. When they were drawing about four miles away, they saw the entire mountain burning and covered with smoke, flames rising to heaven; everything set in place there including the men remained safe and sound. When they had related this to the king of Babylon, who was led to seek forgiveness, both he and the Saracen people greatly grieved about the things which they had done against the Christians. Issuing a command, he ordered the basilica of the glorious sepulcher to be rebuilt. Nevertheless when rebuilt, resembling the earlier one, it was not greater in size or beauty compared with what Helena, mother of Constantine, had accomplished at royal expense. Soon thereafter, famine broke out in every land of the Saracens for three years and an innumerable multitude perished from hunger; men became food, buried in the open for the wild beasts and the birds. There followed a devastation among them by the sword. For, peoples from Arabia spread throughout their lands, slaughtering those who had survived hunger with swords. The king of Babylon, who in his pride had set himself against God, was captured by them and, while still alive, had his stomach cut open and his guts torn out, sending his wicked soul to hell. His stomach, filled with stones, was sewn up and his body thrown in the sea, lead tied around his neck.

What role did Rodulfus Glaber assign to the Jews of Europe in the destruction of the Holy Sepulcher? According to his report, what was the result of their actions? According to Adhémar, what happened to the Muslims who tried to destroy the church in Bethlehem at the site of Christ's birth? Imagine a Christian pilgrim about to set out for Jerusalem when he or she heard rumors about the Holy Sepulcher's destruction: how might that pilgrim have reacted?

36. MILLENNIAL DEVOTION AND PILGRIMAGE TO THE HOLY LAND

In addition to spurring local pilgrimage and devotion to the saints, the "evangelical awakening" of the eleventh century witnessed the growth and intensification of religious travel to Jerusalem and its surroundings. According to the chronicler Rodulfus Glaber (docs. 32 and 35), this upswing in Christian pilgrimage to the Promised Land involved greater numbers and different kinds of people than beforehand. For some observers, he reports, the floods of people visiting the Holy Sepulcher of Christ offered a sign that the end of days approached, when Jerusalem would form the stage for an apocalyptic drama between the faithful and the forces of evil.

Source: trans. J. France, in Rodulfus Glaber, *The Five Books of the Histories* (Oxford: Clarendon Press, 1989), pp. 199, 201, 203, 205.

Book Four

6.18. At this time an innumerable multitude of people from the whole world, greater than any man before could have hoped to see, began to travel to the sepulcher of the Savior at Jerusalem. First to go were the petty people, then those of middling estate, and next the powerful, kings, counts, marquesses, and bishops; finally, and this was something which had never happened before, numerous women, noble and poor, undertook the journey. Many wished to die there before they returned to their own lands. A certain Burgundian called Lethbaud, from the region of Autun, went on this journey in the company of others. When he had seen these most holy of places, he went to the Mount of Olives from where the Savior, before many credible witnesses, ascended into heaven, with the promise that he would return to judge both the quick and the dead. Our pilgrim threw himself to the ground, his arms extended in the form of a cross, and with many tears he exulted in the Lord with indescribable joy. Repeatedly he stood up, raising his body with all his might, extending his arms to heaven and in a loud voice revealing the desires of his heart: "Lord Jesus, who for us and our salvation didst deign to come down from the seat of thy majesty to earth, and who, from this place which I now behold, didst return, still clad in the flesh, to heaven whence thou earnest, I beseech thee by the plenitude of thy goodness, if this year is to be my last, let me not return to my own land but let it come to be accomplished in the sight of this, the place of thy Ascension. I believe that, just as I have followed thee in the body to come to this place, so my soul, unharmed and rejoicing, will follow after thee into heaven." The prayer finished, he returned with his companions to the hostel. It was then dinner-time. The others went to table, but he, with a smiling face, went to bed as though he were feeling very tired and wished to take a little rest. No one knows what he dreamt as he slept, but suddenly he cried out in his sleep: "Glory be to thee, O God! Glory be to thee, O God!" Hearing this, his companions urged him to get up and eat. But he refused, turned over on the other side, and said that he did not feel well; he rested till evening, then, calling together his companions of the journey, he asked for and received the viaticum of the life-giving eucharist, sweetly bade all farewell, and died. Truly he was free from that vanity which inspires so many to undertake the journey simply to gain the prestige of having been to Jerusalem. In the name of the Lord Jesus Christ he faithfully made petition to the Father, and this was granted. His companions, on their return, told this story to us when we were at the monastery of Bèze.

6.19. At the same time Ulric bishop of Orléans undertook this journey; and he told us about a miracle which should not be passed over. On the day of that great sabbath when all the people gathered together to await the holy fire wondrously lit by the power of God, he was amongst them. Evening was drawing in when suddenly, just at the time when the fire was to appear, a Saracen [Muslim], truly an impudent jester, one of the crowd of that race which every year gathers and mixes with the Christians, cried out in the manner of the Christians when the fire is first seen: "Aios Kyrie Eleison [Holy Lord, have mercy upon us]." Then, laughing aloud mockingly he reached out and snatched a candle from the hand of one of the Christians and made to flee. But he was seized by a demon who much troubled him. The Christian followed him and took back his candle. The fellow at once died in agony in the hands of the other Saracens. This event terrified all the Saracens alike, but brought joy and exaltation to the Christians. At this very moment, as is customary, by the power of God the fire burst from one of the seven lamps seen hanging there, and swiftly it ignited the others. The bishop bought this lamp and its oil from Jordan, then patriarch of Jerusalem, for a pound of gold, and took it back with him to his own see, where it provided many benefits for the sick. He also brought back for King Robert [II of France] a substantial portion of the holy cross of the Lord our savior, a present from Constantine, emperor of the Greeks, who also sent a great many silken hangings. The king had sent him by this bishop a sword with a golden hilt, and a reliquary of gold set with precious gems.

6.20. Amongst others at this time, Robert duke of Normandy went to Jerusalem with a great many of his people, bearing many gifts of gold and silver as offerings. He died on his way back at the city of Nicaea, and there he was buried. It was a cause of great distress amongst his people that he had no legitimate child to succeed him in the government of this province. As is well known, he had married a sister of Cnut king of the English, but he so disliked the woman that he divorced her. However, by a concubine he had engendered a son whom he called William after one of his ancestors. Before he departed he constrained all the princes of his dukedom to swear an oath on their honor as warriors: by this they promised to elect him in his stead if he failed to return. Immediately this was unanimously put into effect with the agreement of Henry [I] king of the French. This had been the custom of this people since it first appeared in Gaul, as we noted earlier, to take as princes offspring born of similar unions with concubines; but lest this be regarded as too extreme an abomination, we may compare the case of the sons of Jacob by concubines, who were not for that reason deprived of their honors by their father and indeed, like their brothers, were made patriarchs. Long after, in the last years of the universal monarchy, we read that Constantine, the great pioneer of the Christian faith in the empire, was born of a concubine, Helena.

6.21. When some consulted the more watchful of the age as to what was meant by so many people, in numbers unheard-of in earlier ages, going to Jerusalem, some replied cautiously enough that it could portend nothing other than the advent of the accursed Antichrist who, according to divine testimony, is expected to appear at the end of the world. Then a way would be opened for all peoples to the east where he would appear, and all nations would march against him without delay. In fact then will be fulfilled that prophecy of the Lord, that even the elect will, if it is possible, fall into temptation. We will speak no further of this matter, but we do not deny that the pious labors of the faithful will be then rewarded and paid for by the Just Judge.

What sort of people went on pilgrimage to Jerusalem around the year 1000? What happened to the pilgrim who prayed to Christ that he might finish his life at the place of the Lord's ascension? What happened to the "Saracen" who mocked the Christians during the miracle of the Eastern fire? Based on this account, does Rodulfus Glaber seem to feel that the world might be drawing to an end? If so, how might this belief have shaped his view of pilgrimage to Jerusalem?

37. THE PILGRIMAGE OF RICHARD OF VERDUN

Traveling to Jerusalem in 1027, Richard of Verdun (970–1046), abbot of St-Vanne in northwestern France, numbered among the many European pilgrims who flocked to the Promised Land during the early eleventh century. A well connected, if sometimes controversial, figure due to his apparently profligate spending, Richard showed a particular interest in the cult of saints and sacred relics, gathering numerous remains and objects in his monastery over the course of his career – a devotional interest plainly on display during his travels to the East.

Source: trans. B.E. Whalen, from *Vita Richardi abbatis S. Vitoni Vidunensis*, ed. D.W. Wattenbach, Monumenta Germaniae Historica: Scriptores, vol. 11 (Hannover, 1854), pp. 288–90.

17. ... whereupon, with a great yearning of his mind, he [Richard] began to declare openly to all his desired vow [to go to Jerusalem]. Getting the churches under his care in order, placing honest and obedient brothers in charge of them, this pilgrim of Christ set forth with the blessing and prayer of the bishop [Rambert] from his homeland, with a group of companions accompanying him, religious men of both [higher and lower] ranks, including among them the venerable in life Abbot Ervinus, lured from Triers by the friendship of his [Richard's] sanctity, who became Richard's inseparable

companion. Passing through innumerable trials along the road, through long and difficult labors, through waterless and uninviting wastelands, through the horrors caused by thieves and the terrors caused by Gentiles [non-Christians], he came to Constantinople.

At that point, as it pleased him to spend some time in the city for the purpose of visiting the places of the saints, rumor of his sanctity soon reached the emperor [Constantine VIII] and the patriarch [Alexius I Studites], for light is scarcely able to hide in the shadows. Not unmindful of the Lord's words, he "who receives the just in the name of the just shall receive a just reward," they reverently welcomed and received him with happy spirits; when they talked to each other on friendly terms, they revered the elegance of his bearing, his age, and the sweet and abundant wisdom of this miraculous man of God. Then the emperor, as befitting his station, endowed him with a most precious purple robe and many presents. No less did the patriarch offer him praises, since he was delighted by his [Richard's] mellifluous words, and he gave to him two small fragments of the cross of salvation, encased in pure gold in the shape of a cross, which he wore about his neck during the remainder of his pilgrimage for his own protection. The patriarch also gave him relics of other saints, all of which the venerable father preserved and bestowed upon this church when he returned.

18. Finally, honored with so many praises, comforted by so many gifts, with the blessing of the patriarch and the kindly permission of the emperor, not unmindful of his vows, he devoutly sought to fulfill them, enflamed by the pious affectation of his mind. Traversing such a great distance, he reached the venerable site of his desire, which he greedily drank in. It is not for me to say how much he showered all the places that he saw and passed through with the flood of his tears; let the reader or listener meditate upon this with such sweetness of the heart. When he was in Pilate's palace, he looked upon the column [where Christ was scourged], and pictured in his mind the binding and whipping of the savior, and he called to mind with pious affection the spitting, the blows, the mockeries, and the crown of thorns, and, at the place of the crucifixion at Calvary, the lance, the draught of vinegar, the blasphemy of those passing by, the exclamation of [Christ's] voice and the giving up of the ghost. How much, do you think, did the fountain of his tears erupt with the force of his piety, how much did his heart fill with the grief of his piety, with the pain of his piety? "The stream of a river," said [King] David [in the Book of Psalms], "makes the city of God joyful." So says scripture, that the soul of the just man is the seat of wisdom; if the soul of the just man is the seat of wisdom, how much more is the soul of the just man the city of God? "I will dwell among them," it is said, "and will walk among them." How many tears, do you figure, did he pour forth from the depths

of his heart when he saw the tomb of the prince of life in the garden of his delight, filled with joy, and when he called to mind the joys of the angelic thunder announcing the Lord's resurrection and the special sudarium [the cloth placed over Christ's face in the tomb], set aside from the other linens, his heart filled with faith?

> Thus the servant of the Lord, rightfully blessed by Christ
> afflicting himself, made peace with Christ
> his lips wet with the tears of his piety, pouring forth kisses
> circled about, explored the places of Christ, prostrated himself in prayer .
> and then went to the river Jordan by a speedy course.

In that river, while he bathed, the pledge of the Lord's cross that (as was said above) he wore suspended about his neck fell into the river, coming off his neck without him realizing it. Therefore he bathed and left, and had already gone a little distance with his companions when he took account of himself and realized the loss of that sacred object, so precious as it was to him. Then he suffered a great bitterness of his heart, and returned on the way that he had come without delay to the river, turning his gaze here and there and everywhere, when behold! Glory be to God in the highest! – he saw it, floating on the rolling waves, and coming towards him. Soon, exhilarated with indescribable joy by this divine gift, he gave thanks to all-powerful God and, taking it up with reverence, quickly rejoined the venerable company of his companions.

> After this, the suppliant [man] went up to the countryside of Bethlehem
> turning his thoughts with devout mind to the birthplace of the Lord
> where the ethereal divinity of the Word put on flesh
> betook himself in worship, and afterwards turned toward home.

At last, having looked upon again and again all of the places of Christ's humanity, saluting them with sobbing tears and kissing them sweetly, he made the decision to return to his homeland with his beloved companions.

What route did Richard of Verdun take toward Jerusalem? How was he received by the Byzantine emperor and patriarch, and what did this reception imply about the abbot's status and saintliness? What gifts did the emperor and patriarch give him? How did Richard's experience in the holy places affect him, according to his hagiographer?

38. THE GERMAN PILGRIMAGE OF 1064–65

The turn of the eleventh century had witnessed an upsurge in the number of Western travelers going to Jerusalem for the purposes of religious veneration. Continuing over the following decades, this phenomenon included "mass pilgrimages" of large groups, including both clergy and laity, men and women, and people of different social ranks, sometimes numbering in the hundreds or thousands. The so-called German Pilgrimage of 1064–65, described by contemporary chroniclers in the Annals of Nieder-Altaich *and the* Chronicle of Marianus Scottus, *represents one of the most famous mass pilgrimages of this period.*

Sources: *The Annals of Nieder-Altaich*, trans. B.E. Whalen, from *Annales Altahenses maiores*, ed. E.L.B. Oefele, Monumenta Germaniae Historica: Scriptores in usum scholarum (Hannover, 1891), pp. 66–70; The *Chronicle of Marianus Scottus*, trans. B.E. Whalen, from *Chronicon*, ed. G.H. Pertz, Monumenta Germaniae Historica: Scriptores, vol. 5 (Hanover, 1844), pp. 558–59.

The *Annals of Nieder-Altaich*

[In 1065] the emperor celebrated Christmas at Cologne. At that time, the Christian faith flourished far and wide. All of the prophet's predictions, that only a few had understood before the coming of Christ, shone forth in a clearer light to all the faithful after his birth and passion, including among them, so it seems, that which is fulfilled: "And his tomb shall be glorious." In this same year, a great multitude set out for Jerusalem to worship at the tomb of the Lord, so that whosoever you please could believe the "fullness of the Gentiles" is coming in [meaning the expected conversion of non-Christians before the end of time]. Since so many things occurred that ought to be described about that same journey, I must ask your patience, so that it is not troublesome for anyone if we take some to time to explain just a few of the things that happened. Therefore, among those who set out, these were the leaders: Sigfried, archbishop of Mainz; William, bishop of Utrecht; Otto, bishop of Regensberg; and Gunther, bishop of Bamberg. The latter, although younger in age than the others, was nevertheless not lesser than them in wisdom or in the virtue of his spirit. Although now after his death we cannot think about him without pain and grief, at that time, he was a source of honor and a pillar of the whole kingdom....

A great multitude of counts and princes, rich and poor, apparently greater than twelve thousand in number, followed these prelates. As soon as they crossed over the Morava river, they immediately faced frequent danger from thieves and bandits, but, prudently and cautiously avoiding them, they at last reached the city of Constantinople. There, they comported themselves so honorably in every way, that the imperial arrogance of the Greeks greatly wondered about them. On account of this great spectacle, they wondered greatly at the prelate Gunther and believed him to be the king of the Romans [the people of the German Empire] who had disguised himself as a bishop, since it would be otherwise impossible for him to pass through those kingdoms to visit the sepulcher of the Lord. After leaving there, several days later, they reached Aliquia after various trials and tribulations, as that same bishop Gunther relates, writing from that very place among others to his friends, who were back home: "So it was, brothers, that we passed through fire and water, and the Lord led us to Aliquia, which sacred scripture calls by the name of Laodicea. We suffered the Hungarians, who served us faithlessly, and the Bulgarians, who secretly stole from us; we fled from the Uzos [a Turkish people], who openly raved against us, we witnessed the imperial, Greek arrogance of the people of Constantinople, and we endured the Romans [Byzantines], who raged beyond all humanity as wild beasts. Indeed, we endured all these burdens, but worse burdens were still to come."

While they were staying at Aliquia for several days, behold, many returning from Jerusalem informed them about the innumerable deaths of their companions, displaying their calamities by their fresh and bloody wounds. They declared in no uncertain terms that no one would be able to pass by that route, since the savage people of the Arabs, thirsting after human blood, had occupied all of that land. What to do, therefore, and where to turn? After talking it over, they quickly resolved to place all of their hope in the Lord, foregoing all else, knowing that they belonged to the Lord either dead or alive, and with cheerful disposition, they set out for the holy city through the lands of the pagans. Soon, when they had arrived at a certain city, called Tripoli, and the barbarian ruler saw such a great multitude, he declared that all alike should be cut down by a cruel blade, hoping that he might reap a massive amount of money. Amidst these wicked schemes, however, the divine mercy of the Lord was not lacking for those who confided in him. All at once, storm clouds arose from the sea, which touched upon the city on one side, producing lightning and shaking with thunder and great dread. When this storm lasted up until the sixth day, and the mountain of the seas' waves were rising higher than normal, the pagans, compelled by necessity, yelled and hollered among themselves that the city and its people would soon be submerged in the abyss, since the God of the Christians was fighting on behalf of his people. Fearful of death, the ruler stepped back from his plan. Soon, the commotion of the sea settled, and he granted the Christians leave to proceed.

After suffering these various trials and problems, at last they came through the entire district to the city named Caesarea, where they celebrated the

Lord's [Last] supper, which fell during that year on the 8th kalends of April [24 March]. They rejoiced among themselves as if they had evaded all of the dangers, since from there to Jerusalem they reckoned the journey not more than two days. The following day, that is, Good Friday, around the second hour of the day, when they reached the village of Capharsala, suddenly they fell into the hands of the Arabs, who, just like starving wolves that had desired a meal for a long while, rushed upon them and wretchedly struck them down, tearing apart the first ones whom they found. At first, our people tried to resist, but since they were unarmed, they were quickly forced to flee into the village. Who can explain with words the great calamity and misery, the kinds of innumerable death, and the slaughter of men that took place as they were taking flight? William, the bishop of Trier, was gravely wounded there, stripped of his garments along with many others and cut down in a wretched manner, left lying there on the ground. The three remaining bishops, together with a considerable number of various people took refuge in a certain courtyard, walled with two stone towers, and prepared to defend themselves there for as much time as God might grant to them. The entrance to the courtyard was very narrow, and with the enemy menacing them, they did not manage to unload the burdens of their horses; therefore, they lost their horses and mules with everything that they were carrying.

After their enemies divided up all these things among themselves, soon they returned to relieve those lords of their money. Resolving to take up arms, whatever lay at hand, they bravely fought against them. On this account, their enemies grew even more enraged against them, and attacked more fiercely.... For three days they battled each other ceaselessly with the greatest effort. Even as our people labored – no matter how hungry, thirsty, and without sleep, for they were fighting for their lives and salvation – their enemies tore at them with the ferocity of wolves, for they believed that they had loot hidden in their stomachs (even though time had not allowed for them to swallow anything). Finally, around the ninth hour of the day on holy Easter Sunday, they declared peace between them: eight of the pagans' leaders were allowed to ascend one of the towers, where the three bishops were located, to find out just how great an amount of money would be needed to purchase their lives and their freedom to depart. As soon as they climbed up there, however, the leader [of the Arabs] who seemed to be the chief among them, approached Bishop Gunther, whom he reckoned to be the leader of all [the Christians], unwound the cloth that he wore wound about his head, and looped it around the bishop's neck as he sat there. "Behold," he said, "having captured you alone, I have everyone else in my power, and at this very moment, I might hang you and them equally from a tree, and do what I wish with you all." At this point, it should be observed, that this just man acted boldly like a lion. For when this happened and he understood what had been said through an interpreter, that venerable man was not at all scared by the innumerable and encircling group of his enemies, but right away lashing out with his hand, he struck that pagan to the ground and put his foot on his neck. "Well then," he said, "men, get up and bind all of them as captives with chains, naked, and keep a watch on them with the very spears that they are using to menace us." Immediately, it was done as he had ordered, and in this way the attack of those belligerent pagans ceased on that day. Around the ninth hour of the following day, the local governor of the Babylonian king, who ruled over Ramla, having heard about everything that had happened, came with a great force to liberate our people, even though he was a Gentile [non-Christian]. For he figured that if all of these men perished in such a great slaughter, then no one else would come to the land for the sake of prayer, and therefore he and his men would incur a great loss [of revenues]. When they became aware of his arrival, the Arabs scattered everywhere and took to flight, and he [the governor], after taking charge of those who had been captured and bound, opened the gates for our people to leave. Setting forth, our people reached Ramula, and settled down there for two weeks, invited to stay by the governor and the townspeople.

At last, therefore, on the second Ides of April [12 April], they entered the holy city. Who can explain with mere words the great flood of tears that poured forth; who can explain how pure prayers and sacrifices they offered to God, how they sang with a joyful mind after many longing sighs: "We will worship in that place, where his feet stood"? Fulfilling their vow to the Lord there with intimate devotion for thirteen days, rejoicing, at last they returned to Ramla. Many more Arabs gathered from all sides and, plotting with cruel intentions, blocked every passage by the roads, since they were still yearning to carve the money out of their guts. Our people, however, were not unmindful of this situation; soon, with some merchants giving them a ship, and watching for the right winds, they took to their boat and eight days later, after a favorable voyage, they reached the port of Aliquia. After several days, they proceeded from there, although not without considerable effort and difficulty, and finally after a long time on the roads they joyfully reached the borders of Hungary and the banks of the Danube river. Yet what joy does this deceitful world ever hold or happy ending does it bring in conclusion? They had just crossed that river, and were just rejoicing as they reached their homeland, and behold, the often-mentioned, illustrious bishop Gunther – just as if he already knew the day of his death – bent his knee to the ground on the bank of that river, kissing the earth: "Praise be," he said, "and render thanks to God, who brought me to this place. For, in whatever hour or place he has foreordained my demise, am I certain that the faithful will bear my body to Bamberg." What more is there to say? That very hour, he fell ill, but nevertheless he would not delay from taking to the road until they came to the city named Deserta [Oedenburg]. Not faring well there, as he struggled for a long while with his sickness, knowing for certain that the day of his death was approaching, he made confession to his three fellow bishops and many other men of sacred orders; anointed with the anointment of holy oil, receiving the viaticum of the Lord's body and blood, he died on the tenth kalends of August [23 July]. Lamenting, those faithful counts and fellow bishops raised up his body from there, and, as a great crowd of his faithful daily arrived on the scene, hopeful for something else from him, with great grief nearly all of Bavaria and France bore him to Bamberg and buried him with seemly honor before the altar of St-Gertrude, just as he had planned for while he was still living.

Chronicle of Marianus Scottus

[1064] Many rich and poor, more than seven thousand of them, set out for Jerusalem with the archbishop of Mainz, the bishop of Utrecht, the bishop of Bamberg, and the bishop of Regensberg. In the places where the bishops have their sees, they possessed ritual vestments, and had gold and silver vessels and plates; from these, they managed to supply themselves gloriously with food and drink.

[1065] The Arabs, gathering together when they heard tale of these riches, killed many of the aforementioned men on [Good] Friday. Overwhelmed, our people fled into an empty, fortified town, which was called Carvasalim. Shutting themselves up in there, they defended themselves with stones and clubs against the assault of the Arabs, who were seeking all of their riches, or rather, their money and their lives. Then, one noble soldier, who in no way intended to be denied the sepulcher of the Lord, came forth naked. The Arabs immediately stretched him out flat in the shape of a cross, pinning his hands and feet to the ground with nails, and they cut open the surface of his stomach on two sides, revealing his innards from his stomach up to his gullet, tossing them all over his face, thereby showing just how human guts look. After that, they chopped him up into bits; their leader threw a stone on him first, and everyone else did likewise. Then they said to all of our people, watching inside the fort: "This is what will happen to you, if you don't hand over all of your money!"

Then, when our people promised to surrender their money, keeping only what they needed to survive to reach Christian lands, they sent in the leader of the Arabs with sixteen men, armed with swords. When he saw the glorious bishops with their soldiers, and the ritual vestments they were wearing, and everything else about them, he threw a rope around the bishop of Bamberg's neck (as the pagans are accustomed to do with a convict), as if he were our lord by virtue of his greatness and the comeliness of his body, saying: "You and everything of yours belong to me." The bishop said, through an interpreter: "What are you doing to me?" He responded: "I will suck the precious blood out of your guts, and string you up like a dog in front of this fort." Then the bishop, grabbing him by the head, knocked him to the ground with a single blow; the other men with him were bound. When those who were outside heard all this commotion, they rushed forth against the fort. Those who were bound, however, placed atop the walls with swords up against their necks, beseeched their sons and friends, who got the others to stop the attack. Then a fight broke out among the thieves, many of whom desired money, and many of whom desired the lives of their fathers and friends. Two weeks after Easter, summoned there by some of those who had escaped, the ruler of Ramla arrived on the scene with a strong force, putting the Arabs to flight. He took a payment of fifty gold byzants (that is, a kind of large coin), took captive the leader of the Arabs, who had been a foe of the Saracen king for some time, and led the Christians to Jerusalem, and finally to their boat. God granted them a favorable wind that carried them back to Christian lands; out of the seven thousand who set out, not even two thousand returned.

What were some of the dangers that the German pilgrims faced during their journey? How do these chroniclers portray Muslims, called here Arabs and Saracens? How does the author of the Annals of Nieder-Altaich *celebrate the deeds of Bishop Gunther in particular? Why did the local Muslim governor rescue the beleaguered Christians? Based on this account, how might the participants on the "German pilgrimage" have felt about their experiences? Does it seem likely that the story of their trials would have encouraged or discouraged other pilgrims?*

39. A CANTERBURY MONK AT CONSTANTINOPLE

Along with Jerusalem, Constantinople continued to attract Western pilgrims on the eve of the First Crusade. The relics of the city formed a key part of its attraction. The fragment below describes the pilgrimage of an English monk to the city around 1090, who decided that he would like to bring relics of Saint Andrew back from Constantinople to his homeland.

Source: trans. B.E. Whalen, from Charles H. Haskins, "A Canterbury Monk at Constantinople," *English Historical Review* 25 (1910): 294–95.

In the time when the younger King William was ruling over the English people, and the church of Christ at Canterbury had been devastated by the death of its archbishop, Lanfranc, a certain monk by the name of Joseph went to Jerusalem for the sake of prayer. When he had fulfilled his desire there and set out for home on the usual route with a great crowd of companions, he turned aside from the usual route and his companions, heading instead with only a few friends to Constantinople. For he had heard that there was an incomparable treasury of relics in that location, and he wished to commend himself in person to their blessings. Therefore, with God leading him to that place, when he had arrived and asked where that treasure was kept, he discovered certain men there from his homeland and some friends, who were attached to the household of the emperor. Recognizing them at once, rejoicing he spoke with them, and discovered that those relics were in the emperor's chapel, although it was difficult for anyone to enter inside. The emperor, wishing to safeguard carefully those incomparable prizes, had placed a great number of guards there, including one in particular who oversaw all the others on guard-duty. Because the monk's friends were familiar with that guard and friends with him themselves, it so happened that by their intervention, the guard brought the monk into the chapel and showed him the greatest part of the relics.

When he showed those relics to him, and the monk was venerating each piously, it came to pass that he showed to him some bones of Saint Andrew the apostle, among others. After he told him and affirmed that those were the relics of that apostle, the monk, who had always favored that apostle more dearly, venerated his relics with more devotion. As soon as he saw them, he most devoutly cast himself down onto the floor, and prayed among other ways in this manner: "If it pleasing to almighty God," he said, "might I now keep some of these relics and have them in the place that I desire." The guard heard this, but, because he was Greek, did not really understand what the monk had said, so he asked one of the monk's friends, who was their interpreter, what it was that the monk had said. The interpreter, since he did not dare to reveal to the guard a prayer of this kind, first asked the monk whether he wanted him to tell the guard about it. When he had received permission to speak from him, then at last he explained to the guard that the monk desired this and that. Hearing this, he responded to the monk through the interpreter: "What price might you be willing to pay to someone," he asked, "who could make your desire come true?" The monk said: "I have little funds left from my journey and still have a long way left to go. Nevertheless, if there was someone who could manage to make my wish come true, I would give to them from my funds as much as I could afford to spare. In truth, I would carry off those relics to a place where they would enjoy constant praise. For in my home land, there is a certain bishop's see, where a church was founded in honor of Saint Andrew the apostle. A newly established congregation of monks most devoutly serves God there. If God deigns it worthy to fulfill my wish, I would like to carry away some of the relics to that church." The guard then said: "Go back to your lodgings and send your friend, this interpreter, back to me. Thinking it over, let me know through him what you wish. For it would not do us any good if you were to return here, so that business of this kind not.... [the text breaks off here]

How did the English monk gain access to the imperial treasury of relics? What did he propose to the guardian there? What does this brief story tell us about the desire of Western European pilgrims for Eastern relics? The story of the Canterbury monk ends before its conclusion: does it seem likely that the guard fulfilled his end of the bargain or somehow duped the eager pilgrim?

CHAPTER FIVE

PILGRIMAGE AND HOLY WAR

The crusades represent one of the most famous manifestations of Christian Europe's newly found confidence and expansionary energies during the High Middle Ages. During the First Crusade (1096–99), waves of medieval European warriors and clerics set out with the goal of "liberating" Jerusalem from its state of "bondage" under the Muslims, capturing Jerusalem on 15 July 1099. There remains a great deal of debate about the various factors that caused the First Crusade: according to some chronicles, the mistreatment of Christian pilgrims by the new Turkish rulers of Palestine played a role in encouraging the expedition to the holy places. Contemporary sources often referred to the crusaders themselves simply as "pilgrims," who, similar to other pious travelers to Jerusalem, had sworn a vow to reach the Holy Sepulcher of Christ, marking themselves with the cross as a sign of their pilgrimage. In return for this penitential journey, the crusaders were promised the remission of their sins, popularly understood as a guarantee of entry into heaven for those who died on the expedition. As a result of the First Crusade, Christian Europeans also took control of foreign lands in Syria and Palestine, leading to the creation of "crusader kingdoms" in the region. Over the following centuries, Europeans launched a number of additional campaigns, including the Second Crusade (1145–49) and the Third Crusade (1189–92), which took place after the recapture of Jerusalem by the Muslims in 1187. Further crusading expeditions, large and small, would persist into the late Middle Ages. As a special kind of Christian pilgrimage, the crusades developed into an important part of medieval piety; even those who could not go on crusade could offer donations to fund others who were willing and able to become "soldiers of Christ."

40. PETER THE HERMIT'S PILGRIMAGE

Although most chroniclers of the First Crusade credited Pope Urban II with officially setting the expedition in motion during his "crusade sermon" at the council of Clermont in 1095, others attributed the inspiration for the crusade to a humbler figure named Peter the Hermit. According to crusade historian William of Tyre, who wrote decades after the capture of Jerusalem, during a pilgrimage to Jerusalem Peter spoke to the patriarch of Jerusalem about the city's sorrows and received a divine revelation that God was ready to show mercy for his people and restore the Promised Land to them. Bearing a letter from the patriarch calling for aid, Peter returned to Europe, inspiring the First Crusade.

Source: trans. E.A. Babcock and A.C. Krey, in *A History of Deeds Done Beyond the Sea*, 2 vols. (New York: Columbia University Press, 1943), vol. 1, pp. 79–85, 87.

1.10. In the midst of the insidious perils of these times [the Turkish conquests of the 1070s], it happened that a numerous company of Greeks and Latins, after risking death in a thousand forms in hostile lands, arrived at the city. They had come for the purpose of worshipping at the venerated places, but the keepers of the gates refused them admittance until they should pay the gold piece which was fixed as tribute money. Those who had lost their all upon the way, however, and had with extreme difficulty arrived in physical safety at their longed-for goal, had nothing with which to pay tribute. So it happened that more than 1,000 pilgrims, who had gathered before the city to await the privilege of entering, died of hunger and nakedness. These people, whether living or dead, were an intolerable burden to the wretched citizens. They attempted to keep alive those who survived by furnishing them with such food as they could. They also made an effort to bury the dead, although their own affairs were beyond their strength. Those pilgrims who paid the usual tribute and received permission to enter Jerusalem brought still greater responsibility upon the citizens. For there was danger, as they wandered about incautiously in their eagerness to visit the holy places, that they would be spit upon, or boxed on the ears, or, worst of all, be furtively smothered to death. Consequently, as the pilgrims hastened to the holy places, the citizens followed them in brotherly kindness. Anxious for their life and safety and full of terror lest some unlucky accident befall them, they hoped in this way to prevent such mishaps.

There was a monastery in the city, belonging to the people of Amalfi, which was called, as it is even yet, St-Mary of the Latins. Close by, also, was a hospital with a modest chapel in honor of the blessed patriarch of Alexandria, John the Almoner. This was under the charge of the abbot of the monastery just mentioned. Here aid was given at any time to wretched pilgrims who arrived under such circumstances, the expense being defrayed either by the monastery or from the offerings of the faithful. Scarcely one out of 1,000 pilgrims who came was able to provide for himself. Many had lost their traveling money and were so exhausted by dreadful hardships that they were barely able to reach their destination in safety. Thus neither at home nor abroad was there any rest for the citizens. Death threatened them every day and, what was worse than death, the fear of servitude, harsh and intolerable, ever loomed before them. Another thing caused them extreme distress. Even while they were in the very act of celebrating the holy rites, the enemy would violently force an entrance into the churches which had been restored and preserved with such infinite difficulty. Utterly without reverence for the consecrated places, they sat upon the very altars and struck terror into the hearts of the worshippers with their mad cries and whistlings. They overturned the chalices, trod underfoot the utensils devoted to the divine offices, broke the marble statues, and showered blows and insults upon the clergy. The lord patriarch then in office was dragged from his seat by his hair and beard and thrown to the ground like a mean and abject person. Again and again he was seized and thrust into prison without cause. Treatment fit only for the lowest slave was inflicted upon him in order to torture his people, who suffered with him as with a father.

For 490 years [since the initial Muslim conquest of Jerusalem], as has been stated, this devoted people of God endured cruel bondage with pious long-suffering. With tearful groans and sighs, ever constant in prayer, they cried to God, begging that he would spare them now that their sins were corrected and that, in his great mercy, he would turn away from them the scourge of his wrath. For they had descended into the abyss of evil, whence, "deep call unto deep," the depth of misery to the depth of pity, they deserved to be heard by him, who is the God of all consolation. Finally, the Lord looked with pity upon them from his seat of glory, and, desiring to end such tribulation, determined with fatherly care to comfort them as they desired. In the present work, it is our intention to set down, as a perpetual memorial to the faithful in Christ, the method and ordering of this divine plan by which he intended to relieve the long-continued affliction of his people.

1.11. At the very time when that city beloved of God was undergoing the troubles which we have been describing, there was among the many who journeyed to the venerated places for the sake of devotion and prayer, a certain priest, Peter, from the bishopric of Amiens in the kingdom of the Franks. He was known, both in fact and in name, as the Hermit, and he was drawn to Jerusalem by this same fervor of spirit. As regards the outer man, he was small of stature and insignificant in person; but, in that small body, a greater valor reigned. He was of vivacious disposition and keen and pleasing eye, and he was not lacking in spontaneous eloquence. After he had paid the tribute which, by common custom, was imposed on all Christians who wished to enter the city, he was received as a guest by a certain believer who was himself among the number of Christ's confessors. Peter was a diligent man, and he asked many questions of his host about the condition of the Christians. From him he learned full details, not only about the dangers of the present time, but also about the persecution which their forbears had endured for many years previous. Whatever information was lacking by word of mouth he afterwards supplied by the faithful observation of his own eyes. As he went about to the churches during his stay in the city, his own investigations showed him plainly the truth of that which he had heard from others. Hearing that the patriarch of the city [Simeon II] was a devout and God-fearing man, he desired to confer with him about the conditions then existing in Jerusalem, and he hoped also to obtain more complete information on certain other matters. Accordingly, he went to see him and was admitted to his presence. Through the offices of a faithful interpreter, the two men enjoyed an agreeable conversation. Simeon, the patriarch, perceived from Peter's words that he was a discreet man of varied experience in many matters and of convincing power both in word and deed. He began to explain to him intimately the many woes which were so cruelly afflicting the people of God who dwelt at Jerusalem. Peter's brotherly sympathy was so deeply moved by this recital that he could not restrain his tears. He began to inquire even more earnestly whether it was not possible to find some way out of the troubles which beset them.

The good man replied, "Peter, the Lord, gracious and merciful, refuses to heed our tearful groans and sighs, because of the sins which enchain us. For not yet is our iniquity purged, and therefore, for the present, the scourging ceases not. But, through the ever-abounding mercy of God, the strength of your people, true worshippers of the Lord, is still intact, and their kingdom, the dread of our enemies, flourishes far and wide. If they, in brotherly love, would sympathize with us in our present situation and provide a remedy for the calamities which oppress us; or if they would, at least, intercede for us with Christ, we might hope that our affliction would soon end. We have no hope henceforward of receiving any aid from the empire of the Greeks, although they were more closely connected with us by blood and proximity and have far greater wealth. They are barely able to defend themselves, and their strength has so dwindled away, as your brotherly kindness may have heard, that within a few years, they have lost more than half their empire."

Peter replied, "Know, holy father, that if the church at Rome and the princes of the west had some careful instructor worthy of confidence to tell them about the calamities which you are suffering, without doubt they would endeavor to provide a remedy as quickly as possible by word and deed for these troubles of yours. Write, then, with all diligence to the lord pope and the church at Rome and also to the kings and princes of the West and confirm the letter with the seal of your authority. In fact, I, for the healing of my soul, do not shrink from taking this work upon myself. With God as my authority, I am prepared to visit all, to solicit all, to bear witness to your exceeding great affliction with all diligence, and to invite earnestly one and all without delay to provide a remedy." These words pleased the patriarch and seemed good in his eyes as well as in those of the Christians about him. Accordingly, with many thanks to the man of God for his sympathy, they gave him the writing for which he had asked.

1.12. Truly, thou art great, O God our Lord, and thy mercy is without limit. Verily, kind Jesus, those that trust in thee shall never be dismayed. For whence came such confidence to one so needy and helpless: grim, lacking all the qualities that make for influence and far away from his native land, that he dared to take upon himself a mission beyond his strength, confident that his desire would be successfully accomplished? The only explanation is that he had directed his thoughts toward thee, his protector; that, glowing with ardent love, sympathizing with his brethren, and loving his neighbor as himself, he so acted as to fulfill the law. His own strength was not sufficient, yet charity persuaded him. And although the task which his brethren had imposed upon him seemed difficult and well-nigh impossible, nevertheless, love toward God and toward his neighbor made it easy, because "love is as strong as death." It is "faith which, working through love," will avail in you, and the services which you have rendered are not vain. You did not permit your servant to hesitate long but did manifest yourself to him and encouraged him by a vision of yourself that he might not waver but might rise strengthened to accomplish that work of love.

It happened one day that this servant of the Lord of whom I am speaking was unusually troubled in mind at the thought of returning to his own land and assuming the responsibility of this mission. He accordingly entered the church of the Resurrection of the Lord; turned with deep devotion to the fount of mercy. He passed the night in prayers and vigils and, finally, overcome by the stress of emotion sank upon the pavement and gave way to the sleep which overpowered him. Deep slumber came upon him, as it is wont to do, and he seemed to see our Lord Jesus Christ standing before him, as in a vision, saying: "Rise, Peter, make haste and do without fear the tasks which have been entrusted to you, for I shall be with you. It is time that the holy places were purged and my servants aided." Peter awoke, comforted in the Lord by the vision which he had had and rendered more inclined to obedience. In response to the divine admonition, he delayed no longer but at once energetically prepared to return. After offering the usual prayers, he took leave of the lord patriarch, who gave him his blessing, and then went down to the sea. There he found a merchant ship which was about to sail across to Apulia. He embarked, and after a prosperous voyage arrived at Bari. As he was about to set out thence for Rome, he learned that Pope Urban was in those parts. Accordingly, he presented to him the letter of the patriarch and the Christians at Jerusalem. He described their sufferings and the abominations committed by the unclean people in the holy places and executed with diligence and wisdom the commission entrusted to him.

1.13. ... Kindled with enthusiasm from on high, Peter traversed all Italy [after meeting with Pope Urban II], crossed the Alps, and went about to each of the princes of the West, insisting, rebuking, and censuring. His warning words, aided by divine grace, persuaded some not to delay going to the aid of their brethren who were in such adversity, not to allow the holy places which the Lord had deigned to glorify with his own presence to be profaned longer by the filth of the infidels. Nor was he satisfied to sow this seed among princes alone, but he longed to inspire the common people and men of the lower classes by his pious exhortations to undertake the same duty. As he made his way slowly through kingdoms and nations, devoutly solicitous, he preached the same message to the poorest and most lowly in the faithful execution of his mission. The Lord looked upon his faithful service and granted him such favor that rarely did he call the people together without results. His preaching made him very necessary to the pope, who had decided to follow him beyond the mountains without delay. For in his role of forerunner, he prepared the hearts of his hearers to obey, so that the pope, who wished to persuade them to the same course of action, had less difficulty in attaining his purpose and was able to influence them more readily.

How does William of Tyre describe the situation of Christian pilgrims at Jerusalem during the period before the First Crusade? How did the natives of the city care for pilgrims? Why, according to this account, was the time right for Christians to try to recover control of the holy places? During their meeting, what did Peter the Hermit and the patriarch of Jerusalem discuss? What sort of revelation did Peter receive during his stay in the city? How does William present the relationship between Peter and Pope Urban II as determining their roles in the origins of the crusade?

41. THE CONQUEST OF JERUSALEM IN 1099

After an arduous journey of roughly three years, the armies of the First Crusade conquered Jerusalem on 15 July 1099, completing their "pilgrimage" to liberate the church of the Holy Sepulcher. The following account of the city's capture comes from The Deeds of the Franks, *one of the earliest chronicles of the expedition.*

Source: trans. A.C. Krey, *The First Crusade: The Accounts of Eye-Witnesses and Participants* (Princeton: Princeton University Press, 1921), pp. 249–50, 256–57; revised.

Rejoicing and exulting, we reached the city of Jerusalem on Tuesday, on the third day of the week, the eighth day before the Ides of June, and began to besiege the city in a marvelous manner. Robert the Norman besieged it from the north side, near the church of St-Stephen, which was built on the very spot where that first martyr won eternal happiness by being stoned in Christ's name. Next to the Norman count was Robert, count of Flanders, while Duke Godfrey and Tancred besieged the city from the west. The count of St-Gilles located himself on the south, on Mount Zion, near the church of St-Mary, the mother of the Lord, where Christ once supped with his disciples.

On the third day some of our men, namely Raymond Piletus and Raymond of Turenne, went out on a foraging expedition. They encountered a force of 200 Arabs, and the soldiers of Christ fought these unbelievers. With the Lord's help, they fought so valiantly that they killed many of the enemy and captured 30 horses. On the second day of the following week, we made an attack on the city, and so bravely did we fight that, if scaling ladders had been ready for our use, the city most certainly would have fallen into our hands. As it was, we pulled down the outer wall and placed one ladder against the main wall, upon which some of our men ascended and fought hand to hand with swords and lances against the Saracen [Muslim] defenders of the city. Many of our men were killed in this attack, but more of the enemy.

For a period of ten days during the siege we were not able to buy bread at any price, until a messenger came announcing the arrival of our ships. We also suffered greatly for thirst. In fear and terror we were forced to water our horses and other animals at a distance of six miles from camp. The Pool of Siloam, at the foot of Mount Zion, sustained us, but, nevertheless, water was sold among us very dearly. When the messenger arrived from our ships, the leaders took counsel and decided that armed men should be sent to guard the ships and sailors at the port of Joppa. So one hundred men from the army of Raymond, count of St-Gilles, under Raymond Piletus, Achard of Montemerle, and William of Sabran, left camp in the early dawn and started confidently toward Joppa. 30 of these knights separated themselves from the rest of the band and met 700 Arabs, Turks, and Saracens from the army of the emir. The soldiers of Christ boldly attacked the enemy, whose force was so superior to ours that they soon surrounded us. Achard and some of the poor footmen were killed. While this band was completely surrounded, and all believed that they would be killed, a messenger was sent to Raymond Piletus, who said, "Why do you stand here with these knights? Lo, all of our men are in serious danger from the Arabs, Turks, and Saracens, and may all be dead by this time. Hasten to them and aid them." As soon as they heard this, our men hastened to the scene of battle. When the pagans saw the rest of our knights approaching, they formed themselves into two lines. Our men rushed upon the unbelievers, shouting the name of Christ, each determined to bring down his man. The enemy soon realized that they would not be able to withstand the bravery of the Franks, so they turned their backs and fled in terror. Our men, pursuing them a distance of four miles, killed many of them, but kept one alive to give them information. 103 horses were captured.

During this siege we were so distressed with thirst that we sewed up skins of oxen and buffalos and in these carried water for a distance of six miles. Between fetid water and barley bread we were daily in great want and suffering. Moreover, the Saracens hid in ambush at the watering places and either killed and wounded our animals or drove them away to caverns in the hills....

At length, our leaders decided to beleaguer the city with siege machines, so that we might enter and worship the savior at the Holy Sepulcher. They constructed wooden towers and many other siege machines. Duke Godfrey made a wooden tower and other siege devices, and Count Raymond did the same, although it was necessary to bring wood from a considerable distance. However, when the Saracens saw our men engaged in this work, they greatly strengthened the fortifications of the city and increased the height of the turrets at night. On a certain Sabbath night, the leaders, after having decided which parts of the wall were weakest, dragged the tower and the machines to the eastern side of the city. Moreover, we set up the tower at earliest dawn and equipped and covered it on the first, second, and third days of the week. The count of St-Gilles erected his tower on the plain to the south of the city.

While all this was going on, our water supply was so limited that no one could buy enough water for one denarius to satisfy or quench his thirst. Both day and night, on the fourth and fifth days of the week, we made a determined attack on the city from all sides. However, before we made this assault on the city, the bishops and priests persuaded all, by exhorting and preaching, to honor the Lord by marching around Jerusalem in a great procession, and to prepare for battle by prayer, fasting, and almsgiving. Early on the sixth day of the week we again attacked the city on all sides, but as the assault was unsuccessful, we were all astounded and fearful. However, when the hour approached on which our Lord Jesus Christ deigned to suffer on the cross for us [Good Friday], our knights began to fight bravely in one of the towers – namely, the party with Duke Godfrey and his brother, Count Eustace. One of our knights, named Lethold, clambered up the wall of the city, and no sooner had he ascended than the defenders fled from the walls and through the city. Our men followed, killing and slaying even to the Temple of Solomon, where the slaughter was so great that our men waded in blood up to their ankles.

Count Raymond brought his army and his tower up near the wall from the south, but between the tower and the wall there was a very deep ditch. Then our men took counsel how they might fill it, and had it proclaimed by heralds that anyone who carried three stones to the ditch would receive one denarius. The work of filling it required three days and three nights, and when at length the ditch was filled, they moved the tower up to the wall, but the men defending this portion of the wall fought desperately with stones and fire. When the count heard that the Franks were already in the city, he said to his men, "Why do you loiter? Lo, the Franks are even now within the city." The emir who commanded the Tower of St-David surrendered to the count and opened that gate at which the pilgrims had always been accustomed to pay tribute. But this time the pilgrims entered the city, pursuing and killing the Saracens up to the Temple of Solomon, where the enemy gathered in force. The battle raged throughout the day, so that the Temple was covered with their blood. When the pagans had been overcome, our men seized great numbers, both men and women, either killing them or keeping them captive, as they wished. On the roof of the Temple a great number of pagans of both sexes had assembled, and these were taken under the protection of Tancred and Gaston of Beert. Afterward, the army scattered throughout the city and took possession of the gold and silver, the horses and mules, and the houses filled with goods of all kinds. Later, all of our people went to the sepulcher of the Lord, rejoicing and weeping for joy, and they rendered up the offering that they owed.

What signs are there that the author of this account was familiar with the major pilgrimage sites of Jerusalem? What did the crusaders do when their initial attack on the city failed? When they finally captured Jerusalem, what did they do next? Based on the evidence in this document, were the crusaders acting as pilgrims – or something else?

42. THE RELICS OF SAINT GEORGE AT ANCHIN

During the course of the First Crusade and afterwards, much like pilgrims before them, the crusaders had the chance to acquire Eastern relics from the biblical past and age of the early church, including the lance that pierced Christ's side at Antioch and a portion of the True Cross at Jerusalem. The account below, written by an anonymous cleric from the abbey of Anchin in Lille (in modern France), explains how the crusading count Robert of Flanders brought relics of Saint George to his church when he returned from the capture of Jerusalem.

Source: trans. B.E. Whalen, from *Narratio quomodo reliquiae martyris Georgii ad nos Aquicinensis pervenerunt*, in *Recueil des historiens des croisades: historiens occidentaux*, vol. 5 (Paris, 1841–64), pp. 248–52.

1. In the name of the Father, Son, and Holy Spirit, with few words and a humble style, if I am able, most dear brothers I will explain to you how the East deigned it worthy from on high to visit the church of Anchin through the relics of Saint George. If it pleases anyone, more out of curiosity than piety, to read or listen to what I am about to write, do not be indignant towards me, as if I was presumptuous about my abilities and put down such a great subject with a brief and uncultivated style; rather, if one understands how the virtue of obedience works, in all those things that offend him, let him show me forgiveness instead of scorn. For I do not set about this task with any presumptions about the abilities of my own genius: rather, I am compelled by the authority of my abbot, fully aware (as they say) that I am putting my hand in the fire. Again, I give my reader fair warning, so that they do not remain incredulous about the saint's miracles, which they will hear about from us, but rather let them believe us, and hear what is true through him [God], who always works miracles through his saints. Indeed, we were not informed about this matter from some sort of common or ignorant people, but rather we learned about the things we are describing from Robert the Younger, count of Flanders, who brought the holy relics to our church, and many other men of religion returning with him from Jerusalem, relating things that they saw and not just heard.

2. In that time when the army of Christians set out for Jerusalem from nearly every part of the world, a certain priest named Gerbod took to the road with some others from this country, who set out with the aforementioned ruler. When Christians from everywhere had descended upon Romania [the Byzantine empire, specifically Anatolia], enflamed we believe by the desire for God's home, they began to experience great hunger, after they had consumed nearly everything which they had plundered by fire and sword

from their enemies' towns and fields, and everything which they had brought
with them. At this point, forced by his need, that priest abandoned the army
and came to a certain monastery, where, along with a certain layman who
was a companion in his effort, travel, and hunger, he was kindly received by
the brothers of that place. For as long as he wanted, he was cared for by them
in that place, with all humanity. Since he was quite talkative and clever at
dissimulating what he wanted (I knew him since he was boy), he began to
be on quite intimate terms with them, as if he wanted to lend a hand with
all of their needs: he carefully inquired about each and every one of their
possessions, which they had both within and without. The brothers, as they
were of simple minds or natures, hid absolutely nothing from him, but rather
suspecting nothing ill, told him – dishonest as a priest and as a pilgrim, finding out things for his own benefit – about everything that they possessed.
In particular, they revealed to him a little marble space that contained the
relics of Saint George the martyr, namely his arm with its upper-arm and rib,
along with the remains of many other martyrs. No one was able to open up
this little space, unless they held in their hand a cross, prepared there for that
purpose, as the priests afterwards explained.

3. What more is there to say? The priest, seeing this heavenly treasure
on earth, began to desire it; desiring it, he planned to take it. After getting
everything ready in advance, which might be helpful once he had gotten
started, keeping watch outside the church, he directed his companion, the
layman, to carry out the theft. Again and again, by divine command, that
that cross was struck from his hands, as he was holding it and trying to open
the little chamber (as I said before, no one was able to access the body of
the martyr, unless he held that cross in his hand). Amazed by this new and
unheard of miracle, he threw himself on the ground in prayer. After offering
up many prayers and vows, trembling and humble, he again took up that
cross, and tried once more; trying, he opened it. At last achieving the result
of his desire, he opened the little space and, seizing the relics of Saint George,
along with some others which could be grabbed by someone in such a hurry,
he returned joyfully to the priest. What more is there to say? The priest,
taking the relics from the layman, invited him to take flight along with him.
But, o misery! Blindness struck that priest, who, I believe, did not show the
proper veneration owed to the saints, and he unwillingly returned to that
same church a little while later.

4. Received by those holy brothers much more kindly than he had hoped,
not as he deserved, after he returned what he had taken and confessed his
misdeed, he earned their forgiveness. When they prayed to the Lord for this
penitent, not only did he recover the sight of his eyes that he had lost, but,
through the grace of God (who was already looking out for us in this matter),

he managed to acquire from them the arm of Saint George. Joyful and filled with gladness, he returned to the army with this great treasure. Quickly forgetting what he had experienced, however, he showed no honor to the blessed relics that he bore. On this account, when he began to fall greatly ill through the grace of God, leading him to penance, he called a cleric of Lille named Gunscelin to him and told him about his fault by acting in such a negligent fashion, asking him for forgiveness. Because of the blessed relics, he declared with tears, he had suffered such things, and if he were able to merit forgiveness, he promised with every sort of vow that he would other-wise comport himself in a much more religious manner. After he promised to amend his ways, immediately he returned to pristine health; however, quickly forgetting or rather disregarding what he had promised, "just like a dog to its vomit," the ingrate returned to his accustomed ways. Truly, as the prophet says, "all the ways of the Lord are mercy and truth," for divine com-passion for a long time tolerated someone who sinned so often, not repenting worthily, until in the end, struck by the judgment of God, he collapsed in the middle of his companions, dying all of the sudden. Then a certain layman from Lille, named Gerard, who had been known to the priest back in their homeland and his companion during that pilgrimage, a close friend in all matters, took possession of the relics for himself. When he likewise took ill, he called upon the aforementioned Gunscelin, namely an honest man raised to the honor of the priesthood, and handed over the sacred remains to him, asking forgiveness for the fact that he had presumed to handle them with his impure hands, swearing that this was the reason for his sickness.

5. Why delay anymore? After his health returned, he sought back what he had handed over; seeking it, he got it; getting it and not correcting his ways, he fell dead just like the aforementioned priest. O the blindness! O the presumption! O the temerity of humankind, which during each and every generation, except for a few who fear God, refuses to acknowledge what it needs to do to act well, gathers and ignores the scourges sent upon it. Cer-tainly, similar judgments of omnipotent God's right hand present themselves to me, even from the Old Testament, from whose ceremonies and rites of sacrifices the truth, religion, and sanctity of the sacraments of the present time stand apart, just like the day from the shadow of night. Where do we read this? When the sons of Aaron, Nadab, at Abiu, offered strange fire to the Lord, in the sacrifice of that time, which they had not been commanded to do, fire came forth from the Lord and consumed them, and they died. In the Books of Kings, it is written of Oza that, when he extended his hand over the Ark of the Lord, and placed his hand on it, as the oxen kicked it and made it lean aside, God grew angry and struck him for his temerity, and he died there next to the Ark of God. In truth, brothers! Presumption is a great

sin, a great temerity, as their father – namely, that great mouthpiece of God, Aaron – did not free the former from a horrendous death; and the latter did not at all escape his demise, even though he stepped forward as if devoutly to offer homage. And what shall I say about King Ozia? It is written about him that he sought out the Lord and it so happened that he was righteous in the Lord's eyes, and that his name spread far and wide, because God was with him and offered him strength. Nevertheless, after doing so much good, with an elated heart, neglecting his Lord, when he wanted to burn incense (which was not his duty), as it says in scripture, he was struck with a most foul leprous wound and he remained a leper until the day of his death. Thus, it should not be surprising, in this time when the worship of our religion is more pure and holy, that those forbidden such presumption, who sinned in a similar manner – I say again, it should not be surprising – die in a similar manner; except for the fact that divine judgment laid low those living under the austerity of the [Old Testament] law at the beginning of their sin, while the patience of God tolerated those residing under the grace of the Gospel for a long time, trying to lead them to repentance.

6. But now let us return to the flow of our story, so that we do not seem to make this digression any longer than it needs to be. Therefore, Count Robert, when he heard about the demise and cause of death of his man Gerard of Lille, as we just described, laid claim to all of his possessions for himself, and he placed the sacred relics with honor, as was suitable, or rather as he was able, in his tent before his own eyes. Indeed, it would be too long a tale to explain all the great many things that God revealed through his saint during the journey. When the guardians, in whose care the count had placed him [the saint], again grew sick, they left off their watch; at last, he was asked by Sannard, his chaplain, a catholic and religious man, with many prayers, that he might watch over the saint. Or to tell about how the count, when he was returning home with all his men, was seized from the depths of the sea, or so I might say, from the jaws of death, by the merits of the saint, and, cast upon a certain island by the force of the winds, lost the sacred relics with the golden reliquary in which they had been placed. Grieving to the depths of his soul on this account, nevertheless, by the grace of God, he received them back from a certain barbarian, a resident of that land, returning to port and giving thanks. As I said, it would take too long to explain all these things and many others, which God deigned it worthy to reveal on the journey through his saint....

7. When the count returned from his service to God to his home country, and, on account of their honor and love, everyone rushed forth to greet him, he handed over the aforesaid relics, that is the arm of Saint George, to Lord Haimeric, abbot of the monastery of Anchin, who hastened forth to greet

him with other abbots. Afterwards, when he came to visit our flock and humbly commended himself with prayers, with his own hands he placed it [the arm] on the altar of our Lord and savior. Therefore, as the prophet says, since we are bidden to "praise God in his saints," we rightfully ought to show the devotion of our praise, offering up the sacrifice our service to the honor of God, and the veneration of such a great martyr, and all of his saints, so that we might glorify the miraculous Lord in his saints, and honor his saints, made miraculous through the Lord, for our means. Indeed, piety demands this for faith, so that we do not only extol the most abundant bestower of grace, worthy of devout praises, but we also take care to honor and show favor to the receivers of that grace, and to a certain extent, his helpers in the divine labors. Most dear brothers! We, his humble and lowly servant, give thanks to our savior, and for such great favors devoutly repeat "Glory to God in the highest," for whom there is honor and glory, power and command throughout the ages. Amen.

When and why did the priest Gerbod set out on his journey to Jerusalem? When and where did he first encounter the relics of Saint George? What happened when he tried to take them for himself? After his return to the crusader camp, why did God punish Gerbod and eventually strike him dead? What does the author of this account seem to be saying about the proper veneration owed to the saints? How did the relics of Saint George eventually make their way to the monastery at Anchin?

43. MONASTIC CRITICISMS OF CRUSADING AND PILGRIMAGE

Although the call for the First Crusade generated great enthusiasm around Europe, not everyone approved of the idea that Christian believers should drop everything and rush off to Jerusalem. As the crusaders set out, and over the following decades, bishops such as Anselm of Canterbury (1033–1109) and abbots such as Geoffrey of Vendôme (1093–1132) spoke out in particular against monks who intended to leave their monasteries without proper permission from their superiors in the company of crusaders or other pilgrims.

Sources: Letters of Saint Anselm, trans. B.E. Whalen, from *S. Anselmi: Opera Omnia*, ed. F.S. Schmitt, 6 vols. (Edinburgh: Thomas Nelson & Sons, 1940–61), vol. 4, pp. 85–86, vol. 5, p. 355; Letters of Geoffrey of Vendôme, trans. B.E. Whalen, from *Goffridi abbatis Vindocinensis, S. Priscae cardinalis, epistolae*, in Patrologia Latina, ed. J.-P. Migne, vol. 157 (Paris, 1841–64), cols. 127–28, 162–63.

Letters of Saint Anselm

195. Anselm, by grace of God archbishop, greetings to bishop Osmund. Many ill things are being said about the abbot of Cerne [in Dorchester], including among them the fact that he encourages his monks to go to Jerusalem – and has already sent one who is but a young boy – and that he wickedly takes away church properties and pawns them, and also that he wanders about various places like a frivolous youth, gambling, passing through villages even with women and only a single companion, so that he has become a shameful joke in people's eyes. In addition, he is making preparations for himself to go to Jerusalem, and has already bought a boat for this purpose with his fellows, handing over thirty *solidi* [coins]. There are other things that I might say about him, too shameful to speak about.

Therefore, it has been ordered on the part of the king, at his command, and ours, for your sanctity to investigate this situation, in as much as it pertains to you, as diligently as possible, and take steps to correct it as expeditiously as you can. Settle this matter, so that it is not allowed for him to alienate church properties and, if any liturgical vessels are taken outside the church, see that they are returned. It should not be allowed for him to wander about indiscriminately, nor should he send his monks to Jerusalem or go there himself; or rather, to go into confusion and damnation. If you discover anything else that needs to be corrected or enforced, manage the situation as securely as you are able, so that neither he nor his monks nor the church with its properties fall into perdition on his account, until the king returns and what ought to be done about these things can be settled by him. Also, let the command be given to all the monasteries in your diocese that no monk should presume to set out on the journey to Jerusalem, and prohibit this on pain of excommunication. I beg of you, that you command the bishop of Exeter, the bishop of Bath, and the bishop of Worchester on behalf of the king and us, that they prohibit this in their diocese, for the Apostolic [see] prohibits it. Farewell.

410. Anselm, servant of the church of Canterbury, to his beloved brother P., monk at the monastery at Saint Martin at Sées, greetings and may you always be consoled and steered by the grace of God. I hear, my dearest friend, that you desire to set out for Jerusalem. On this account, let me say to you right up front that your desire is not a good one and will do nothing for the salvation of your soul. For it is contrary to your vow, whereby you made a promise openly before God to remain steadfast in the monastery, in which you accepted the habit of a monk. It also runs contrary to your obedience to the Apostolic [see of Rome], which has commanded by its great authority that a monk should not presume to set out on this journey, unless there

remains behind some other religious person who is capable of watching over the church of God and teaching the people – and this should be done only by the council of one's bishop and in obedience to him. I was on hand when the Apostolic [pontiff] promulgated this decree. For it is against the obedience owed to your abbot, who has made his will clear in this matter, that he dislikes and denounces this desire as a danger to your soul.

Letters of Geoffrey of Vendôme

21. To the venerable brother and fellow abbot, Odo, greetings and affection from brother Geoffrey, his heartfelt friend. An unflattering rumor has reached our ears that you have the desire of returning to Jerusalem. It should be enough that you have seen Jerusalem once, although if you had never seen it, this diabolic deceitfulness would not have been born against you, nor would the pardon of God be necessary for you. Indeed, it is hardly possible to observe the faith of the monastic profession when one is going to Jerusalem; rather, one violates it. For, just as it is enjoined upon the laity to go to Jerusalem, it is forbidden for monks by the Apostolic see. I know this myself, just like someone who was actually there to hear the words of the lord pope Urban, when he bid the laity to set out on the pilgrimage, and prohibited monks from making that same pilgrimage. When Saint Benedict [of Nursia] mentions [in the Benedictine Rule] monks who wandered here and there, he is speaking about those who renounced the world at that time, professing themselves to be in the service of God, but not remaining steadfast somewhere in their profession. In truth, those who render their profession in a certain place, where first they professed themselves, carry the cross of the Lord, for it is necessary to *follow* the Lord, not to seek a pilgrimage to his sepulcher. Therefore, let us not deviate from the path of our profession under the excuse of taking the path to Jerusalem, lest, while we seek a false happiness, we find misery for the body and the soul. Out of a carnal love for your brother who is in Jerusalem (and by chance might already be dead), for however long a delay it takes you to reach there, your attention will at least be turned toward forbidden things, and the care of your spiritual sons and brothers abandoned – whose care you undertook with the promise of your faith, and for whom you will be expected to render an account to the Lord. For it is not the faithful deed of a good woman to fall asleep and expose her children, whom once she vigilantly guarded, to the offspring of a boar. By this trickery of Satan, many who renounced the devil with their first regeneration [of baptism], and renounced the devil and the world together with their second [regeneration of their monastic vows], have already set out for the Promised Land, but returned in their hearts to Egypt and, despising manna, sought flesh-pots and other things that are contrary to

the divine law. For so they had pieces of meat; but found in the pieces of meat the hook and nets used to capture the beasts. These men are comparable to that unfaithful messenger the raven, who, out of a desire for a carcass, spurned the bidding of holy Noah. Earlier, indeed, like the dove, they received the olive-branch and returned with it to the ark, staying in the ark, but then they flew out the window of the ark, into which they had already flown by the faith of their baptism and their monastic profession, never to return. As I do not wish in any way whatsoever to be a man among their number, therefore all the less do I wish to be a guardian and shepherd of the Lord's flock, lest by chance it happens – may God prevent it – that the guardian becomes a thief, the shepherd a wolf. Farewell, and let it please you to hold fast to what I have written in good spirit.

24. To the most beloved father Hildebert, venerable bishop of Le Mans, Geoffrey, humble servant of the monastery of Vendôme, affectionate greet-ings. You have informed us that a monk named John has returned from Jerusalem. It would have been quite better for him to have lived well in his monastery. Not all who see the terrestrial Jerusalem, but rather all those who act well, merit the Jerusalem that is placed in the heavens. What he related to you would have displeased us less, if he had first come to us, as he should have. The license that you require from us for him to live among you is harmful, not beneficial for his soul. First, he ought to be reconciled through the regular satisfaction [of penance] to his monastery, which he disobediently abandoned, rather than being worthy of communion with your sanctity or any other catholic person. Let him come, therefore, to his monastery and confess that he had acted less than perfectly, and let him follow not punish-ment but medicine for his imperfection. Whatever your sanctity might ask of us after that, our humility might carry through. Let him not fear to go there; let him not hasten fearfully, where there is no fear. Certainly, it behooves us to heal this wounded man, rather than make his wounds worse, since it is read that the highest pastor carried his weary sheep, did not cast it aside. In as much as possible, his infirmity ought to be borne with compassion, so that he might choose to be sick rather than allow the cure of piety to heal his infirmity. If he does not acquiesce to us, calling him diligently, if he flees the repeatedly offered and shown remedy of your paternal affection, if he despises the womb of maternal sweetness, so we might excommunicate him as sacrilegious until he renders satisfaction, to the extent that the [monastic] rule teaches and commands.

What evidence do Anselm's and Geoffrey's letters provide that Pope Urban II, when calling the First Crusade, had foreseen the possible disruptions it might cause for monastic life? In what ways did leaving on crusade or pilgrimage without proper permission represent a violation of one's monastic vows? How do Anselm and Geoffrey suggest that journeying to the "earthly" Jerusalem could endanger a monk's soul, rather than save it?

44. THE PILGRIMAGES OF BOHEMOND OF TARANTO

The Norman warrior Bohemond of Taranto numbered among the leading figures of the First Crusade. By all accounts, he was ambitious, fierce, and cunning, and he did not disguise his desire to create a new lordship for himself in the East during the crusade. At the same time, like other crusaders, Bohemond carried out his own acts of pious devotion as a pilgrim. The first selection below, written by the chronicler Fulcher of Chartres, describes Bohemond's arrival at Jerusalem about six months after the capture of the city (Bohemond had remained behind at Antioch, seized by the crusaders in July 1098). The second selection, written by an anonymous hagiographer, recounts his pilgrimage to the shrine of St-Leonard in France in 1105, fulfilling a vow that he had made after being captured in battle by his Muslim enemies.

Sources: Bohemond at Jerusalem, trans. A.C. Krey, in *The First Crusade: The Accounts of Eye-Witnesses and Participants* (Princeton: Princeton University Press, 1921), pp. 272–75, revised; Bohemond at the Shrine of St-Leonard, trans. B.E. Whalen, from *Miracula sancti Leonardi*, in *Acta Sanctorum*, vol. 67/3 (Paris: Apud Victorem Palme, 1863), pp. 160–63.

Bohemond at Jerusalem

Lord Bohemond, a wise and energetic man, was then ruling in Antioch, while Baldwin, a brother of the aforesaid Godfrey, ruled Edessa and the neighboring lands across the Euphrates river. When these two heard that Jerusalem had been taken by those who had set out as their companions, they were most joyful and humbly gave thanks to God. If those who preceded them had done well and successfully, however, it is not to be doubted that these two, with their forces, were to partake of the glory, even though they followed later. For it was necessary that the land and territories taken with such difficulty from the Turks should be carefully guarded. These, if left unguarded, might be recovered in a renewed attack by the Turks, who were now driven back to Persia. In this case, great harm would befall all the Franks going to Jerusalem, as well as returning. Perhaps divine providence, knowing that Bohemond and Baldwin would be more useful to the army in what remained to be done, rather than in what was already done, had delayed them.... Setting out and passing to the left of Antioch, he [Baldwin] came to Laodicaea, where he bought provisions for the journey, reloaded the pack animals, and set out. It was the month of November. After we had passed by Gibellum, we overtook Bohemond camped in his tents before the city of Valenium. There was with him a certain archbishop of Pisa, Daimbert by name, who, with some Tuscans and Italians, had come by ship to the port of Laodicaea, and who was there waiting to go with us. The bishop of Apulia was also there. With Lord Baldwin there was a third bishop. We estimated the number of those thus assembled in friendship to be 25,000 of both sexes, foot-soldiers as well as knights. When we had reached the interior territories of the Saracens [Muslims], we were unable to obtain from the wicked inhabitants of the region any bread or food of any kind. There was no one who would give or sell it to us, and, as our provisions were being more and more used up, it happened that many were cruelly tortured by hunger. Horses, too, and mules suffered doubly for lack of food. They traveled, but they ate not.... Thus for the love of God we endured this and many other ills, such as hunger, cold, and heavy rains. Many, lacking bread, ate horses, mules, and camels. Besides the excessive cold, we were tormented very often by showers of rain; and the heat of the sun was not sufficient to enable us to dry our wet clothes thoroughly before another rain would harass us for four or five days. Then I saw many who had no tents die from exposure to the cold rain. I, Fulcher of Chartres, who was with them, saw many persons of both sexes and a great many beasts die from the very cold rain one day. It would be long to tell and tedious to listen to all the details of their suffering; for no trouble or sorrow escaped the people of God. Often, many Franks were killed by the Saracens who lurked along the way in narrow paths, or wherever our men went in search of food. You might have seen mounted knights of noble birth become simple foot-soldiers, after having lost their horses in one way or another. As the baggage animals failed, you might have seen sheep and goats, stolen from the Saracens, heavily laden with baggage, which by its weight skinned their backs. Twice on the way, and no oftener, we had bread and grain, bought at exorbitant prices from the people of Tripoli and Caesarea. From this it is manifest that one can scarcely get any great good without great labor. It was indeed a great blessing when we finally arrived at Jerusalem. When we reached there, our long fatigue was forgotten. When we viewed the much longed for holy of holies, we were filled with indescribable joy. Oh, how often we recalled to mind that prophecy of [King] David which says, "We shall worship in the place where his feet have stood!" We beheld that prophecy truly fulfilled in us, although it likewise pertains to many others. To that place, indeed, did we go up, "the tribes, the tribes of the Lord, to confess his name" in his holy place. On the day of our entrance into

Jerusalem, the retreating sun, having fulfilled its winter descent, resumed its ascending course.

After we had visited the Lord's sepulcher and his glorious temple and many other sacred places, on the fourth day we went to Bethlehem, in order that, as we were about to celebrate the anniversary of the nativity of our Lord, we might that very night be watchers in the stable where the holy mother laid Jesus, and there assist in the devotions. All that night we filled with appropriate devotions; and in the third hour, after three masses had been celebrated, we returned to Jerusalem. Oh, what a stench there then was around the wall of the city, inside and outside, from the dead bodies of the Saracens, massacred by our companions during the capture of the city, wherever they had hunted them down! After we and our beasts had been refreshed for some time with a much needed rest, and after the duke and other leaders had chosen Daimbert, mentioned above, to be patriarch in the church of the Holy Sepulcher, we got new supplies of provisions, and, loading our mules, we went down again to the river Jordan. Some of the army, the last to arrive, chose to remain in Jerusalem; others who had come first preferred to go with us, but Duke Godfrey continued energetically to rule the territory of Jerusalem.

Bohemond at the Shrine of St-Leonard

After the death of the most saintly and glorious confessor of Christ, our lord Leonard, it came to pass that a war broke out in the lands of Jerusalem between the Christians and the Saracens, as the former sought to wipe out the squalor of the latter's perfidy from that most sacred region where the Lord our God, Jesus Christ, was born and suffered for us. Although the Christian army had at its head three of the bravest and strongest leaders and soldiers, Baldwin, Bohemond, and Richard [of Salerno], it happened that Bohemond and Richard were captured by the barbarians along with a multitude of Christians during that very long and difficult battle. While they were held captive in chains for a long time, in a certain city named Flagonia, Baldwin, who was their leader in the aforementioned battle, arranged a pact with the Saracens: that they might accept a certain weight of gold (the equivalent to how much Bohemond himself weighed), and in a secure place agreed to by both sides, the barbarians would release Bohemond alone and restore him to his freedom. However, when the promised amount of gold was partially lacking, because some of the Christians did not wish to contribute, meaning that Bohemond remained in captivity for a long while afterwards, a certain pilgrim came to visit him and spoke to him thus: "Who are you and where do you come from?" When he explained who he was and where he came from, the pilgrim gave him such sound advice as this: "Why," he said, "do you not swear a vow to God and Saint Leonard the confessor, whose body is entombed in the region of Aquitaine, by whose merits many are freed from the bondage of their chains? So you, if you pray to him with all your heart, beyond a doubt, at once you will enjoy his aid."

When Bohemond heard this, he swore a vow to God and the aforesaid Saint Leonard, that, if by the saint's merits, God snatched him up from captivity among that barbaric people and brought him safe and sound to the shores of the Latin Christians' lands, he would quickly hurry with many prayers and offerings to visit his [Leonard's] body and the place where he was buried in the ground. After he swore and said these things, on the next night, Saint Leonard appeared to him. When he made the sign of the cross, all of the chains upon Bohemond and his companions burst asunder; and again, when he made the sign of the cross, the doors of the prison and city opened, with the guards realizing nothing. So he brought them safe and sound into the region of Jerusalem, bidding them to follow him without fear. At dawn, they were greeted with honor by Baldwin and the other Christians, rejoicing and giving thanks to the almighty God and to Jesus Christ his son and also to the Holy Spirit, who had deigned it worthy to free them through [the merits of] the most blessed confessor, Leonard.

A little while later, after he amassed a great deal of silver and gold, Bohemond set out for Aquitaine to visit the body of Saint Leonard. When he had come to the place where his most sacred body rests, pouring forth great thanks and praise to God and Saint Leonard for snatching him and his companions up from their chains, and that they had judged it worth to rescue him from the imprisoning squalor of that perfidious and barbaric people in the land of Christendom. Shedding copious tears, he gave many gifts for the restoration of the church and had chains of silver and gold hung over the body of the blessed confessor of Christ, Leonard, which he ordered to be made much like those which plagued him in that barbaric captivity and bondage, to the praise and glory of our Lord Jesus Christ and the memory of his liberation by the most glorious confessor Leonard, with him granting this, who lives with the Father, Son, and Holy Spirit, and reigns throughout the ages. Amen.

What holy sites did Bohemond and his companions visit when they finally reached Jerusalem? Can you think of any other reasons, besides religious veneration, why he might have wanted to visit Jerusalem in the aftermath of the crusade? What sort of miracles accompanied Bohemond's liberation from captivity by Saint Leonard? How did he show his thanks to the saint?

45. THE TRAVELS OF SAEWULF

In the wake of the First Crusade, "traditional" pilgrimage to Jerusalem continued in greater volume than before, as Christians came from Europe to visit the holy places recently captured by their co-religionists. One such pilgrim, Saewulf, journeyed from England to Jerusalem around 1102, visiting the church of the Holy Sepulcher and the "Temple of the Lord," a church founded by the crusaders in the Dome of the Rock, the famous seventh-century mosque.

Source: revised by S.J. Allen and E. Amt, in *The Crusades: A Reader*, ed. S.J. Allen and E. Amt (Peterborough, ON: Broadview Press, 2003), pp. 99–102, from the translation by T. Wright, in *Early Travels in Palestine* (London: Henry G. Bohn, 1848), pp. 31, 34, 36–40, 44, 46–48.

I, Saewulf, though conscious of my own unworthiness, went to offer up my prayers at the Holy Sepulcher.... After leaving the isle of Cyprus, we were tossed about by tempestuous weather for seven days and seven nights, being forced back one night almost to the spot from which we sailed; but after much suffering, by divine mercy, at sunrise on the eighth day, we saw before us the coast of the port of Joppa, which filled us with an unexpected and extraordinary joy. Thus, after a course of 13 weeks ... we put into the port of Joppa, with great rejoicings and thanksgivings, on a Sunday ... I was suddenly seized with a great desire of landing, and, having hired a boat, went into it, with all my companions; but, before I had reached the shore, the sea was troubled, and became continually more tempestuous. We landed, however, with God's grace, without hurt, and entering the city weary and hungry, we secured a lodging, and reposed ourselves that night....

We went up from Joppa to the city of Jerusalem, a journey of two days, by a mountainous road, very rough, and dangerous on account of the Saracens [Muslims], who lie in wait in the caves of the mountains to surprise those less capable of resisting by the smallness of their company, or the weary, who may chance to lag behind their companions. At one moment, you see them on every side; at another, they are altogether invisible, as may be witnessed by anybody traveling there. Numbers of human bodies lie scattered in the way, and by the wayside, torn to pieces by wild beasts. Some may, perhaps, wonder that the bodies of Christians are allowed to remain unburied, but it is not surprising when we consider that there is not much earth on the hard rock to dig a grave; and if earth were not wanting, who would be so simple as to leave his company, and go alone to dig a grave for a companion? Indeed, if he did so, he would be digging a grave for himself rather than for the dead man. For on that road, not only the poor and weak, but the rich and strong, are surrounded with perils.... We, however, with all our company, reached the end of our journey in safety. Blessed be the Lord, who did not turn away my prayer, and has not turned his mercy from me....

The entrance to the city of Jerusalem is from the west, under the citadel of King David, by the gate which is called the gate of David. The first place to be visited is the church of the Holy Sepulcher ... not only because the streets lead most directly to it, but because it is more celebrated than all the other churches; and that rightly and justly, for all the things which were foretold and fore-written by the holy prophets of our savior Jesus Christ were there actually fulfilled. The church itself was royally and magnificently built, after the discovery of our Lord's cross, by the archbishop Maximus, with the patronage of the emperor Constantine, and his mother Helena. In the middle of this church is our Lord's sepulcher, surrounded by a very strong wall and roof, lest the rain should fall upon the holy sepulcher, for the church above is open to the sky.... In the court of the church of our Lord's sepulcher are seen some very holy places, namely, the prison in which our Lord Jesus Christ was confined after he was betrayed ... then, a little above, appears the place where the holy cross and the other crosses were found, where afterwards a large church was built in honor of Queen Helena, but which has since been utterly destroyed by the pagans; and below, not far from the prison, stands the marble column to which our Lord Jesus Christ was bound in the common hall, and scourged with most cruel stripes. Near this is the place where our Lord was stripped of his garments by the soldiers; and next, the place where he was clad in a purple vest by the soldiers, and crowned with the crown of thorns, and they cast lots for his garments. Next we ascend Mount Calvary, where the patriarch Abraham raised an altar, and prepared, by God's command, to sacrifice his own son [Isaac]; there afterwards the son of God, whom he [Isaac] prefigured, was offered up as a sacrifice to God the Father for the redemption of the world. The rock of that mountain remains a witness of our Lord's passion, being much cracked near the foss [crevice] in which our Lord's cross was fixed....

We descend from our Lord's sepulcher, about the distance of two arbalest-shots, to the Temple of the Lord, which is to the east of the Holy Sepulcher, the court of which is of great length and breadth, having many gates; but the principal gate, which is in front of the Temple, is called "the beautiful," on account of its elaborate workmanship and variety of colors.... In the middle of [the] Temple is seen a high and large rock, hollowed beneath, in which was the Holy of Holies. In this place Solomon placed the ark of the Covenant, having the manna and the rod of Aaron ... and the two tablets of the Testament [the Ten Commandments] ... here the child Jesus was circumcised on the eighth day, and named Jesus, which is interpreted as "savior"; here the Lord Jesus was offered by his parents, with the Virgin Mary, on the day of her purification, and received by the aged Simeon; here, also, when Jesus was twelve years of age, he was found sitting in the midst of the doctors, hearing and interrogating them, as we read in the Gospel; here afterwards he cast out the oxen, and sheep, and pigeons, saying, "My house shall be a house of prayer" and here he said to the Jews, "Destroy this temple, and in three days I will raise it up"....

The city of Bethlehem in Judea is six miles to the north of Jerusalem. The Saracens have left nothing there habitable, but everything is destroyed (as in the other holy places outside the walls of the city of Jerusalem) except the monastery of the blessed Virgin Mary, which is a large and noble building.... The city of Nazareth of Galilee, where the blessed Virgin Mary received the salutation of our Lord's nativity from the angel, is about four days' journey from Jerusalem.... The city of Nazareth is entirely laid waste and overthrown by the Saracens; but the place of the annunciation of our Lord is indicated by a very noble monastery.... Having, to the best of our power, visited and paid our devotion at all the holy places in the city of Jerusalem and the surrounding country, we took ship at Joppa on the day of Pentecost, on our return; but, fearing to meet the fleet of the Saracens, we did not venture out into the open sea by the same course we came, but sailed along the coast by several cities, some of which have fallen into the hands of the Franks, while others still remain in the power of the Saracens....

By what route did Saewulf reach Jerusalem? Where else did he visit during his stay there? How might Christian rule over the region have changed his pilgrimage experience? What evidence does his account provide that the crusader conquest of the region did not necessarily mean more security for Christian pilgrims?

46. PILGRIMAGE FROM RUSSIA TO THE HOLY LAND

By the late tenth century, Christianity had begun to spread from the Byzantine Empire into the northern region of Kiev, home to a people called the Rus. Over the following generations, the Christian church spread throughout these areas of modern day Ukraine and Russia, which developed their own Christian rites and traditions, including pilgrimage. The account below of the abbot Daniel, later bishop of Suriev, is the earliest known record of a Russian pilgrim to Jerusalem. Daniel visited the holy place between 1106 and 1107, during the early years of the crusader kingdom of Jerusalem.

Source: trans. (from the French version) C.W. Wilson, in *The Pilgrimage of the Russian Abbot Daniel in the Holy Land*, Palestine Pilgrims' Text Society, vol. 4 (London, 1895), pp. 1–14.

I, Daniel, an unworthy abbot of Russia, the least among the monks, ill at ease by reason of my many sins and the insufficiency of my good works, was seized first with the idea, and then with an impatient yearning to behold the sacred city of Jerusalem and the Promised Land. By the grace of God I reached the holy city of Jerusalem, and saw the holy places: I visited the whole of Galilee and all the sacred places around the holy city of Jerusalem, which Christ our God pressed with his feet, and where he manifested himself by marvelous miracles. I have seen all these places with my sinful eyes; and God in his mercy has deigned to show me all that I have for so many years ardently longed to see. My brothers, my fathers, my lords, forgive me, a sinner, and pardon my ignorance and the simplicity of the description (which I am about to make) of the holy city of Jerusalem, of that blessed land, and of the road that leads to the holy places. He who accomplishes this journey in humility, and in the fear of God, will never offend against the divine mercy; whereas I followed that hallowed road unworthily, in all feebleness and indolence, without abstinence, and giving myself up to every vice. But in the hope that the mercy of God and your prayers on my behalf may gain the pardon of our Lord Jesus Christ for my innumerable sins, I have described that road and the holy places with no pride as in anything meritorious. This thought is indeed far from me, for I have done nothing good during the journey; and it is only out of love for those holy places that I have written down what I saw with my own eyes, so as to remember all that God allowed me to see, notwithstanding my unworthiness. Fearing the example of that idle servant who buried his master's talent without rendering it profitable, I have written this for the faithful, so that, upon hearing the description of the holy places, they might be mentally transported to them, from the depths of their souls, and thus obtain from God the same reward as those who have visited them.

Many virtuous people, by practicing good works and charity to the poor, reach the holy places, without leaving their homes, and so render themselves worthy of a greater recompense from our God and Savior Jesus Christ. Others, of whom I am the chief, after having visited the holy city of Jerusalem and the holy places, pride themselves as if they had done something meritorious, and thus lose the fruit of their labor. And again, others who have made the pilgrimage return without having seen many valuable things, so eager were they to return home; for this journey cannot be made quickly, nor can all the holy places in Jerusalem and other localities be hurried through.

I then, unworthy Abbot Daniel, arriving at Jerusalem, stayed for 16 months in the *metochia* [a lodging or hospice for pilgrims] of the Laura of St-Sabbas, and was thus able to visit and explore all the holy places. Now it is impossible to visit and explore all the sacred places without a good guide and an interpreter; I therefore gave all that I could out of my small means as a reward to those who were thoroughly acquainted with, and able to show me, the holy places of the city and other localities, so that I might see every detail; in this, accordingly, I was successful.

By God's grace, I found in the Laura of St-Sabbas a very pious man of advanced age, who was well versed in the scriptures. God inclined the heart of this holy man to love unworthy me; and it was he who, with great care, showed me all the holy places, both in Jerusalem and the whole country, and who took me to the Lake of Tiberias, Tabor, Nazareth, Hebron, and the [river] Jordan. And out of affection for me, although suffering great fatigue, he conducted me to the large number of holy places of which I shall speak later....

The holy city of Jerusalem lies in arid valleys, in the midst of high rocky mountains. It is only on approaching the city that one sees, first, the Tower of David, then advancing a little, the Mount of Olives, the holy of holies, the church of the Resurrection, in which is the Holy Sepulcher; and, finally, the whole city. About a *verst* [about 3,500 feet] in front of Jerusalem there is a flattish mountain, upon reaching which every traveler dismounts, and, making the sign of the cross, adores the Holy Resurrection in sight of the city. Every Christian is filled with an immense joy at sight of the holy city of Jerusalem; and tears are shed by the faithful. None can choose but weep when they see the places so ardently longed for, where Christ our God endured the Passion for the remission of our sins; and thus, full of this deep joy, the journey to Jerusalem is continued on foot. To the left, near the road, there is the church of the first martyr, Saint Stephen; it was at this place that he was stoned by the Jews; they show also his tomb here. Just here there is a flat rocky mountain which split at the time of Christ's crucifixion. The place is called "Gehenna," and is a stone's throw from the city wall. After that the pilgrims, full of joy, enter the holy city of Jerusalem through the gate near the house of David; this gate faces towards Bethlehem and is called the Gate of Benjamin. On entering the city there is a road traversing it, which to the right leads to the holy of holies, and to the left to the Holy Resurrection containing the Holy Sepulcher.

The church of the Resurrection is of circular form; it contains 12 monolithic columns and 6 pillars, and is paved with very beautiful marble slabs. There are 6 entrances, and galleries with 16 columns. Under the ceiling, above the galleries, the holy prophets are represented in mosaic as if they were alive; the altar is surmounted by a figure of Christ in mosaic. At the high altar there is an "Exaltation of Adam" in mosaic; and the mosaic of the arch above represents the Ascension of our Lord. There is a [scene of the] "Annunciation" in mosaic on the pillars on either side of the altar. The dome of the church is not closed by a stone vault, but is formed of a framework of wooden beams, so that the church is open at the top. The Holy Sepulcher is beneath this open dome.

Here is the description of the Holy Sepulcher: it is a small cave hewn in the rock, having an entrance so low that a man can scarcely get through by going on bended knees; its height is inconsiderable, and its dimensions, equal in length and breadth, do not amount to more than four cubits. When one has entered the grotto by the little entrance, one sees on the right hand a sort of bench, cut in the rock of the cavern, upon which the body of our Lord Jesus Christ was laid; it is now covered by marble slabs. This sacred rock, which all Christians kiss, can be seen through three small round openings on one side. There are five large oil-lamps burning night and day suspended in the sepulcher of our Lord. The holy bench upon which the body of Christ rested is four cubits in length, two in width, and one-and-a-half in height. Three feet in front of the entrance to the cavern there is the stone upon which the angel sat who appeared to the women and announced to them the resurrection of Christ. The holy grotto is cased externally with beautiful marble, like a raised platform, and is surrounded by 12 columns of similar marble. It is surmounted by a beautiful turret resting on pillars, and terminating in a cupola, covered with silver-gilt plates, which bears on its summit a figure of Christ in silver, above the ordinary height; this was made by the Franks. This turret, which is exactly under the open dome, has three doors skillfully executed in trellis-work; it is by these doors that one enters the Holy Sepulcher. It is this grotto, then, which served as the Lord's Sepulcher; and I have described it according to the testimony of the oldest inhabitants, who thoroughly know the holy places.

The church of the Resurrection is round in form and measures 30 *sagenes* [a *sagene* equals about seven feet each way]. It contains spacious apartments in the upper part, in which the patriarch [of Jerusalem] lives. They count 12 *sagenes* from the entrance of the tomb to the wall of the high altar. Behind the altar, outside the wall, is the "navel of the earth," which is covered by a small building on [the vault of] which Christ is represented in mosaic, with this inscription: "The sole of my foot serves as a measure for the heaven and for the earth." It is 12 *sagenes* from the "navel of the earth" to the place of the crucifixion of our Lord and to the end. The place of crucifixion is towards the east, upon a rounded rock, like a little hill, higher than a lance. On the summit of it, in the middle, a socket-hole is excavated, one cubit deep, and less than a foot in circumference; it is here that the cross of our Lord was erected. Beneath this rock lies the skull of the first man, Adam. At the time of our Lord's crucifixion, when he gave up the ghost on the cross, the veil of the Temple was rent, and the rock cleaves asunder, and the rock above

Adam's skull opened, and the blood and water which flowed from Christ's side ran down through the fissure upon the skull, thus washing away the sins of men. The fissure exists to this day, and this holy token is to be seen to the right of the place of crucifixion.

Although Daniel is the first known Russian pilgrim to Jerusalem, are there any signs in his account that other Russians had gone there before him? What does he say about those who did not go on actual pilgrimages to the holy places, but rather did good works and helped the poor? Why did he obtain a guide to the city when he arrived at Jerusalem, and where did he stay? What holy sites did he visit? Are there any differences evident between Daniel's account and those of contemporary pilgrims from Western Europe?

47. THE TOMB OF THE PATRIARCHS

Around the time that they conquered Jerusalem, the crusaders also seized Hebron, an important pilgrimage site for Jews, Muslims, and Christians due to its association with the tomb of the biblical patriarchs Abraham, Isaac, and Jacob. In 1119, the Latin clergy installed at the site claimed to have discovered the bodily remains of the patriarchs and their wives. The account below, written decades later by an anonymous cleric of Hebron, explains that miraculous event and its significance in God's plan for history.

Source: trans. B.E. Whalen, in B.E. Whalen, "*The Discovery of the Holy Patriarchs:* Relics, Ecclesiastical Politics, and Sacred History in Twelfth-Century Crusader Palestine," *Historical Reflections/Réflexions Historiques* 27 (2001): 157–76.

With your affection compelling me, nay more, with the Holy Spirit urging me, most dear brothers who are at Cariatarbe [Hebron], wishing to obey your commands by no means did I put off undertaking the work charged to me. Having at once taken up the writing tablet in accordance with your bidding, however, I rather feared to describe how the bodies of the holy patriarchs, namely Abraham, Isaac and Jacob, were discovered: a difficult work indeed, but worthy of being committed to remembrance. Whereupon, while granted I know that I am not sufficiently able to provide this account by my own merits, assured by your prayers I undertook that which you encouraged, yet with a fair amount of peril. For when I recall in how many things I have failed and consider how much this matter ought to be celebrated with praise, I fear greatly to heap sin upon sin, since the Lord checks the sinner after a question, saying: "Why do you recite my statutes and take my covenant on your lips? In truth you hate discipline and have thrust my words behind you."

Nevertheless, on the other hand, I do not mistrust the memory of him saying: "The sinner who shall have turned to me at any hour, I shall not remember any of his offenses." In him, therefore, I place all my hope; to him I flee with all my strength; to him alone, who made the deaf to hear and the mute to speak, do I commit the sails of my fearful ship with all devotion. For I know that he said: "Open your mouth and I shall fill it." Far be it that I proclaim myself to be of such merit; nevertheless "God is powerful enough to raise the sons of Abraham from the stones." Therefore you, most dear brothers, since you wished me to undertake so great a task, appeal to God with your prayers and urge the remembrance of our redeemer, so that he who found it worthy to reveal the bodies of the saints to us may also find it worthy to place in my mouth right and well sounding words, by which I may worthily explain the discovery of the saints to their own praise and glory. In truth, I, who also learned about events that happened during the reign of the emperor Theodosius from a certain Greek monk of Mount Sinai, will make clear that which was related to me by the very discoverers themselves, namely Arnulf and Odo, men of religion serving God there under a canonical rule: gathering these things together in one place and adding nothing of my own, granted with a rustic style, yet most truthful, with the help of God who lives and reigns forever and ever. Amen.

1.1. None of the faithful who have fully and carefully read the Book of Genesis doubt that the holy patriarchs, Abraham, Isaac, and Jacob, were buried with their wives in Hebron, a city of Judea formerly called by the other name of Arbe. For it is read at the end of that same book that when Jacob was growing old in Egypt, he called his twelve sons, to each of whom he gave his own blessing. And he commanded them saying: "Behold, I am about to be gathered to my people; raise me up from here and carry me to Hebron, and bury me there with my fathers in the double cave, which Abraham bought with a field from Ephron the Hittite for the possession of a tomb. And they buried him there with Sara his wife. There Isaac was buried with Rebecca. There lies Leah buried." When Jacob died, his sons did as he had commanded them, bearing him embalmed with perfumes to Hebron and placing him in the tomb of his fathers.

It is also said that Adam – the First Man – was buried there, which can be plainly understood from the Book of Joshua, where it is written: "Joshua gave to Caleb, son of Jephunneh, Hebron, where Adam the Great was buried." Saint Ambrose attests to this in his book *On the Creation of Adam*, saying: "Adam, first of all men, was formed in the valley of Hebron. From that same place he was taken into paradise, from which he was expelled on account of his disobedience, cast down into the valley of tears from which he had been taken, and, having died there, was buried by his sons in a double cave." Not unreasonably, therefore, did the ancients wish to name that place Cariatarbe, that is the "Four Tombs," since those four men are said to be buried in that same place. That valley is also called the "valley of lamentation and blessing," lamentation because Adam wept there on account of his son, whom Cain had killed, and blessing since the Lord blessed Abraham in that place, saying: "Blessing you, I shall bless you and I shall multiply you, and likewise in your seed all peoples shall be blessed." These matters, most dear brothers, we have recalled at length, yet nevertheless appropriately, lest by chance there be one (let it not be so!) who doubts it is thus as we have said. However, since there are some who know of the double cave by name but are altogether ignorant about what kind of place it is, we judge it worthy of further explanation (as we see it), so that when people hear about the marvelous difficulties of the place itself, they will confess that the patriarchs were not discovered without a divine miracle.

1.2. The building of the very structure attests to how great among the ancients was the worth, reverence, and excellence of this venerable place, in which the bodies of the saints rest. For a high and strong wall with a wondrous appearance surrounds it, made in a marvelous manner from large square and polished stones, having on the inside a height of eighteen cubits and a breadth of forty-nine. The floor on the inside is seen to be similar, wonderfully and beautifully constructed from large square stones, so solid and strong that any sort of great building could be raised atop it. The hardness of the stones of each structure exceeds any kind of marble. Moreover, this entire work is so joined and interconnected that the smallest stone in it could not be removed without an enormous effort. Six pyramids are contained inside, built in honor of the holy patriarchs, Abraham, Isaac, Jacob, and their wives, alternating opposite to one another: that is, the pyramids of the men are opposite the pyramids of the women and each one opposite that of his spouse. Those which are called by the name of blessed Abraham and blessed Sara are in the middle; those of Isaac and Rebecca on the eastern side; and those of Jacob and Leah are to the west.

The double cave is situated deep beneath the pyramid of Saint Abraham, nearly 14 cubits under the floor. Certain people assert that Jacob and Esau were the builders of this very wondrous work, but it is perilous to affirm strongly what is not known from truth. One thing we know for sure, that it was made on account of reverence for the saints. This also ought to be known: that city of Cariatarbe, which is Hebron, is remembered to have belonged to the priests [the Levites] from that time when the Promised Land was divided by lot among the sons of Israel. For so it is written in the Book of Joshua: "Joshua gave to the sons of Aaron, the priests, Cariatarbe, which is called Ebron in the hill country of Judea along with its surrounding suburbs;

and its fields and villages he gave to Caleph, son of Jephone, for his possession. Naturally it was appropriate that people venerated and respected those
priests from whom the highest priest, that is Christ, was later to be born. So
we believe that priests of the tribe of David [the author seems confused here;
the Jewish priesthood was from the tribe of the Levites] stood in that same
place until the arrival of Christ, and that they remained there afterwards up
until the time of Titus and Vespasian, rulers of the Romans.

1.3. Moreover, during the reign of those aforesaid rulers, a not inconsiderable persecution arose against the impious Jews, so great that scarcely a Jew,
or none at all, was able to be found in all the Promised Land who was not
shamefully sold to foreigners or violently put to the sword by them. So it
happened that all of Judea was reduced "into a wasteland nor was there one
who lived in it," except for a few faithful, who, hiding in the mountains out
of fear of the unbelievers, stayed alive on the roots of plants: They were made
paupers on account of God so they might merit being eternally enriched
by him. Seeing what had happened and that all the land was empty of its
inhabitants, coming forth from their caves these people then occupied the
holy places that the Lord had sanctified by his presence. Serving him in those
places day and night by keeping vigils, fasting, praying and afflicting their
own bodies for love of the heavenly kingdom, they poured forth diligent
prayers to God, so they might be free without fear from the hand of their
enemies and serve Him in sanctity and justice.

And there gathered around them Christians of various ranks: bishops,
priests, deacons and subdeacons awaiting consolation from the Lord, even
prepared to hand over their bodies for punishment on account of God. Holding counsel amongst themselves, they elected bishops and archbishops in each
of those cities where they lived, namely Caesarea, Jerusalem, Bethsan and
many others. In Hebron also they chose an archbishop and with him ministers of the priesthood, confirming and approving by the testimony of many
that it had formerly been the metropolitan city of the Philistines. Josephus
himself and Eusebius of Caesarea, besides Jerome, also affirm this. Many
bishops and priests were seized by the infidels and, having suffered diverse
punishments, in the end they were miserably dismembered.

1.4. And so, after many years passed, when the most pious emperor Theodosius was reigning the Christian churches were opened. The faith of the
Gospel sprouted and the number of Christian people grew, with faithful
ministers of Christ scattering the seed of the divine word to unknowing
peoples throughout the world. With a great crowd of believers gathered
about him, Theodosius began to seek the bodies of holy martyrs, who had
been killed by his predecessors (iniquitous emperors) or their followers in
many parts of the world, especially in the East, and he began to bring them

to Constantinople and build basilicas in their honor. Indeed, a considerable inquiry was made about the blessed patriarchs Abraham, Isaac, and Jacob. After holding counsel with the wise men of his kingdom, he sent a large number of men with bishops and priests into Judea to seek the sacrosanct bones of the holy patriarchs with diligent care and (if they were in any way able) to bear them with honor to him at Constantinople. He furthermore ordered that the blessed archbishop who presided over Cariatarbe at that time should aid them with the greatest zeal. For he himself, the most Christian emperor in the East, ruled all the way to Alexandria and beyond, nor was there one at that time who disturbed Christians, for throughout all that land there were Greek Christians.

O pious presumption! For so much did that your mind presume about the compassion of God, believing it possible to obtain something which at that point it did not merit and, piously unknowing, it attempted to oppose the will of God. Consider with how many afflictions he tormented himself, who desired to have so great a treasure. Indeed, he copiously wept in prayer every night. Burning with the ardent desire for those holy relics, among those prayers that he frequently poured forth to God, he asked this first and foremost: that God find it appropriate to grant his desire. Nor did so many and such great holy relics suffice for him, namely the bodies of six apostles and blessed Luke the Evangelist, also of blessed Stephen the protomartyr and many others – not only martyrs, but also confessors and virgins – which blessed Helena had gathered together with fitting honor in her basilica. For as he said: "By no means does it suffice for me, unless I have the bodies of the holy patriarchs." Although he was disappointed in his desire, nevertheless, because God did not wish his prayers to remain unfulfilled, He gave to him a precious treasure: namely the body of blessed Joseph, son of Israel, as the following will show.

1.5. Therefore, coming into Judea with great pomp, the men who had been sent by Theodosius inquired as to Hebron's whereabouts. When they had arrived there, they spoke to the archbishop of that same place. Peacefully greeting him on the part of Theodosius and making known the reason for their journey, they humbly asked that he show them the double cave. When he heard this, bursting into tears as he was a man of dovelike simplicity, the priest responded to them after careful consideration, saying: "It is most troublesome, my sons, what you require. Indeed, I am not acquainted with the double cave by sight, but am by no means ignorant of where the bodies of those holy men are said to be buried. Behold! It is held to be underneath these walls." For he had shown the walls to them, and he added: "Remain with me for several days and rest, since you are tired from the labor of your long journey. Meanwhile, let us humbly offer prayers directed to God, so that he himself might deign it appropriate to reveal to us this hidden treasure. Let his will be done – without his aid, we will accomplish nothing."

So they acquiesced to him, and he received them kindly in his house, ministering to them those things which were needed. Meanwhile, they prepared strong iron stakes for raising up the floor stones and shovels for digging up the earth, hiring paid workers to help them. On the designated day they came to the door of the sanctuary, but when they presumed to enter therein, God so struck them with blindness that even with their eyes open they could see nothing, nor by any means could they manage to reach the door. When they tried next to touch the wall and feel their way in, their hands stuck to the wall, nor were they able to proceed any farther. Indeed, they could not go forwards but they could easily go backwards, and if at some point they retreated, they were immediately restored to their former vision. They were at once equally distressed with shame and amazement, and they wondered amongst themselves at what had happened to them. After return-ing to their lodgings, supposing that by chance that this was happening to them on account of their sins, they confessed their faults to those priests who had come with them and so returned to the work begun: Yet nonetheless did all-powerful God carry out his own miracles among them. Seeing this, the inhabitants of this place praised and glorified the ever-living God, who alone makes wondrous things. O, how great was their grief! How many prayers did they pour forth to the universal God amid their tearful groans! For they feared lest by chance, following the commands of their ruler, they be deprived of such holy patronage.

1.6. Despite the differences, let us compare (if it is pleasing) what then happened to the ancient miracle that the Lord made for the blessed Lot in So-dom. When he took angels into his hospitality, men of that city surrounded his home so they might enter and carry out their accursed crimes. These men, however, wished to enter the sanctuary of the blessed patriarchs so they might piously and honorably remove their bodies. The former men were blinded for the sake of evil, so that they might altogether perish; the latter men were blinded for the sake of goodness, so that repenting of their sins they might be saved. The former men were thrust into hell with great horror; the latter men, bearing with them a most precious treasure (even if it was not the one that they wished for), returned to their homeland with the greatest joy: they were about to benefit even more from so great a miracle. Nor, do I think, did this happen without a reason. For it would be unworthy that those men, to whom God had granted in their lifetimes the land of Canaan as a gift, be exiled from it, albeit with the most appropriate veneration. O, the wondrous providence of God, that the saints might be discovered by the Christian faithful in the very place where they had been buried, and venerated by them with the highest praises in that same place for all remaining time, just as they are now. [With the assistance of the bishop of Hebron, the Greek envoys find and acquire the relics of Joseph, son of Jacob, joyfully returning with them to Constantinople.]

1.8. ... These deeds we related as having happened under Emperor Theodosius, most dear brothers, were truthfully related to us by a certain John, a monk of Mount Sinai, and a certain Syrian priest, both men of religion. We therefore insert them in this work so that, when you hear how the bones of the holy patriarchs were discovered by the Latins – which were not able to be found by such great and very religious men, nay more, by a hundred generations already passed – it might be clearly understood how much benevolence the creator of all things, God, has shown to them more than other peoples; and furthermore, so that people who say that Hebron is not a metropolitan city [the seat of a bishop] might reflect and repent, not wishing to believe Eusebius of Caesarea, Jerome, the confessor of Christ, and Josephus also – so they might at least assent to those things which are contained in Greek books, as we have written.

After some time, when the most pious Theodosius had died, for the purgation of the sins of the Christian people the Saracens [Muslims] burst forth from their borders, directing their forces against Judea. When this was discovered, the majority of the Greeks fled to Constantinople, living in that place and within its lands; certain others, whom the love of Christ had firmly bound together, remained there under the barbarians to worship at the holy places. Those who lived at Cariatarbe, however, fled with the others, hiding the entrance of that most sacred sanctuary so it would never be thought there had been an entrance into it. Bursting in, the barbarians seized all that region and Jerusalem, which God favors. Their priests took possession of the Temple of the Lord, which was in that place, and the city of Hebron. While those who arrived at Hebron wondered at the strong and beautiful composition of the sanctuary's walls, and at the fact that no entrance was apparent for going in, certain Jews who had stayed in that region under the rule of the Greeks came to them and said: "Give us your pledge that we might live together among you and allow us to build a synagogue before the entrance, and we will show you where you ought to make a door." And so it was done. It is too great a matter, however, to tell how that people (while granted they were infidels) honorably kept that place: how none of them, unless barefoot and with washed feet, would presume to enter into it, and how inside they built with miraculous workmanship a house of prayer [a mosque], for they wondrously decorated everything with gold and silver and silk cloth. Or to tell in what manner, after many years, the creator and the redeemer of all things took all that region from those aforesaid unbelievers and gave it back to the

Latin Christians [the crusaders]; or how the archbishop of Apamea altogether plundered the site of the holy patriarchs after Jerusalem was captured by the Franks through the virtue of God; or how a community of the Lord's clerics, under the apostolic rule, was established by the Latins in that same place to serve the Lord. Let us turn our pen (as we promised) to that story which God, by his grace, found worthy to manifest in our times.

2.1. In the twenty-first year of the kingdom of the Franks, there presided at Cariatarbe a certain man of pious memory by the name of Ranier, first prior of the Latins, who was venerable in virtue and praiseworthy in all things. On account of his devotion to God, he held himself in such low regard that, as much as he was thought to be exercising a position of authority over others, he seemed to be a servant to those under him, obviously imitating the pious teacher who said: "I did not come to be ministered unto but to minister." Thus many men gathered about him wishing to serve God under his teaching, among whom were Odo and Arnulf, priests of the Lord, by whose relation I learned that which I am telling. More than all others, these three, namely the prior and the two men named above, devoted themselves as much to prayers and nocturns as to vigils. Constantly afflicting themselves with tearful moans, they beseeched almighty God that he might grant to them that which he had previously denied to so many and such great people. Finally, God heard them and granted that which they had asked of him. Look, most dear brothers, how much the ceaseless prayer of the just can do! For these men were just and that which they asked for was just, and so it was given to them; if they had not been just, by no means would they have obtained what they wished for.

2.2. On a certain day in the month of June, when the regular canons were resting in their cells after midday as was customary, a certain brother of that same church (who was a scribe by training) entered into the church fleeing the heat of summer and lay down on the floor next to the pyramid of blessed Isaac. At that spot there was a little crack between two great floor-stones, from which a light and fragrant (nevertheless cold) breeze was escaping through an underground passage. As he was lying there, he caught the breeze coming from underneath in his bosom. As if playing, he began to drop through that little crack some small stones, which he heard fall into the depths, and he judged that there was some cistern or cavern there. Taking up a rod, he tied a long, strong string on its end, and a little piece of lead to the end of that string. Lowering it in, he measured eleven cubits in depth. By chance the prior was then absent, for burdened with certain business he had gone to Jerusalem. When the brothers awoke from their sleep and Nones [the ninth hour of the divine office, about three o'clock] was sung, this brother told them what he had found. Hearing this, they suspected that it was the entrance to the double cave. Waiting for two or three days and diligently praying to God that he might direct their labor to a good end, they meanwhile prepared iron tools which were necessary for cutting through the stones, for they were naturally very hard and nearly impervious to any iron. When a space of two or three days had passed, by the common counsel of all the brothers and with the permission of the lord who ruled there at that same time, named Baldwin, they took up that laborious work in the name of the Holy Trinity: yet with a fair amount of fear. For they were afraid lest by chance, on account of their sins, the Lord of the heavens and the earth did not wish to aid them. Therefore, more and more the priests exerted themselves by celebrating solemn masses, as did other clerics by reading the psalters, and laymen just as much by praying to the ruler of all creation that he might be appeased concerning their injustices, and, pleased with their supplications, he might deign it appropriate to bring that which they had begun to a conclusion in accordance with their prayers.

2.3. Although the stone-cutters were overwhelmed by great fatigue from cutting for many days, when the stones were finally cut and removed the mouth and entrance of a cave appeared. When it was opened, everyone wished to enter as they were all burning with desire. Since the place was not able to hold them all at once, however, they decided that the aforesaid Odo – as he seemed older than them all and was, after the prior, first canon of that same place – should enter first of all, figuring it appropriate that, if destiny brought it about, the fathers of many people might be discovered by an older man and by age their own father. Willingly undertaking this, he was lowered in by the brothers with a rope, but not finding a passageway by which he might proceed any farther, he called for them to pull him back up. So he was pulled out. On the following day they lowered in Arnulf, having given him a torch for naturally it was a very dark place. He began to wonder to himself what this place could be, for he saw that both walls were as one, so that you might think it was made from a single stone, and that all this work was similar to the wall above. At this point he did not know what to do and was disturbed by an incredible grief of his spirit, especially since no way lay open for him to proceed. Finally, having renewed his courage (for he was a sensible man), he took up an iron hammer and began to strike here and there to see if he might hear some empty space. Striking the wall on the east side, he heard a noise resonating from within, as if it were hollow.

2.4. Then, with his hope somewhat restored, he ordered some men to be lowered in who might remove the great stone by which the underground passage was blocked. When they were lowered in, they were barely able to move it after a space of four days. After the stone was removed, there appeared something like a large water-channel, nevertheless dry, having a height of eleven cubits, a length of seventeen, and a width of one. Entering into it and diligently looking about, yet finding entirely nothing, they wondered at this work and were afflicted by a great sadness. What a miraculous thing! Both the walls on the right and left side were composed of square and polished stones, equally firm as those above. At this point those who were present were overcome more by a grief of the spirit than a pain of the body. Yet Arnulf, whose mind, so to speak, was already conscious of finding the relics of the saints, took up a hammer as before and began to strike here and there, so that he might by chance hear what he had heard earlier. After hearing the sound of a hollow space before him, he encouraged the others who were with him to labor more zealously, showing them another stone which they ought to move. And so they exerted themselves for another four days in order to remove it. Looking through the hole they had made, they saw a little chamber in the shape of a basilica, built with an admirable workmanship in a round shape and enclosed from above by a single stone, with enough space inside to hold nearly thirty men. After seeing this, weeping in an excess of great joy, they gave glory to the Lord but in no way did they presume to enter it. For they figured that the relics of the saints were in that place and therefore they waited for their superior to return from Jerusalem. When he did get back, they told him what had happened. O, how he was filled with such a great exaltation of heart, when he heard that which he was wishing for! However, since he had not been present at the beginning of this undertaking, grieving he cried out that he was wretched.

2.5. After calling a council of the brothers that same day, they decided that they would enter into that place after Nones, with all the brothers aroused from their sleep, on that very day. Once they had diligently investigated what was in there, they might better know what they ought to do next. And so it was done. Coming to that place at the appointed hour and removing the stone from the opening of the discovered basilica, they entered: yet they did not at all find what they thought they would. Whereupon they were greatly dumbfounded and wondered at that little chamber. Indeed, it ought to be marveled at still today, since such a kind of place is either scarcely able to be found or not at all, especially underground. While the prior himself and those who had entered with him were considering whether they would be able to find the entrance to the double cave anywhere, Arnulf turned back to the opening of the basilica. Carefully looking at its entrance, he noticed a small stone in the shape of a wedge inserted into the natural rock, which he ordered to be removed. When it was removed, the entrance into that much desired cave appeared. Then they all tearfully gave thanks to God, beseeching him to find it worthy to reveal to them what was inside, similar to that wise woman who "having lost a coin, lights a lamp and overturns her house, diligently seeking until she finds it." For they overturned their house – namely, the tomb of the patriarchs – and lit a lamp of prayers and afflictions, offering gifts welcome to God, and they acquired from him what they sought in his name. O, the truthful promise of God, which disappoints no one, for it is said: "Whatever you shall have asked the Father in my name, he will give to you."

2.6. Therefore, after the cave was opened on the seventh kalends of July [25 June 1119], in the name of obedience and penance the prior commanded Arnulf, who had labored the most, to enter and thus bring his labor all the way to completion. Nor was there delay. Taking a candle in his hand, fortifying himself with the sign of the sacred cross and singing "Kyrie eleison" in a high-sounding voice, not without fear he entered. Thinking to himself, lest by chance Baldwin, the defender of that same place, suspect that there was a treasure of gold or silver inside, he encouraged the prior to advise Baldwin to go in there along with him. Accordingly, the prior asked Baldwin. Acquiescing to the prior's entreaties, Baldwin entered but seized by fear he fled at once. Searching, Arnulf circled about the cave to see if he might find the bones of the saints, and in that hour he found nothing except earth sprinkled as if with blood. Turning back, he announced this to those who awaited him outside. Hearing this they all departed, filled with a great sadness.

2.7. On the following day, the prior advised Arnulf to enter the cave again and search about on all sides, digging up the earth with the greatest care. Following the commands of his master, he took a staff in his hand and entered. When he dug at the earth with the staff, he discovered the bones of blessed Jacob: at this point, not knowing whose they were, he gathered them together in one place. Thereupon, proceeding further and looking more diligently, he saw the opening of a second cave at the head of holy Jacob, in which were the bones of the blessed Abraham and Isaac: at that time it was closed, but when he had opened it, there was a cavern. After entering into it he discovered in its depths a most sacred body marked as that of holy Abraham, and at his feet the bones of blessed Isaac his son. For they had not all been buried in one cave, as some claim, but rather Abraham and Isaac in the inner one and Jacob in the outer one. Arnulf, who had discovered this greatest and incomparable treasure, went forth from the cave and announced to the prior and the brothers that he had discovered the relics of the blessed patriarchs. Hearing what they had awaited for a long time with the greatest expectation, they praised God with exulting spirits in hymns and songs. Taking water and wine, Arnulf washed the bones of the saints' relics and placed the relics of each father individually onto wooden boards that they had prepared for this purpose. Then he put them back down there and departed. Whereupon the prior, after everyone left, diligently sealed the entrance so that no one might enter without his leave.

2.8. Indeed, on another day, when some of them were entering in there for the sake of prayer, they saw – on the right of one going in – some traces of letters carved on a certain stone, which they showed to the others; however, at that point, they were not able to figure out what they meant. Raising up that one stone and finding nothing except earth and figuring that the letters were not carved there without a reason, they dug at the wall on the opposite side – to the left of one entering the cave – and discovered on the sixth kalends of August [27 July] some fifteen earthenware vessels filled with the bones of the dead. Whose they were, truthfully they did not know; nevertheless, it ought to be believed that they were the relics of some of the first leaders of Israel.

2.9. With all this done, the prior set out for Jerusalem to tell Warmund of pious memory, the patriarch who at that time presided there, about the discovery of the saints, and to ask that he come to Cariatarbe for the elevation of the patriarchs' bodies. With benevolent spirit, Warmund promised many times that he would come; however, not using good judgment, he disappointed the one to whom he had sworn that he would come. So the prior, seeing that he was fooled by the patriarch, revealed the precious relics of the holy patriarchs with appropriate honor on the day before the Nones of October [6 October] with a great multitude of people present who had gathered from Jerusalem and the neighboring cities for the celebration of the saints. With clerics chanting in high voices and singing "Te Deum laudamus" [we praise you, God], and with the cloister purified by a ceremonial procession, he displayed them for viewing to the eager people. Blessed are you, Lord God, who hid these things from the wise and the prudent, and revealed them to the meek! O how great was everyone's exultation! How much weeping there was out of an excess of joy, when those blessed bones were kissed, which had never been granted to any other people. Therefore, after all these rituals were carried out, commending themselves to the holy protection of the blessed patriarchs, everyone returned home with joy.

Consider the first part of this account, where the anonymous author offers a history of Hebron from the time of Abraham until the crusader conquest: what does his presentation imply about the relationship of the Jews to the site? What about Greek Christians and Muslims? Why did God prevent any other people from discovering the relics of the patriarchs before the arrival of the Latin crusaders? As seen in previous documents, Hebron was an important pilgrimage site for Jews, Christians, and Muslims: how might pilgrims from all three religious traditions have reacted to the news that the Latin canons at the site had discovered the patriarchs' remains?

48. RICHARD OF CORNWALL'S CRUSADE

In addition to large-scale crusading expeditions to Jerusalem, Egypt, or other locations in the eastern Mediterranean, smaller contingents of "armed pilgrims" continued to set out for the Promised Land, intending to support the remaining Christians in the region, to fight the "infidels," and to perform acts of pious veneration at the holy places. One such force left England in 1240 under the leadership of Earl Richard of Cornwall (1209–72), brother of King Henry III (r. 1216–72). The account below, written by chronicler Matthew Paris, includes a letter written by Richard himself back to his compatriots in England, who were eager to hear news of his journey.

Source: trans. J.A. Giles, in Matthew Paris's *English History*, vol. 1 (London: Henry G. Bohn, 1852), pp. 287–90, 308–9, 362–69; revised.

Earl Richard and the Other Nobles Set Sail

In this year Earl Richard, after he made all the necessary preparations for his journey to Jerusalem, went to the abbey of St-Albans, entering the chapter-house and begging the assistance of the prayers of the brotherhood. From there he went to London, between Ascension and Whit Sunday, and said farewell to the king, his brother, the legate, and the rest of the nobles, after which he hastened his steps towards Dover. The king took the earl's son Henry, and also his possessions, into his care. The legate, and a great number of nobles, prelates, and religious men, accompanied him on his journey to the sea-coast, where they devoutly entrusted him to divine guidance. Brother Theodoric, however, a prior of the Hospitallers, still attended him as his inseparable companion and guide. A great many nobles of England set sail about this same time, including among others William Longuespee, earl of Salisbury, and a great many others too numerous to mention, and a great many barons and knights who adhered to them as their leaders and chiefs.

The King of France Receives Earl Richard with Great Honor

After Earl Richard safely arrived on the shores of the continent, he entered the French territories and made his way towards the king [Louis IX]. As he drew near, however, the king, with his mother B[lanche] and many of his nobles, came to meet him with rejoicing and entertained him in his palace, feasting with him as his beloved relation and loading him with royal presents. On the earl's departure, he also sent his marshal as a protector and guide to him through the whole of his territory, who bountifully and honorably supplied the necessary things for the journey and lodgings for him and his followers until he had safely passed the Rhone. The citizens of Avignon, too, came to meet him with great demonstrations of joy and freely offered to procure him entertainment in their city at their own expense. He afterwards took boats at Vienne, determining to sail down the Rhone to the city of Arles, but the citizens of Vienne and other neighboring cities asked Earl Richard to sell them his passage-boats, for which they would give him three times their value. When the earl refused to do so, stating that he was not a merchant, they seized and detained them by force. The earl, however, much offended, pursued his journey as he could, and arrived at the city of Arles. The citizens of Vienne afterwards repenting, although late, of this enormous offence of theirs, sent the vessels that they had taken away from the earl to him at Beaucaire, but the earl, in his indignation, destroyed them all. The count of Toulouse was greatly vexed at this injury having been inflicted on Earl Richard in his dominions, for they were relations ...

Earl Richard Visits St-Gilles

When Earl Richard had arrived thus far, knowing that he was not far from the city of St-Gilles, he hastened to that place to pay his devotions so that, in the same way as he had done a short while before at the general chapter of the Cistercians, he might commend himself in all humility to their prayers. In his innate munificence, he bestowed on them a yearly income of 20 marks for the improvement of the condition of the community, so, with the favor of Saint Gilles, he might more safely pass through the dangers of the sea.

The Pope Forbids Earl Richard to Set Sail

When Earl Richard had arrived at St-Gilles, he was met by a legate and the archbishop of Arles, who forbade him by authority of the pope to set sail. The earl was greatly astonished by this and replied that he had once believed there was truth in the words of the apostolic see [of Rome], and in the preachers whom it sent, but being greatly vexed at this prohibition, he said; "I have made all the necessary preparations for my passage, have bidden farewell to my friends, have sent my money and arms in advance of me, and have got my ships ready and loaded them with provisions. Now the tone is altered. Just as I have arrived at the seacoast and am about to embark, the pope, who is called the successor and vicar of Jesus Christ, who is said to have never broken his word, forbids me to proceed on the service of Christ, although I am now ready for all emergencies." Seeing that they could not prevent him from setting sail, the legates advised him to leave the port of Marseilles and to put to sea from the port of Aigues Mortes, which latter place was abhorred by the whole army, owing to its foul and sickly state. Therefore, they dissuaded the earl from doing so. Despite the false and ambiguous arguments of the legates, detesting the duplicity of the Roman church, with great bitterness of spirit he adhered to his purpose of sailing from Marseilles. He then went, in the first place, to Roche, where he prepared and loaded his ships. He also sent word to the emperor by special messengers, namely, the knight Robert de Twenge and others, informing him of his condition, and the pope's cunning devices. On the week before the octaves of the Nativity of Saint Mary, he put to sea.

Earl Richard Arrives at the Holy Land after a Prosperous Voyage

During this time, Earl Richard, who had been on his voyage to the Holy Land, at length arrived safely on the twelfth day after Michaelmas at the port of Acre, together with the whole of his own fleet, as well as the foreign fleet which had joined him. When he landed, he was received with great joy by the prelates and clerks in procession, clothed in their sacred robes, and by chiefs and knights, who came to meet him with due reverence, amidst the applause of the people, the ringing of bells, the chanting of the clergy, and the music of cymbals and harps with attendant bands of dancers. In this way, at his arrival, all seemed to be united with the inhabitants of heaven and were refreshed with inexpressible joy and exultation, for, raising their hands toward heaven, they cried: "Blessed is he who comes in the name of the Lord." On the third day after he had landed, he caused a proclamation to be made in Acre by the voice of a herald, that no Christian pilgrim should take his departure owing to a want of money, but that all were to stay and fight boldly for Christ, and they would be supported for pay by him.

Earl Richard's Letters Containing an Account of His Pilgrimage

About this time, the friends of Earl Richard, anxious about his proceedings, were fully informed about them by the following letter from him:

"Richard, earl of Cornwall and count of Poitou, to the noble, venerable, and well-beloved masters in Christ, B. de Rivers, earl of Devon, the abbot of Beaulieu, and Robert, clerk, health and every good wish, with sincere affection. Of the great desolation and grief of which the Holy Land has long been the seat, and how difficult a matter has been its reparation and relief since the catastrophe at Gaza, wise men are sensible. Experience of the truth has reached those dwelling near and report has carried to those at a distance, and but that the present letter might disclose our secret, and being opened on the way to you give occasion to a sinister interpretation, many things would be explained in it which now sleep and lie concealed in the bottom of our heart. From the time when kings and kingdoms turned aside from Jerusalem, owing to its being divided and held by iniquitous and unjust possessors, we have been consumed with no small grief and cannot altogether be silent, but must loosen our tongue in bitter complaint, as there is no pleasant matter to occupy it. For the sword of compassion has pierced to our soul, so as not to be able to contain itself. For some time past, indeed, in the Holy Land, discord has reigned instead of peace, schism instead of union, hatred instead of affection, and justice has been totally excluded. Of such seed there have been many planters in that land, and many have become collectors of the fruit springing from it, but I hope they are now eradicated."

"There is no one among all of its beloved ones to console it. For twin brothers, disagreeing in the bosom of their mother, whose business it was to defend her, becoming proud in their affluence, have nourished and fomented these humors at the roots, and caused the branches of it to spread far and wide. For an abundance of good things produces such an itching after mutual contention, that the reprimands of the father who presides over the see of Peter [the pope] are encountered with the utmost indifference, provided that the stronger party dazzle the world with their renown. To the pacification of these discordant parties we have applied no small portion of care, but, as yet, the footsteps of peace leave no impression, inasmuch as the followers of discord do not acquiesce in the words of peace. Those who have money easily allure others to them as long as it lasts, but when the time for vindicating the modesty of their mother arrives, they leave the peace-makers, and feigning secret impediments, show no regard to bring consolation to their mother. From this cause, and the great number of the Gallic cavalry, almost twice as numerous as the Saracens [Muslims], utterly prostrated by evil habits, the enemies of the cross were so unexpectedly encouraged that a small body of them thought little or nothing of numbers of us. Owing to this, on our first arrival here, the nobles who were thought likely to help us were taking their departure, and it appeared to be a serious and difficult matter to relieve the country. Yet, the divine clemency, when it wills it, suffers injuries to be without their remedies and sorrow to be without means of consolation."

"For when we were expecting, on our arrival here, in conjunction with the rest of the Christians, to the utmost of our power, as was incumbent upon us, according to our vow, to revenge the insults offered to the cross on the enemies of that cross, by attacking their territory and afterwards occupying and restoring them to good condition, behold the king of Navarre, then the head and chief of the army, and the count of Brittany, although aware of our approach for 15 days before we arrived at Acre, took their departure with an immense host. Before they left, however, in order that they might appear to have done something, they made a kind of truce with Nazir, the lord of Crach, by which it was agreed that he should give up all the prisoners taken at Gaza, whom he had in his custody or power, together with some lands contained in the conditions of the truce, as a security for which he gave his son and brothers as hostages, fixing on a term of 40 days for fulfilling the terms of the truce. Before that period, however, had elapsed, the said king and count departed, paying no heed to the time agreed on, or to the terms of the truce. Within this said period, namely, on Saint Dionysius's eve [9 October 1240], we, as we have before informed you, arrived at Acre. By the general advice of all, we at once sent to the aforesaid Nazir, to ask him if he could observe towards us the truce he had made with the said king, and we received word in reply, that he would willingly do so if possible, owing to his respect for the said king of Navarre, although he should gain but little by it. We therefore, by the advice of the nobles, awaited the completion of the term fixed on to see the result. At the expiration of the term, however, we received another message from him, stating that he could on no account abide by the aforesaid agreement. On hearing this, by the common consent of all, we betook ourselves to Joppa to improve with all possible caution the condition of the Holy Land, which had deteriorated from the aforesaid causes. At this place a man of rank and power came to us on the part of the sultan of Babylon, and told us that his lord was willing to enter into a truce with us if we pleased. After hearing and perfectly understanding what was to be set forth to us by him, and having with all sincerity invoked the grace of God, we, by the advice of the duke of Burgundy, Count Walter de Brienne, the master of the Hospitallers, and other nobles, in fact, the chief part of the army, agreed to the under-mentioned terms of truce, which, although at our first arrival appeared to be a difficult matter to accomplish, is yet a praiseworthy one, and productive of advantage to the Holy Land, since it is a source of delight and security to the poor people and to travelers, advantageous and agreeable to the middle classes of the inhabitants, and useful and honorable to the rich and to religious men. Nor did it appear to us, on looking at the melancholy condition of surrounding events, that we could then employ ourselves more advantageously than in releasing the wretched prisoners from captivity, as there was a deficiency of men and things (although we alone still had money about us), and profiting by the time of the truce to strengthen and fortify against the Saracens the cities and castles that had become ruinous. We have thought it proper to insert the names of the places and territories which were given up in accordance with the terms of the truce, although it may be tedious to you, lest perchance some evil interpreter may ascribe our deeds by way of glory to others or perversely or maliciously pervert their character"…. [A detailed list of various cities, territories, and fortifications in the region of Jerusalem follows.]

"… All this territory, with the castles therein before named, the Christians are allowed to fortify during the truce if they wish. The noble captives taken at Gaza are also to be restored, and all the prisoners taken in the war with the French are to be released on both sides. As soon as the aforesaid truce was arranged, we took our way to Ascalon, and that the time might not hang idly on our hands, by the advice of all the Christian chiefs we began to fortify a large castle. From that place we sent messengers to the sultan of Babylon, to induce him to swear to observe the said truce, if he would do so, and at the same time to send the aforesaid prisoners. He, however, for what reason we know not, detained our messengers, without giving us any reply, from Saint Andrew's day [30 November] until the Thursday after Candlemas [2 February]. During this time, as we afterwards found by his letters, he, by the advice of his nobles, swore to keep the said truce. We, during all this time, remained at Ascalon, assiduously intent on building the aforesaid castle, which, by God's favor has, in a short time, progressed so far that at the time of dispatching these presents, it is already adorned and entirely surrounded by a double wall with lofty towers and ramparts, with four square stones and carved marble columns, and everything which pertains to a castle, except a fosse round it, which will, God willing, be completed without fail, within a month from Easter. And this was not done without good reason, for as we could not be certain that the truce would be confirmed, we thought it best to employ our time in building and fortifying this castle; so that if the truce should be broken by any casualty, we might have, in the march and in the very entrance of their territory, this place, which was formerly under their dominion, as a safe and strong place of refuge, if it were necessary for us to retreat there. And those who remained therein would have no occasion to fear the result of a siege, for although the besiegers could cut off all assistance and provisions from them by land, yet all necessaries could reach them by sea…. On Saint George's day [23 April], then, after peace had been sworn to be observed on both sides, and after the truce had been confirmed, we received according to the terms of the truce, all the Christian captives whom we had been so long expecting. After duly completing these matters, we took leave of the Holy Land in peace, and on the festival of the finding of the Holy Cross we embarked at Acre to return home. Owing to the fair wind failing us on the voyage, and being much fatigued, we landed at Trapani in Sicily, on the octaves of Saint John. At that place we heard of the capture and detention of some of our bishops, and of other lamentable sufferings of the church. Therefore, in order to restore peace as far as we were able, among those at variance, and to urge with all our power the release of captives, and to give comfort to our mother, we turned aside from our course, and went to the court of Rome. As soon as, by God's favor, the Lord disposes all events, we purpose returning to England with all possible speed."

What route did Earl Richard take to reach the Holy Land? Whom did he encounter during his journey and what problems did he face? When he writes to his friends back in England, what complaints does he have about his fellow Christians in the holy places? What concern does he show for pilgrims, travelers, and other Christians? Richard never actually went to Jerusalem itself, but he presents his "pilgrimage" as a success: how does he make this claim? Based on the evidence here, was Richard of Cornwall a pilgrim, a crusader, or something in between?

CHAPTER SIX

PILGRIMAGE AND MEDIEVAL SOCIETY

Historians commonly identify the "High Middle Ages," meaning from around the years 1050 to 1300, as a period of confidence and maturity for medieval European Christian civilization, one that witnessed the emergence of newly effective governing institutions, both secular and ecclesiastical, thriving cities and renewed commercial life, the origins of the university, and the building of monumental "Gothic" cathedrals, among many other noteworthy developments. In many ways, the notion of Christendom as the community of Catholic believers assembled under the spiritual authority of Rome came into its own during this expansionary era. Alongside the flourishing cult of saints and relics, pilgrimage formed part of the fabric of this dynamic medieval Christian society. Pilgrims took to the roads, sometimes visiting local shrines, sometimes heading for major devotional sites such as the church of Saint James at Compostela or the city of Rome. Firmly embedded in a wider set of devotional traditions, pilgrimage required pragmatic arrangements for transporting, feeding, and housing pious travelers. Monks and clerics recorded stories about the saints and their miracles to attract further visitors (and, with them, pious donations). As the European economy and society boomed, so did Christian pilgrimage. In this period of effervescence, pilgrimage also manifested some of the limits and challenges faced by the Christian society of medieval Europe, which, despite (or perhaps because of) its relative security and prosperity, showed an increasingly anxious concern with the definition and regulation of proper religious beliefs and practices.

49. GUIBERT OF NOGENT, *ON THE SAINTS AND THEIR RELICS*

Around 1125, exegete, chronicler, and theologian Guibert, abbot of Nogent, completed his tract On the Saints and their Relics, *which criticized many common devotional practices relating to the veneration of the saints and their bodily remains. Although Guibert did not entirely doubt the miraculous power of the saints, he identified what he saw as common forms of abuse and fraud perpetrated in their names, above all where the transfer and fabrication of relics were concerned. Guibert's tract did not circulate widely in the twelfth century, but his work provides a powerful critique of popular trends in Christian piety, anticipating later medieval and early modern criticisms of relics and pilgrimage.*

Source: trans. T. Head, in *Medieval Hagiography: An Anthology*, ed. T. Head (New York: Garland Publishing, 2000), pp. 417–22.

... But let us be finished with those [saints] whose very obscurity deprives them of authority, and turn instead to those [saints] whom the certitude of faith upholds. Surely the errors [told about] them are also endless! For some say that they have the relics of a certain saint, while others claim to have the same relics. Let us take the example of the head of John the Baptist: the people of Constantinople say that they possess it, but the monks of Angely claim to have the very same head. What greater absurdity can be preached about this man than that he be said by two groups to have two heads? But let us be done with absurdities and attend to the matter at hand. Since it is certain that a head is not able to be duplicated, and thus that the two groups are unable to have [what they claim], it is obvious that one group or the other has resorted to lies. When two sides contend with each other arrogantly and falsely about a pious matter, they substitute a devilish behavior for a godly one. Thus both the deceivers and the deceived vainly venerate the very relic about which they boast. Behold how, when some unworthy object is venerated, the whole crowd of supporters is subjected to a long chain of false reasoning. And even if one head is not that of John the Baptist, but in fact that of some other saint, still the claims made about it are no less sinful lies.

Why am I going on about the head of John the Baptist, when each day I hear the same thing said about innumerable bodies of other saints? When my predecessor, the bishop of Amiens, transferred what he thought to be the body of Saint Firminus the martyr from one casket to another, he failed to discover any document inside, not even a single letter of testimony as to who lay there. I have heard this with my own ears from the bishop of Arras, and even from [his successor as] bishop of Amiens. For which reason the bishop forthwith had an inscription made on a leaden plate, which would lie in the reliquary: "This is Firminus the martyr, bishop of Amiens." Not long afterward, the incident was repeated in a similar manner at the monastery of St-Denis. Relics were taken forth from their resting place in order to be placed in a more ornate shrine, which had been prepared by the abbot. When the skull was unwrapped along with the bones, a slip of parchment was found in the martyr's nostrils, on which it was written that *this* body was Firminus, the martyr of Amiens. Things are not as those from Amiens claimed them to be in this matter, for written testimonies give voice to a contrary claim and reason, if you please, takes the seat of judgment. Will not the inscription placed on that metal plate by the bishop be judged legally null and void? Does his claim become valid merely by being written down? Surely those from St-Denis would object, and they at least have [older] writings on their side. So we see that those people who venerate a patron saint about whom they are unsure are always in great danger, even if that patron turns out to be ancient. For if that patron is not a saint, they have committed an enormous sacrilege. What is a greater sacrilege than to venerate as holy something that is not? For only those things which pertain to God are divine. And what pertains to God more than those who are united in one body with God? I have heard [a story] which will throw light on our concerns and help us to make judgments about those matters we are discussing. A certain Odo — bishop of Bayeux, bastard son of Robert, count of the Normans, and thus the natural brother of William, the senior king of the English — ardently wished to possess [the relics] of his holy predecessor Exuperius, which were enshrined with great honor in the city of Corbeil. He paid a hundred pounds to the guardian of the church in which the saint was enshrined in order that he might receive [relics of the] saint from him. The custodian, cunningly asking the bishop to wait for him, dug up the tomb of a certain peasant who was also named Exuperius. The bishop asked him whether what had been brought [to him] were [the relics of] Saint Exuperius and even demanded an oath from the guardian. The guardian said, "I swear under oath to you that this is the body of Exuperius, but I can say nothing about his being a saint, since that title has been given to many people whose reputation is far from being saintly." Thus the bishop, deceived by the thief, did nothing. When the townspeople learned how he had turned their patron into merchandise, the guardian became the object of scorn. When pressed by them, he responded, "Go back and check the seals of the saint's tomb, and if you do not find them unbroken, I will pay recompense." Behold how this acquisition of false [relics] by the bishop brought dishonor on all religion, by profanely promoting this peasant Exuperius to sainthood and placing his bones on the sacred altar of God, which may never be rid of this blasphemy. My memory is full of many similar events done in every quarter, but I lack both the time and the strength to recount them. Fraudulent deals are frequently struck – not so much in the case of whole bodies, as in the case of limbs and parts of bodies – and common bones are thus distributed to be venerated as the relics of the saints. These things are clearly done by those who, according to the apostle, "suppose gain to be godliness" and turn those very things which should serve for the salvation of their souls into the excrement of bags of money.

But all such practices stem from a perverse root, which is nothing other than that [the bodies of the saints] are deprived of that which all [who share in] human nature ought to be accorded as a common lot. For if it is more certain than certainty itself that the origin of humanity comes from the earth and, because of original sin, [humanity] will according to the law return to that same earth when the penalty of death is paid, it is most certainly said to human beings: "You are dust, and to dust you shall return." As far as I know, God has not said to anyone yet living or to come: "You are gold or silver, and to gold or silver you shall return." So why, I ask, should a human being be removed from the natural elements (still less by the order of God) and be enclosed in gold or silver cases, which are not required for purposes of preservation.... No matter what type of coffin you use to seek to ward off the touch of the earth, you will become earth, whether you wish it or not. And why should anyone be granted the dignity of being enclosed in gold or silver, when the Son of God is buried in the lowliest rock? From the earliest centuries not even the proudest of kings has attempted such a thing; not a single example comes to my mind. Even when they invested infinite amounts of treasure in their tombs, I do not remember having read that they exchanged pure marble for coffins of gold or silver. What sort of an attempt is it to emulate God – certainly not one according to reason! – when faith, bearing no true fruit but bringing forth much that is unseemly, produces in our age [a practice] which we are unable to find in any other religion, indeed in any display of wealth, in this world? Surely if the bodies of the saints remained in the places assigned them by nature – that is, in their graves – then errors of the sort I have encountered would not exist. But, as it is, these bodies are removed from their tombs, their limbs carried in every direction, and, under the pretext of piety, opportunities arise to display them. Such a degree of wickedness has entered this practice and the uprightness of its original intention has been so distorted, that a general avarice has corrupted [a practice] which had been begun in good faith.... What judgment will be imposed on those whose only reason is avarice, [those] who cause the bodies of the saints to have no rest and to be scattered about, even, as I have said, having them displayed on a daily basis for the sole reason of obtaining offerings? For they are accustomed to cover the bare bones of the saints in boxes made of ivory and silver, and then, when requests flow in on them, they uncover [those bones] at certain times and places....

Edmund was a king and martyr of no small renown among the English, whose zeal in the care of his body I wish other saints would imitate. To this very day he remains in a sleeplike state and will not allow anyone to see or touch him. Although I will not mention those things which may be read in his *Passion*, [I will tell how] in our own time an abbot of [Bury St Edmunds], being more than a little curious, wondered whether the saint's head, which had once been cut off, was now reunited to the body, as popular opinion held. After having undertaken a fast with one of his monks, he tried, with that monk's help, to separate the neck [of the saint] from the shoulders. But he was instantly punished for his attempt with so great an infirmity that no movement remained in either of his hands. If [the saints] were allowed to rest in their graves, without any exchanges or transactions over their bodies and relics, then all dispute would cease. If the tombs of all the saints remained untouched, as is just, then one group of people would not be able to say that they had a certain relic which another group also claimed to possess. If all the saints were to rest unmoving in the earth to which they had been consigned, then frauds such as we have reported above concerning the distribution of their broken parts could not take place and unworthy people would not be held in high regard [as saints].

A question might also be posed by some people concerning relics: when they are honored as belonging to one saint but are those of another, and are not what they are thought to be, will something disastrous happen to the people who venerate [those relics], as is often thought? I do not agree. For our Lord says of the saints, "That they may be one, even as we are one." Their union under Christ as head provides them, as it were, an identity of body and they join together to be one in spirit with God. Among the bones of those who truly are saints, there is no error if the bones of some saints are honored as being the bones of others who are recognized as their fellow members in the body of their Creator. According to this opinion, it does not seem to be problematic that the festival of the Four Crowned Martyrs is observed through the authority of Rome under the names of five other martyrs.

But, given this, someone will doubtless ask whether God hears those simple folk when he is invoked by them through [the intercession of] those who do not number among the saints. One would answer that, although a person might annoy God when praying to him through [a saint] of uncertain status, nevertheless when a person prays faithfully believing someone who is not [a saint] to be [a saint], then that person still pleases God. For the sake of argument, let us suppose that there is a person who thinks that giving alms is a sin. If that person were knowingly to give alms, and that person were to have done this deed with full attention to conscience, then that person would sin, even though for anyone else to act in this manner would be a good deed. Let us then take the case of people who value as a saint someone whom they have heard called a saint, but who is not truly numbered among the saints. If such people were to ask the aid of the [false] saint wholeheartedly and in accord with the faith, and if the entire intention of their prayer were to be fixed upon God, who is both the seed and the fruit of prayer, then – no matter the manner in which the soul may seem to have erred through simplicity concerning the choice of intercessor – their prayer would be honored [by God], for what is done with good intentions is never denied a good reward. If you receive a prophet in the name of a prophet, that is one who has only the name of a just man and prophet with none of the reality, then you share in the full merit of the prophet and just man, although the person who only has the name of just man and prophet, and who merely pretends [to possess] their habits, is himself left bereft [of any merit]. Surely many barely literate persons are frequently mistaken in their prayers, but the divine ear judges intentions rather than words. For if when you pray "Lord may the power of the Holy Spirit be with us," you were to say *absit* [be away from us] rather than *assit* [be with us], yet do so earnestly, it would not harm you. God is not overly attentive to grammar. No voice comes to him, that his heart does not embrace.

On what specific grounds does Guibert criticize the transfer of relics from one place to another? What signs are there in his tract that he disapproves of the lavish display of relics? Why does Guibert fear that the veneration of the saints might detract from the worship of God? Imagine that his criticisms of the cult of saints and relics were embraced by many of his contemporaries in the Roman church: what impact might this have had on twelfth-century traditions of pilgrimage to various churches and shrines around Europe?

50. ACCOMMODATING PILGRIMS AT THE CHURCH OF ST-DENIS

In terms of church architecture, the twelfth century is famous for the emergence of the "Gothic" style, which featured technical developments that allowed for larger, stained-glass windows, filling churches with radiant light. Some of the first steps toward the Gothic style were taken by Abbot Suger of St-Denis (ca 1081–1151) during his redesign and expansion of the basilica of St-Denis outside Paris. As seen in the selection below, written by Suger himself, he justified his renovations by describing the large crowds of pilgrims who visited the site to venerate the holy relics there, dangerously overfilling the church. One can imagine similar scenes at other important churches around Western Europe during the twelfth century.

Source: trans. E. Panofsky, in *Abbot Suger on the Abbey Church of St-Denis and Its Art Treasures*, ed. E. Panofsky and G. Panofsky-Suerel, 2nd ed. (Princeton: Princeton University Press, 1946), pp. 87–98.

When the glorious and famous king of the Franks, Dagobert, notable for his royal magnanimity in the administration of his kingdom and yet less devoted to the church of God, had fled to the village of Catulliacum [St-Denis] in order to evade the intolerable wrath of his father Clothaire the Great, and when he had learned that the venerable images of the holy martyrs who rested there – appearing to him as very beautiful men clad in snow-white garments – requested his service and unhesitatingly promised him their aid with words and deeds, he decreed with admirable affection that a basilica of the saints be built with regal magnificence. When he had constructed this [basilica] with a marvelous variety of marble columns he enriched it incalculably with treasures of purest gold and silver and hung on its walls, columns, and arches tapestries woven of gold and richly adorned with a variety of pearls, so that it might seem to excel the ornaments of all other churches and, blooming with incomparable luster and adorned with every terrestrial beauty, might shine with inestimable splendor. Only one thing was wanting in him: that he did not allow for the size that was necessary. Not that anything was lacking in his devotion or good will; but perhaps there existed thus far, at that time of the early church, no [church] either greater or [even] equal in size; or perhaps [he thought that] a smallish one – reflecting the splendor of gleaming gold and gems to the admiring eye more keenly and delightfully because they were nearer – would glow with greater radiance than if it were built larger.

Through a fortunate circumstance attending this singular smallness – the number of the faithful growing and frequently gathering to seek the intercession of the saints – the aforesaid basilica had come to suffer grave inconveniences. Often on feast days, completely filled, it disgorged through all its doors the excess of the crowds as they moved in opposite directions, and the outward pressure of the foremost ones not only prevented those attempting to enter from entering but also expelled those who had already entered. At times you could see, a marvel to behold, that the crowded multitude offered so much resistance to those who strove to flock in to worship and kiss the holy relic the nail and crown of the Lord, that no one among the countless thousands of people because of their very density could move a foot; that no one, because of their very congestion, could [do] anything but stand like a marble statue, stay benumbed or, as a last resort, scream. The distress of the women, however, was so great and so intolerable that you could see with horror how they, squeezed in by the mass of strong men as in a winepress, exhibited bloodless faces as in imagined death; how they cried out horribly as though in labor; how several of them, miserably trodden underfoot [but then] lifted by the pious assistance of men above the heads of the crowd, marched forward as though upon a pavement; and how many others, gasping with their last breath, panted in the cloisters of the brethren to the despair of everyone. Moreover the brethren who were showing the tokens of the passion of our Lord to the visitors had to yield to their anger and rioting and many a time, having no place to turn, escaped with the relics through the windows. When I was instructed by the brethren as a schoolboy I used to hear of this; in my youth I deplored it from without; in my mature years I zealously strove to have it corrected. But when it pleased him who separated me from my mother's womb, and called me by his grace, to place insignificant me, although my merits were against it, at the head of the important administration of this sacred church; then, impelled to a correction of the aforesaid inconvenience only by the ineffable mercy of almighty God and by the aid of the holy martyrs our patron saints, we resolved to hasten with all our soul and all the affection of our mind, to the enlargement of the aforesaid place – we who would never have presumed to set our hand to it, not even to think of it, had not so great, so necessary, so useful and honorable an occasion demanded it.

How does Suger describe the original church built at St-Denis? How does he portray the basilica during the days when crowds of pilgrims filled it, including, specifically, female visitors? What led him to commission the architectural changes to the church? Based on this description, would the dangerous crowds of pilgrims probably have encouraged or discouraged pilgrims from visiting St-Denis?

51. MIRACLES AT THE SHRINE OF THOMAS BECKET

On 29 December 1170, after years of contention with the English ruler Henry II, Archbishop Thomas Becket of Canterbury was murdered by four of the king's knights in the cathedral church at Canterbury. Becket's remains immediately began to attract pilgrims and visitors seeking the healing power of the saint. Becket, canonized in 1173, emerged as one of the most popular saints in medieval England, where his shrine became a pilgrimage destination of unrivaled popularity. The selections below describe a number of healing miracles from the year 1171, recorded by Benedict of Canterbury, the first of several monks to memorialize the saint's deeds.

Source: trans. J. Shinners, in *Medieval Popular Religion 1000–1500*, ed. J. Shinners, 2nd ed. (Peterborough, ON: Broadview Press, 2007), pp. 165–70, from J.C. Robertson, *Materials for the History of Thomas Becket, Archbishop of Canterbury*, Roll Series 67 (London: Longman & Co., 1876), vol. 2, pp. 61–69, 74.

2.7. Edilda, a woman from Canterbury, was left at the shrine, carried with the help of three women. It had now been about a year and half since she could stand on her foot. During that whole time she had lived as if on the brink of death, confined to bed. The disease was especially severe in her left knee, which through the contraction of the muscles prevented her from walking. Her knee reeled with pain if the woman happened to touch it even lightly with her hand. She was carried to the martyr by three women, as we said, and propped on a staff; she returned home with her pain relieved. In witness of her recovered health, before us all with her upraised fist she struck her knee a hard blow, which since the second year of her illness she could not touch because of the pain. The people saw her walking about and praised the Lord; they were filled with wonder and amazed over what had happened to her. But we refrain from discussing why she remained lame and did not regain complete health, considering it more prudent to keep totally silent about God's secret judgments than to draw rash conclusions from them.

2.8. But we know that he who strengthened that woman's weak knee was capable of making her feet and soles completely firm so that she could have walked normally, just as we have no doubt that he did grant this to Wlviva, a woman from Canterbury. Satan had bound her for three years already, and she was bent over, unable to walk anywhere without a crutch. She fell down before the saint for a short prayer and, with the pain gone from her loins, she rose standing straight up without her crutch, wanting no longer to carry the thing that had once supported her.

2.9. Edmund, a young man born in Canterbury and well known there, brought himself to the shrine guided by one eye alone: he had only the appearance of a left eye for it had no power of vision. On his left side he also had something growing inside that seemed congealed and very heavy which, shifting up and down, had tormented him for nearly two years causing him unbelievable stabs of pain and amazing torture. It was pushing him toward death, which was apparent just by his pale and withered look. A drop of [Becket's] most holy blood was put in his eye, and he drank an infusion: the blood and water. Miraculous power of that drink! Going a good distance away from the tomb, he threw himself down on his face; he turned himself on his side and began thrashing around and screaming; he kept getting up but could not stand because of his weakened gait. He sank down on his face dashing it against the stone, and it seemed as if he had come there only to his harm. He whom divine power was healing you would have thought insane. Finally he collapsed into sleep. He lay on his back sleeping. The saint of God stood next to him while he slept and, grabbing him by the shoulder, shook him and said, "Get up, go on." He instantly awoke and felt that the shifting thing that had been twisting inside him was being forced up to the bottom of his throat. Nearly choking, he threw his hand to his throat, wanting to feel what it was. Then instantly, as if some small inner sack had burst, by some divine power it was expelled from his mouth. It seemed to him to have the taste of bitter gall. Immediately he got up, threw down his cloak, and proceeded to the martyr's tomb to give thanks. Having received a complete cure of his eye and his body, through love of the martyr he took the cross [vowed] that he would go to Jerusalem, and all the people who saw it praised God.

2.10. We realize that what happened to a woman named Muriel deserved no less praise or glory. Debilitated by a grave illness for two years or more, she thought that only the remedy of death would put an end to her suffering. When her husband realized the things that God's martyr was gloriously doing, he offered his sick wife a drink of that health-giving drink [Becket's blood mixed with water]. She drank it, and by degrees over the course of three days began to suffer more than usual from weakness. By the third day she had weakened to the point of death, so much so that she was taken out of her bed lest, contrary to the custom of the Christian religion, she die lying on a comfortable feather bed. A priest was summoned with the greatest haste to administer extreme unction to her. But she suddenly was nauseous and vomited up what was making her sick; for that whole day at regular intervals she did not stop vomiting. It was discovered that she was spitting up an enormous number of cherry stones, plum pits, and acorns – cooled in the woman's stomach, some of them had even sprouted! Some of these were shown to us, which left us awestruck both that the woman had carried the pits of these fruits in her stomach for such a long time and that the pits could germinate there. There can be no doubt that they would have hastened her death if the draft of that holy liquid had not come to her aid. Thus the woman was cured, snatched, as it were, from the very jaws of death. And though, as we said, she was so incapacitated that she had been unable to set foot out of her house for more than two years, the next day, through the strength bestowed on her by God, she went on foot to the martyr. And all the people rejoiced together at the things he had gloriously done.

2.11. The Lord added another miracle to this one, though for a less serious illness. (Why do I say less serious? The sickness someone endures never seems small.) We knew a certain lady named Ethelburga, full of good works and charity, who had suffered for many days from a serious gout in her left arm and shoulder. Deprived of the use of her left arm, she arranged to have a candle made to the measure of the arm's length in honor of the martyr. You should have seen how the martyr responded to the woman through the action of grace, because the Lord promised to those turning to him, "Before you can call me, I will say to you, 'Look, here I am.'" For she had scarcely begun to measure her arm with a thread than she announced that she felt all the pain receding. And so she had the candle made, offered it to the martyr, and regained full health.

2.12. Robert, a blacksmith from the Isle of Thanet, also found the grace of healing, but the vision that preceded the gift of his cure is no less wonderful. He had been blind for at least two years; the loss of his livelihood troubled him more than his lost sight. But then, after our venerable father had been called home from exile, around the time when he was called to heaven from the exile of this world [29 December], this man heard this oracle in a dream: "Go, Robert, to Christ Church Canterbury; a monk will put milk in your eyes and you will recover your sight." But at first he thought he was deluded; he neither believed the promise nor obeyed the command. Yet later, when he heard that God's saint practically glittered with miracles, he recalled what he had heard and, equating this sweetest lamb's innocent blood to milk's sweetness, he began to hope for a cure. With the guidance of his wife and daughter (for we understand they accompanied him), he arrived where he had been ordered to go. After daubing his eyes with the longed-for blood of the martyr, he prostrated himself in prayer. While facedown, he felt his head racked by what seemed like a loud thunderclap and he regained his sight. Getting up, he publicly preached God's grace.

2.13. But what is easier: to restore health to the body or the mind? He who restored sight to physical eyes restored sanity to the young man, Henry of Fordwich. He had been insane for some days and had accidentally wounded his friends due to his pain. With his hands bound behind him, he was dragged to the saint. He was presented to the saint even though he was struggling and shouting. He remained there insane for the whole day, but as the light of the sun waned, he started gradually to recover the light of reason. He spent the night in the church and went back home in the morning completely recovered.

2.14. We received a woman from the vicinity of the same town who not only could not hear but was also troubled by an unbearable pain in the head. That universal medicine of the sick – water mixed with the blood – was poured into her stopped ears; she was also given some to drink, and then she threw herself into prayer. While she prayed she suffered more bitterly than before and she thought [she heard] many twigs being snapped in pieces inside her head. She asked those standing around whether they heard the noise in her head. But while she was being racked this way, she cried out to the Lord and he heard her. For as she shouted, a great deal of matter flowed out of her ears, as if some inner abscess had ruptured. The matter was followed by blood, and the blood by the gift of her lost hearing.

2.15. Eilward, a man from Tenham, for some years had lost the pleasures of the sense of smell and could smell absolutely nothing. He entered that place where rests that good odor of the anointed one, that sweet victim, that scented tree, whose aroma the whole world now senses; but before he had reached that fragrant flower of England, there came to him the sweetest perfume filling his nostrils, and he rejoiced to recover his sense of smell.

2.16. We think that it should not be forgotten that, while many people obtained a longed-for healing, one person was denied outright. For the holy father [Becket] came to a crippled boy who had gone seeking a favor from the martyr and had fallen asleep with his head resting on top of the tomb. "Why are you lying on me?" he asked. "You certainly will not be healed. Go away. I'll do nothing for you." These words woke him up and he told us and his mother what he had heard with great sadness of heart. Convinced by the adamancy of the [saint's] words, he had himself taken elsewhere. Still, we urged him to press on with his prayers, and he agreed; but time passed and he did not regain his health....

2.18. With regard to these other cures, it first occurs to us to speak about what Agnes, a Canterbury woman, gained from the Water of Saint Thomas – for this is what the people of the surrounding region called it: "Saint Thomas's Water," or "Canterbury Water." Thus, an uncontrollable pain seized this woman's face, and a horrible tumor disfigured it; her mouth, twisted on one side, betrayed the shape of nature corrupted. An excess of phlegm constantly and copiously flowing from her mouth caused her much embarrassment without any relief from the pain or the tumor. At last the inner part of her face became infected, with the result that it was necessary for the woman to have milk instead of solid food. Since she was unable to eat food, she sustained herself with little sips of liquid. But for the last three days she had stopped drinking even these since she was so squeezed by pain. You would not have endured the stink that issued from her putrefying face. Into her fifth week of pain, the woman was thirsty and drank some of the saint's water. O miraculous water, which quenched not only the thirst but the pain of its drinker! O miraculous water, which quenched not only the pain but shrunk the tumor! I am about to tell you something astonishing.

A basin used to be put to the woman's mouth to catch the phlegm. Lying prone with her mouth open, the woman was being coaxed to take care of the phlegm running out of her mouth. But when she lay back down after a swallow of water, from her mouth appeared the rather large head of a worm shaped like a red-hot coal, one and half inches long with a tail like a very sharp awl and crawling on four feet. By its speed it showed such tenacity that some said it had come from the Enemy [the Devil]. It was drowned in the bowl of phlegm, so it was thought, but when [the bowl was] put up to an upper window, it was not visible. Thus the patient's pain ceased and in a brief time her swollen face returned to its normal state....

2.24. What are we to say about Saxeva of Dover? Did not her joy wane as her pain waxed? From Christmas to Easter she continually experienced what the opposite of health is through a cramp in her bowels and a pain in her arm. A mental pain afflicted her as much as her physical suffering, for she was unable to work but ashamed to beg. Her spirit grew weary of life. She fled to the martyr, prayed to him, and slept. The martyr revealed his presence to the sleeper. "Rise," he said, "offer your candle." Leaping up, she discovered herself cured. She obeyed his order and showed herself so healthy and agile that she said with exaggeration that she was strong enough to fly.

What sort of people came to the shrine of Thomas Becket at Canterbury? Where did they come from? What kind of problems were they experiencing? How does Benedict of Canterbury try to convince his readers of the saint's miraculous powers? Did pilgrims seeking cures at the shrine always get what they prayed for? What do the descriptions of illness given in this account indicate about the level of medical knowledge possessed by the monks who celebrated Saint Thomas's miracles?

52. *THE MARVELS OF ROME*

Writing in the early thirteenth century, the English cleric and university master Gregorius, who had apparently traveled to Rome on ecclesiastical business, composed a description of the city's noteworthy sites and attractions. Rather than focusing on Rome's Christian pilgrimage sites, he showed an uncommon interest in the city's classical structures and "pagan" landscape, demonstrating that Rome's appeal to travelers was not limited to saints' shrines and churches. Even Gregorius, however, did not ignore Rome's popularity among devotional travelers, commenting – with a sometimes cutting tone – on the presence of pilgrims in the city.

Source: trans. J. Osborne, in *Master Gregorius: The Marvels of Rome* (Toronto: Pontifical Institute of Mediaeval Studies, 1987), pp. 17–35.

Prologue

Here begins Master Gregory's prologue concerning the wonders which once were or still are in Rome, of which the traces or the memory remain alive to this day. At the special request of my comrades, specifically Master Martin, Lord Thomas, and several others whom I greatly respect, I have been constrained to set down on parchment those things which I have seen in Rome that are most worthy of admiration. I fear however that my poorly composed report may disturb your sacred study and interrupt the delights of holy scripture, and I blush to offend ears accustomed to the lectures of the foremost scholars with my unpolished prose. After all, who wouldn't think twice about inviting to a plain and frugal repast guests who are accustomed to delicacies? That explains why my lazy hand has had to be prodded to take up the promised task, for often, just as I was about to pick up my pen, my mind would shrink from the subject when I considered the poverty of my disordered discourse. However, the wishes of my colleagues have finally overcome my bashfulness. In order not to delay the promised truth I have taken up the pen in my awkward clumsy hand, and I have set forth the work, as best I can, in the following manner.

The prologue ends. Here begins the account of the wonders of the city of Rome, which have been fashioned either by magic craft or by human labor.

1. I strongly recommend the wonderful panorama of the whole city. There is so great a forest of towers, and so many palatial buildings, that no one has counted them. When I saw it for the first time, at a distance from the slope of the hill, my mind was struck by those words which Julius Caesar uttered after he had conquered the Gauls, flown across the Alps, and was greatly "admiring ... the walls of Rome":

Home of the gods, have men abandoned you without a fight?
What city will they then defend? Heaven be thanked.

and so on. And a little later:

The city which could have held the throng of assembled
humanity was abandoned by a cowardly hand

and invoking the name of Rome, he called it

the image of the highest divinity.

After I had spent some time admiring this stunningly picturesque sight, I thanked God, mighty throughout the entire world, who had here rendered the works of man wondrously and indescribably beautiful. For although all of Rome lies in ruins, nothing intact can be compared to this. And thus someone has said:

Rome, although you are almost a total ruin, you have no equal;
shattered you can teach us, whole how greatly you would speak!

I believe this ruin teaches us clearly that all temporal things will soon pass away, especially as Rome, the epitome of earthly glory, languishes and declines so much every day....

3. Let me begin with an account of the city's bronze statues. Concerning the first bronze statue: The first bronze statue is a bull, like the one which, according to legend, Jupiter used to fool Europa. This statue projects from the fortifications of the Castle of Crescentius, and is so skillfully made that it appears to its viewers likely to bellow and move.

4. Concerning the second statue: There is another bronze statue in front of the papal palace: an immense horse, with a rider whom the pilgrims call Theodoric, although the Roman people say he is Constantine, and the cardinals and clerks of the Roman curia call him Marcus or Quintus Quirinus. In ages past this memorial, made with extraordinary skill, stood on four bronze columns in front of the altar of Jupiter on the Capitoline, but blessed [Pope] Gregory [the Great] took down the horse and rider, and placed the four columns in the church of St-John Lateran. The horse and rider were set up outside the papal palace by the Roman people. The horse, the rider, and the columns were lavishly gilded, but in many places the gold has fallen victim to Roman avarice, and time has also taken its toll. The rider raises his right hand, as if to address the people or to give orders; his left hand holds a rein, which turns the horse's head aside to the right, as if he were about to ride away in another direction. A little bird, which they call a cuckoo, sits between the ears of the horse, and under the hoofs there is a sort of dwarf, who is being trodden upon. He makes a wonderful image of the agonies of death.

Just as this admirable work has been assigned different names, so too have a variety of reasons been proposed for its manufacture. I shall give a wide berth to the worthless stories of the pilgrims and the Romans in this regard, and shall record what I've been told by the elders, the cardinals, and the men of greatest learning. Those who call him Marcus give this account of its origin. There was a certain king of the Miseni, a dwarf, who was more skillful than any other man in the perverse arts of magic. After he had subjugated the neighboring kings, he attacked the Romans, whom he easily defeated in several encounters. For his magic so blunted his enemy's strength and the keenness of their weapons that they completely lost the will to fight, and their weapons the power to inflict wounds. Because he defeated the Romans easily in every engagement, they were reluctant to leave their fortifications, and eventually found themselves surrounded by a tight blockade. Penned up in this way, they were unable to obtain any reinforcements.

Every day before dawn this magician would come out of his camp alone, and while the loud cry of a bird could be heard coming from the camp, he would practice his magic arts alone in a field. By certain secret words and powerful spells he made it impossible for the Romans to muster their strength and defeat him. When the Romans became aware of this, and when they realized that he made a habit of leaving his camp in this manner, they approached a certain soldier named Marcus, a man brimming with energy, and promised him the highest honors if he would brave the danger and lift the siege of the city. They offered him its lordship if he could save it, and promised him an eternal memorial. He agreed and that night they made an opening through the wall and its outer earthwork so that this soldier and his horse could pass through to the spot where the king came out. Then they explained their plan. Marcus was to go out by night, and when he discovered that the king of the Miseni had left his camp, he was not to attack him with his weapons, since these had no power to hurt the king, but to seize him and carry him back inside the walls. Marcus gave his complete assent and in the middle of the night he passed through the wall. Vigilantly he waited for dawn, and as usual the cuckoo began to sing, a sign of light in the eastern sky. Thus alerted, he mounted his horse, caught sight of the king, who was just beginning to perform his magic rites, and making a great charge, he seized him. Captured in a manner he had not foreseen, the magician was then carried back inside the wall, and fearing that any delay might allow their captive to free himself by his magic craft, Marcus trampled him to death beneath the hoofs of his horse as everyone looked on; for the king could not be harmed by weapons. Then they opened the gates and fell upon the army, which, demoralized by the demise of its king, had begun to take flight; and in that fight a great many were captured or killed. Never have the spoils of battle so greatly enriched the Roman treasury, and because of the benefits gained from Marcus' participation, a memorial was put up in his honor as agreed. The horse, which had contributed its speed, and the bird, who had heralded the dawn, were also included; and the trampled dwarf was set beneath the horse's feet, where he had fallen....

6. Concerning the third bronze statue: The third statue is that of the Colossus, which some think to be a statue of the sun, while others call it the image of Rome. What is particularly astounding about this piece is how so great a mass could have been cast, how it was raised, and how it could stand. For its

height, as I have discovered it written, was 126 feet. This enormous monument stood on the island of Herodius at the Colosseum, 15 feet higher than the loftiest points in the city. It held a sphere in its right hand, and a sword in its left, the sphere representing the world and the sword military prowess. The Romans entrusted the sword to the left hand and the sphere to the right because it is more virtuous to rule than to conquer. As a philosopher [Lucan] has said: "It's easier to get to the top of the ladder than it is to stay there."

The sphere was given to the side of strength and the sword to the side of weakness for no other reason than this: that it's less praiseworthy to conquer the world than it is to keep it conquered. This bronze image was completely gilded with imperial gold and it shone in the darkness. The strangest thing of all about it was that it turned continuously in a motion equal to that of the sun, which it therefore always faced, and because of this many believed that it was the image of the sun. While Rome flourished, every visitor to the city worshipped it on bended knee, offering honor to Rome by worshipping its image. But after all the statues in Rome were pulled down and broken, blessed Gregory destroyed it in the following manner. Because such a great mass could not be toppled even by enormous effort and force, he commanded that a large fire should be lit under the statue, and this reduced the gigantic figure to its former formless state. The head, and the right hand holding the sphere, did however survive the fire, and these make a wonderful sight for onlookers, elevated on two marble columns in front of the papal palace. Although of horrific size, one can nonetheless admire in them the great skill of their maker, and indeed nothing of the perfect beauty of the human head or hand is lacking in any part. It's quite amazing how the fluid craftsmanship can simulate soft hairs in solid bronze, and if you look at it intently, transfixed by its splendor, it gives the appearance of being about to move and speak. They say that no other statue was ever made in the city with such care or expense....

8. Concerning a great many statues: Among all the strange works which were once in Rome, the multitude of statues known as the "Salvation of the Citizens" is to be much admired. By magic art, statues were dedicated to all those peoples who were subject to Roman rule, and indeed there was no race or region under Roman authority which did not have its statue in this particular hall. A large portion of its walls still stand, and the vaults seem stark and inaccessible.

In this hall these statues stood in a row, each one having written on its breast the name of the race which it represented, and each wearing around its neck a bell made of silver, because silver is more resonant than other metals. And there were priests who watched over them, ever vigilant both by day and by night. If any nation dared to rise in rebellion against Roman rule, its statue would immediately move, causing the bell to ring, and at once a priest would write down its name and convey this to the government. Above this hall of statues there was a bronze soldier on horseback who would move in conjunction with the statue, aiming his lance at the race whose image had stirred. Warned in this unequivocal manner, without delay the Romans would dispatch an army to suppress that nation's rebellion, and they would often forestall their enemies before they could prepare their weapons and supplies, thus subjugating them easily and without bloodshed. They say moreover that in the same hall there was an inextinguishable fire. When the artificer of this wonderful work was asked how long it would burn, he replied that it would last until a virgin gave birth. I'm told that the hall and the soldier collapsed in a great heap on the night that Christ was born of the Virgin, and that its magic artificial fire was justly extinguished when the true eternal light made its appearance. We can also believe that the evil enemy lost its ability to deceive mankind when God took human form....

16. Concerning the Temple of Pallas: The Temple of Pallas was once a remarkable structure. Although demolished by the exertions of the Christians and crumbling with age, it hasn't been entirely destroyed, and the part which remains is used by the cardinals as a storehouse. There is a great heap of broken statues there, but also one of Pallas bearing arms which still projects above the highest vault. Although disfigured by the loss of her head, spectators consider her a wonderful sight. This statue was greatly venerated by the ancient Romans. Christians were led to it, and those who didn't worship Pallas on bended knee were executed by various means. Hippolytus and his family were brought to this image or idol, and when he paid it no obeisance he suffered martyrdom, torn apart by horses.

17. I can't leave out the palace of the divine Augustus, for the excellence of this vast dwelling equals that of its founder. Built entirely of marble, it has supplied a great deal of precious material for the construction of Rome's churches; but as so little of it remains, I shall say very little about it. A small portion of the throne does however survive, and on it I found this inscription: "the house of the divine and most merciful Augustus." For although he ruled the city and the entire world, he always avoided the title "Lord."...

22. Concerning the triumphal arch of Augustus: Not far from this temple is the triumphal arch of Caesar Augustus, on which I found this inscription written:

Because Augustus restored a conquered world to Roman rule, regaining
it for the Republic, the Roman people erected this monument;

in other words it was a timeless memorial to record for posterity his many victories and great triumphs. The arch itself is multiple and constructed of marble, and on its stone platforms, which project outwards quite a distance, statues were placed of military commanders and those who had either distinguished themselves on campaign or fallen in the thick of battle. Among these the portrait of Augustus, larger than the others and carved with wonderful skill, is preeminent, and one can see where he triumphs and where he overcomes his foes. All over the arch there are reliefs depicting the army and cursed war, and if you look closely the battles seem very realistic. The battle of Actium is cleverly depicted, in which Caesar emerging from the struggle with a greater victory than he had expected, pursues Cleopatra's fleeing galley. It is captured, Cleopatra is brought before him, and after applying the asps to her breasts the proud woman, carved in Parthian marble, pales on the point of death. Caesar Augustus attained the highest honors from this war, and this is how he celebrated his triumph: four white horses led by four of the most noble Romans drew a golden chariot, in which he sat, dressed in a toga embroidered with gold and jewels. In front of him stretched a long procession of captured kings, chiefs and princes, their hands bound behind their backs, along with countless other distinguished displays. His wars and achievements were spoken of in every language to be found in Rome, and the city's populace did not cease to celebrate his victory. It was even depicted in pictures, so that those who could not hear of his glory might see it. And with great celebration and indescribable joy he was led all the way to the Tarpeian rock on the Capitoline hill, where he presented both the weapons which he had borne in battle himself and those which he had captured from his enemies, hanging them up in the rotunda as a record of his great victory: There the Senate, the senatorial fathers, and the Roman people presented to him the last province, so that the fame of his triumph and the glory of his victory would be made known throughout the entire world. All these things which I have mentioned are shown in the carved reliefs on the arch....

27. Concerning the pyramids, which is to say the tombs of the mighty: Now I shall add a few words about the pyramids, the tombs of the mighty, of enormous size and height, and rising to a point in the manner of a cone. The first of these which I encountered was the tomb of Romulus, which stands by the castle of Crescentius near the church of St-Peter. The pilgrims erroneously claim that this is the grain heap of the apostle Peter, which was transformed into a stone hill of the same size when Nero confiscated it. It's an utterly worthless tale, typical of those told by pilgrims. Hidden inside every pyramid is a marble sarcophagus, with carved reliefs on all sides, in which the body of the deceased was placed....

29. There are many pyramids in Rome, but of all of them the one which deserves the greatest admiration is the pyramid of Julius Caesar, made of a single porphyry block. It's indeed a marvel how a block of stone of such height could have been cut, or have been raised, or remain standing; for they

say that its height is 250 feet. At the top there is a bronze sphere, in which Julius Caesar's ashes and bones are deposited. Someone marveling at it has commented:

> If it be one stone, tell me how it was raised.
> If there be many stones, tell me where they join.

They say that it stands on the spot where a certain person encountered Julius, who was on his way to an assembly, and offered him a letter revealing the conspiracy. This warned, among other things, that he would die cruelly if he entered the assembly or the Capitol that day. Caesar took the letter, but said to the man: "At the moment I am going to speak with my astrologer, and I shall read your letter after the assembly." The astrologer was present who had predicted that Caesar would die on the first day of the month, and Caesar called to him saying: "Today is the first of the month, and I'm still alive!" The astrologer replied, "It is indeed the first day of the month, but it has not yet passed, and I hope that my prediction will be proved wrong." And immediately Caesar tuned away and entered the Capitol, where he expired after receiving 24 stab wounds from Brutus, Cassius, and their cronies. However I prefer to believe Marius Suetonius, who says that he was killed by the hilts of their swords, which left no visible wounds, and they say that because of this he was received into the company of the gods. Maro writes this as his epitaph:

> The radiant figure marvels at the unaccustomed splendor of Olympus.
> In the woodlands I was Oaphnis, known from here to the stars.
> Keeper of a handsome flock, though I was even fairer!

and so forth. In his left hand they found the letter warning him of the conspiracy. And so Caesar, lord and master of the world, who assumed power after first suppressing liberty, now reposes in this bronze sphere, his body reduced to ashes. The pilgrims call this pyramid "Saint Peter's needle," and they make great efforts to crawl underneath it, where the stone rests on four bronze lions, claiming falsely that those who manage to do so are cleansed from their sins, having made a true penance.

What sort of sites in Rome interested Master Gregorius? How well educated was he in the classical history of Rome and its rulers? What signs are there in his account of tensions between the city's pagan past and its importance as a center of Christian devotion? What seems to have been his attitude toward many of the pilgrims who visited Rome?

53. A MIRACLE OF MARY MAGDALENE

During the High Middle Ages, a number of shrines, churches, and monasteries assumed considerable importance as centers of worship along the pilgrimage routes from northern Europe to Rome and especially to Saint James of Compostela. The monastery of Vézelay in Burgundy, which claimed to possess holy relics of Mary Magdalene, emerged as a particularly important center of devotion in its own right. The following miracle story comes from a thirteenth-century collection of documents, intended to bolster and celebrate her cult.

Source: trans. B.E. Whalen, from *Le dossier Vézelien de Marie Madeleine: Invention et translation des reliques en 1265-1267*, ed. V. Saxer, Subsidia Hagiographica, vol. 57 (Brussels: Société des Bollandistes, 1975), pp. 242–43.

Our word cannot begin to do justice to the magnitude of the miracles wrought by that favored woman of God, since there are more beyond even those recounted by brother Vincent in book 24, chapter 153 of his *Mirror of History*, and by brother James of Genoa in his *Golden Legend*, and also those things written down in various volumes kept in that same very monastery [of Vézelay]. Nevertheless, out of devotion toward the faithful, we judge it worthy of inserting one here, omitting the others for the sake of brevity.

How a Breton Trusting in Her Spared Himself from a Shipwreck

There was a certain noble Breton [a man from Brittany], endowed with great expanses of property, who was devout and constant in his praise of the blessed Mary Magdalene, so that he venerated her with the greatest affection along with his wife, children and entire family, and asked her with daily prayers to come to his aid. He always fasted most devoutly on the feast-day of her vigils with his entire household, and was accustomed to prepare a great meal on her feast-day for the poor and pilgrims. On that same day, he would forgive his debtors the debts owed to him, offer forgiveness for those who sinned against him, and celebrate that special, noble feast-day among all the solemnities of the saints. Moreover, among his continual prayers, it was asked of God especially that he never allow that man to meet his demise without performing true penance and a confession of his sins. It so happened, therefore, that the aforesaid nobleman, setting out for England, suffered a shipwreck. When the waves pounced upon all of his companions, he also was tossed about in the ocean waves. Soon, as he anticipated the coming of death rushing upon him, from the depths of his fearful grief, he took courage: "O blessed Mary

Magdalene, surely I have often beseeched your sanctity, so that you would never allow me to leave this world without performing true penance and confessing my sins? Behold, now I am dying, and I am not able to confess my sins." He had not yet finished this bemoaning of his heart, when a beautiful and well clad woman took a hold of his right arm and calmed the sea from its turbulent waves; nevertheless, she only carried him alone, light as a baby, from among all the others safe and sound to the shore, from which he had set out, nearly forty stades distant from the place of the shipwreck (from the day of his birth, he had never learned how to swim). Therefore, returning home, that man preached about the miracles of that holy helper throughout that land, and, as had been foreordained to him by her, lived in his body only for another ten days, receiving true penance (as he had asked) and making arrangements for his properties.

How did the noble Breton show his devotion to Mary Magdalene (in particular, how did he treat the poor and pilgrims)? What did he ask of her in his time of need? What did she do for him?

54. THE *PILGRIM'S GUIDE TO ST-JAMES OF COMPOSTELA*

According to a tradition that dates back to the sixth century, after his martyrdom in Palestine, the body of the apostle Saint James was miraculously transported to Spain, where James had already spent time spreading the Gospel. By the ninth century, the church at Compostela, in northwestern Spain, claimed to be James's burial place. By the High Middle Ages, Compostela had emerged alongside Rome as one of the most important religious destinations within Europe, the terminus of a vast network of pilgrimage routes that included places like Conques (doc. 33) and Vézelay (doc. 53). The selections below come from the twelfth-century Pilgrim's Guide *to the shrine of St-James, apparently the product of multiple authors but commonly attributed in its final form to a French cleric from Poitou named Aimery Picaud.*

Source: abridged by M.-A. Stouck, in *Medieval Saints: A Reader*, ed. M.-A. Stouck (Peterborough, ON: Broadview Press, 1999), pp. 313–27, from the translation by J. Hogarth, *The Pilgrim's Guide: A 12th-Century Guide for the Pilgrims to St. James of Compostella* (London: Confraternity of St. James, 1992), pp. 3–88.

1. Of the Roads to St-James

There are four roads leading to St-James which join to form one road at Puente la Reina, in the territory of Spain. One runs by way of St-Giles [St-Gilles du Gard] and Montpellier and Toulouse and the Somport pass; another by St-Mary of Le Puy and St-Faith of Conques and St-Peter of Moissac; the third by St-Mary Magdalene of Vézelay and St-Leonard of Limousin [St-Leonard de Noblat] and the town of Perigueux; and the fourth by St-Martin of Tours and St-Hilary of Poitiers and St-John of Angely [St-Jean d'Angely] and St-Eutropius of Saintes and the town of Bordeaux.

The roads which go by St-Faith, by St-Leonard and by St-Martin join at Ostabat and after crossing the pass of Cize [through the Pyrennes] meet the road over the Somport pass at Puente la Reina; and from there a single road leads to St-James.

4. Of the World's Three Hospices

The Lord established in this world three columns most necessary for the support of the poor: the hospice in Jerusalem, the hospice of Mont-Joux [on the Great St-Bernard pass] and the hospice of Santa Cristina on the Somport pass. These hospices were sites in places where they were necessary: they are holy places, houses of God, places of refreshment for holy pilgrims, of rest for the needy, of comfort for the sick, of salvation for the dead, of help for the living. Those who built these most holy places will without doubt possess the kingdom of God.

5. Of the Names of Those Who Repaired the Road to St-James

These are the names of those who, in the time of Diego [Gelmirez] archbishop of St-James, and Alfonso, emperor of Spain and Galicia, and Pope Callistus, repaired the road to St-James, from Rabanal to Puertomarin, for the love of God and his apostle, before the year 1120, in the reign of Alfonso [I] of Aragon and Louis [VI] the Fat, king of France: Andrew, Roger, Avitus, Fortus, Arnold, Stephen and Peter, who rebuilt the bridge over the Mino which had been demolished by Queen Urraca. May the souls of these men and those who worked with them rest in eternal peace!

These are the rivers on the road to St-James from the pass of Cize and the Somport pass. From the Somport pass there flows down a river of pure water, the Aragon, which irrigates Spain. From the pass of Cize there flows a river of pure water which many call the Runa and which flows down towards

Pamplona. At Puente la Reina there are both the Arga and the Runa. At a place called Lorca, to the east, there flows a stream known as the Salt River. Beware of drinking from it or of watering your horse in it, for this river brings death. On its banks, while we were going to St-James, we found two Navarrese sitting there sharpening their knives; for they are accustomed to flay pilgrims' horses which die after drinking the water. In answer to our question they lied, saying that the water was good and drinkable. Accordingly we watered our horses in the river, and at once two of them died and were forthwith skinned by the two men.

Through Estella flows the river Ega, the water of which is sweet, pure, and excellent. At the village of Los Arcos is a stream which causes death, and between Los Arcos and the first hospice beyond the village is another stream which is fatal to both horses and men who drink it. At the village of Torres del Rio, in Navarrese territory, is a river which also is fatal to horses and men, and there is another river that brings death at the village of Cuevas.

At Logrono is a large river called the Ebro, with pure water and an abundance of fish. All the rivers between Estella and Logrono have water which brings death to men and beasts who drink it, and the fish in these streams are likewise poisonous. Do not eat, in Spain or Galicia, the fish commonly known as barbus [barbel] or the one which the Poitevins call alose [shad] and the Italians clipia or an eel or a tench: if you do you will assuredly die or fall sick. And anyone who eats any great quantity of these and does not fall sick must have a stronger constitution than other people or must have lived in the country for a long time; for all kinds of fish, beef and pork in Spain and Galicia make foreigners ill.

Those rivers which are sweet and good for drinking are the following: the Pisuerga, which flows at the Puente de Itero; the Carrion, at Carrion de los Condes; the Cea at Sahagun; the Elsa at Mamilla de las Mulas; the Porma, at the large bridge [the Puente de Villarente] between Mamilla and Leon, the Torio, which flows through Leon, below the Jewish quarter; the Bernesga, on the far side of Leon in the direction of Astorga; the Sil at Ponferrada, in a green valley; the Cua at Cacabelos; the Burbia at the bridge of Villafranca del Bierzo; the Valcarce, which flows down the valley of that name; the Mino at Puertomarin; and a river in wooded country two miles from the city of St-James, at a place called Lavacolla, in which French pilgrims traveling to St-James are accustomed, for love of the apostle, to take off their clothes and cleanse not only their private parts but the whole of their body. The river Sar, which flows between the Mount of Joy [Monte del Gozo] and the city of St-James, is held to be clean; so too is the Sarela, which flows on the other side of the town, to the west.

I have described these rivers so that pilgrims going to St-James may take care to avoid drinking bad water and may choose water that is good for them and for their horses.

7. Of the Names of the Countries and the Characteristics of the Peoples on the Road to St-James

Going to St-James on the Toulouse road we come first, after crossing the Garonne, into Gascony, and then, going over the Somport pass, enter Aragon and then Navarre, which extends as far as the bridge over the Arga [Puente la Riellna] and beyond. If, however, we take the road over the pass of Cize we come, after Tours, into Poitou, a fertile and excellent region, full of all delights. The men of Poitou are strong and warlike, skilled in the use of bows and arrows and of lances in war, valiant in battle, swift runners, elegant in their attire, handsome of face, ready of tongue, generous and hospitable. Then comes Saintonge; and from there, after crossing an arm of the sea and the river Caronne, we come into the territory of Bordeaux, which has excellent wine and an abundance of fish but an uncouth manner of speech. The speech of Saintonge is also uncouth, but that of Bordeaux is more so.

Then, for travelers who are already tired, there is a three days' journey through the Landes of Bordeaux. This is a desolate country, lacking in everything: there is neither bread nor wine nor meat nor fish nor water nor any springs. There are few villages on this sandy plain, though it has honey, millet, panic [a kind of millet], and pigs in plenty. If you are going through the Landes in summer be sure to protect your face from the huge flies, called guespe [wasps] and tavones [horse flies], which are particularly abundant in this region. And if you do not watch your feet carefully, you will sink up to your knees in the sea sand which is found everywhere here.

After passing through this region you come into Gascony, a land well supplied with white bread and excellent red wine, woods and meadows, rivers and springs of pure water. The Gascons are loud-mouthed, talkative, given to mockery, libidinous, drunken, greedy eaters, clad in rags and poverty-stricken; but they are skilled fighters and notable for their hospitality to the poor. They take their meals without a table, sitting round the fire, and all drink out of the same cup. They eat and drink a great deal and are ill clad; nor do they scruple to sleep all together in a scanty litter of rotting straw, the servants along with the master and mistress.

Leaving this country the road to St-James crosses two rivers near the village of St-Jean de Sorde, one on the right and the other on the left; one is called a *gave*, the other a river, and they both must be crossed by boat.

Accursed be their boatmen! For although the rivers are quite narrow these men are in the habit of taking a piece of money for each person, rich or poor, when they ferry across, and for a horse they exact four, unworthily and by force. Their boat is small, made from a single tree trunk, ill-suited to carry horses: and so when you get into the boat you must take care not to fall into the water. You will do well to hold on to your horse's bridle and let it swim behind the boat. Nor should you go into a boat that has too many passengers, for if it is overloaded it will at once capsize. Often, too, having taken their passengers' money, the boatmen take such a number of other pilgrims on board that the boat overturns and the pilgrims are drowned; and then the wicked boatmen are delighted and appropriate the possessions of the dead.

Then, round the pass of Cize is the Basque country with the town of Bayonne, on the coast to the north. Here a barbarous tongue is spoken; the country is wooded and hilly, short of bread, wine, and all other foodstuffs, except only apples, cider and milk. In this country there are wicked toll-collectors – near the pass of Cize and at Ostabat and St-Jean and St-Michel-Pied-de-Port – may they be accursed. They come out to meet pilgrims with two or three cudgels to exact tribute by improper use of force; and if any traveler refuses to give the money they demand they strike him with their cudgels and take the money, abusing him and rummaging in his very breeches. They are ruthless people, and their country is no less hostile, with its forests and its wildness; the ferocity of their aspect and the barbarity of their language strike terror into the hearts of those who encounter them. Although they should levy tribute only on merchants they exact it unjustly from pilgrims and all travelers. When custom requires that the duty to be paid on a particular object is four or six pieces of money they charge eight or twelve – double the proper amount.

We urge and demand, therefore, that these toll-collectors, together with the king of Aragon and the other rich men who receive the proceeds of the tolls and all those who are in league with them, to wit Raymond de Soule, Vivien d'Aigremont and the Vicomte de St-Michel, with all their posterity, and also the ferrymen already mentioned and Arnauld de la Guigne, with his posterity, and the other lords of the two rivers, who unjustly receive the money collected by the ferrymen, and also the priests who, knowing what they do, admit them to confession and the Eucharist, celebrate divine service for them and receive them in church – we demand that all these men should be excommunicated until they have expiated their offenses by a long and public penance and have moderated their demands for tribute, and that the sentence of excommunication should be made public not only in their own episcopal see but also in the basilica of St-James, in presence of the pilgrims.

And if any prelate should pardon them, either from benevolence or for his own profit, may he be struck with the sword of anathema!

It should be said that the toll-collectors are not entitled to levy any kind of tribute on pilgrims and that ferrymen are properly entitled to charge only an obol [half a penny] for taking over two men – that is, if they are rich – and for a horse a piece of money; for a poor man they may charge nothing at all. Moreover the ferrymen are required to have boats amply large enough to accommodate both men and horses.

Still in the Basque country, the road to St-James goes over a most lofty mountain known as the Portus Cisere tribute [pass of Cize], so called either because it is the gateway of Spain or because necessary goods are transported over the pass from one country to the other. It is a journey of eight miles up to the pass and another eight down from it. The mountain is so high that it seems to touch the sky, and a man who has climbed it feels that he could indeed reach the sky with his hand. From the summit can be seen the Sea of Brittany and the Western Sea [the Atlantic Ocean], and the bounds of the three countries of Castile, Aragon, and France. On the highest point of the mountain is the place known as the Cross of Charles, because it was here that Charlemagne, advancing into Spain with his armies, cleared a passage with the aid of axes and picks and mattocks and other implements, set up the Lord's cross and, kneeling with his face turned towards Galicia, prayed to God and Saint James. And so pilgrims are accustomed to kneel here in prayer, looking towards the country of Saint James, and each then sets up a cross. Sometimes as many as a thousand crosses are to be seen here, and so the place is known as the first station for prayer on the road to St-James. On this mountain, before Christianity was fully established in Spain, the impious Navarrese and the Basques were accustomed not only to rob pilgrims going to St-James but to ride them like asses and kill them. Near the mountain, to the north, is a valley known as the Valley of Charles [Valcarlos] in which Charlemagne was encamped with his armies when his warriors were killed at Roncesvalles. This is the road used by many pilgrims who do not wish to climb the mountain.

Below the pass on the other side of the mountain are the hospice and the church containing the rock which Roland, that most valiant hero, split from top to bottom with a triple stroke of his sword. Beyond this is Roncesvalles, scene of the great battle in which King Marsile [the Muslim king of Spain in the Chanson de Roland], Roland, Oliver and 40,000 other warriors, both Christians and Saracens, were killed.

After this valley comes Navarre, which is well supplied with bread and wine, milk and livestock. The Navarrese and the Basques resemble one another in appearance, diet, dress and language; but the Basques have a fairer complexion than the Navarrese. The Navarrese wear short black garments reaching only to the knee, after the manner of the Scots. Their shoes, which they call lavarcas, are made of hairy untanned leather; they are tied on with thongs, and cover only the sole of the foot, leaving the upper part bare. They wear dark-colored woolen cloaks, fringed like traveling cloaks, which reach to the elbow and are known as saias. Coarsely dressed, they also eat and drink coarsely; in Navarre the whole household – master and servant, mistress and maid – eat from the same pot, in which all the food is mixed together, using their hands instead of spoons, and drink from the same cup. Watching them eat, you are reminded of dogs or pigs greedily gulping down their food; and when you hear them speaking it is like the barking of dogs. Their language is utterly barbarous: they call God Urcia, the Mother of God Andrea Maria, bread orgui, wine ardum, meat aragui, fish arraign, a house echea, the master of the house iaona, the mistress Andrea, a church elicera, the priest belaterra (which means "good earth"), corn gari, water uric, the king ereguia, and Saint James Jaona domne Jacue. This is a barbarous people, different from all other peoples in customs and in race, malignant, dark in color, ugly of face, debauched, perverse, faithless, dishonorable, corrupt, lustful, drunken, skilled in all forms of violence, fierce and savage, dishonest and false, impious and coarse, cruel and quarrelsome, incapable of any good impulses, past masters of all vices and iniquities. They resemble the Getae [the people who lived around the mouth of the Danube, and whose name was synonymous in Roman times for ferocity] and the Saracens [Muslims] in their malignance, and are in every way hostile to our French people. A Navarrese or a Basque will kill a Frenchman for a penny if he can. In some parts of the region, in Biscay and Alava, when the Navarrese are warming themselves, men show their private parts to women and women to men. The Navarrese fornicate shamelessly with their beasts, and it is said that a Navarrese will put a padlock on his she-mule and his mare lest another man should get at them. He also libidinously kisses the vulva of a woman or a she-mule.

The Navarrese, therefore, are condemned by all right-minded people. But they are good in battle, though not in besieging fortresses; and they are regular in the payment of tithes and accustomed to make offerings to the altar. Every day, when a Navarrese goes to church, he makes an offering to God of bread, wine, corn or some other substance. Wherever a Navarrese or Basque goes he has a horn round his neck like a hunter and carries two or three javelins, which he calls auconas. When he goes into his house or returns there he whistles like a kite; and when he is hiding in secret places or in some solitary spot with robbery in mind and wants to summon his companions without attracting notice he hoots like an owl or howls like a wolf.

It is commonly said that the Basques are descended from the Scots; for they resemble them in customs and in appearance. Julius Caesar is said to have sent three peoples – the Nubians [perhaps the Numiani, another British tribe], the Scots, and the tailed men of Cornwall – into Spain to make war on the peoples of Spain who refused to pay him tribute, telling them to kill all males and to spare only the women. These peoples came to Spain by sea and after destroying their ships devastated the country by fire and sword, from Barcelona to Saragossa and from Bayonne to Mount Oca. They were unable to advance any further, for the Castilians united and drove them out of their territory. In their flight they came to the coastal mountains between Najera and Pamplona and Bayonne, on the seaward side in Biscay and Alava, where they settled down and built many fortresses. Having killed all the men they took their wives by violence and had children by them, who later became known as Navarrese – the name being interpreted as non verus [not true], that is not engendered of a pure race or legitimate stock. The Navarrese also used to derive their name from a town called Naddaver [possibly Nadabar, in Ethiopia] in the country from which they originally came: a town which was converted to the Lord in early times by the preaching of Matthew, the apostle and evangelist. Leaving Navarre, the route runs through the forest of Oca and continues through Spanish territory – Castile and the Campos – in the direction of Burgos. This is a country full of treasures, of gold and silver, fortunate in producing fodder and sturdy horses and with an abundance of bread, wine, meat, fish, milk, and honey. It is, however, lacking in trees and the people are wicked and vicious.

Then, after crossing the territory of Leon and going over the passes of Monte Irago [Foncebadon] and Cebrero, you come into Galicia, a well wooded and well watered region with rivers and meadows and fine orchards, excellent fruit and clear springs, but with few towns and villages or culti-vated fields. There is little wheaten bread or wine but ample supplies of rye bread and cider, cattle and horses, milk, honey and sea fish both large and small. The country is rich in gold, silver, cloths, animal furs from the forests and other riches, as well as precious Saracen wares. The Galicians are more like our French people in their customs than any other of the uncultivated races of Spain, but they have the reputation of being violent-tempered and quarrelsome.

8. Of the Bodies of Saints Which Rest on the Road to St-James and Are To Be Visited by Pilgrims

Pilgrims going to St-James by way of St-Gilles must in the first place pay honor to the body of the blessed Trophimus the Confessor in Arles. Saint Paul refers to him in his epistle to Timothy; he was consecrated as a bishop by Paul and sent by him to preach the Gospel in Arles for the first time [in fact, the shrine was dedicated to Trophime, the fourth-century bishop of Arles]. It was from this most clear spring, we are told by Pope Zosimus, that the whole of France received the waters of the faith. His feast is celebrated on 29 December. Also to be visited in Arles is the body of the blessed Caesarius [the sixth-century archbishop of Arles], bishop and martyr, who instituted a rule for nuns in that city. His feast is celebrated on 1 November. In the cemetery of Arles pilgrims should seek out the relics of the blessed bishop Honoratus [of Arles], whose feast is celebrated on 16 January. In his venerable and magnificent basilica rests the body of the blessed Genesius, that most precious martyr. In the village of Trinquetaille near Arles, between two arms of the Rhone, is a magnificent tall marble column, standing behind the church of St-Genesius, to which it is said he was tied by the faithless people before being beheaded; it is still stained red with his blood. Immediately after his execution the saint took his head and threw it into the Rhone; his body was carried down by the river to the basilica of St-Honoratus, where it was given honorable burial. His head floated down the river to the sea and was conveyed under angelic guidance to Cartagena in Spain where it now gloriously rests, performing numerous miracles. The saint's feast is celebrated on 25 August.

The pilgrim must then visit the cemetery near Arles known as Aliscamps and, as the custom is, intercede for the dead with prayers, psalms and alms. The cemetery is a mile long and a mile wide, and in no other cemetery can be found so many and such large marble tombs. They are of different forms and bear ancient inscriptions in Latin script but in unintelligible language. The further you look the more sarcophagi you see. In this cemetery there are seven churches. If, in anyone of them, a priest celebrates the Eucharist for the dead, or a layman has a mass said for them, or a clerk reads the Psalter, they will be sure on the day of resurrection before God to find these pious dead helping them to obtain salvation; for many are the holy martyrs and confessors who rest here, and whose souls dwell amid the joys of Paradise. Their memory is celebrated, according to custom, on the Monday after the Easter octave. A visit must also be paid, with a most attentive eye, to the venerable body of the blessed Aegidius the most pious confessor and abbot [Saint Giles, an eighth-century hermit and one of the most popular saints of the Middle Ages]; for this most blessed saint, famed in all the countries of the world, must be venerated by all, worthily honored by all and loved, invoked and supplicated by all. After the prophets and the apostles none among the blessed is worthier than he, none is more holy, none is more glorious, none is readier to help. It is he, more than any of the other saints, who comes most rapidly to the help of the needy and the afflicted and the suffering who call on his aid. What a fine and profitable act it is to visit his tomb! Anyone who prays to him with all his heart will assuredly be granted his help that very day. I have had personal experience of what I say: once in this saint's town I saw a man who, on the very day that he had invoked this blessed confessor, escaped from a house belonging to a cobbler named Peyrot just before it collapsed and was reduced to rubble. Who will spend most time at his place of burial? Who will worship God in his most holy basilica? Who will most frequently embrace his sarcophagus? Who will kiss his venerable altar or tell the story of his most pious life?...

Such is the tomb of the blessed Aegidius, confessor, in which his venerable body rests with honor. May they blush with shame, those Hungarians who claim to have his body; may they be dismayed, those monks of Chamalières, who think they have his whole body; may they be confounded, those men of St-Seine who assert that they possess his head; may they be struck with fear, those Normans of Coutances who boast that they have his whole body; for his most holy bones, as many have borne witness, could not be removed from his own town. Certain men attempted by force to carry off the venerable arm of the blessed confessor to distant lands, but were quite unable to remove it....

Those Burgundians and Germans who go to St-James by the Le Puy road should venerate the relics of the blessed Faith [Foy], virgin and martyr, whose soul, after her beheading on the hill town of Agen, was borne up to heaven in the form of a dove by choirs of angels and crowned with the laurels of immortality. When the blessed Caprasius [Caprais], bishop of Agen, heard this while hiding in a cave to escape the rage of persecution, he found the courage to face martyrdom, hastened to the place where the blessed virgin had suffered and himself gained the palm of martyrdom, bearing himself most valiantly and even reproaching his executioners for their slowness.

Thereafter the most precious body of the blessed Faith [Foy], virgin and martyr, was honorably buried by Christians in the valley commonly known as Conques. Over her tomb was built a handsome basilica, in which the rule of Saint Benedict is strictly observed to this day for the glory of God. Many benefits are granted both to the sick and to those who are in good health. In front of the basilica is an excellent spring, the virtues of which are too great to be told. The saint's feast is celebrated on 6 October. Then, on the road to St-James by way of St-Leonard [de Noblat], the most holy body of the blessed Mary Magdalene is above all to be venerated [at Vézelay]. This is that glorious Mary who in the house of Simon the Leper watered the Savior's feet with her tears, wiped them with her hair, kissed them and anointed them with a precious ointment. Accordingly her many sins were forgiven her, for she had greatly loved Jesus Christ her redeemer, who loves all men. It was she who after the Lord's ascension left Jerusalem with the blessed Maximinus and other disciples of the Lord, sailed to Provence and landed at the port of Marseilles. She lived the life of a hermit in that country for some years and was then buried in Aix by Maximinus, who had become bishop of the town. Much later a sanctified monk named Badilo translated her most precious relics to Vézelay where they now rest in an honorable tomb. There a large and beautiful basilica and an abbey were built; there sinners have their faults remitted by God for love of the saint, the blind have their sight restored, the tongues of the dumb are loosed, the lame are cured of their lameness, those possessed by devils are delivered and ineffable benefits are granted to many of the faithful. The saint's feast is celebrated on 22 July....

Pilgrims traveling on this road should also pay honor, on the banks of the Loire to the venerable body of the blessed Martin [of Tours], bishop and confessor, who gloriously brought three dead men back to life and is reported to have restored lepers, men possessed by devils, the sick, the lunatic and the demoniac, and sufferers from other diseases, to the health they desired. The shrine containing his most sacred remains, in the city of Tours, is resplendent with a profusion of gold, silver and precious stones and is graced by numerous miracles. Over it a great and splendid basilica, in the likeness of the church of St-James, has been built. The sick come to it and are made well, the possessed are delivered, the blind see, the lame stand upright, all kinds of sickness are cured and all those who ask for the saint's intercession are fully satisfied. His glorious renown, therefore, is spread throughout the world in well merited eulogies, for the honor of Christ. His feast is celebrated on 11 November....

Also to be visited is the venerable head of the blessed John the Baptist, which was brought by certain religious men from Jerusalem to a place called Angely in Poitou. There a great and magnificent basilica was built and dedicated to him, and in this his most sacred head is venerated night and day by a choir of a 100 monks and has wrought countless miracles. While the head was being transported by sea and by land it gave many proofs of its miraculous power: on the sea it warded off numerous perils, and on land it brought dead men back to life. Accordingly it is believed to be indeed the head of the venerable Forerunner. It was found on 24 February in the time of the emperor Marcian, when the Forerunner first revealed to two monks the place where his head was concealed....

Finally and above all, pilgrims are to visit and pay the greatest veneration to the most holy body of the blessed apostle James in the city of Compostella. May the saints mentioned here and all the other saints of God intercede for us, through their merits and their prayers, with our Lord Jesus Christ, who lives and reigns with the Father and the Holy Ghost, God from eternity to eternity. Amen....

9. Of the Body and Altar of Saint James

... So far we have spoken of the characteristics of the church: we must now consider the venerable altar of the apostle. In this venerable basilica, according to tradition, the revered body of the blessed James rests under the magnificent altar set up in his honor. It is enclosed in a marble tomb which lies within a fine vaulted sepulcher of admirable workmanship and fitting size. That the body is immutably fixed there we know from the evidence of Saint Theodomir, bishop of the city, who discovered it and was unable to move it from the spot. May they blush for shame, therefore, those envious people beyond the mountains who claim to have some part of it or to possess relics of it! For the body of the saint is here in its entirety – divinely illuminated by paradisiac carbuncles, constantly honored by divine fragrances, radiant in the light of celestial candles, and devoutly attended by watching angels.

Pilgrims, whether poor or rich, returning from St-James or going there must be received with charity and compassion; for whosoever receives them and gives them hospitality has for his guest not only Saint James but our Lord himself. As the Lord says in his Gospel: "He that receives you, receives me." Many are those who have incurred the wrath of God because they would not take in the pilgrims of Saint James and the needy.

A weaver in Nantua, a town between Geneva and Lyons, refused bread to a pilgrim of Saint James who asked for it; and at once he saw his cloth fall to the ground, rent asunder. At Villeneuve a poor pilgrim of Saint James asked for alms, for the love of God and the blessed James, from a woman who was keeping bread under hot ashes. She told him that she had no bread: whereupon the pilgrim said, "May the bread that you have turn into stone!" The pilgrim had left the house and gone some distance on his way when the wicked woman went to take her bread out of the ashes and found a round stone in the place where the bread had been. Struck with remorse, she set out to look for the pilgrim, but could not find him.

At Poitiers two valiant French pilgrims, returning from St-James in great need, asked for hospitality, for the love of God and Saint James, in the street running from the house of Jean Gautier to the church of St-Porchaire, but found none. Finally, at the last house in the street, by the church, they were taken in by a poor man; and that night, by the operation of divine vengeance, a fierce fire broke out and quickly destroyed the whole street, beginning with the house where they had first asked for hospitality and going right up to the house where they were taken in. Some thousand houses were destroyed, but the one where the servants of God were taken in was, by grace, spared. Thus we learn that the pilgrims of St-James, whether rich or poor, should be given hospitality and a considerate reception. Here ends the fourth book of the apostle Saint James. Glory be to him who has written it and to him who reads it.

What is the attitude of the guide's author toward the peoples living along the pilgrim-age route to Compostela, such as the Gascons and the Navarrese? What were some of the problems and dangers confronting pilgrims en route to the shrine of St-James (and how did the people living along the route take advantage of the pilgrims)? What other places does the guide recommend that pilgrims visit? What evidence do you see that the author of this guide has personally experienced some of the pilgrimage spots? What sort of accommodations and other forms of assistance were available for pilgrims? What hap-pened to people living along the pilgrimage routes who did not help pilgrims in need?

55. LITURGY FOR PILGRIMS AND CRUSADERS

As pilgrimage and crusading became increasingly formalized and widespread practices in medieval European society, the Catholic church developed ritual blessings for those about to set out on their pilgrimage or crusade. The selection below, from a common English liturgical tradition of the High Middle Ages, also includes a description of the medieval pilgrim's "classic" symbols: the scrip (purse) and staff.

Source: revised and extended by S.J. Allen and E. Amt, in *The Crusades: A Reader*, ed. S.J. Allen and E. Amt (Peterborough, ON: Broadview Press, 2003), pp. 193–96, from the translation by F.E. Warren, in *The Sarum Missal in English* (London: De La More Press, 1911), pp. 166–73.

Psalm [25]: Unto you, O Lord, will I lift up my soul. My God, I have put my trust in you. O let me not be confounded, neither let my enemies triumph over me....

Psalm [51]: Have mercy upon me, O God, according to your loving kindness: according unto the multitude of your tender mercies blot out my transgres-sions. Wash me thoroughly from my iniquity, and cleanse me from my sin....

Psalm [91]: Who dwells under the defense of the most high, shall abide under the shadow of the Almighty. I will say unto the Lord, you are my hope, and my stronghold; my God, in him will I trust....

After each Psalm: Glory be to the Father, and to the Son, and to the Holy Ghost. As it was in the beginning, is now, and ever shall be, world without end. Amen.

Lord, have mercy upon us.

Christ, have mercy upon us.

Lord, have mercy upon us.

Our Father, which art in heaven, hallowed be thy name. Thy kingdom come. Thy will be done, in earth as it is in heaven. Give us this day our daily bread. And forgive us our trespasses, as we forgive them that trespass against us.

[Versicle] And lead us not into temptation,

[Response] But deliver us from evil.

V. I said, Lord, be merciful unto me;

R. Heal my soul, for I have sinned against you.

V. The Lord show you his ways;

R. And teach you his paths.

V. The Lord direct your steps according to his word;

R. That no unrighteousness get the dominion over you.

V. O that your ways were made so direct;

R. That you might keep the statutes of the Lord.

V. The Lord uphold your goings in his paths;

R. That your footsteps slip not.

V. Blessed be the Lord God daily;

R. The God of our salvation prosper your way before you.

V. The good angel of the Lord accompany you;

R. And dispose your way and your actions aright, that you may return again to your own place with joy.

V. Blessed are those that are undefiled in the way;

R. And walk in the law of the Lord.

V. Let the enemy have no advantage against you;

R. And let not the son of wickedness approach to hurt you.

V. O Lord, arise, help us,

R. And deliver us for your name's sake.

V. Turn us again, O Lord God of hosts;

R. And show the light of thy countenance upon us, and we shall be whole.

V. Lord, hear my prayer;

R. And let my crying come unto you.

V. The Lord be with you.

R. And with thy spirit.

Let us pray. Assist us, O Lord, in these our supplications, and dispose the way of thy servant N[ame] towards the attainment of salvation, that among all the changes and chances of the journey through life, he may ever be defended by thy help.... O God, who leads unto life, and guards with your fatherly protection them that trust in you, we beseech you that you would grant unto these your servants N[ames] here present, going forth from among us, an escort of angels; that they, being protected by your aid, may be shaken by no fear of evil, nor be depressed by any lingering adversity, nor be troubled by any enemy lying in wait to assail them; but that having prosperously accomplished the course of their appointed journey, they may return unto their homes; and having been received back in safety, may pay due thanks unto your name....

Here shall the pilgrims rise from their prostration, and the blessing of the scrip and staff shall follow, thus:

[V.] The Lord be with you.
[R.] And with thy spirit.

Let us pray.

O Lord Jesus Christ, who of your unspeakable mercy, and at the bidding of the Father, and with the cooperation of the Holy Ghost, did will to come down from heaven, and to seek the sheep that was lost through the wiles of the Devil, and to bear it back on your own shoulders to the flock of the heavenly country, and did command the sons of mother church by prayer to ask, by holy living to seek, and by knocking to persevere, that they may be able to find more quickly the rewards of saving life: we humbly beseech you that you would vouchsafe to sanctify and bless (+) these scrips (or this scrip), and these staves (or this staff), that whosoever, for the love of your name, shall desire to wear the same, like the armor of humility, at his side, or to hang it from his neck, or to carry it in his hands, and so on his pilgrimage to seek the prayers of the saints, with the accompaniment of humble devotion, may be found worthy, through the protecting defense of thy right hand, to attain unto the joys of the everlasting vision, through thee, O Savior of the world....

Here the priest shall sprinkle the scrip with holy water, and place it on the neck of the pilgrim, saying:

In the name of our Lord Jesus Christ receive this scrip, the habit of thy pilgrimage that after being well chastened thou mayest be found worthy both to reach in safety the thresholds of the saints, whither you desire to go; and that when thy journey is finished you may return to us in safety....

Let it be done to each person, if there be more than one. Then shall the priest deliver the staff to each one, saying:

Receive this staff for the support of thy journey, and for the labor of your pilgrimage; that you may be able to overcome all the hosts of the enemy, and to arrive in safety at the thresholds of the saints, whither you desire to go; and that when your journey has been obediently accomplished, you may again return to us with joy....

And thus let him say to others, if there be more than one.

Blessing of a cross for one on a pilgrimage to Jerusalem:

[V.] The Lord be with you.
[R.] And with thy spirit.

O God of unconquered power, and boundless pity, the entire aid and consolation of pilgrims, who give to your servants most invincible armor: we pray to you that you would vouchsafe to bless this cross, which is humbly dedicated to you; that the banner of the venerated cross, the figure whereof has been depicted upon it, may be a most invincible strength to your servant against the wickedest temptation of the ancient enemy; that it may be a defense by the way, a guard in thy house, and a protection to us everywhere....

Here shall holy water be sprinkled upon the dress [the clothing bearing the cross]. Then if any of those present be about to journey to Jerusalem, a vestment shall be given to him marked with the cross, the priest saying thus:

Receive this vestment, marked with the cross of our Lord and Savior, that through it there may accompany you safety, blessing, and strength for a prosperous journey to the sepulcher of [Christ]....

And thus shall it be done to the rest, if there be more than one present. The branding of a cross upon the flesh of pilgrims going to Jerusalem has been forbidden by canon law under pain of the greater excommunication. This done, there shall be said a mass for travelers, after the manner of a simple feast of nine lessons.

What does this liturgical ceremony suggest about the meaning of pilgrimage for those about to undertake it? How might it have made them feel? What about the priest who performed the rite? What does this liturgical performance imply about the relationship between "pilgrimage" and "crusading"? Why might the branding of a cross as a sign of pilgrimage have been forbidden? This text suggests that the Lord is a shepherd caring for pilgrims like lost sheep: what does this imagery imply about pilgrimage?

56. MEDIEVAL *EXEMPLA* AND PILGRIMAGE

During the thirteenth century, as part of an intensified effort to educate the laity in proper religious values and morals, clerics and monks such as James of Vitry and Caesarius of Heisterbach produced collections of exempla, *miraculous stories intended to exemplify for listeners proper behavior and to scare them with the consequences of misdeeds, while offering an entertaining tale in the bargain. Among many other subjects, medieval* exempla *extolled the benefits of pilgrimage and warned potential pilgrims about what might happen if they failed to fulfill their vows.*

Sources: James of Vitry, trans. J. Powell, from *The Exempla or Illustrative Stories from the Sermones Vulgares of James of Vitry*, ed. T.F. Crane (New York: Burt Franklin, 1971), pp. 47, 59–60; Caesarius of Heisterbach, trans. B.E. Whalen, from *Caesarii Heisterbacensis monachi, Dialogus miraculorum*, ed. J.M. Heberle, 2 vols. (1851; Ridgewood, NJ: Gregg Press, 1996), vol. 1, pp. 324, 326–27, 377–78; vol. 2, pp. 130–33, 218–19.

James of Vitry

102. Indeed, we have seen certain men who seem to be extremely devout and promise much to God when they are sick and afflicted, who oblige and bind themselves by a vow, yet afterwards when they recover they do not fulfill what they have promised. This was just the case with a certain pilgrim who, while he was traveling to the church of St-Michael [in Normandy], which is situated near to the sea, he saw the great waves of the sea rushing toward him and began to shout: "Saint Michael, rescue me from this danger, and I will give you a cow." As the sea drew ever nearer and almost drowned him, he began to shout even more: "Saint Michael, help me in this time of need, and I will give you a cow with its calf." When the sea receded, however, once he was safe, he said: *"Ne la vache ne le veel,"* that is, "Neither the cow nor the calf for you."

108. Behold, see how God values pilgrims and cares for those who, out of love for him, abandon the shared comfort of parents and relatives. In the life of the fathers, we read that there were two brothers, one who committed

himself to a pilgrimage, and the other who remained at home. It so happened that the pilgrim died and angels were escorting his soul; when he was about to enter heaven, there was some debate about him, and one [of the angels] said to the Lord: "He was a little negligent, but since he was a pilgrim, you should allow him to enter." Then his brother died. A certain old man, who had seen the angels come for the pilgrim, saw none come on the scene for his brother and asked the Lord why this was the case. The Lord responded: "The divine voice was calling, and the pilgrim had no consolation of friendship from relatives or friends." We discover in scripture many other examples of the consolation of pilgrims, and the virtue of the cross, and also the merit and reward of those signed with the cross, who offer themselves and their own to our Lord Jesus Christ....

Caesarius of Heisterbach

5.39. There was once two wealthy and honest men from Cologne, especially good friends with each other, one named Sistappus and the other Godefridus, who set out on the road together for [the church of] St-James [of Compostela]. One day, they were riding along alone since the other brothers had gone ahead. At the entrance into a certain forest, the Devil, who was envious of their friendship and harmony, seized Godfrey's rather thick staff hanging off of his back and broke it into two. When he could see no one thereabouts, he grew upset and cried out to his companion: "Hey there brother, why did you break my staff?" When he [Sistappus] denied it under oath, as Godefridus himself related to me, he grew so angry with him that he could scarcely keep his hands from beating him to a pulp. At last, by the grace of God and the merits of the blessed apostle, he came to his senses, and did penance before his best friend; the Devil, the head of all discord, fled in confusion.

5.42. There was once a certain soldier named Mengoz, who learned to speak French when he was growing up in France. When he grew gravely ill, in the hope of getting better, he made a vow to go on pilgrimage to [the church of] St-Remigius of Rheims, but he did not carry it out. This vow-breaker returned to his home-country. After a few days passed, another soldier, a noble man named Guldolphus born in the village of Sefflingen, who had undertaken a forty-day fast, proposed to go to the Cistercian General Chapter [meeting] and, recognizing Mengoz, asked him to join him as a companion on his pilgrimage. He gratefully agreed. When they had together reached the town of Tricastrum, located near Dijon, and had sat down to dinner in the manner of penitents in that land, Saint Remigius, bishop of Rheims, appeared in a bishop's garb before his transgressor, saying: "Mengoz, why did you not fulfill your vow?" The soldier, in truth, was terrified both by the reproach of this vision and his [unfulfilled] vow. Soon, the Devil arrived on the scene, adding some words of dissuasion to these words of admonition, saying: "There is no rush, you can fulfill your vow as you are able." Without another word, he seized the man by the feet, and dragged him on his stomach mercilessly across the pavement, so that his face was cut in four places and his blood poured forth all over the ground. When Guldolphus saw him dragged around in this way, but could not see who was doing the dragging (as he himself personally told me), he jumped up all agitated and wrapped his arms around the soldier; as strong as he was and is, he could barely manage to keep him still. When he learned from him the cause of his guilt and punishment, he said: "I advise you to fulfill your vow." When he [Mengoz] responded that he did not have the funds, he [Guldolphus] gave to him a sterling silver coin, so that he would not neglect to fulfill his vow....

6.25. It was not all that long ago, when a group of pilgrims was heading from Germany to the threshold of St-James [of Compostela], that a false brother joined them one night. The next morning, when he followed them coming out of the hostel to the gate of the city, he grabbed a hold of one of them, crying out that this man had stolen his horse from him. They were forced by the judge to return to the hostel. When all of the pilgrims swore that the man, whom the wicked one accused, was a simple and good person, the judge wisely acted as follows: when the thief [the false accuser] was not present, he had all of the saddles and reins removed from the horses, and had them led into the stable. After this, he said to the thief: "Enter and lead out your horse." He entered, and brought out a horse, but not the same one that he had said had been stolen from him at the gate. For, at that point, he had not carefully looked the horse over. Everyone laughed, and explained to the judge whose horse had been brought out, and that wretch was hung on the gallows. Now do you see how God protects those who walk in simplicity and punishes those acting badly?

8.58. There was once a man from lower Utrecht, who set out for [the church of] St-James with his son. It so happened, if I recall correctly, that in a certain place his host lost something – I do not know exactly what – and suspecting him, openly accused him of theft before the city's judge. He denied it, saying that "God knows and Saint James is my witness, that I have never been a thief, nor am I a thief's companion." The judge did not believe his words, and condemned the innocent man by a sentence of hanging. The son, seeing his father condemned and that the testimony of his brothers had achieved nothing for him, weeping and wailing, said to the judge: "I ask you, lord, insofar as it is the will of God and Saint James, to hang me and let my father go free, for I know that he is innocent." The judge, finally overcome by his tears and insistence, absolved the father and hung him. Very sad, the father continued on his way with his companions. Visiting the threshold of St-James, he prayed to him on behalf of his son's soul. Afterwards he returned to the place of the hanging, and he said to his brothers: "Behold, brothers, my son! I beg you, that we might pause here a little while, until I can take him down and bury him." The son, hearing his father's voice, replied: "Father, come forward happily, for I still live." Taken down by him, and asked what was the source of such a great miracle, he said: "Saint James the apostle, from the hour when I was strung up on the gallows until this very moment, held me up with his own hands. I did not hunger, thirst, or feel any pain; I have never felt better all the days of my life." At once, they set out together for the [church of the] blessed apostle, the son fulfilling his vow and the father once again giving thanks, before returning safely to the city of Utrecht. This very miracle was widely known and greatly celebrated in that city, as was told to us by William, our monk, a canon [member of the regular clergy] there.

8.59. In a town called Holenbach, there once lived a soldier named Gerard. His nephews are still living, and scarcely anyone can be found in that same town who would deny the miracle that I am about to relate. This man honored Saint Thomas the apostle more passionately, more specially than all the other saints, so that he would not deny alms to any pauper asking for them in his [the apostle's] name. He customarily offered to him many private services, so that there were prayers, fasts, and the celebration of masses. One day, with God permitting it, the enemy of all good, the Devil, pounding on that soldier's door in a pilgrim's guise and garb, asked him for shelter in the name of Saint Thomas. After he entered with all haste, since he was freezing and pretended to be catching a cold, Gerard handed over to him his rather nice, furry cloak, which he used to cover himself when lying down. The next morning, when the person who seemed to be a pilgrim did not appear, and his longed-for cloak was nowhere to be found, angry with her husband, the wife said: "You are often fooled by wandering beggars of this kind, and still never leave off your superstitions." He responded to her, with a calm demeanor: "Do not get upset; Saint Thomas will surely restore this lost item to us." The devil had done this so that the soldier, through the loss of his cloak, might be provoked to impatience and dampen the favor in his heart for the apostle. But rather, what the Devil has prepared for his ruin brought the soldier to glory, whereupon the latter was enflamed even more eagerly [toward the saint], and the former thrown into confusion and punished.

For, after a little time had passed, Gerard wished to go to the threshold of St-Thomas; when he was getting prepared [for this purpose], before his wife's eyes, he divided a golden collar into two parts, and holding them up together before her, he gave one to her and kept the other for himself, saying:

"You should believe in this sign. I ask that you wait for me to return for five years, after which you can marry whom you will." And she promised this to him. Following an incredibly long journey, with the greatest effort and great expense, he at last reached the city of Saint Thomas the apostle [in India]. There, he was officially greeted by the citizens and received with much affection, as if he were one of them and most well known among them. Giving thanks to the blessed apostle, he entered into his shrine, and prayed that he might commend himself, his wife, and all of their belongings into his care. After this, mindful of his end, and realizing that the five years were up that very day, he groaned and said: "Oh, my wife shall marry another man".... Looking about, very sad, he saw the aforesaid demon walking up in his cloak. The demon said: "Do you recognize me, Gerard?" "No," he replied, "I do not recognize you, but I do my cloak." The demon responded: "I am the one who asked you for hospitality in the name of the apostle and stole your cloak, on account of which I am greatly punished." And he added: "I am the Devil, and it has been commanded to me that, before men retire for the night, I will carry you to your house, because your wife is marrying another man, and is already settling down into marriage with him." Picking him up, over part of the day, he transferred him from India to Germany, from the rising to the setting of the sun, and around twilight placed him down safely without a mark upon him in his own courtyard. Looking like a barbarian, he entered into his house. When he saw his own wife sitting with her spouse, with her watching, he approached and dropped part of the collar into her drinking cup before stepping back. When she saw it, quickly pulled it out, and joined it together with the part given to her, she realized that this was her husband. Immediately, she jumped up and rushed into his arms, proclaimed that this was her man, Gerard, and bid farewell to her [other] husband. Nevertheless, Gerard allowed him to spend the night in a respectable fashion. Behold, it is evident in this as much as the aforesaid miracle, how these [miracles] favor and glorify those showing favor to the blessed apostle!

What does the story about the pilgrim who reneged on his promise to Saint Michael seem to say about the fickle nature of some religious travelers? What evidence do the exempla *provide that monks and clerics were concerned about the fulfillment of pilgrimage vows? What happens to those who refuse or hesitate to carry out a promised pilgrimage? What role do demons and the Devil play in tempting unwary believers away from their obligations? How do God and the saints protect the faithful, who remain steadfast in their vows and faith?*

57. JEWISH HOST DESECRATION AND CHRISTIAN VENERATION

In 1215 at the Fourth Lateran Council, the Roman church formally defined the doctrine of transubstantiation as the real change of the Eucharistic bread and wine into the flesh and blood of Christ (despite its continued appearance as bread and wine). Responding, perhaps, to doubts about this teaching, Christians in the thirteenth and fourteenth centuries accused Jews of stealing and violating the Eucharist, confirming its reality as the body of Christ when their mistreatment of the host produced blood and other visible effects. Such desecrated hosts became relics in their own right, creating a new sacred attraction for Christian believers and pilgrims. The anonymous account below describes one such supposed incident at Paris in 1290.

Source: trans. M. Bazemore, from *De miraculo hostiae a Judeao Parisiis anno domini MCCXC multis ignomiis affectae*, in *Recueil des historiens des Gaules et de la France*, ed. M. Bouquet, vol. 22 (Paris, 1904), pp. 32–33.

Formerly, God conferred great benefits on his people [the Jews], but those things which the divine bounty has showed and shows daily to us Christians are immeasurable. It was not enough for him to change the children of wrath by nature into children of God by the sacrament of baptism, unless he remains with us until the completion of the world, nourishing us with his own flesh and blood. When, in the sacrament of the Eucharist, we receive in our members his body and blood we become Christ-bearers, joined to him just as our limbs unite to the head. Taught by the Lord in the past about the necessity of the Eucharist for the life of the soul, just as their venomous, odious parents turned away from [this teaching], so the children of the poisonous Jews remain doubtful of it. See for yourself: in the year of our Lord 1290, on 11 April, Easter day (greatly celebrated by the Parisians far and above all other cities), a certain down-on-her-luck woman, a commoner, had pawned her clothes to a Jew for the pledge of 30 Parisian *solidi*. When she wanted to reclaim them, so that she might appear fashionable before her neighbors, the Jew promised to return them for free, if she would bring to him the thing that the woman claimed was her God. The greedy woman promised to do so. When she received the most holy body of Christ at the church of St-Medericus with the others ready [to take the Eucharist], she took it hidden in her mouth to the Jew, from whom she received her clothes free of charge.

"I will know," said the cruel merchant, "whether those things which the insane Christians blather about this matter are true." So he grabbed a bread knife and, placing the most holy body of Christ on a chest, pierced it with dire blows, whence he perceived sacred blood to flow copiously. This deed was witnessed by his wife and children. His wife, upon seeing this stupendous miracle, stood astonished. The Jew, frightened as well, but feeling no remorse, again seized the host and attacked it with hammer and nails, causing the sweet-smelling blood to flow as before. His wife admonished him to stop what he was doing, to little avail. He then threw the most holy host into a large fire, from which it emerged whole, flying throughout the house. Trying once more in vain to rip it to shreds with a knife, he attacked the host, which always remained whole, with all his strength, finally hanging it from a little hook near the washroom. The Jew then threw it, abundantly flowing with blood as before, into a cauldron of boiling water, which became like blood; elevated again by the power of its majesty, it showed itself to the Jew in the form of the body of the crucified Lord, at whose appearance, while his wife and children wept contritely before this prodigious event, he went completely mad and fled into his bedroom.

He who considers this event will with astonishment praise divine mercy and speak of it as if it were another resurrection of the Lord (although granted, once he rose from the dead, he was never to die again). Indeed, that sacrosanct host, after being stabbed, pierced, scourged, burnt by the flames, torn, speared, and thrown into a cauldron of boiling water, unblemished and whole, lies with honor in the church of St-John in Grève, covered by a small piece of the Lord's clothing, and to the greater glory of the Lord, adorned with a small piece of the Cross. With their own eyes, the faithful can look at the aforementioned breadknife and the blood that miraculously flowed forth from the wound and the container of ashes in which it arrived, in the church of the Brothers of Blessed Mary of Charity, in the same neighborhood.

This is how these deeds done in the house came to the notice of the people. At the hour of the high mass, when the signal was given by the bell in the church of the Crusaders that the gathering people might adore the sacrosanct body of Christ, the son of the Jew, going outside, asked those passing by where they were running. They declared that they were going to the venerable mystery of the sacrosant body of Christ. The boy told the Christians that they would vainly seek in that church their God, whom his father had beaten, scourged, afflicted with injury, and treated with evil. Hearing this and eager to find out the truth of it, a certain woman, full of horror and armed with the sign of the cross, charged into the house of the Jew and saw this second martyrdom of the Lord's flesh. Immediately, the sacrosanct host, consecrated and unharmed, leapt into the tinder-box which the woman carried about for making a fire. Clutching it close to her bosom, with great reverence, she brought it for safekeeping to a priest of St-John in Grève. Moreover, that woman, when she attempted to leave, as though bound in chains could not exit the church until she handed over to the priest that [host] which she bore, witnessed by many who had gathered around, already attracted by the rumor of this deed. The woman told them about what she had seen. Whereupon the priest undertook to tell the bishop of Paris. The whole of the city rushed to the spectacle. The Jew was joined with his wife and children in chains. Brought to the presence of the bishop and men distinguished by ecclesiastical dignity, the Jew confessed to the crime; he was warned that he should repent, for it is written, "I desire not the death of the wicked, but more that he should change his ways and live," and he might hope for pardon, as when God prayed formerly for those who crucified him. The woman and children were converted to the Christian faith. The obstinate Jew, condemned to be cremated by fire, was led to the place of punishment; when the executioner wanted to place him on the fire he exclaimed: "Woe is me, who was caught so unawares that I was not able to make use of my defenses!" Asked what he meant by these "defenses," the Jew responded, "I have a book in my home, which, were I to have it with me, God would make it so that you could not burn me." At the command of the overseer [of the execution], the book was brought by his assistants, bound to the Jew, and placed under the flame; both were reduced to ashes, just as easy as it was difficult for the Jew to be converted from his infidelity. Then, with the crowd of people standing around, the bishop of Paris investigated the place where the miracle occurred, as described. He marked with holy anointing of chrism the wife of the Jew, his son and his daughter, who were cleansed by baptism. Many other Jews, too, so moved by the evident miracle, converted to the faith, securing the sacrament of baptism. Moreover, in that spot where such a crime was savagely perpetrated, Raynerius Flamingus, a citizen of Paris, undertook the building of a chapel where the miracle was expressed, at his own expense in the year 1294; with Guido of Joinville making the arrangements, he bestowed it upon the brothers of Blessed Mary of Charity of the diocese of Catalonia. Philip, king of the Franks, called the Fair, enlarged the home near the aforementioned chapel in the year of our Lord 1299. Truly, the aforementioned brothers of the order established a commemoration of so great a miracle to be celebrated solemnly each year on Whitsunday.

Why, according to this text, did the poor Christian woman secretly bring the Eucharist to the Jew in question? What did he do to the host, and what did his actions seem to reveal about the nature of the Eucharist? Informed of this sacrilege, how did the Christian community of Paris (including the clergy) respond? How did this accusation against the host-desecrating Jew lead to the creation of new relics and Christian devotional sites?

CHAPTER SEVEN

PILGRIMAGE AND THE WIDER WORLD

During the High Middle Ages, the Christian inhabitants of Europe realized that the world was a much larger place than they had previously imagined, filled with non-Christians as well as with a variety of Christian peoples. A number of factors contributed to Europe's broadening horizons at this time, including the lasting legacy of the crusades and the expansion of commercial activities by Italian city-states. In particular, the rise of the Mongol Empire in the thirteenth century created new opportunities for European merchants and missionaries to travel across central Asia, sometimes even reaching distant "Cathay" (China). Such long-distance travel worked both ways, also bringing Eastern Christians to the Middle East and Europe. During this same era, Muslim travelers continued to make the Hajj (a pilgrimage to Mecca, required of every capable believer at least once in his or her lifetime) and other devotional journeys, traveling the same networks of roads and sea-lanes that connected Africa, Europe, and Asia. Christians, Muslims, Jews, and others traveled around the known world, crossing each other's paths as they did so. In this cosmopolitan environment, traditional Christian pilgrimage from Europe to Jerusalem continued unabated. For many Christian travelers, however, their visit to the Promised Land formed but one stage of farther-reaching voyages that were made for adventure, diplomacy, or profit. A pilgrimage to Jerusalem, still the mark of a pious Christian, could seem for some an obligatory stop on a world tour as much as a spiritual experience.

58. MUHAMMAD AL-IDRISI'S DESCRIPTION OF JERUSALEM

Due in part to their inheritance of classical Greek knowledge, and in part to their own travels throughout far-flung Islamic lands, Muslims in the High Middle Ages far excelled contemporary Europeans in their knowledge of the wider world. Writing around 1154, Muhammad al-Idrisi, who worked for the Christian ruler Roger II of Sicily, included the following description of Jerusalem in his geographical work. Apparently, he borrowed much of his information from a Christian guide to the holy places, written in Arabic.

Source: trans. J. Wilkinson, with J. Hill and W.F. Ryan, in *Jerusalem Pilgrimage 1099-1185*, ed. J. Wilkinson, J. Hill, and W.F. Ryan (London: The Hayluyt Society, 1988), pp. 223–27.

The Holy City, a beautiful city of ancient foundation, lasting forever: it was anciently called Aelia. It stands on a mountain, and you ascend to it from all sides. In plan it is long, and its length stretches from west to east.

The gate of the Oratory is on its western side; and this is the gate over which is the cupola of David – peace be upon him.

The gate of Mercy is on the eastern side of the city. It is closed, and is only opened at the feast of Olive-Branches.

Sion Gate is on the south of the city.

The gate of the Crow's Pillars lies to the north of the city. When you enter by the gate of the Oratory which as aforesaid is the western gate, you go eastward through a street that leads to the great church known as the church of the Resurrection, which the Muslims call the Dunghill. This is a church to which pilgrimage is made from all parts of the Greek [Byzantine] Empire, both from the eastern lands and the western. You may enter by a gate at the west end, and the interior thereof occupies the center space under a dome which covers the whole of the church. This is one of the wonders of the world. The church itself lies lower than this gate, but you cannot descend thereto from this side.

Another gate opens on the north side, and through this you may descend to the lower part of the church by thirty steps. This gate is called the gate of St-Mary.

When you have descended into the interior of the church you come on the most venerated Holy Sepulcher. It has two gates, and above it is a vaulted dome of very solid construction, beautifully built, and splendidly ornamented. Of these two gates, one is toward the north, facing the gate of St-Mary, and the other is toward the south, facing which is the gate of the Crucifixion. Above this gate is the bell-tower of the church.

Over against this, on the east, is a great and venerable church, where the Franks of the Greek Empire have their worship and services. To the east of this blessed church, but bearing somewhat to the south, is the prison in which the Lord messiah was incarcerated; also the place of the crucifixion.

Now as to the great dome, it is of a vast size and is open to the sky. Inside the dome, and all round it, are painted pictures of the prophets, and of the Lord messiah, and of the lady Maryam [Mary], his mother, and of John the Baptist. Over the Holy Sepulcher lamps are suspended, and above the place [of the grave] in particular are three lamps of gold.

On leaving the great church and going eastwards, you come to the holy house built by Solomon, the son of David. This, in the time of the Jews, was a mosque [place of prayer] to which pilgrimage was made, but it was taken out of their hands and they were driven from thence; but when the days of Islam came, under the kings of the Muslims, the spot came once more to be venerated, as the Masjid al-Aksa.

The Masjid al-Aksa is the Great Mosque, and in the whole earth there is no mosque of greater dimensions than this, unless it be the Friday mosque at Cordova, in Andalusia [Muslim Spain], which they say has a greater extent of roof than has the Aksa, but the court of the Aksa mosque is certainly larger than is that of the mosque at Cordova. [The court of] the Masjid al-Aksa is four-sided, its length measures 200 fathoms, and its breadth is 180 fathoms.

In that half [of the court] which lies towards the prayer-niche [the main building of the Aksa mosque] is roofed with domes of stone set on many rows of columns. The other half is a court, and is not roofed over. In the center of the court rises the mighty dome known as the Dome of the Rock. This dome is overlaid with gold mosaic, and is of most beautiful workmanship, erected by the Muslim caliphs. In its midst is the rock, which is said to have fallen down [from heaven]. It is a mass of stone of the height of a platform, and occupies the center under the dome. The extremity of one of its sides rises above the floor to half a man's height or more, while the other side lies even with the ground. The length of the rock is nearly equal to its breadth, and is some ten ells and odd by the like. You may descend into the interior thereof, and go down into a dark chamber, like a cellar, the length of which is ten ells, by five in the width, and the ceiling is above a man's height up. No one can enter this chamber except with a lamp to light him.

The dome has four gates. The western gate has opposite to it an altar whereon the children of Israel offer up their sacrifices. Near the eastern gate of the dome is the church which is called the Holy of Holies; it is of an admirable construction.

[The gate] to the south faces the roofed-in portion [of the Masjid al-Aksa], which same was in former times the place of prayer of the Muslims. Since it was conquered by the Greeks [the crusaders], and it has remained in their hands even down to the time of the writing of this book, they have converted this roofed-in portion of the mosque into chambers wherein are lodged those companies of men known as ad-Dawiyyah, whose name signifies "Servants of God's House" [the Templars]. Opposite to the northern gate [of the Dome of the Rock] is a beautiful garden, planted with all sorts of trees, and round this garden is set a colonnade of marble, of most wondrous workmanship. In the further part of this garden is a place of assembly, where the priests and deacons take their repasts.

Leaving the mosque you come, on the eastern side, to the gate of Mercy, which is now closed, as we·have said before; but near to this gate is another, which is open. It is called the gate of the Tribes, and through it there is much coming and going. When you have passed out by the gate of the Tribes you reach the limits of the archery ground, and find there a large church, and very beautiful, dedicated to the lady Mary, and the place is known as Gethsemane. At this place also is her tomb, on the edge of the Mount of Olives. Between it and the gate of the Tribes is the space of about a mile.

On the road ascending the Mount of Olives is a magnificent church, beautifully and solidly built, which is called the church of Pater Noster; and on the summit of the mount is another church, beautiful and grand likewise, in which men and women enclose themselves, seeking thereby to obtain favor with Allah — be he exalted! In this aforementioned mount, on the eastern part, and bearing rather to the south, is the tomb of Lazarus, whom the Lord messiah raised again to life. Two miles distant from the Mount of Olives stands the village from which they brought the she ass on which the Lord messiah rode on his entry into Jerusalem. The place is now in ruins, and no one lives there.

From the Tomb of Lazarus you take the road down to the Valley of the Jordan, and between the valley and the Holy City is the distance of a day's journey. Before reaching the river Jordan is the city of Jericho, lying three miles distant from the bed of the river.

On the banks of the Jordan stands a magnificent church, called after Saint John, where the Greek monks dwell.

The river Jordan flows out from the lake of Tiberias, and falls into the lake of Sodom and Gomorrah, and these were two cities of the people of Lot which God overwhelmed because of the sins of their inhabitants. The land lying to the south of the river Jordan is one continuous desert.

Now as to what lies adjacent to the holy city on the southern quarter: When you go out by the gate of Sion you pass a distance of a stone's throw and come to the Church of Sion, which is a beautiful church, and fortified.

In it is the guest-chamber wherein the Lord messiah ate with the disciples, and the table is there remaining even unto the present day. The people assemble here on [Maundy] Thursday.

From the gate of Sion you descend into a ravine called the Valley of Gehenna. On the edge of this ravine is a church called after the name of Peter, and down in the ravine is the Spring of Siloam which is the spring where the Lord messiah cured the infirmity of the blind man, who before that had no eyes. Going south from this said spring is the field wherein strangers are buried, and it is a piece of ground which the Lord bought for this purpose; and nearby to it are many habitations cut out in the rock wherein men enclose themselves for the purposes of devotion.

Bethlehem is the place where the Lord messiah was born, and it lies six miles distant from Jerusalem. Half-way down the road is the tomb of Rachel, the mother of Joseph and of Benjamin, the two sons of Jacob — peace be upon them all. The tomb is covered by 12 stones, and above it is a dome vaulted over with stone. At Bethlehem is a church that is beautifully built, of solid foundations, spacious and finely ornamented even to the uttermost, so that not among all other churches can its equal be seen. It is situated on a low-lying ground. The gate thereof is toward the west, and there are marble columns of perfect beauty. In one angle of the choir, towards the north, is a cave wherein the Lord messiah was born. It lies below the church, and in the cave is the manger wherein the messiah was found. As you go out from Bethlehem you see toward the east the church of the Angels who told the good news of the birth of the Lord Messiah to the shepherds.

What sites and structures around Jerusalem does al-Idrisi include in his description of the holy places? What evidence does this text provide that the crusaders were still ruling over the city when he wrote his account? How would you describe the presentation of sacred spots associated with the "Lord messiah" (Jesus Christ)? Imagine that al-Idrisi had a chance to speak with a Christian pilgrim to Jerusalem about the city's holy sites: what might they say to each other?

59. THE ITINERARY OF BENJAMIN OF TUDELA

Although not a pilgrim in the traditional sense of the word, the twelfth-century Jewish traveler Benjamin of Tudela, who began his journey in Spain in the late 1160s, visited many of the major religious sites in the Middle East, including the cities of Jerusalem and Hebron. His travel account offers us a valuable Jewish perspective on the "Promised Land" during a period when the crusaders still controlled the region.

Source: revised by S.J. Allen and E. Amt, in *The Crusades: A Reader,* ed. S.J. Allen and E. Amt (Peterborough, ON: Broadview Press, 2003), pp. 116–20, from the translation by M.N. Adler, *The Itinerary of Benjamin of Tudela: Critical Text, Translation, and Commentary,* ed. M.N. Adler (New York: Philipp Feldheim, 1907), pp. 124–27.

[From Tarsus] it is two days' journey to Antioch the great, situated on the river Orontes.... This is the great city which Antiochus the king built. The city lies by a lofty mountain, which is surrounded by the city wall. At the top of the mountain is a well, from which a man appointed for that purpose directs the water by means of 20 subterranean passages to the houses of the great men of the city. The other part of the city is surrounded by the river. It is a strongly fortified city, and is under the sway of Prince Bohemond the Poitevin, surnamed "le Baube" [the Stammerer]. Ten Jews dwell here, engaged in glass-making, and at their head are Rabbi Mordecai, Rabbi Chayim, and Rabbi Samuel. From here it is two days' journey to Leda, or Ladikiya, where there are about 100 Jews, at their head being Rabbi Chayim and Rabbi Joseph.

From there, it is two days' journey to Gebela, which is Baal-Gad, at the foot of Lebanon. In the neighborhood dwells a people called Al-Hashishim [the Assassins]. They do not believe in the religion of Islam, but follow one of their own folk, whom they regard as their prophet, and all that he tells them to do they carry out, whether for death or life. They call him the sheik "Al-Hashishim," and he is known as their elder. At his word these mountaineers go out and come in. Their principal seat is Kadmus, which is Kedemoth in the land of Sihon. They are faithful to each other, but a source of terror to their neighbors, killing even kings at the cost of their own lives. The extent of their land is eight days' journey. And they are at war with the sons of Edom who are called the Franks, and with the ruler of Tripoli.... At Tripoli in years gone by there was an earthquake, when many gentiles [non-Jews] and Jews perished, for houses and walls fell upon them. There was great destruction at that time throughout the land of Israel, and more than 20,000 souls perished.

From there, it is a day's journey to Jubail, which borders on the land of the children of Ammon, and here there are about 150 Jews. The place is under the rule of the Genoese, the name of the governor being William Embriacus.... There are about 200 Jews there, at their head being Rabbi Meir, Rabbi Jacob, and Rabbi Simchah. The place is situated on the sea-border of the land of Israel. From there it is two days' journey to Beirut or Beeroth, where there are about 50 Jews, at their head being Rabbi Solomon, Rabbi Obadiah, and Rabbi Joseph. Thence it is one day's journey to Sidon, a large city, with about 20 Jews. Ten miles from there a people dwell who are at war with the men of Sidon; they are called Druses and are pagans of a lawless character. They inhabit the mountains and the clefts of the rocks; they have no king or ruler, but dwell independently in these high places, and their border extends to Mount Hermon, which is a three days' journey. They are steeped in vice.... There are no resident Jews among them, but a certain number of Jewish handicraftsmen and dyers come among them for the sake of trade, and then return, the people being favorable to the Jews. They roam over the mountains and hills, and no man can do battle with them.

From Sidon it is half a day's journey to Sarfend, which belongs to Sidon. From there, it is a half-day to New Tyre, which is a very fine city, with a harbor in its midst. At night-time those that levy dues throw iron chains from tower to tower, so that no man can go forth by boat or in any other way to rob the ships by night. There is no harbor like this in the whole world. Tyre is a beautiful city. It contains about 500 Jews, some of them scholars of the Talmud, at their head being Rabbi Ephraim of Tyre, the Dayan, Rabbi Meir from Carcassonne, and Rabbi Abraham, head of the congregation. The Jews own seagoing vessels, and there are glass-makers amongst them who make that fine Tyrian glassware which is prized in all countries. In the vicinity is found sugar of a high class, for men plant it here, and people come from all lands to buy it. A man can ascend the walls of New Tyre and see ancient Tyre, which the sea has now covered, lying at a stone's throw from the new city. And should one care to go forth by boat, one can see the castles, market-places, streets, and palaces in the bed of the sea. New Tyre is a busy place of commerce, to which merchants flock from all quarters.

One day's journey brings one to Acre, the Acco of old, which is on the borders of Asher; it is the commencement of the land of Israel. Situated by the Great [Mediterranean] Sea, it possesses a large harbor for all the pilgrims who come to Jerusalem by ship. A stream runs in front of it, called the brook of Kedumim. About 200 Jews live there, at their head being Rabbi Zadok, Rabbi Japheth, and Rabbi Jonah. From there it is three parasangs [a parasang might equal about three miles] to Haifa ... on the seaboard, and on the other

side is Mount Carmel, at the foot of which there are many Jewish graves.
On the mountain is the cave of Elijah, where the Christians have erected
a structure called St-Elias. On the top of the mountain can be recognized
the overthrown altar which Elijah repaired in the days of Ahab. The site of
the altar is circular, about four cubits remain thereof, and at the foot of the
mountain the brook Kishon flows. From here it is four parasangs to Capernaum, which is the village of Nahum....

Six parasangs from here is Caesarea ... and here there are about 200 Jews
and 200 Cuthim. These [Cuthim] are the Jews of Shomron, who are called
Samaritans. The city is fair and beautiful, and lies by the sea. It was built
by Caesar, and called after him Caesarea. Thence it is half a day's journey
to Kako.... There are no Jews here. From there it is half a day's journey to
Sebastiya, which is the city of Samaria, and here the ruins of the palace of
Ahab the son of Omri may be seen. It was formerly a well-fortified city by
the mountainside, with streams of water. It is still a land of brooks of water,
gardens, orchards, vineyards, and olive groves, but no Jews dwell here. From
there it is two parasangs to Nablus ... where there are no Jews; the place is
situated in the valley between Mount Gerizim and Mount Ebal, and contains
about 1,000 Cuthim, who observe the written law of Moses alone, and are
called Samaritans. They have priests of the seed [of Aaron], and they call
them Aaronim, who do not intermarry with Cuthim, but wed only among
themselves. These priests offer sacrifices, and bring burnt-offerings in their
place of assembly on Mount Gerizim, as it is written in their law – "And you
shall set the blessing on Mount Gerizim." They say that this is the proper
site of the Temple. On Passover and the other festivals they offer up burnt-
offerings on the altar which they have built on Mount Gerizim, as it is written in their law – "You shall set up the stones upon Mount Gerizim, of the
stones which Joshua and the children of Israel set up at the Jordan." They say
that they are descended from the tribe of Ephraim. And in the midst of them
is the grave of Joseph, the son of Jacob our father, as it is written – "and the
bones of Joseph buried they in Shechem"....

From [Gibeon the Great] it is three parasangs to Jerusalem, which is a
small city, fortified by three walls. It is full of people whom the [Muslims] call
Jacobites, Syrians, Greeks, Georgians, and Franks, and people of all tongues.
It contains a dyeing-house, for which the Jews pay a small rent annually to
the king, on condition that besides the Jews no other dyers be allowed in
Jerusalem. There are about 200 Jews [or, alternatively, about four Jews] who
dwell under the Tower of David in one corner of the city. The lower portion
of the wall of the Tower of David, to the extent of about ten cubits, is part of
the ancient foundation set up by our ancestors, the remaining portion having
been built by the Muslims. There is no structure in the whole city stronger

than the Tower of David. The city also contains two buildings, from one of which – the hospital – there issue forth 400 knights; and therein all the sick who come thither are lodged and cared for in life and in death. The other building is called the Temple of Solomon; it is the palace built by Solomon the king of Israel. 300 knights are quartered there, and issue from there every day for military exercise, besides those who come from the land of the Franks and the other parts of Christendom, having taken upon themselves to serve there a year or two until their vow is fulfilled. In Jerusalem is the great church called the [Holy] Sepulcher, and here is the burial-place of Jesus, unto which the Christians make pilgrimages.

Jerusalem has four gates: the gate of Abraham, the gate of David, the gate of Zion, and the gate of Gushpat, which is the gate of Jehoshaphat, facing our ancient Temple, now called the Temple of the Lord. Upon the site of the sanctuary Omar ben al-Khataab erected an edifice with a very large and magnificent cupola, into which the gentiles do not bring any image or effigy, but they merely come there to pray. In front of this place is the western wall, which is one of the walls of the Holy of Holies. This is called the gate of Mercy, and thither come all the Jews to pray before the wall of the court of the Temple. In Jerusalem, attached to the palace which belonged to Solomon, are the stables built by him, forming a very substantial structure, composed of large stones, and the like of it is not to be seen anywhere in the world. There is also visible up to this day the pool used by the [ancient Jewish] priests before offering their sacrifices, and the Jews coming thither write their names upon the wall. The gate of Jehoshaphat leads to the valley of Jehoshaphat, which is the gathering-place of nations. Here is the pillar called Absalom's Hand, and the sepulcher of King Uzziah.

In the neighborhood is also a great spring, called the Waters of Siloam, connected with the brook of Kidron. Over the spring is a large structure dating from the time of our ancestors, but little water is found, and the people of Jerusalem for the most part drink the rainwater, which they collect in cisterns in their houses.... In front of Jerusalem is Mount Sion, on which there is no building, except a place of worship belonging to the Christians. Facing Jerusalem for a distance of three miles are the cemeteries belonging to the Israelites, who in the days of old buried their dead in caves, and upon each sepulcher is a dated inscription, but the Christians destroy the sepulchers, employing the stones thereof in building their houses. These sepulchers reach as far as Zelzah in the territory of Benjamin. Around Jerusalem are high mountains.... From Jerusalem it is two parasangs to Bethlehem, which is called by the Christians Beth-Leon, and close thereto, at a distance of about half a mile, at the parting of the way, is the pillar of Rachel's grave, which is made up of 11 stones, corresponding with the number of the sons of Jacob.

Upon it is a cupola resting on four columns, and all the Jews that pass by carve their names upon the stones of the pillar. At Bethlehem there are two Jewish dyers. It is a land of brooks of water, and contains wells and fountains. At a distance of six parasangs is St-Abram de Bron, which is Hebron; the old city stood on the mountain, but is now in ruins; and in the valley by the field of Machpelah lies the present city. Here there is the great church called St-Abram, and this was a Jewish place of worship at the time of the Muslim rule, but the gentiles have erected there six tombs, respectively called those of Abraham and Sarah, Isaac and Rebekah, Jacob and Leah. The custodians tell the [Christian] pilgrims that these are the tombs of the patriarchs, for which information the pilgrims give them money. If a Jew comes, however, and gives a special reward, the custodian of the cave opens unto him a gate of iron, which was constructed by our forefathers, and then he is able to descend below by means of steps, holding a lighted candle in his hand. He then reaches a cave, in which nothing is to be found, and a cave beyond, which is likewise empty, but when he reaches the third cave behold there are six sepulchers, those of Abraham, Isaac, and Jacob, respectively facing those of Sarah, Rebekah, and Leah. And upon the graves are inscriptions cut in stone; upon the grave of Abraham is engraved "This is the grave of Abraham"; upon that of Isaac, "This is the grave of Isaac, the son of Abraham our father"; upon that of Jacob, "This is the grave of Jacob, the son of Isaac, the son of Abraham our father"; and upon the others, "This is the grave of Sarah"; "This is the grave of Rebekah"; and "This is the grave of Leah." A lamp burns day and night upon the graves in the cave. One finds there many casks filled with the bones of Israelites, as the members of the house of Israel were wont to bring the bones of their fathers thither and to deposit them there to this day....

What most interested Benjamin of Tudela during his travels? What sort of "holy sites" appealed to him and why? What knowledge does he show about non-Jewish communities and religious practices, including Muslims and Christians? Compare Benjamin's description of the "Tomb of the Patriarchs" at Hebron with that of the anonymous, twelfth-century Latin cleric (doc. 47): what do their similarities and differences seem to suggest about the importance of the site to Jewish, Christian, and Muslim visitors?

60. RABBAN SAUMA'S JOURNEY FROM
· THE EAST

In the mid-1260s, a Nestorian Christian named Rabban Bar Sauma, born in the outskirts of Khanbaliq [modern-day Beijing], set out with his companion Rabban Marcos on a pilgrimage to Jerusalem. Unable to reach the city due to political turbulence, they stopped in Persia, where Rabban Marcos was eventually elected catholicus or patriarch of the Nestorian church, taking the name of Mar Yaballaha III. At this same time, the Mongol ruler of Persia, Arghun, desired to send a legate to the pope of Rome and Christian rulers of Europe to inquire about the possibility of an alliance against the Islamic Mamluk dynasty. In 1287, Rabban Sauma undertook this task in the name of the Mongol ruler and catholicus, visiting Constantinople, Rome, and France before his return to Persia in 1288. In the selection below, from the History of Mar Yaballaha III, *we see that Rabban's interests during his journey extended beyond diplomacy to include holy sites, saints' shrines, and relics, as well as witnessing religious ceremonies.*

Source: trans. J.A. Montgomery, in *The History of Mar Yaballaha III, Nestorian Patriarch and of his Vicar Bar Sauma*, Records of Civilization: Sources and Studies (New York: Columbia University Press, 1927), pp. 51–73.

Now Mar Yaballaha was advanced in his [Arghun's] presence, and day by day his honor increased before the king and the queen. For he pulled down the church of Mar Shallita in Maragha and restored it at great expense, and replacing the [roof] timbers he made it into two naves. At the side he made the cell of its vicar. And his affection was very warm for the family of King Arghun, because he loved the Christians with all his heart. And he was minded to go and subjugate the lands of Palestine and Syria [saying]: "that if the western kings, who are Christians, do not help me, my desire cannot be fulfilled." So he desired of the *catholicus* that he should give him a wise man, one useful and fit for the embassy, to send him to those kings. And when the *catholicus* saw that there was none acquainted with the languages except Rabban Sauma, since he was competent for this, he commissioned him to go.

Then Rabban Sauma said: "I am desirous of this and eager for it." And King Arghun at once wrote recommendations for him to the kings of the Greeks and the Franks, that is, the Romans, and *yarliks*, and letters, with gifts for each king separately. And he gave Rabban Sauma 2000 pounds of gold, along with 30 goodly steeds and a tablet. And when he came to the monastery to receive a letter from Mar Yaballaha the *catholicus* and to bid him goodbye, the *catholicus* gave him his permission to go. And when the time of departure came, he [the *catholicus*] was unhappy, for he said: "What will become of this? For you have been the manager of the monastery, and you know well that with your departure my undertakings will fall into confusion." And after he had spoken thus they separated from one another with weeping. And documents and presents that were befitting he sent with him to the reverend pope, gifts commensurate to his ability.

And Rabban Sauma started off, and there went with him certain eminent priests and deacons of the monastery. He arrived at the land of the Romans [the Byzantine Empire] on the shores of the sea ... and he saw the church. And he embarked in a ship. And his companions with him in the ship were more than 300 souls. And every day he used to exhort them with a discourse on the faith. And many of the people in the ship were Romans [Byzantines] and by reason of the flavor of his discourse they honored him not a little. And after some days he reached the great city of Constantinople. And before he entered, he sent two pages to the royal court to announce that King Arghun's ambassador was come. And the king commanded that certain should go out to meet them and bring them in with joy and honor. And when Rabban Sauma entered, he appointed a house, that is a mansion, for his stay. And after he was rested, he came to king *basilios* [the Byzantine emperor Andronikos II]. And after he greeted him, the king asked him: "How are you after the fatigue of the sea and the weariness of the journey?" He answered: "With the sight of the Christian king weariness is banished and fatigue dismissed. For I was eager to see your kingdom that our Lord preserves!"

And after they were regaled with food and drink, he desired of the king that he might see the churches and the shrines of the fathers and the relics of the saints there. The king put him in the hands of his royal officers, and they showed him everything that was there. First, he went into the great church of [Hagia] Sophia, which has 360 gates, which are all finished in marble. It is impossible to describe the dome over the altar to one who has not seen it, or to tell the extent of its height and width. There is in the church a picture of the lady Mary, which Luke the Evangelist painted. And he saw too the hand of John the Baptist, and the relics of Lazarus and Mary Magdalene, and the stone that was set upon our Lord's tomb, when Joseph the Counselor took him down from the cross; and Mary wept on that stone and to the present her tears are moist, and as often as its moisture is wiped off, it becomes moist again. Moreover he saw the jar of stone in which our Lord changed the water to wine at Cana of Galilee; and the sarcophagus of one of the holy women, which is brought forth every year, and every sick person who is placed under it is healed; [and] the sarcophagus of Mar [blessed] John Chrysostom. And he saw the stone on which Simon Peter sat when the cock crowed; and the tomb of the victorious king Constantine, which is reddish; and the tomb of [Emperor] Justinian, which is of a green color; and the stations of the 318 Fathers [of the Council of Nicaea], which are all set in one large church, and their bodies are not corrupted because they confirmed the faith; and also many shrines of the holy fathers. And he saw many amulets and icons figured in bronze and stone.

Then Rabban Sauma went in to the king and said: "The king live forever! I acknowledge the grace of our Lord in that I have been deemed worthy of the sight of these holy shrines. And now, if the king permits, I will proceed to fulfill the orders of King Arghun, his orders that I go to the lands of the Franks." Then the king treated him kindly and presented him with gifts of gold and silver. And thence he went to embark on the sea. And he saw on the shore of the sea a monastery of the Romans, and there were deposited in their treasury two silver caskets, in one of which was the head of John Chrysostom, in the other that of the reverend pope [Sylvester I] who baptized King [Emperor] Constantine. And he embarked, and got out on the broad sea. And he saw in it a mountain from which all day long smoke ascends and by night fire is exhibited, and none can approach its neighborhood for the smell of the sulfur. For people say that the "Great Serpent" is there, after whom that sea is called Athlia. For that sea is a terror, many thousands of men have perished in it. At the end of two months he gained the shore of the sea, after much travail and weariness and discomfort. [Passing through Naples on his way to Rome, Rabban Sauma learns that the current pope, Honorius IV, had recently died.]

... After some days they reached great Rome. They entered the church of Peter and Paul, for the monastery of the see of the reverend pope is there. After the death of the reverend pope there were 12 men conducting the [apostolic] see called cardinals [cardinal bishops]. And when they were in council to elect a pope, Rabban Sauma sent word to them that "we are ambassadors from King Arghun and the *catholicus* of the East." Then the cardinals bade them enter. And the Frank, who came in with Rabban Sauma instructed them that when they entered the monastery of the reverend pope, there was an altar there which they should worship, and from there go and salute the cardinals. And they did so. As it pleased the cardinals, when Rabban Sauma entered, none rose in his presence, for it was not the custom of these 12 men to do so because of the dignity of the see. And they sat Rabban Sauma alongside of them. One of them asked him: "How are you after the toil of travel?" He answered: "By your prayers I am happy and content." And he said to him: "Why have you come here?" He said to him: "The Mongols with the *catholicus* of the East have sent me to the reverend pope on behalf of Jerusalem. And he has sent letters with me." They said to him: "Content yourself at present, and later we shall speak with one another." And they assigned him quarters and lodged him there.

After three days the cardinals sent and called him. When he came to them, they began to ask him: "What is this region? And why have you come?" And he said so and so. They said to him: "Where does the *catholicus* live? And who of the apostles taught your region?" He answered them: "Mar Thomas and Mar Addai and Mar Mari taught our region, and we hold to the ordinances they gave us until now." They said to him: "Where is the see of the *catholicus*?" He said: "In Baghdad." They responded: "What are you there?" He answered: "I am the deacon of the monastery and master of the students and visitator-general." They said: "We are surprised that you are a Christian and a deacon of the patriarchal see of the East, and yet you come on an embassy of the king of the Mongols." He said: "Know, my fathers, that many of our fathers went to the lands of the Mongols and Turks and Chinese and taught them. And today there are many Mongol Christians. Indeed some of the children of the king and queen are baptized and confess the Christ. They have churches with them in the camp. And they honor the Christians greatly, and there are also many believers among them. The king, since he is assiduous in affection for the *catholicus* and is desirous to conquer Palestine and the lands of Syria, desires your help because of the captivity of Jerusalem. For this purpose he has chosen and sent me. And since I am a Christian, my word should be credible with you." They said to him: "What is your creed and what doctrine do you confess – that which the reverend pope accepts today or another?" He replied: "As for us Easterners, none has come to us from the pope, for the holy apostles whom I have named taught us, and up to the present we hold fast to what they committed to us." They said to him: "How do you believe? Expound your creed."

He answered them: "I believe in one God, hidden, eternal, without beginning and without end, Father and Son and Holy Spirit, three equal persons [of the Trinity], inseparable, in whom there is not a first or second, nor a younger and elder, who are in one nature but in three persons, the Father begetter, the Son begotten, the Spirit proceeding; that at the end of the time one of the persons of the royal Trinity, to wit, the Son, clothed himself with perfect man, Jesus Christ, of the holy Virgin Mary, and was united with him personally and in him redeemed the world; who in his Godhead was eternally of the Father, and in his humanity in time was born of Mary, a unity not to be dissolved nor broken forever, a unity without intermixture or confusion or articulation; and this Son is of a unity, perfect God and perfect man, two natures and two persons, one personality"....

And they terminated his discourse with many arguments. But they honored him for his discourse.

Then he said to them: "I have come from far lands not to dispute nor to expound the themes of the faith; but to receive a benediction from the reverend pope and to the shrines of the saints have I come, and to declare the business of the king and the *catholicus*. If it be agreeable to you that we leave the discussion and you make arrangement and appoint someone who will show me the churches here and the shrines of the saints, you will confer a great favor upon your servant and disciple." Then they called the governor of the city and certain monks and ordered them to show him the churches and the places of the saints there. And so they went forth at once, and they saw the places which we will now record.

First, they went into the church of Peter and Paul. Now beneath the throne [tribune] is a chapel, and there is deposited the body of Saint Peter. And above the throne is the altar; and the altar which is in that great temple has four gates, and at each gate carved doors of iron. And on the altar the reverend pope consecrates [celebrates the Eucharist], and none but he presides at the service of that altar. Afterwards they saw that throne of Mar Peter, on which they seat the reverend pope when they consecrate him. And further they saw the pure piece of garment in which our Lord left his portrait, sending it to King Abgar of Edessa. But the majesty of that church and its glory cannot be told. It stands on 108 pillars. And there is in it another altar at which their king of kings receives ordination – and he is called emperor king of kings – from the pope. For they say that after the service [prayers] the reverend pope takes the crown with his feet and invests him, and he [the pope] puts it [the crown] on his head – so that the priesthood may dominate over royalty, they say.

After they had seen all the churches and monasteries in great Rome, they went out of the city to the church of Mar Paul the apostle, for his tomb is also beneath the altar, and the chain with which Paul was bound, having been brought there, is there. Also there is deposited in that altar a casket of gold in which is placed the head of the martyr Stephen and the hand of Mar Ananias who baptized Paul. Also the staff of the apostle Paul is there. From there they went to the place where the apostle Paul was crowned [with martyrdom]. And they say that when his head was cut off, it leaped up three times, and each time it called "Christ, Christ," and from the three places where it fell there issued water at each place and it is good for cures and relief of all who are afflicted. And there is a great church there, and in it the bones of illustrious martyrs and fathers; and they received benediction from them. Further, they went to the church of the Lady Mary and that of Mar John [the]

Baptist. And they saw in it [the latter] the coat of our Lord which was not sewn. And there is in this church the table upon which our Lord consecrated the Eucharist and gave it to his disciples. And every year the reverend pope celebrates the mysteries of Passover [Maundy Thursday] on this table. And there are in this church four pillars of brass, the thickness of each six cubits, which they say the kings brought from Jerusalem. And they saw there the font in which King Constantine the Conqueror [Constantine I] was baptized, of dark [black] polished stone. The pillars of this church are 140 in number, of white marble, for the church is large and wide. They saw the place where Simon Cephas argued with Simon, in which the latter fell and his bones were broken. From there they went to the church of the Lady Mary, and they brought out to them the casket of crystal [beryl] in which is the garment of the lady Mary, and the piece of wood on which our Lord slept when he was a child. And they saw the head of the apostle Matthew in a casket of silver. Also they saw the foot of the apostle Philip and the arm of James the son of Zebedee in the church of the Apostles there. And after this they saw buildings which word of speech cannot relate, and the narrative concerning the buildings would cause a prolongation of the story in any attempt to relate them, therefore I will excuse myself.

Afterwards Rabban Sauma and his companions returned to the cardinals, and he made his acknowledgments that they had deemed him worthy of the sight of those sanctuaries and of the benedictions that come from them. And Rabban Sauma asked leave of them to go to the king in Rome. They said: "We cannot give you a reply [to your commission] until a pope is in office." And from there they went to the land of Tuszekan [apparently, Tuscany], and were given honors. And from there they came to Genoa. Now there is no king in that place, but the people institute as chief over it for the government one whom they desire. When they heard that an ambassador of King Arghun had arrived, the chief went out with all the crowd and brought them into the city with honor. And there was there a great church with the name of Senalornia the Saint. And in it was the holy body of Mar John [the] Baptist in a casket of pure silver. And they saw also a bowl of six-sided emeralds, and those people told them that this is that in which our Lord and his disciples ate the Passover, and when Jerusalem was taken it was brought here. And from there they came to the land of Onbar [apparently, Lombardy]. And the people there saw that they were not fasting on the first Saturday [the sabbath] of the Fast [Lent]. And when they asked them, "Why do you do so, and separate yourselves from all Christians?," they answered: "This is our custom. When we were first instructed, our ancestors were weak in faith and were not able to fast; their teachers bade them to fast forty days."

After this they went to the land of Paris to King Francis [Phillip IV]. And the king sent out many people to meet them, and they brought them into the city with honor and great acclaim. Now his lands extended for a month's length and more. And he assigned them a lodging place. And after three days King Francis sent an officer to Rabban Sauma and summoned him. And when he came in, he rose up before him and honored him, and he said to him: "For what have you come, and who sent you?" He said to him: "King Arghun and the *catholicus* of the East have sent me on behalf of Jerusalem." And he declared to him all that he knew, and gave him the letters he had with him, and the presents, that is, the gifts, which he brought. King Francis answered him: "If the Mongols, although they are not Christians, are fighting with the Arabs because of the captivity of Jerusalem, it still more behooves us to fight and go forth in force, if our Lord wills." Rabban Sauma said to him: "Now that we have seen your praiseworthy majesty and have viewed the glory of your power with the eye of flesh, we ask of you that you give orders that the citizens show us the churches and the shrines and the relics of the saints, and all that is to be found with you and not anywhere else, so that when we return we can tell and declare in the lands what we have seen." Then the king gave orders to his officers to "go and show them all the marvels which we have, and afterwards I will show them what I have." And so those officials went out with them. And they remained a full month in that great city of Paris, and saw everything in it.

Now there are there 30,000 students [at the University of Paris], who study in ecclesiastical subjects, that is interpretation, and in subjects outside of this: the exegesis, that is interpretation, of all the holy scriptures, and wisdom, that is philosophy, and rhetoric, along with medicine and geometry and arithmetic and the science of the planets and stars, which they are very assiduous to write up. And they all receive stipends from the king. Further, they saw a great church where the coffins of the kings lie. And their effigies in gold and silver are upon their tombs. There are in the service of the tombs of those kings 500 monks who eat and drink at the king's cost, and they are diligent in fast and prayer at the tombs of those kings. And the crowns and arms of these kings along with their clothing are alongside these tombs. Indeed, they saw everything worthy of praise and honor.

Afterwards the king sent and called them, and they came to him at the church. And they saw him standing by the altar and they greeted him. And he asked Rabban Sauma: "Now you have seen what we have, does there remain anything else beside?" Then he made his acknowledgments. Forthwith, he went up with the king to an upper chamber of gold, which the king opened. And he brought out of it a casket of crystal [beryl], in which was set the Crown of Thorns, which the Jews set upon the head of our Lord when they crucified him. The crown was visible in the casket before it was opened, because of the translucency of the crystal. Furthermore, there was in it a relic of the wood of the cross. And the king said to them that "when our ancestors took Constantinople [during the Fourth Crusade] and despoiled Jerusalem, they brought these benedictions from there." And we blessed the king. Then we persuaded him to give us orders to leave. Then he said to us: "I will send with you one of the great officers at my side to give King Arghun a reply." And he gave him gifts and fine garments. [Rabba Sauma next travels to Gascony to meet with the English king, Edward I, before visiting Genoa and finally returning to Rome, where a new pope, Nicholas IV, has been elected.]

... And Rabban Sauma went in at once to the reverend pope. He was seated on his throne. And he [Bar Sauma] presented himself with homage and kissed his feet and hands. And he retired backwards with his hands clasped. He said to the reverend pope: "May your throne be established, O father, forever, and blessed may it be above all kings and peoples, and may peace reign in thy days in the whole church to the ends of the earth! Now that I have seen thy face it has brightened my eyes that I do not come heartbroken to the lands. I acknowledge the grace of God that he has counted me worthy of the sight of thee." And he presented to him the gift of King Arghun along with his letters and also the gift of Mar Yaballaha the *catholicus*, that is, "the blessing," and his letters. And the reverend pope was glad and rejoiced, and he honored Rabban Sauma more than was usual. And he said to him: "It will be well if thou celebrate the season with us and see our custom," for that day was the middle of the Dominical Fast [Lent]. He replied: "Your command is high and lofty." And the reverend pope assigned an abode for his sojourn, and appointed attendants to give him all he desired. After some days Rabban Sauma said to the reverend pope: "I desire to consecrate [the Eucharist] that you too may see our custom." And he bade him to consecrate, as he requested. And on that day a great congregation assembled to see how the ambassador of the Mongols consecrates. And when they saw, they rejoiced and said: "The language is different, but the rite is one." Now that same day when he consecrated was the Sunday of [the antiphon] "Who is the Healer?" [the fifth Sunday of Lent]. When he had solemnized the mysteries, he went in to the reverend pope and greeted him. And he said to Rabban Sauma: "May God receive thy offering and bless thee and pardon thy faults and sins!" And Rabban Sauma said: "With the pardon of my faults and sins which I have received from you, O father, I desire of thy fatherliness, O holy father, that I may receive the communion from your hands, so that I may have complete forgiveness." And he said: "It shall be so."

When Sunday came again, that is, Hosanna Sunday [Palm Sunday], there assembled in the morning thousands and tens of thousands without number before the throne [of the pope], and they brought olive branches. And he blessed them; he gave the blessing to the cardinals, and then to the metropolitans, and then to the bishops, and then to the officials, and then he shed it on all the people. And he arose from the throne, and with rejoicing they brought him to the church. And he entered the chancel and changed his vestments and put on the crimson garments of the rite, which were embroidered with gold and gems and hyacinths and pearls, down to the shoes of his feet, that is, his sandals. And he entered the sanctuary, and came to the pulpit, and he preached and exhorted the people. And he consecrated the mysteries. He gave Rabban Sauma the communion first, after he had confessed his sinfulness, and he absolved him from his faults and sins and those of his ancestors. He rejoiced greatly to receive communion from the hand of the reverend pope, and he received the communion with tears and weeping, acknowledging the grace of God and thinking upon the mercy poured out upon him.

Afterwards on Holy Passover [Maundy Thursday] the reverend pope came to the church of St-John the Baptist, after a great congregation had assembled, and he went up to the great upper room there, all furnished and decorated. Before the room was a great lobby. And there went in with him the cardinals and metropolitans and bishops. And they began with service; and when it was finished, the reverend pope made an allocution and preached to the people, as was the custom. And there was not a sound heard from the multitude of people, except for the "Amen"; and when "Amen" was said, the earth trembled from their cries. From there he went down to the front of the altar and made a quantity of chrism oil, that is, oil of anointing. And afterwards he consecrated the Atoning mysteries, and gave communion to the people. And he went forth from there and came into the great nave. And he distributed and gave to the holy fathers to each one 2 leaves of gold and 30 sheets of silver. And he departed. And the reverend pope assembled the monks of his monastery, and he washed their feet, and wiped them with a cloth that was girt about his loins, to the last. When the full rite of Passover was accomplished, at noon he gave a great dinner. And the servants set before each man his portion of food. And those who sat there were 2,000 more or less. And when they removed the food, there remained [but] three hours of the day.

On the next day, which was the passion of our redeemer [Good Friday], the reverend pope put on a black cassock, and all the clergy likewise; and they went out barefoot, and came to the church of the Adorable Cross. The reverend pope worshipped and kissed it [the cross], and he gave it to each one of the clergy. When the crowd saw it, they uncovered their heads and kneeled on their knees and worshipped it. He preached and discoursed to the people. And when the cross had turned around in the four directions, and when the service was finished, he brought some of the host [Eucharist] of the Passover [Maundy Thursday] and put wine with it. And the reverend pope received the communion alone, for it is not the custom for Christians to offer the offering on the day of the passion of our redeemer. Then he returned to his monastery.

On the day of the Sabbath of Light [the night before Easter Sunday], the pope went to the church, and they read the books of the prophets and the prophecies about the Christ. And they placed a font and set about it branches of myrtle. And the reverend pope consecrated the baptismal water himself, and he baptized three children and signed them [with the sign of the cross]. And he entered the chancel, and he put off his vestments of the passion, and put on the robes of his function, the value of which passes telling. And he consecrated the mysteries.

On the Sunday of the resurrection [Easter Sunday] the reverend pope entered the holy church of the Lady Mary. And they greeted one another, he and the cardinals and the metropolitans and the bishops and the crowds; and they kissed one another on the mouth. And he celebrated the mysteries, and they received the communion. And he entered the monastery and he made a great feast and celebration without stint. On New Sunday [the first Sunday after Easter] the reverend pope held an ordination, and he ordained three bishops. And Rabban Sauma's party saw their ritual. And they celebrated the blessed feasts with them.

When all this had taken place, he desired of the reverend pope permission to depart. But he said to him: "It is our desire that you remain with us, and you shall be in our company, and we will keep you as the apple of our eye." But Rabban Sauma replied: "I, O father, have come on an embassy to do you service. If my coming were of my own desire, in the outer gate of your monastery would I accomplish the days of this my life of vanity in your service. But when I return I will declare to the kings there the favors you have done to my weakness. I think it will be a great satisfaction to the Christians. But I desire of your holiness that you give me as alms of some of the relics you have." The reverend pope said: "If it were our custom to give everyone these relics, although they were mountains high, they would soon be finished off by the myriads. But since you have come from a far country, we will give you a few." And he gave him a small relic from the garment of our Lord Christ, and from the *poikile* [bonnet] of the Lady Mary, and small relics of the saints there. And he sent to Mar Yaballaha a crown of pure gold for his head, adorned with very precious stones, and clothing for the vestments of his function, red and embroidered with gold, and shoes sewn with small pearls, and boots, and also a ring from his own finger; and letters patent which contained authorization of his patriarchate over all the easterners. And to Rabban Sauma he gave letters patent as visitor over all Christians. And he blessed him. And he allotted to him for the expenses of his journey 1,500 pounds, 21 of red gold. And to King Arghun he sent some gifts. And he embraced and kissed Rabban Sauma and dismissed him. And Rabban Sauma rendered thanks to our Lord that he had deemed him worthy of such boons.

Again he crossed the seas from whither he had gone. And he arrived safely at King Arghun's in soundness of body and preservation of soul. He gave him the documents of blessing along with the presents which he brought from the reverend pope as well as from all the kings of the Franks. And he told him how they had received him with love, and had warmly listened to the dispatches he brought. He narrated the marvels he had seen and the might of the empire. King Arghun rejoiced and was delighted, and he thanked him and said to him: "We have put thee to great trouble, seeing thou art an old man. Therefore we will not let you be separated from us. But we will establish a church in our royal court, and you shall serve and pray in it." Rabban Sauma said: "If milord the king will command, let Mar Yaballaha the *catholicus* come and receive the gifts which the reverend pope has sent him and the articles for divine worship which he has donated to him, and he shall be the institutor of the church which the king establishes in the royal court, and he shall consecrate it." And these things came to pass just so. And since it was not our purpose to relate and compose things which Rabban Sauma did and saw, we have somewhat abbreviated what he himself wrote in Persian. And these things which are here recorded have been added and abbreviated in proportion to the aim of the undertaking.

What were some of the specific reasons that the Mongol king sent Rabban Sauma as his ambassador to the Byzantine emperor, pope, and European kings? What were some of the holy sites that Rabban Sauma visited during his stays in Constantinople and Rome? What evidence does this text provide about differences between Nestorian Christians and members of the Western Roman church over what they believed and how they practiced their faith? Does Rabban Sauma's veneration toward the saints seem similar to or different from that of the Christian pilgrims from Europe featured in other documents? What seems to have driven him more, his responsibilities as a diplomat or his piety as a Christian believer (and are these two roles incompatible or complementary)?

61. IBN BATTUTA ON THE PILGRIMAGE SITES OF MECCA

One of the most famous and far-ranging travelers of the Middle Ages was not a Christian, but rather a Muslim named Abu 'Abdallah Ibn Battuta (ca 1304–80). Born in Morocco and educated in Islamic religious law, over the course of his life Ibn Battuta traveled from western Africa to Arabia, to the Asian steppes and India, and perhaps as far as China, before returning home to Morocco (followed by further travels to Spain and sub-Saharan Africa). He began his wanderings in 1325 by making a pilgrimage to the holy places of Mecca. Ibn Battuta would make such a pilgrimage (the Hajj) to Mecca several more times during his various travels. The selections below, from his Rhila or account of his voyages, include a description of Mecca and its surroundings, some of which he borrowed from the twelfth-century writings of Ibn Jubayr.

Source: trans. H.A.R. Gibb, in *The Travels of Ibn Battuta (A.D. 1325–1354)*, ed. H.A.R. Gibb, Works Issued by the Hakluyt Society (Cambridge: Cambridge University Press, 1958), vol. 110, pp. 190–96, 211–17.

The Venerable City of Mecca

Mecca is a large town, compactly built and oblong in shape, situated in the hollow of a valley which is so shut in by hills that the visitor to her sees nothing of her until he actually reaches her. These hills that overlook her are of no exceeding elevation. The "two rugged hills" of them are the Hill of Abu Qubais, on the southern side of the town, and the Hill of Qu'aiqi'an on its [western] side. To the north of the town is the Red Hill (al-Jabal al-Ahmar), and on the side of Abu Qubais are Greater Ajyad and Lesser Ajyad, both of which are ravines, and al-Khandama, a mountain; this will be described later. All the places of the pilgrimage ceremonies – Mina, Arafa, and al-Muzdalifah – lie to the east of Mecca (God ennoble her). At Mecca the city gates are three in number: Bab al-Ma'la, in the highest [northern] part of the town; Bab al-Shubaika, in its lowest part, known also as Bab al-Zahir and Bab al-'Umra – this is on the western side, and through it lies the road to al-Madina the Illustrious, Cairo, Syria, and Judda; it is from it also that one sets out to al-Tan'im, as will be described later, and Bab al-Masfal, which is situated on the southern side, and is the gate through which Khalid b. al-Walid (God pleased with him) entered on the day of the conquest [when Muhammad and his earliest followers returned from exile in Medina to Mecca].

Mecca (God ennoble her), as God has related in his glorious Book, citing the words of his prophet al-Khalil, lies "in a valley bare of corn," but the blessed prayer [of Abraham] has anticipated her needs, so that every delicacy is brought to her, and the fruits of every kind are gathered for her. I myself have eaten there fruits, such as grapes, figs, peaches, and fresh dates, that have not their equal in the world; likewise the melons which are transported to her have none to compare with them for flavor and sweetness. The flesh-meats in Mecca are fat and exceedingly delicious in taste. All the commodities that are dispersed in different countries find assembly in her. Fruits and vegetables are carried to her from al-Ta'if and Wadi Nakhla and the bottom of Marr, through a bounteous provision of God for the dwellers in his secure sanctuary and the sojourners at his ancient house.

The Sacred Mosque

The Sacred Mosque lies in the midst of the city and occupies an extensive area; its length from east to west is more than four hundred cubits (this figure is given by al-Azraqi) and its breadth is approximately the same. The most venerable Ka'ba stands in the middle of it. The aspect of the mosque is [so] exquisite, its outward sight [so] beautiful [that] no tongue could presume to describe its attractions, and no voice of description do justice to the charm of its perfection. The height of its walls is about twenty cubits, and the roof [of its colonnades] is supported by tall pillars, arranged in a triple row, of most substantial and beautiful construction. Its three aisles are arranged on a marvelous plan, which makes them appear like a single aisle. The number of marble pillars which it contains is 490, exclusive of the plaster pillars which are in the Dar al-Nadwa annexed to the sanctuary. This building is incorporated in the colonnade running [from west] to north, and opposite it are the Maqam [of Ibrahim] and the 'Iraqi angle [of the Ka'ba]; its court is contiguous to and entered from the colonnade mentioned. Along the wall of this colonnade is a series of small platforms beneath vaulted arcades; these are occupied by teachers of the Qur'an, copyists, and tailors. On the wall of the parallel colonnade to this there are platforms resembling these; the other colonnades have at the foot of their walls platforms without arcades. By the Bab Ibrahim there is [another] extension from the [south-]western colonnade, in which there are plaster columns. The Caliph al-Mahdi Muhammad, son of the Caliph Abu Ja'far al-Manur (God be pleased with both), has to his credit a number of noble activities in regard to the extension of the Sacred Mosque and the perfection of its construction, and on the highest part of the wall of the western colonnade is an inscription: "The servant of God Muhammad al-Mahdi, commander of the faithful (God justify him), commanded the enlargement of the sacred mosque for the pilgrims to the House of God and the visitors thereto in the year one hundred and sixty-seven" [after the *Hijra*=783–784 CE].

The Illustrious and Venerable Ka'ba

The Ka'ba stands out in the middle of the mosque – a square-shaped building, whose height is on 3 sides 28 cubits and on the fourth side, that between the Black Stone and the Yamanite angle, 29 cubits. The breadth of that side of it which extends from the 'Iraqi angle to the black stone is fifty-four spans, and so also is the breadth of the side which runs parallel to it, from the Yamanite angle to the Syrian angle; the breadth of that side of it which extends from the 'Iraqi angle to the Syrian angle, within the Hijr [the "enclosure"], is forty-eight spans, and so also is the breadth of the side parallel to it, [from the Yamanite angle to the black stone, the same as that] from the Syrian angle to the 'Iraqi angle; but measured round the outside of the Hijr the length of this side is 120 spans, and the circuit is always made outside the Hijr. It is constructed of hard brown stones cemented together in the most admirable, substantial, and solid manner, so that the days may not change it nor long ages affect it.

The door of the venerable Ka'ba is in the side which is between the Black Stone and the 'Iraqi angle. Between it and the Black Stone is [a space of] ten spans, and that place is the so-called Multazam where prayers are answered. The height of the door [sill] above the ground is eleven and a half spans and the breadth of the wall in which it is set is five spans. The door is covered with plates of silver exquisitely fabricated, and both its jambs and its lintel also are plated with silver. It has two great rings made of silver, through which passes a bolt.

The holy door is opened every Friday after the [mid-day] prayer and it is opened also on the anniversary of the birthday of the Prophet (God bless and give him peace). The ceremony which they use in opening it is as follows. They bring up a bench resembling a mimbar, which has steps and wooden legs with four rollers upon which the bench runs, and place it against the wall of the illustrious Ka'ba so that its top step adjoins the holy threshold. When this is done, the chief of the Shaibis mounts the steps, carrying in his hand the holy key, and accompanied by the doorkeepers. The latter take hold of [and draw aside] the curtain which is hung over the door of the Ka'ba and is known by the name of the Veil, while their chief opens the door. When he opens it, he kisses the illustrious threshold, enters the house alone, closes the door, and remains there as long as he requires to make a prayer of two bowings. Then the rest of the Shaibis enter, close the door also, and make their prayers. After this the door is opened, and the people rush to gain admission. During the preliminaries they stand facing the holy door with downcast eyes and hands outstretched to God most high, and when it is opened they shout the Takbir and cry "O God, open unto us the gates of your mercy and your forgiveness, O most Merciful of the merciful."

The interior of the illustrious Ka'ba is paved with marble inlaid with arabesques and its walls have a similar facing. It has three tall pillars, exceedingly high and made of teak; between each pillar and the next is a distance of four paces, and they stand [lengthwise] in the middle of the space inside the illustrious Ka'ba, the central one being opposite to the mid-point of the side between the [Yamanite] and Syrian angles. The hangings of the illustrious Ka'ba are of black silk, with inscriptions in white; they gleam upon its walls with light and brilliance and clothe it entirely from the top to the ground.

One of the marvelous "signs" in connection with the holy Ka'ba is this: its door is opened at a time when the sanctuary is choked with a multitude of peoples whom none can number save God, who has created them and sustained them, yet they enter it – the whole body of them – and it is not too narrow to contain them. Another of its marvels is that it is never at any time, whether by night or day, without some worshipper engaged in making the circuit, and none has ever reported that he has seen it at any time without worshippers. Yet another marvel is this: that the pigeons of Mecca, in spite of their number, and the other kinds of birds as well, do not alight upon it, nor do they pass over it in their flight. You can see the pigeons flying over the whole sanctuary, but when they come to level with the illustrious Ka'ba, they deflect their course from it to one side, and do not pass over it. It is said that no bird ever alights on it unless it be suffering from some disease, and in that case it either dies on the instant or is healed of its disease – magnified be He who has distinguished it by nobility and holiness and hath clothed it with respect and veneration.

The Mountains around Mecca

... Another of these hills is Jabal Hira, to the north of Mecca (God ennoble her) and about a league distant from it. It dominates Mina, soaring into the air and high-summited. The apostle of God [Muhammad] (God bless and give him peace) used frequently to devote himself to religious exercises in it before his prophetic call, and it was here that the truth came to him from his Lord and the divine revelations began. This too is the mountain which quaked beneath the apostle of God (God bless and give him peace), and to which the apostle of God (God bless and give him peace) said: "Be still, for on you are none other than a prophet and a veracious one and a martyr." There is some difference as to the persons who actually were with him on that day, and one tradition relates that the ten [companions] were with him. Another tradition relates that Jabal Thabir also quaked beneath him.

Another of them is Jabal Thawr, at the distance of one league from Mecca (God most high ennoble her) on the road to al-Yaman. In it is the cave which served as a refuge to the apostle of God (God bless and give him peace) when he quitted Mecca (God ennoble her) as an emigrant, accompanied by [Abu Bakr] al-Siddiq (God be pleased with him), as is related in the Exalted Book. It is stated by al-Azraqi in his book that this mountain called the Apostle of God (God bless and give him peace) by his name and said: "To me, O Muhammad, to me, for I have given refuge before you to 70 prophets." Then when the apostle of God (God bless and give him peace) entered the cave and became secure in it, accompanied by his friend al-Siddiq, the spider spun her web at that moment over the door of the cave and the dove made a nest and hatched her eggs in it by the will of God most high. The polytheists [of Mecca], who had with them a man skilled in tracking footsteps, came at length to the cave and said "Here the track stops," but when they saw the spider with its web spun over the mouth of the cave and the dove hatching out its eggs, they said "No one has gone in here" and turned back. Then [Abu Bakr] al-Siddiq said "O apostle of God, what if they had come in upon us from there?" He replied, "We should have gone out here," and pointed with his blessed hand to the other end, where there was no door; and straightway there was opened in it a door by the power of the king and giver of all. The people make a point of visiting this blessed cave, and try to enter it through the doorway by which the Prophet (God bless and give him peace) gained entry into it, for the sake of the blessing it confers; there are some of them who manage it, but some of them do not succeed and stick in it until they are pulled out with a ruthless tug. Others perform a prayer in front of the cave, without entering it. The folk of those parts say that anyone who is true-born can enter it, but he who is born of adultery cannot do so, and so many people avoid making the attempt because it is liable to end in shame and disgrace.

Ibn Juzayy remarks: "I have been told by certain of our shrewd-minded shaikhs who have made the pilgrimage that the cause of the difficulty in entering is that inside it, close to this cleft by which entrance is gained, there is a large stone lying transversely [across the passage]. When anyone [tries to] enter through this cleft lying flat on his face, his head comes up against that stone, so that he can neither draw himself in nor twist himself upwards, seeing that his face and chest are close to the ground. The man who does this is the one who sticks and cannot get free without suffering some discomfort and being pulled out. But if one enters through the cleft lying on his back, he can manage it, because when his head reaches the transverse stone, he raises his head and rises into a sitting position. He then has his back supported by the transverse stone, his middle in the cleft, and his legs outside the cave, and all he has to do is to stand upright inside the cave....

"... The following incident happened on this mountain to two of my associates, one of them the esteemed jurist Abu Muhammad 'Abdallah b.

Farhan of Tuzar in Ifriqiya, the other Abu'l-'Abbas Ahmad of Wadi Ash [Guadix] in Andalusia [Iberia]. They proposed [to visit the cave] during the period of their residence in Mecca (God Most High ennoble her), in the year seven hundred and twenty-eight [1350–51 CE], and went off alone, without getting some guide who knew the way to it to accompany them. They lost themselves in consequence, missed the way to the cave, and followed another track, which came to a sudden end. This was at the time when the heat grows violent and summer is at its most ardent. When the water they had with them was exhausted and they had not yet reached the cave, they began to make their way back to Mecca (God most high ennoble her). They found a track and followed it up, but it led to another mountain. The heat beat down upon them, thirst tormented them, and they came face to face with death. The jurist Abu Muhammad ibn Farhan was finally unable to walk any further, and threw himself upon the ground. The Andalusian managed to save himself, for he had some remnant of strength left, and he continued to follow the paths on those hills until the road led him to Ajyad. He then came into Mecca (God Most High ennoble her), sought me out and told me the whole story and about 'Abdallah al-Tuzari and his breakdown on the mountain. It was then about the close of day. This 'Abdallah had a cousin named Hasan, who lived in Wadi Nakhla but was at that moment in Mecca. I informed him what had happened to his cousin, and then sought out the pious shaikh, the imam Abu 'Abdallah Mhammad b. 'Abd al-Rahman known as Khalil, the imam of the Malikites (God profit us by him) and reported his case to him also. He sent out in search of him a company of Meccans who were familiar with those hills and rock-paths. To return to 'Abdallah al-Tuzari, he had betaken himself, when his companions left him, to a large rock, seeking the shelter of its shade, and he remained in this state of exhaustion and thirst, with the carrion-crows flying over his head and waiting for his death. When the daylight was gone and darkness fell, he recovered some strength, and refreshed by the cool of the night he rose at dawn to his feet and descended from the hillside to the bottom of a wadi, which was sheltered by the mountains from the rays of the sun. He kept on walking until an ass appeared within his view, and making in its direction he found a Bedouin tent. When he saw it, he fell to the ground and was unable to rise. He was seen by the woman of the tent, and as her husband had gone to fetch water, she gave him what water she had with her. It did not quench his thirst, and when her husband came back he gave him a whole skin of water without quenching his thirst either. The man set him on an ass which he had and brought him to Mecca, where he arrived at length at the time of the afternoon prayer on the following day, as emaciated as if he had risen from a grave."

The Meccans: Their Good Qualities

The citizens of Mecca are given to well-doing, of consummate generosity and good disposition, liberal to the poor and to those who have renounced the world, and kindly towards strangers. One of their generous customs is that when any of them makes a feast, he begins by giving food to the poor brethren who have devoted themselves to the religious life and are sojourning at the Sanctuary, first inviting them with courtesy, kindness and delicacy, and then giving them to eat. The majority of these destitute devotees are to be found by the public ovens, where the people bake their bread. When anyone has his bread baked and takes it away to his house, the destitute follow him up and he gives each one of them whatever he assigns to him, sending none away disappointed. Even if he has but a single loaf, he gives away a third or a half of it, conceding it cheerfully and without a grudging attitude.

Another good habit of theirs is that orphan children make a practice of sitting in the bazaar, each with two baskets, one large and one small (the Meccans call a basket by the name of *miktal*). A man of the townsfolk of Mecca comes to the bazaar, where he buys grain, meat and vegetables, and passes these to a boy, who puts the grain in one of his baskets and the meat and vegetables in the other, and takes them to the man's house, so that his meal may be prepared from them. Meanwhile the man goes about his devotions and his business. There is no instance related of any of the boys having ever abused their trust in this matter – on the contrary he delivers what he has been given to carry, with the most scrupulous honesty. They receive for this a fixed fee of a few coppers.

The Meccans are elegant and clean in their dress, and as they mostly wear white their garments always appear spotless and snowy. They use perfume freely, paint their eyes with kuhl, and are constantly picking their teeth with slips of green arak-wood. The Meccan women are of rare and surpassing beauty, pious and chaste. They too make much use of perfumes, to such a degree that a woman will spend the night hungry and buy perfume with the price [of her food]. They make a practice of performing the circuit of the House on the eve of each Friday, and come in their finest apparel, and the sanctuary is saturated with the smell of their perfume. When one of these women goes away, the odor of the perfume clings as an effluvium to the place after she has gone.

The citizens of Mecca observe various excellent customs at the pilgrimage season and other periods of the year, and we shall speak of these, if God most high will, when we finish our account of its distinguished men and residents.

The Qadi and Khatib of Mecca, the Imam of the Pilgrimage Ceremony and the Learned and Pious Citizens

The qadi of Mecca is the learned, pious, and devout Najm al-Din Muham-mad, [grand]son of the learned imam Muhyi al-Din al-Tabari, a worthy man, liberal in his alms and charities to the [poor] sojourners, of fine character, much given to performing the circuit and to contemplation of the illustrious Ka'ba. He distributes an immense quantity of food on the occasion of the great festivals, especially on the birthday of the apostle of God (God bless and give him peace), for on that day he distributes food to the Sharifs, notables, and poor brethren of Mecca, the servitors of the illustrious Sanctuary, and all the sojourners. The Sultan of Egypt, al-Malik al-Nasir (God's mercy upon him) held him in high honor, and all the sultan's alms, together with the alms of his emirs, used to pass through his hands. His son Shihab al-Din is [also] a worthy man, and it is he who is now qadi of Mecca (God ennoble her).

The preacher of Mecca and imam at the Station of Ibrahim (upon him be peace) is the chaste and fluent orator, the solitaire of his age, Baha al-Din al-Tabari. He is one of those preachers whose equal in effective mastery of language and excellence of diction is not to be found in the inhabited world. It was told me that he composes a fresh allocution for every Friday, and never afterwards repeats it.

The imam of the pilgrimage ceremony, who is also imam of the Mali-kites in the illustrious Sanctuary is the learned shaikh and jurist, the pious, humble, and celebrated Abu 'Abdallah Muhammad, son of the jurist-imam the pious and abstinent Abu Zaid 'Abd al-Rahman. This is the man who is widely known as Khalil (God profit us by him and prolong his life to our enjoyment). His family comes from the district of al-Jarid in Ifriqiya, where they are known as the Banu Hayyun, being one of the notable families of that part, but his birthplace, and that of his father, was in Mecca (God ennoble her). He is one of the leading citizens of Mecca, nay rather its unique personality and pole, by common consent of all parties, schools and sects. He is immersed in his devotions at all times, modest, generous-minded, of fine character, full of sympathy, never turning away disappointed any who beg his charity.

What places and structures does Ibn Battuta identify as holy sites in and around Mecca for Islamic pilgrims? What sort of devotional practices did pious Muslims carry out there? What were some of the dangers or possible problems faced by pilgrims to the city? How did the religious leaders and people of Mecca care for such large numbers of travel-ers? Compare this document with some of the Christian pilgrimage accounts featured above: what seems more important, their similarities or differences?

62. THE PILGRIMAGE OF MANSA MUSA

*In 1324, the Islamic sultan of Mali in sub-Saharan western Africa, Mansa Musa,
set out on the Hajj to Mecca. As the ruler of Mali, a gold-producing region, Mansa
Musa had considerable wealth at his disposal and made quite an impression on the
locals when he passed through Egypt on his way to Mecca. His reputation even reached
Christian ears in Spain. The two selections below, describing his pilgrimage, come from
the fourteenth-century Arabic chronicles of Ibn al-'Umari (1301–49) and Ibn Khaldun
(1332–1406), who based their accounts on the oral reports of those who witnessed the
famous passage of the sultan from Mali.*

Source: trans. J.F.P. Hopkins, in *Corpus of Early Arabic Sources for West African History*, ed. J.F.P.
Hopkins (Cambridge: Cambridge University Press, 1981), pp. 267–72, 322–23.

Al-'Umari

The emir Abu 'l-Hasan 'Ali b. Amir Hajib told me that he was often in the
company of sultan Musa the king of this country when he came to Egypt on
the pilgrimage [to Mecca]. He was staying in [the] Qarafa [district of Cairo]
and Ibn Amir Hajib was governor of Old Cairo and Qarafa at that time. A
friendship grew up between them and this sultan Musa told him a great deal
about himself and his country and the people of the Sudan who were his
neighbors. One of the things which he told him was that his country was
very extensive and contiguous with the ocean. By his sword and his armies
he had conquered 24 cities each with its surrounding district with villages
and estates. It is a country rich in livestock – cattle, sheep, goats, horses,
mules – and different kinds of poultry – geese, doves, chickens. The inhabitants of his country are numerous, a vast concourse, but compared with the
peoples of the Sudan who are their neighbors and penetrate far to the south
they are like a white birth-mark on a black cow. He has a truce with the
gold-plant people, who pay him tribute.

Ibn Amir Hajib said that he asked him about the gold-plant, and he said:
"It is found in two forms. One is found in the spring and blossoms after the
rains in open country. It has leaves like the najil grass and its roots are gold.
The other kind is found all the year round at known sites on the banks of
the Nile and is dug up. There are holes there and roots of gold are found like
stones or gravel and gathered up. Both kinds are known as tibr but the first is
of superior fineness and worth more." Sultan Musa told Ibn Amir Hajib that
gold was his prerogative and he collected the crop as a tribute except for what
the people of that country took by theft....

Ibn Amir Hajib said also that the blazon of this king is yellow on a red ground. Standards are unfurled over him wherever he rides on horseback; they are very big flags. The ceremonial for him who presents himself to the king or who receives a favor is that he bares the front of his head and makes the juk-beating gesture towards the ground with his right hand as the Tatars [Mongols] do; if a more profound obeisance is required he grovels before the king. "I have seen this (says Ibn Amir Hajib) with my own eyes." A custom of this sultan is that he does not eat in the presence of anybody, be he who he may, but eats always alone. And it is a custom of his people that if one of them should have reared a beautiful daughter he offers her to the king as a concubine and he possesses her without a marriage ceremony as slaves are possessed, and this in spite of the fact that Islam has triumphed among them and that they follow the Malikite school [of Islamic religious law] and that this sultan Musa was pious and assiduous in prayer, Qur'an reading, and mentioning God.

I said to him (said Ibn Amir Hajib) that this was not permissible for a Muslim, whether in law or reason, and he said: "Not even for kings?" and I replied: "No! Not even for kings! Ask the scholars!" He said: "By God, I did not know that. I hereby leave it and abandon it utterly!"

I saw that this sultan Musa loved virtue and people of virtue. He left his kingdom and appointed as his deputy there his son Muhammad and emigrated to God and his messenger [Muhammad]. He accomplished the obligations of the pilgrimage, visited [the tomb of] the Prophet [at Medina] (God's blessing and peace be upon him!) and returned to his country with the intention of handing over his sovereignty to his son and abandoning it entirely to him and returning to Mecca the Venerated to remain there as a dweller near the sanctuary; but death overtook him, may God (who is great) have mercy upon him....

This sultan Musa, during his stay in Egypt both before and after his journey to the noble Hijaz [the region surrounding Mecca], maintained a uniform attitude of worship and turning towards God. It was as though he were standing before him because of his continual presence in his mind. He and all those with him behaved in the same manner and were well-dressed, grave, and dignified. He was noble and generous and performed many acts of charity and kindness. He had left his country with 100 loads of gold which he spent during his pilgrimage on the tribes who lay along his route from his country to Egypt, while he was in Egypt, and again from Egypt to the noble Hijaz and back. As a consequence he needed to borrow money in Egypt and pledged his credit with the merchants at a very high rate of gain so that they made 700 dinars profit on 300. Later he paid them back amply. He sent to me 500 mithqals of gold by way of honorarium. The currency in the land of Takrur consists of cowries, and the merchants, whose principal import these are, make big profits on them. Here ends what Ibn Amir Hajib said.

From the beginning of my coming to stay in Egypt I heard talk of the arrival of this sultan Musa on his pilgrimage and found the people of Cairo eager to recount what they had seen of the Africans' prodigal spending. I asked the emir Abu 'l-'Abbas Ahmad b. al-Hak the mihmandar [an official in charge of important guests] and he told me of the opulence, manly virtues, and piety of this sultan. "When I went out to meet him (he said), that is, on behalf of the mighty sultan al-Malik al-Nasir, he did me extreme honor and treated me with the greatest courtesy. He addressed me, however, only through an interpreter despite his perfect ability to speak in the Arabic tongue. Then he forwarded to the royal treasury many loads of un-worked native gold and other valuables. I tried to persuade him to go up to the citadel to meet the sultan, but he refused persistently, saying: 'I came for the pilgrimage and nothing else. I do not wish to mix anything else with my pilgrimage.' He had begun to use this argument but I realized that the audience was repugnant to him because he would be obliged to kiss the ground and the sultan's hand. I continued to cajole him and he continued to make excuses but the sultan's protocol demanded that I should bring him into the royal presence, so I kept on at him till he agreed.

When we came in the sultan's presence we said to him: 'Kiss the ground!' but he refused outright saying: 'How may this be?' Then an intelligent man who was with him whispered to him something we could not understand and he said: 'I make obeisance to God who created me!,' then he prostrated himself and went forward to the sultan. The sultan half rose to greet him and sat him by his side. They conversed together for a long time, then sultan Musa went out. The sultan sent to him several complete suits of honor for himself, his courtiers, and all those who had come with him, and saddled and bridled horses for himself and his chief courtiers. His robe of honor consisted of an Alexandrian open-fronted cloak embellished with tard wahsh, cloth containing much gold thread and miniver fur, bordered with beaver fur and embroidered with metallic thread, along with golden fastenings, a silken skull-cap with caliphal emblems, a gold-inlaid belt, a damascened sword, a kerchief [embroidered] with pure gold, standards, and two horses saddled and bridled and equipped with decorated mule[-type] saddles. He also furnished him with accommodation and abundant supplies during his stay.

When the time to leave for the pilgrimage came round the sultan sent to him a large sum of money with ordinary and thoroughbred camels complete with saddles and equipment to serve as mounts for him, and purchased abundant supplies for his entourage and others who had come with him. He arranged for deposits of fodder to be placed along the road and ordered the caravan commanders to treat him with honor and respect. On his return I received him and supervised his accommodation. The sultan continued to supply him with provisions and lodgings and he sent gifts from the noble Hijaz to the sultan as a blessing. The sultan accepted them and sent in exchange complete suits of honor for him and his courtiers together with other gifts, various kinds of Alexandrian cloth, and other precious objects. Then he returned to his country.

This man flooded Cairo with his benefactions. He left no court emir nor holder of a royal office without the gift of a load of gold. The people of Cairo made incalculable profits out of him and his suite in buying and selling and giving and taking. They exchanged gold until they depressed its value in Egypt and caused its price to fall.... Muhanna' b. 'Abd al-Baqi al-'Ujrumi the guide informed me that he accompanied sultan Musa when he made the pilgrimage and that the sultan was very open-handed towards the pilgrims and the inhabitants of the holy places. He and his companions maintained great pomp and dressed magnificently during the journey. He gave away much wealth in alms. 'About 200 mithqals of gold fell to me,' said Muhanna', 'and he gave other sums to my companions.' Muhanna' waxed eloquent in describing the sultan's generosity, magnanimity, and opulence."

Ibn Khaldun

The kingdom of the Sudan in the desert of the Maghreb, in the First and Second Climes, was divided among many nations of the Sudan. The first among them, nearest to the Atlantic, was a nation called Susu. They ruled over Ghana and embraced Islam at the time of the Conquest.... Conditions changed with the passing of time and the people of Mali took possession of the country which is [both] beyond and before them of the lands of Susu and Kawkaw. The last country that they conquered was the land of Takrur. Their kingdom became extremely powerful, and their town of BNY [the precise name of this town is not clear from the manuscript] became the capital of the land of the Sudan in the west. They embraced Islam long ago and some of their kings performed the pilgrimage.

The first among them to do so was Barmandar. I have heard from some of their eminent men that they pronounce his name Barmandana. The kings after him followed his example in performing the pilgrimage. Then Mansa Wali son of Mari Jata went on the pilgrimage during the reign of al-Zahir Baybars. The next one among them on the pilgrimage was Sakurah, their freed slave, who had usurped their kingship. It was he who conquered the town of Kawkaw. Then he went on the pilgrimage during the reign of al-Nasir. After

him Mansa Musa made the pilgrimage, as is recounted in their history in dealing with the Berber dynasties, in the account of the Sanhaja and the dynasty
of the Lamtuna, one of their peoples.

When Mansa Musa left the land of the Maghreb for the pilgrimage he
followed the desert route, and came out near the pyramids in Egypt. He sent
a rich present to al-Nasir. It is said that it included 50,000 dinars. Al-Nasir
accommodated him at al-Qarafa 'l-Kubra and gave it to him as a fief. The
sultan received him in his audience room, talked to him, gave him a gift,
and supplied him with provisions. He gave him horses and camels, and sent
along with him emirs to serve him until he performed his religious duty in
the year 724 [1324 CE]. On his return journey in the Hijaz he was stricken
by a disaster from which his fate rescued him. It so happened that on the way
he strayed from the group and the caravan and was left alone with his people
away from the Arabs. This route was completely unknown to them, and they
could not find the way to a settlement or come upon a watering place. They
went towards the horizon until they came out at al-Suways [Suez]. They were
eating fish whenever they could find some and the Bedouin were snatching
up the stragglers until they were saved. The sultan then again bestowed honors upon him and was generous in his gifts. It is said that he had prepared
in his country for his expenses a hundred loads of gold, each load weighing
three qintars. This was all exhausted, and he could not meet his expenses.
He therefore borrowed money from the principal merchants. Among those
merchants who were in his company were the Banu 'l-Kuwayk, who gave
him a loan of 50,000 dinars. He sold to them the palace which the sultan
had bestowed on him as a gift. He [the sultan] approved it. Siraj al-Din b.
al-Kuwayk sent his vizier along with him to collect what he had loaned to
him but the vizier died there. Siraj al-Din sent another [emissary] with his
son. He [the emissary] died but the son, Fakhr al-Din Abu Ja'far, got back
some of it. Mansa Musa died before he [Siraj al-Din] died, so they obtained
nothing [more] from him.

According to these Arabic chronicles, what are some of the reasons that the pilgrimage of
Mansa Musa so impressed the people of Egypt? How did Mansa Musa behave during
his devotional journey? How was he received by the Egyptian sultan, and what arrange-
ments were made for continuing his pilgrimage to Mecca? According to these reports, was
he the first ruler of Mali to make the Hajj?

63. RUY GONZALEZ DE CLAVIJO AT CONSTANTINOPLE

Starting in the 1360s, after the collapse of the Mongol Empire, a new power arose in central Asia under the Islamic warlord Timur or Tamerlane. Much like his Mongol predecessors, Tamerlane tried to establish diplomatic ties with European rulers, including Henry III of Castile. In 1403, a Spanish nobleman named Ruy Gonzalez de Clavijo and his companions set out from Henry's court in the company of Tamerlane's returning ambassador, Muhammad al-Kazi. Writing in Spanish, Clavijo left a detailed account of his journey, stretching from Seville to Samarkand (in modern-day Uzbekistan). In the selection below, he describes the time that his party spent at Constantinople, where they visited the city's numerous churches and holy sites.

Source: trans. C.R. Markham, in *Narrative of the Embassy of Ruy Gonzalez de Clavijo to the Court of Timour at Samarcand* (1859; rpt. New York: Burt Franklin, 1970), pp. 29–49.

On Sunday, 28 October, the emperor of Constantinople [Manuel II Palaiologos] sent for the ambassadors, and they went from Pera to Constantinople in a boat, and found a crowd of people waiting for them, and horses to convey them to the palace. The emperor had just returned from hearing mass, and he received them very well, in a chamber apart, which was lofty and covered with carpets, on one of which there was the skin of a leopard, and in the back part pillows were placed, embroidered with gold. Having conversed with the ambassadors for some time, the emperor ordered them to return to their lodgings, and he sent them a large stag, which had been brought in by some of his huntsmen. The emperor had with him, the empress his wife and three small children, the eldest being about eight years old. On the following Monday he sent some courtiers to the ambassadors, to answer what they had said to him.

On Tuesday, 30 October, the ambassadors sent to the emperor to say that, as they were desirous of seeing the city, and the churches and relics which it contained, they hoped that he would graciously order them to be shown; and the emperor directed his son-in-law, a Genoese named Dario, who was married to one of his illegitimate daughters, to accompany them, and show them what they wanted.

The first thing they went to see was the church of St-John the Baptist, which they call St-John of the Stone, and which is near the emperor's palace. On the top of the first doorway of this church there was a very rich figure of Saint John, well designed in mosaic; and near this doorway there was a lofty capital, raised on four arches; and the roof and walls are covered with beautiful images and figures in mosaic. This mosaic work is made of very small stones, which are covered with fine gilt, and blue, white, green, or red enamel, according to the color which is required to depict the figures, so that this work is very marvelous to behold.

Beyond this place there is a great court, surrounded by houses, and containing many cypress trees: and opposite the door into the body of the church there is a beautiful fountain, under a canopy raised upon eight white marble pillars, and the pipe of the fountain is of white stone. The body of the church is very lofty, and near the entrance there are three small chapels, each containing an altar, and the door of the center chapel is plated with silver; and by the side of the door there are four marble columns inlaid with small jaspers, and silver crosses, and precious stones: and there are curtains of silk across these doors, placed there that the priest may not be seen when he goes in to say mass. The roof is very rich, and inlaid with mosaics. On the roof of the body of the church there is a figure of God the Father; and the walls are inlaid in the same manner nearly to the ground; and the floor is enriched with jaspers. The chapel was surrounded by seats of carved wood, and between each chair there was a brazier with ashes, into which the people spit, that they may not spit on the ground; and there are many lamps of silver and of glass.

There are many relics in this church, of which the emperor keeps the key. On this day the ambassadors were shown the left arm of Saint John the Baptist, from the shoulder to the hand. This arm was withered, so that the skin and bone alone remained, and the joints of the elbow and the hand were adorned with jewels set in gold. This church also contains many relics of Jesus Christ; but the ambassadors were not shown them on that day, because the emperor had gone out hunting, and had left the keys of the church with the empress, but he forgot to give her the keys of the place where these relics were kept. But on another day they were shown, as will presently be related. This church belongs to a monastery, and the monks have a very large hall, in the middle of which there is a table of white marble, 30 paces long, and there are many wooden seats round it; and there are three other small tables. Within the precincts of this monastery there are gardens, and vineyards, and other things which there is not space to describe.

The same day they went to see another church called Peribelico, dedicated to Saint Mary. At the entrance to this church there is a great court, containing many cypresses, walnut trees, elms, and other trees. The outer walls of the church are covered with images and other figures, in gold, blue, and other colors. On the left hand side of the entrance to the church there are many figures, and amongst them an image of Saint Mary, with one of the emperor and another of the empress on each side. At the feet of the image of Saint Mary there are representations of 30 castles and cities, with the names of Grecian cities written under them. They say that these cities and castles formerly belonged to this church, having been given by an emperor called Romanus, who lies interred here. At the feet of the image there were certain documents written in steel, and sealed with seals of wax and lead, which described the privileges enjoyed by this church over those cities and castles.

There are five altars in the body of the church; which is very large and lofty, supported on pillars of various colored marble, and the walls and floor are inlaid with jasper; and the ceiling is inlaid with very rich mosaics. On the left hand side, at the end of the church, there is a handsome stone monument, where the body of the emperor Romanus is interred: they said that this monument was formerly covered with gold and precious stones, but that when the Latins captured this city, ninety years ago [in fact, just under 200 years earlier], they plundered this tomb. In this church there is another great stone tomb, in which another emperor is interred, and this church also contains the other arm of the blessed Saint John the Baptist, which was shown to the ambassadors. This was the right arm, and it was fresh and healthy; and, though they say that the whole body of the blessed Saint John was destroyed, except one finger of the right arm, with which he pointed when he said "Ecce agnus Dei" ["Behold the lamb of God"], yet certainly the whole of this arm was fresh and in good preservation, but it wanted the thumb. The reason given by the monks for the thumb being gone was this – they say that at the time when idolatry prevailed in the city of Antioch, there was a terrible dragon, to which one person was given every year, to be eaten. They drew lots who should be the victim, and the person on whom the lot fell, could not be excused from being eaten by the dragon. Once the lot fell upon the daughter of a good man, and when he saw that his daughter must be given up to the dragon, he was very sad, and gave her to a church of Christian nuns, who were then in that city, saying to the nuns, that he had heard that God had performed many miracles through Saint John, and that he wished to believe, and to adore the arm of that saint, which they possessed. He prayed that, in addition to the other miracles which God had performed through him, he would save the girl from being eaten by this ferocious dragon, and deliver her from danger. The nuns, taking compassion on him, showed him the arm, on which he threw himself down to worship it, and bit off its thumb, without letting the nuns see him. When the people were going to give the maiden to the dragon, and the monster opened its mouth to eat her, the good man threw the thumb of the blessed saint into its mouth; upon which the dragon turned round, and fled, which was a great miracle: and that man was converted to the faith of our Lord Jesus Christ.

In this same church they were shown a small cross, a *palmo* [a palm] in length, ornamented with gold, with a small crucifix; and it was placed in a recess which was covered with gold, so that it could be taken out and replaced at pleasure. They say that it is made of the wood of the true cross, on which our Lord Jesus Christ was placed, and its color is black. It was made when the blessed Saint Helen, mother of Constantine, who built this city, brought the whole of the true cross from Jerusalem to Constantinople. They were also shown the body of the blessed Saint Gregory, which was whole and undecayed. Outside the church there is a cloister, where there are many beautiful representations of history, among which is the root of Jesse, showing the lineage whence came the blessed Virgin Mary. It was figured in mosaic; and was so wonderful, so rich, and so well drawn, that it surpassed all the other works. There are many monks belonging to the church, who showed the above things to the ambassadors; and also took them into a very large and lofty refectory, in the midst of which there was a table of white marble, very well made, being thirty-five *palmos* long, and the floor was of marble flags. At the end of this refectory there were two small tables of white marble, and the ceiling was covered with mosaic work; and on the walls pictures were represented in mosaic work, from the salutation of the blessed Virgin Mary by Saint Gabriel, to the birth of Jesus Christ our God, together with his journeys with his disciples, and all his blessed life, until he was crucified. In this refectory there were many flag stones, made to place meat and other food upon; and in the monastery there were many cells, where the monks live; and gardens, and water, and vineyards, so that this monastery is like a large town....

On the same day the ambassadors went to see the church which is called St-Sophia, which is the largest, most honored, and most privileged of all the churches in the city; and it has canons who do duty as if it was a cathedral, and a patriarch, whom the Greeks call Marpollit. In a court, in front of the church, there are nine very large white marble pillars, the largest I ever beheld, and it is said that a great palace used to stand on the top of them, where the patriarch and his clergy held their meetings. In this same court, in front of the church, a wonderfully high stone column stands, on the top of which there is a horse made of copper, of the size of four large horses put together; and on its back there is the figure of an armed knight, also of copper, with a great plume on his head, resembling the tail of a peacock. The horse has chains of iron round its body, secured to the column, to prevent it from falling, or being moved by the wind. This horse is very well made, and one fore and one hind leg is raised, as if it was in the act of prancing. The knight, on its back, has his right arm raised, with the hand open, while the reins are held with the left arm. This column, horse, and knight, are so large and high, that it is wonderful to see them. This marvelous horse is said to have been placed here by the emperor Justinian, who erected the column, and performed great and notable deeds against the Turks, in his time.

At the entrance to this church, under an arch, there is a small but very rich and beautiful chapel, raised upon four marble columns; and opposite this chapel is the door of the church. It is very large and high, and covered with brass, and in front of it there is a small court, containing some high terraces; beyond which there is another door covered with brass, like the first. Within this door there is a broad and lofty nave, with a ceiling of wood, and on the left hand there are very large and well built cloisters, adorned with slabs of marble and jasper of various colors. The body of the church contains five lofty doors, all covered with brass, and the center one is the largest. The body of the church is the loftiest, most rich, and most beautiful that can be seen in the whole world. It is surrounded by three large and broad naves, which are joined to it, so that mass may be heard in all parts of the church. The arches of the naves are of green jasper, and unite the roofs of the nave with that of the body of the church; but the summit of the latter rises much higher than that of the naves. It is dome shaped, and very high, so that a man must have good eyes who looks up from beneath; and the church is 105 paces long, by 93 broad; and the dome is supported by 4 pillars, very large and thick, covered with flags of many colored jaspers; and from pillar to pillar there are arches of green jasper, which are very high and sustain the dome. In the arches there are four very large slabs, two on the right hand and two on the left, which are colored with a substance made from a powder, artificially, and called porphyry. The dome is covered with very rich mosaic work, and, over the high altar, the image of God the Father, very large, is wrought in mosaics of many colors; but it is so high up, that it only looks about the size of a man, or a little larger, though really it is so large that it measures three *palmos* between the eyes; but to him who looks at it, it does not appear to be more nor less than a man, and that is owing to the very great height it is placed above the ground....

Afterwards, on Thursday, 1 November, the ambassadors went to Constantinople, and soon found Master Ilario, and others of the household of the emperor, at the gate of Quinigo, where they were waiting. They then mounted on horseback, and went to see a church called Santa Maria de la Cherne, which is within the city, and opposite to a ruined castle, which used to be a lodging used by the emperors. The said castle was destroyed by an emperor, because he found his son in it, in a manner that will be related to you presently.

This church of Santa Maria de la Cherne used to be a chapel of the emperor's, and the interior consists of three naves, the center one being the largest and most lofty, and the other two being lower. They are vaulted, and the arches connect them together. These naves are adorned in the following manner. They are raised on great pillars of green jasper, and their bases are of white marble, inlaid with many figures. The ceilings and the walls, half way up, are covered with flags of jasper of many colors, with many figures and beautiful works artificially wrought upon them. The ceiling of the center nave is very rich, made of timber in squares and beams, all gilded with very fine gold; and though parts of the church were much out of repair, this gilded ceiling looked as fresh and as beautiful as if it was just finished. In the center nave there was a rich altar and a pulpit, also very rich; and all the furniture of the church is very rich and costly, and the roof was all covered with lead.

On the same day the ambassadors went to see the relics in the church of St-John the Baptist, which were not shown to them before, for want of the keys. When they arrived at the church, the monks robed themselves and lighted many candles, and took the keys, singing and chanting all the time. They then ascended to a sort of tower, where the relics were; and with them there was a knight of the emperor's household. They then came forth chanting very mournful hymns, with lighted tapers, and many incense bearers before them, and they placed the relics on a high table covered with a silken cloth, in the body of the church. The relics were contained in a colored chest, which was sealed with two seals of white wax, on two plates of silver. They opened it, and took out two large silver gilt plates, which were placed on the top of the relics. They then produced a bag of white dimity, sealed with wax, which they opened, and took out a small round golden casket, in which was the bread which our Lord Jesus Christ gave to Judas at the last supper, as a sign who it was who should betray him, but he was unable to eat it. It was wrapped in a red crape cover, and sealed with two waxen seals, and the bread was about three fingers in breadth.

They then took out a gold casket smaller than the first, in which there was a crystal case, which was fixed in the casket, and which contained some of the blood of our Lord Jesus Christ, which flowed from his side, when it was pierced by Longinus. They also took out another small golden casket, the top of which was pierced like a grater, and it contained the blood which flowed from a crucifix in the city of Beirut, when a Jew once attempted to injure it. They also showed a little case of glass, which had a cover, and a little golden chain attached to it; in which was a small red crape cover containing some hairs of the beard of our Lord Jesus Christ, being those which the Jews pulled out, when they crucified him. There was also a piece of the stone on which our Lord was placed, when he was taken down from the cross. They then showed a square silver casket, two and a half *palmos* long, which was sealed with six seals made of six plates of silver, and it was opened with a silver key. They took out of it a board, which was covered with gold, and on it was the iron of the lance with which Longinus pierced our Lord Jesus Christ. It was as fine as a thorn, and of well tempered iron, and the handle was bored through, being about a *palmo* and two fingers long; and the blood on it was as fresh as if the deed which was done with it had just been committed. It was fixed on the board, which was covered with gold, and the iron was not bright, but quite dim. There was also fixed on this board, a piece of the cane which they gave our Lord Jesus Christ, when he was before Pilate. It was a *palmo* and a half long; and near it there was also a piece of the sponge with which Jesus Christ, our God, was given gall and vinegar, when he was on the cross. In the same case with this board, there was the garment of Jesus Christ, for which the knights of Pilate cast lots. It was folded, and sealed, that people who came to see it might not cut bits off, as had been done before, but one sleeve was left outside the seals. The garment was of a red dimity, like muslin, and the sleeve was narrow, and it was doubled to the elbow. It had three little buttons, made like twisted cords, like the knots on a doublet, and the buttons, and the sleeve, and all that could be seen of the skirt, seemed to be of a dark rose color; and it did not look as if it had been woven, but as if it had been worked with a needle, for the strings looked twisted in network, and very tight. When the ambassadors went to see these relics, the people of the city, who knew it, came also, and they all cried very loudly, and said their prayers....

This city of Constantinople contains many great churches and monasteries, but most of them are in ruins; though it seems clear that, in former times, when the city was in its youth, it was the most renowned city in the world. They say that even now there are 3,000 churches, large and small; and within the city there are fountains and wells of sweet water; and in a part below the church which is dedicated to the Holy Apostle, there is a bridge reaching from one valley to another, over houses and gardens, by which water used to come, for the irrigation of those gardens. In a street which leads to one of the gates of the city, opposite Pera, there is a pair of stocks fixed in the ground, for men who are to be imprisoned, or who break any of the city regulations, or who sell meat or bread with false weights. Such persons are taken to this place, and left there day and night, exposed to the weather. Between the city walls and the sea, opposite Pera, there are many houses, in which many things are sold, and warehouses. The city of Constantinople is near the sea, as you have been told, and two sides face the sea; and in front is the city of Pera. Between the two cities is the port, and Constantinople is thus like Seville, and Pera is like Triana, with the port and the ships between them; and the Greeks do not call it Constantinople as we do, but Escomboli.

Pera is a small city, but well peopled and surrounded with a wall, and it contains good and handsome houses. It is inhabited by Genoese, and is a lordship of Genoa. It is peopled by Genoese and Greeks, and is so close to the sea, that between the wall and the water there is not sufficient breadth for a carrack to pass.... The said ambassadors were in the city of Pera, from the Wednesday on which they arrived to Tuesday, 13 November, for during all that time they could not find a vessel to take them to Trebizond; and, as the winter was approaching, and the sea is very dangerous for navigating during the winter, they took a galliot to prevent further delay, the master of which was a Genoese named Nicolo Socato, and they caused him to obtain sailors and provisions; and they intended to have sailed on the said Thursday, had not several accidents prevented them.

What were some of the holy sites that Clavijo and his company visited during their stay in Constantinople? What sort of relics did they see? Why do you think that these ambassadors were so interested in churches and saints' shrines? How did the increasing power of the Ottoman Turks in the region complicate Christian travel? What evidence does this account offer that Ruy and his companions were dependent upon others (such as the Genoese) to successfully complete their itinerary?

64. PERO TAFUR AT JERUSALEM

Born in Cordoba, Spain, the wanderer Pero Tafur traveled widely around the Mediterranean world from 1435 to 1439, including visits to Ceuta in northern Africa, Rome, and Jerusalem. Years later, writing in Spanish, he left an account of his journey, including a description of his visit to the Holy Land under Turkish rule.

Source: trans. M. Letts, in *Pero Tafur: Travels and Adventures 1435–1439* (New York: Harper and Brothers, 1926), pp. 48–62.

On Ascension day, after receiving the blessing, we departed and set sail at noon, and took the left side of the gulf towards Esclavonia [Dalmatia], the greater part of which is Venetian, and all along the coast there are many safe harbors and islands and ports for taking in provisions. The next day we came to a town called Parenzo, and from there we sailed for Zara, a town of the Venetians. Thence we reached Ragusa which is under the dominion of the emperor. All this time we kept passing islands belonging to Esclavonia, some populated and some uninhabited. The country is very mountainous and bare; and the inhabitants are the tallest I have ever seen, but what a barbarous people they are! In these parts are bred the best falcons in the world, except the Norwegian, and it is said that silver is to be found in many places.

We continued our voyage along the Gulf, passing Valona, a large city, which had recently fallen into the hands of the Turks, and then, leaving Esclavonia, we sailed by Albania, which is part of the same coast, and left Italy and the Cape of Spartivento on the right hand. The Gulf of Venice runs for 800 miles between Italy and Esclavonia, and at the end of it is the island of Corfu, which the Venetians call their door, although Venice is in fact 800 miles away. On the right hand is that part of Italy called Apulia and the Tierra di Lavoro, and, on the left, Esclavonia, formerly called Dalmatia, and a great part of Albania. The island of Corfu is inhabited by Greeks. Not long ago King Ladislaus of Naples took it and held it with the intention of capturing Jerusalem, of which he called himself king, and it is said that in his necessity he sold the island to the Venetians who now possess it. We remained there two days, waiting for a favorable wind, and on the third day we departed, sailing for Modone, which is in Greece. This day we passed the Gulf of Patras on the left hand, and much enjoyed the sight of it. Here the city of Corinth is situated, a very ancient place with magnificent buildings, now much depopulated. This gulf strikes inland, and with the other gulf which enters from the other side it forms the peninsula of Morea, which in ancient times was called Achaia. It is governed by the emperor of Constantinople, and is the patrimony of the eldest son whom they call despot of Morea. These two gulfs eat so far into the land that they say there is not a space of two miles between them. An emperor of Constantinople once wished to make the peninsula into an island, but he changed his mind on the advice of his counselors. Nevertheless, he enclosed it with a very strong wall which can be seen to this day....

On the third day [from the harbor of Candia] we reached the island [of Rhodes], and found there certain galleys and ships belonging to the king of Aragon, but we armed ourselves and displayed our pennons for Jerusalem, and when they saw these they left us at once and sailed away.... The city of Rhodes is flat, but fortified with a moat and wall, and on one side is a place apart where the Knights Hospitallers of Jerusalem have their residence, which is called the Collachium, and in it is the hospital from which they take their name. It is one of the most magnificent houses of piety which I have ever seen, and, indeed, in the matter of building and embellishments and supplies it could not be improved. The knights receive anyone who is sick, and a patient dying there is absolved from sin and punishment, and even for those who visit the hospital there are certain indulgences. This hospital is situated just as one enters the Collachium on the left hand, and it was built by Don Anton de Fluvian, Grand Master of the knights, who was a Catalan by birth. From there we went to see the city, passing many streets and houses of the knights, among them certain hostels where foreigners eat and have their places of meeting, each nation apart from the others, and a knight has charge of each one of these hostels, and provides for the necessities of the inmates according to their religion. At the end of the knights' quarter, on the left hand, is the church of St-John, to which they constantly resort to say their office, and where they hold their council. In this church there are many relics, including, so they say, the basin in which our Lord washed his hands, and a large share of the money for which he was sold, some of the thorns, a nail of the cross, and many others, and when they elect the Grand Master, the knights swear on these relics that, truly and without favor, they will elect the one most worthy to hold that office. In front of this church is the house of the Grand Master, an ordinary dwelling and not rich. There the master is attended by twelve knights, called companions, who take counsel with him and eat always at his board.

Every day throughout the year the knights have to give food to twelve poor people and serve them with their own hands, except when they are occupied with the sick or are absent. There is another hostel which is for the reception of pilgrims for Jerusalem, and here they lodge everyone according to his station, and everything is provided except food. There is also a church where certain chaplains are charged with the duty of saying mass for the pilgrims, and all this is done to keep them from the common inns. The knights visit them there, and anyone who desires to take a guest with him may do so with leave of the marshal. The island of Rhodes is reasonably well supplied with bread and wine, and with gardens. Most of the gardens are for the service of the master's table, and he portions them out among the twelve companions who are with him. There is also a fortress in the island called Judigo. Much might be related of this noble company of knights, but I leave them now to speak of other things.

We departed from Rhodes [and reached the port of Jaffa].... When the pilgrim ship arrives at Jaffa the fact is known almost at once to the prior of Mount Sion, who sends two or three [Franciscan] friars to the governor of Jerusalem who return with the sultan's safe-conduct. They take the pilgrims ashore and deliver their names in writing to the governor, and they themselves retain another list, and in this manner all fear of imposture is avoided. As one disembarks, there are Moors [Muslims] ready with asses which the pilgrims ride all the time that they are in the Holy Land. Two ducats is the price fixed for the hire, and this cannot be increased or diminished. The governor and the friars travel with the pilgrims to Rama, a great place, five leagues from Jaffa, where there is a hostel founded for pilgrims by Duke Godfrey of Bouillon when he took the Holy Sepulcher [during the First Crusade]. It is well provided with many apartments, some for men and some for women, and we remained there one day. The next morning we traveled two miles to the monastery of St-George, where his body is said to be, and where he is believed to have slain the dragon, but others say that he slew it at Beirut which is the port of Damascus. That day we slept at a place five leagues from there, close to a castle called Emmaus, and the following day we left early and traveled another five leagues to the city of Jerusalem, of which we obtained a good prospect some four leagues off. We could see a number of buildings, as well as Mount Sion, and the castles of King David, and the Holy Sepulcher which is a very lofty church.

As we entered Jerusalem the Christians, both Greeks and other nations, came out to receive us and carried us to a great square in front of the Holy Sepulcher where we prayed, but they did not let us go in. They then took us to a hostel, likewise founded by Duke Godfrey of Bouillon, where we found an abundance of food cooked in various ways, which the Greeks make ready and sell to the Christians. Not long after, the prior of Mount Sion came with his friars, bringing with them ten or twelve knights who are accustomed to live in the monastery, and we were very comfortably lodged. The prior left two friars who were to accompany us from that day onwards and show us the sights in Jerusalem and the vicinity. This monastery of Mount Sion is situated on one side of the city on the highest point, and in it are many places where our Lord worked great miracles. There is also a lofty tower in the vault of which, when the disciples were gathered together, our Lord appeared to them in tongues of fire – this was the feast of Pentecost. From here one can see the sea of Sodom and Gomorrah, which they call the Dead Sea, where once were five cities. Beneath this tower is also a chapel where our Lord appeared to Saint Thomas the apostle and told him to put his hand into his side, and many other things also happened in this place. At the entrance, in the center of a street, is the house of the Virgin Mary, and close to it, behind the monastery, is the place where our Lord partook of the Last Supper with his disciples. This day we rested there, and the next day we heard mass in the Holy Sepulcher, which is only open once a year, and there they took count of us according to the list which they made at Jaffa. Each pilgrim paid seven ducats and a half, and with the two paid for the beasts, and certain payments made in small coin in the holy places – eleven of these coins being worth a ducat – each pilgrim paid twelve and a half ducats as tolls.

As we were preparing to enter the Holy Sepulcher, there came out to meet us in procession all those Christians who had been locked up there since the year before, that is to say the Catholics (three Franciscan friars), the Greeks, the Jacobite Christians, the Armenians, those of Cinturia, India and the Copts, in all seven different kinds of Christians, and we joined the procession and went into the Holy Sepulcher. This is a great church, exceeding lofty, with an immense opening through which the light enters. Within is another smaller chapel, in which is the Holy Sepulcher itself, and this is so small that there is no room in it, except for the priest who says mass and the server. After worshipping there we went with the procession to Mount Calvary, where our Lord was crucified, which is 12 or 15 paces from that place. This is a great rock upon which stands a chapel, most richly ornamented with mosaic work. The hole in which the cross was placed is still to be seen, as well as the holes where the crosses of the two thieves stood. After praying there, we descended to the place where Christ was anointed, and thence to the room where he was detained before the crucifixion. Afterwards we saw the place where Saint Helena found the cross, as well as the spot which our Lord indicated as the center of the world. Adjoining is the dwelling of the friars, where the relics are kept, and where our Lord appeared to St. Mary Magdalene as a gardener. At the entrance is a great hall hung with pennons and flags of many kings and Christian princes, and here the knights set up their arms. All these things and many more are to be seen on the way in from this cemetery, and all the holy relics are there and each one of the aforesaid Christians has a separate chapel.

We left the procession and heard mass, and then had dinner, which the Greeks had prepared for us very well for our money. That day the Moors and Christians had license to display goods for us to buy, and we rested a day and night, hearing divine offices, each one in the manner of his country. Here is the tomb of Godfrey de Bouillon, with an inscription engraved on a stone as follows. [The inscription is missing.] Close to this is the tomb of Baldwin, his brother, made in the same manner, with this inscription. [The inscription is missing.] The following day, when we had heard mass, they opened the doors and let us out after counting us, and sent us to our hostel. That day we saw the Campo Santo and the Valley of Jehoshaphat, where is the sepulcher of the Virgin Mary, which is an underground vault reached by fifteen or twenty steps. The Franciscans are the guardians. Here we paid certain monies. From there we went to the place where our Lord was taken in the garden, and afterwards to the Mount of Olives, where Christ ascended to heaven. There is a notable church here, with a stone with the imprint of his foot upon it. We saw also the place where the disciples, being gathered together, composed the [Apostles'] creed, and from there we continued to the spot where Christ uttered the Paternoster [Our Father]. Close by is the elder-tree where Judas hanged himself. Then, as we returned to Jerusalem, we passed the place where the wood of the Cross was kept for a long time, and not far off is the site of the stoning of Saint Stephen. We entered the city close by the Golden Gate, which adjoins the Temple of Solomon, and passed the pool where the angel troubled the waters, and the sick were healed. Then we saw the houses of Pilate and Caiaphas where Christ was judged. Here they still sentence people to death. We saw also the street called Amargura, where our Lord carried the cross on his shoulders, which is a covered way. Here the rain water is collected and stored in cisterns from which the people drink, for the city is badly supplied with water. This day we slept at our hostel....

The next morning we came to Jericho, 15 leagues from Jerusalem. There is here a great valley, and a vast plain through which the river Jordan flows to the place where our Lord baptized Saint John the Baptist, and was baptized of him. A stone cross in the water marks the spot. Here we all bathed, and a German gentleman belonging to our party perished by drowning. This is a place of the greatest sanctity.

The pilgrims had to return that night to sleep at Jericho and to go the next day to Quarantana, where our Lord fasted. But I arranged with a Moor to take me to the desert of Arabia, three leagues farther on, where Saint John preached, and where the first hermit, Saint Anthony, as well as other holy fathers, retired to live, and from there I returned by the Dead Sea, where were Sodom and Gomorrah and three other cities, five cities in all, which were overthrown for the sin of sodomy. The water is so foul that it cannot be described, and they say that no fish can breed there and that no birds frequent the place. The Moor who traveled with me told me a great marvel: that the river Jordan enters the lake and emerges at the other side without mixing with the fetid waters, and that in the midst of the lake one can drink of the sweet water of the river. All about this valley there are certain tall and very straight trees, much burdened with a fruit like citrons, and if one touches them with the fingers, however lightly, they break and a smoke comes out, and the evil smell remains on the hand all that day.

The following day I returned and dined at Jericho, which is a village with about 100 inhabitants, and there I gathered some of those roses which are beneficial to women in labor, and saw many holy places associated with our Lord. At the head of that river is the province called Bethany-trans-Jordan. That night I slept at the mountain where our Lord fasted where I again joined the pilgrims. This is a very high mountain range, in the center of which there are some small chapels, and there is a road for the ascent, made by Saint Helena to do honor to the place. But as we were ascending, a squire of France, going to the assistance of a lady, fell headlong from the mountain and was dashed in pieces on the rocks below, for the place is very perilous to climb. We then descended, and by another and easier route we reached the very summit where our Lord was tempted by the devil. We then returned and came to a fountain where the people from Jericho had brought food to sell to us. We remained there that night, and the next morning we took up the corpse of that squire and carried it to the before-mentioned house on the mountain, and there we buried it, after which we remained there that day....

That night I bargained with a renegade [a former Christian who had converted to Islam], a native of Portugal and offered him two ducats if he would get me into the Temple of Solomon [the Dome of the Rock] and he consented. At one o'clock in the night I entered, dressed in his clothes and saw the Temple which is a single nave the whole ornamented with gold mosaic work. The floor and walls are of the most beautiful white stones, and the place is hung with so many lamps that they all seemed to be joined together. The roof above is quite flat and is covered with lead. They say, in truth, that when Solomon built it, it was the most magnificent building in the whole world. Afterwards it was destroyed and rebuilt, but today, without doubt, it is still unmatched. If I had been recognized there as a Christian I should have been killed immediately. Not long ago this Temple was a consecrated church, but a favorite of the sultan prevailed on him to take it and turn it into a mosque. The renegade who had escorted me now returned with me to Mount Sion where the friars mourned for me as one already dead, since I had not come at the appointed time, and they rejoiced greatly to see me again, as did also the gentlemen of my company.

We had ordained to go the next day to hear mass and to remain a day and night in the Holy Sepulcher. Accordingly, we arrived at daybreak, and they opened the doors with the same ceremonies as before. That day we confessed and received the sacrament, and I dubbed three gentlemen knights of the Holy Sepulcher, two Germans and a Frenchman, and we placed our arms in the accustomed place and took some of the relics which the guardian gave us, and the next day at dawn we heard mass and departed. We spent the whole of this day and the next in visiting holy places and in preparation for our departure. I had been enquiring as to the possibility of visiting Saint Catherine's monastery on Mount Sinai, which is close to the Red Sea, but learned that the escort with the camels had already departed with an ambassador from Turkey to the Sultan at Babylonia, so that my journey could not be undertaken. I was willing to remain there until next year, if needs be, but the guardian advised me to go to Cyprus to see the cardinal, brother of the old king, stating that he would give me a safe-conduct for Babylonia and that I could reach Mount Sinai from there, and I decided to do this.

Does Pero Tafur seem exclusively interested in religious sites and structures? According to his account, what did the Hospitallers at Rhodes do to help care for pilgrims and other travelers? What procedures were in place for the arrival of Christian pilgrims in the Holy Land (in particular, how did the Muslim governor interact with such pilgrims)? What sort of reception did Tafur and his companions receive by the Christians at Jerusalem? What role did the payment of fees and other expenses play in shaping their pilgrimage experience?

CHAPTER EIGHT

PILGRIMAGE AND PIETY IN THE LATE MIDDLE AGES

By the fourteenth and fifteenth centuries, like other common medieval devotional practices, Christian pilgrimage both within and beyond Europe continued unabated. In conjunction with the increasingly widespread availability of indulgences — meaning the formulaic forgiveness of the penance or punishment owed for sins in this world and the next — the continued centrality of pilgrimage to Christian society seemed beyond question. Nevertheless, more readily and intensely than ever before, some Christians began to question and criticize the cult of saints, indulgences, relic devotion, and other popular traditions, pilgrimage among them. In a world marked by new forms of religious expression for the laity, the increasing use of vernacular languages for literary production, and the rise of Christian humanism, pilgrimage endured and displayed new forms of creative expression, even as it found itself subject to growing criticisms, some made through humorous satire, others with devastating directness. At the close of the Middle Ages and the dawn of the early modern era, the European tradition of Christian pilgrimage did not come to end, but rather, like so many other aspects of medieval culture, religion, and society, persisted while adapting to changing circumstances.

65. THE JUBILEE YEAR OF 1300

In 1300, Pope Boniface VIII (1294–1303) declared a plenary indulgence for anyone worshipping at the churches of Rome during that year. The result was a flood of pilgrims, apparently numbering in the hundreds of thousands, to the holy city. The success of this "Jubilee Year" led to the declaration of another in 1350, signaling the widespread appeal of such plenary indulgences to pilgrims and other pious Christians.

Source: trans. J. Shinners, in *Medieval Popular Religion 1000-1500*, ed. J. Shinners, 2nd ed. (Peterborough, ON: Broadview Press, 2007), p. 402.

The faithful account of our ancestors holds that great remissions of sins and indulgences are granted to those going to the honorable basilica of [Peter], the prince of the apostles in the city [of Rome]. We, therefore, who by virtue of the duty of our office most willingly strive for and attend to the salvation of everyone, by apostolic authority confirm, approve, and also renew and, by this present document, fortify with our patronage these kinds of remissions and indulgences, holding them each and every one valid and pleasing. But for the most blessed apostles Peter and Paul to be more fully honored as the faithful visit their basilicas in the city more devoutly, and for the faithful to consider themselves even more sated with the largess of spiritual favors through frequent visits of this kind, we – through the mercy of Almighty God, the merits of his same apostles, the authority granted by the counsel of our brothers, and the plenitude of apostolic power – in the current year 1300 (dating from last Christmas) and each centennial to follow do grant and will grant not just full and generous but the fullest possible pardon of all their sins to all who, truly contrite and confessed, reverently visit and will visit these basilicas in this present year and in each centennial to follow. We order that whoever wishes to share in this indulgence granted by us must go to the basilicas at least once a day for at least thirty days successively or at intervals if they are Romans; if they are pilgrims or outsiders, for fifteen days in a similar way. A more effective indulgence will result and someone will be more rewarded who will visit these basilicas more frequently and devoutly. May no act of men in general infringe on this record of our confirmation, approval, renewal, concession, and decree, etc. Given at Rome at Saint Peter's, 22 February, in the sixth year of our pontificate [1300].

By what authority did Pope Boniface VIII declare the "Jubilee Year" of 1300? What was the ultimate source of the forgiveness promised by him in this decree? What exactly did pilgrims have to do in order to merit the "remission of sins" promised in this indulgence? What does the decree's distinction between local and long-distance pilgrimage imply about the nature of devotional travel?

66. PILGRIMAGE AND SATIRE: *THE CANTERBURY TALES*

The most famous pilgrimage of the late Middle Ages never actually happened: the one presented in The Canterbury Tales *by English author Geoffrey Chaucer (1343–1400), who wrote his masterpiece in Middle English. Embracing the idea of pilgrimage as a metaphor for transitory human experience, Chaucer imagined a fictional group of pilgrims who were traveling to the shrine of Thomas Becket (doc. 51). During the course of their journey, each member of the band tells a story to amuse his fellow travelers, creating a vast, satirical panorama of medieval life.*

Source: abridged by M.-A. Stouck, in *Medieval Saints: A Reader*, ed. M.-A. Stouck (Peterborough, ON: Broadview Press, 1999), pp. 328–34, from the translation by D. Wright, in Geoffrey Chaucer, *The Canterbury Tales* (London: Fontana Press, 1964), pp. 5–21.

When the sweet showers of April have pierced the dryness of March to its root and soaked every vein in moisture whose quickening force engenders the flower; when Zephyr [the warm west wind] with his sweet breath has given life to tender shoots in each wood and field; when the young sun has run his half-course in the [Zodiacal] sign of the Ram; when, nature prompting their instincts, small birds who sleep through the night with one eye open make their music – then people long to go on pilgrimages, and pious wanderers to visit strange lands and far-off shrines in different countries. In England especially they come from every shire's end to Canterbury to seek out the holy blessed martyr Saint Thomas à Becket, who helped them when they were sick.

It happened one day at this time of year, while I was lodging at the Tabard in Southwark, ready and eager to go on my pilgrimage to Canterbury, a company of 29 people arrived in the hostelry at nightfall. They were of various sorts, accidentally brought together in companionship, all pilgrims wishing to ride to Canterbury. The rooms and stables were commodious and we were very well looked after. In short, by the time the sun had gone down I had talked with everyone of them and soon became one of their company. We agreed to rise early to set out on the journey I am going to tell you about. But nevertheless before I take the story further it seems right to me to describe, while I have the time and opportunity, the sort and condition of each of them as they appeared to me: who they were, of what rank, and how dressed. I shall begin with the Knight.

The Knight was a very distinguished man. From the beginning of his career he had loved chivalry, loyalty, honorable dealing, generosity, and good breeding. He had fought bravely in the king's service, besides which he had traveled further than most men in heathen as well as in Christian lands. Wherever he went he was honored for his valor. He was at Alexandria when it fell. When he served in Prussia he was generally given the seat of honor above the knights of all other nations; no Christian soldier of his rank had fought oftener in the raids on Russia and Lithuania. And he had been in Granada at the siege of Algeciras, fought in Benmarin and at the conquests of Ayas and Attalia, besides taking part in many armed expeditions in the eastern Mediterranean. He had been in 15 pitched battles and fought 3 times for the faith in the lists at Tramassene, and each time killed his foe. This same distinguished Knight had also fought at one time for the king of Palathia against another heathen enemy in Turkey. He was always outstandingly successful; yet though distinguished he was prudent, and his bearing as modest as a maid's. In his whole life he never spoke discourteously to any kind of man. He was a true and perfect noble knight. But, speaking of his equipment, his horses were good, yet he was not gaily dressed. He wore a tunic of thick cotton cloth, rust-marked from his coat of mail; for he had just come back from his travels and was making his pilgrimage to render thanks....

There was a remarkably fine-looking Monk, who acted as estate-steward to his monastery and loved hunting: a manly man, well fitted to be an abbot. He kept plenty of fine horses in his stable, and when he went out riding people could hear the bells on his bridle jingling in the whistling wind as clear and loud as the chapel bell of the small convent of which he was the head. Because the Rule of Saint Maur or of Saint Benedict was old-fashioned and somewhat strict, this Monk neglected the old precepts and followed the modern custom. He did not give two pins for the text which says hunters cannot be holy men, or that a monk who is heedless of his rule – that is to say a monk out of his cloister – is like a fish out of water. In his view this saying was not worth a bean; and I told him his opinion was sound. Why should he study and addle his wits with everlasting poring over a book in cloisters, or work with his hands, or toil as Saint Augustine [of Hippo] commanded? How is the world to be served? Let Saint Augustine keep his hard labor for himself! Therefore the Monk, whose whole pleasure lay in riding and the hunting of the hare (over which he spared no expense) remained a hard rider and kept greyhounds swift as birds. I saw that his sleeves were edged with costly grey fur, the finest in the land. He had an elaborate golden brooch with a love-knot at the larger end to fasten his hood beneath his chin. His bald head shone like glass; and so did his face, as if it had been anointed. He was a plump and personable dignitary, with prominent, restless eyes which sparkled like fire beneath a pot. His boots were supple and his horse in perfect condition. To be sure he was a fine looking prelate, no pale and wasting ghost! His favorite dish was a fat roast swan. The horse he rode was as brown as a berry....

Among the rest were a Haberdasher, a Carpenter, a Weaver, a Dyer, and a Tapestry-Maker, all dressed in uniform livery belonging to a rich and honorable guild. Their apparel was new and freshly trimmed; their knives were not tipped with brass but finely mounted with wrought silver to match their belts and purses. Each seemed a proper burgess worthy of a place on the dais of a guildhall; and every one of them had the ability and judgment, besides sufficient property and income, to become an alderman. In this they would have the hearty assent of their wives – else the ladies would certainly be much to blame. For it is very pleasant to be called "Madam" and take precedence at church festivals, and have one's mantle carried in state.

They had taken a Cook with them for the occasion, to boil chickens with marrowbones, tart flavoring-powder and spice. Well did he know the taste of London ale! He knew how to roast, fry, seethe, broil, make soup, and bake pies. But it was the greatest pity, so I thought, that he'd got an ulcer on his shin. For he made chicken-pudding with the best of them....

There was among us a worthy Wife from near Bath, but she was a bit deaf, which was a pity. At cloth-making she beat even the weavers of Ypres and Ghent. There was not a woman in her parish who dared go in front of her when she went to the offertory; if anybody did, you may be sure it put her into such a rage she was out of all patience. Her kerchiefs were of the finest texture; I daresay those she wore upon her head on Sundays weighed ten pounds. Her stockings were of the finest scarlet, tightly drawn up above glossy new shoes; her face was bold, handsome, and florid. She had been a respectable woman all her life, having married five husbands in church (apart from other loves in youth of which there is no need to speak at present). She had visited Jerusalem three times and crossed many foreign rivers, had been to Rome, Boulogne, the shrine of St-James of Compostela in Galicia, and Cologne; so she knew a lot about traveling around – the truth is, she was gap-toothed [a sign of luck, travel, and a lascivious disposition]. She rode comfortably upon an ambling horse, her head well covered with a wimple and a hat the size of a shield or buckler. An outer skirt covered her great hips, while on her feet she wore a pair of sharp spurs. In company she laughed and rattled away. No doubt she knew all the cures for love, for at that game she was past mistress....

With him [the Summoner] rode a worthy Pardoner [a seller of papal indulgences] of Rouncival at Charing Cross, his friend and bosom companion, who had come straight from the Vatican at Rome. He loudly caroled "Come hither, love, to me," while the Summoner sang the bass louder than the loudest trumpet. This pardoner's hair was waxy yellow and hung down as sleek as a hank of flax; such locks of hair as he possessed fell in meager clusters spread over his shoulders, where it lay in thinly scattered strands. For comfort he wore no hood; it was packed in his bag. With his hair loose and uncovered except for a cap, he thought he was riding in the latest style. He had great staring eyes like a hare's. Upon his cap he'd sewn a small replica of Saint Veronica's handkerchief. His wallet lay on his lap in front of him, chockfull of pardons from Rome. He'd a thin goat-like voice and no vestige or prospect of a beard; and his skin was smooth as if just shaven. I took him for a gelding or a mare. But for his profession, from Berwick down to Ware there was not another pardoner to touch him. For in his wallet he kept a pillow-slip which, he said, was our Lady's veil. He claimed to have a bit of the sail belonging to Saint Peter when he tried to walk on the waves and Jesus Christ caught hold of him. He had a brass cross set with pebbles and a glass reliquary full of pigs' bones. Yet when he came across some poor country parson he could make more money with these relics in a day than the parson got in two months, and thus by means of barefaced flattery and hocus-pocus he made the parson and the people his dupes. To do him justice, in church at any rate he was a fine ecclesiastic. Well could he read a lesson or a parable; but best of all he sang the offertory hymn, because after it was sung he knew he must preach, as he well knew how, to wheedle money from the congregation with his smooth tongue. Therefore he sang all the louder and merrier.

Now I have told you in a few words the class of person, dress, and number of our party and the reason why it assembled in this excellent inn at Southwark, the Tabard hard by the Bell. And now it's time to tell you how we comported ourselves the night of our arrival at the inn; and afterwards I'll speak of our journey and the rest of our pilgrimage. But first I must beg you to be good enough not to put it down to my lack of refinement if in this matter I use plain language to give an account of their conversation and behavior and when reporting their actual words. For you know as well as I do that whoever repeats a story told by another must reproduce as nearly as he can every word entrusted to him, no matter how uncouth or free the language; or else falsify the tale, or invent, or find new words for it. Be the man his brother, he may not shrink, but whatever words are used he also must use.

In the Bible the language of Christ himself is outspoken; but as you well know, it's no breach of taste. Besides Plato says (as anyone who can read him may see), "The words must relate to the action." Also I beg you to forgive me if in this account I have not paid due attention to people's rank and the order in which they should appear. My wits aren't too bright, as you may suppose.

Our Host welcomed each of us with open arms and soon led us to our places at the supper-table. He served us with the finest viands; the wine was strong and we were in a mood to drink. Our Host was a striking-looking fellow, a fit master of ceremonies for any hall. He was a big man with prominent eyes (there's no better-looking burgess in Cheapside), racy in his talk, shrewd yet civil; a proper man in every respect. What's more, he was a bit of a wag, for after supper, when we'd settled our bills, among other things he began to talk of amusing us, saying: "Ladies and gentlemen, you're all most heartily welcome, for on my honor I'm telling you no lie when I say I've not seen such a jolly company as this under my roof at any one time this year. I'd like to provide you with some entertainment if I knew how to set about it ... and I've just thought of a game that will amuse you and not cost a penny."

"You're off to Canterbury – Godspeed, and the blessed martyr reward you! And you mean to entertain yourselves by telling stories on the way, I'll be bound; for there's certainly no sense or fun in riding along as dumb as stones; and so, as I said before, I'll devise a game that'll give you some amusement. If pleases you all to accept my decision unanimously and to do as I'll tell you when you ride off tomorrow, then I swear by my father's soul you can have my head if you don't enjoy yourselves! Not another word – hands up, everyone!"

It did not take us long to make up our minds. We saw no point in deliberating, but agreed to his proposal without further argument and asked him to give what commands he liked.

"Ladies and gentlemen," began the Host, "do yourselves a good turn and listen to what I say, and please don't turn up your noses at it. This is the point in a nutshell: each of you, to make the road seem shorter, shall tell two stories on the journey – I mean two on the way to Canterbury and two others on the way home – tales of once upon a time. Whoever tells his story best – that's to say whoever spins the most edifying and amusing tale – is to be given a dinner at the expense of the rest of us, here in this inn and under this roof, when we return from Canterbury. And just to make it the more fun for you I'll gladly ride with you myself at my own cost and be your guide. Anybody who gainsays my judgment shall pay all our expenses on the road! Now if you agree, let me know here and now without more ado, and make my arrangements early."

The matter was agreed; we gave our promises gladly, begging him to do as he proposed and be our leader, judge and arbiter of our tales, and arrange a dinner at a set price. We agreed to be ruled by his decision in every respect; thus we unanimously submitted ourselves to his judgment. Thereupon, more wine was fetched, and when we had drunk it we all went to bed without further delay.

Next morning our Host rose up at break of day, roused us all and gathered us together in a flock. We rode off at little more than a walking-pace until we came to the watering-place of Saint Thomas, where our Host reined his horse and said, "Attention, please, ladies and gentlemen! You know what you promised; remember? If you're of the same mind this morning as you were last night, then let's see who's to tell the first tale. Whoever rebels against my ruling must pay for everything we spend upon the road, or may I never drink another drop! Now let's draw lots before going further. Sir Knight," said he, "will your honor draw lots, for that is my decree. Come nearer, my lady Prioress, and you too, Master Scholar; lay aside that diffidence and come out of your brown study – all hands draw lots."

Upon this everybody began drawing lots, and in fine, whether by luck, or fate, or chance, the truth is that to everyone's delight the lot fell to the Knight. Now he must tell his tale, as was right and proper according to the bargain I've described. What more can I say? And when that good man saw how things were, he very sensibly obeyed the promise he had freely given and said, "Since I must begin the game, why, then, welcome be the luck of the draw, in God's name! Now let us ride on; and listen to what I say." With that we began to ride forward on our way, and at once he cheerfully began his tale, which went like this....

According to the narrator, at what time of year did people want to go on pilgrimage, and why? Does this band of pilgrims seem a particularly pious group of travelers? Consider how the narrator describes the clothing of the Monk: why does he focus on this subject? Where else had the Wife gone on pilgrimage, and what sort of person does she seem to be? How does the narrator describe the Pardoner and his relics? How might this presentation of the pilgrims bound for Canterbury suggest a broader critique of the cult of saints, indulgences, and pilgrimage?

67. MARGERY KEMPE'S PILGRIMAGE TO JERUSALEM

Englishwoman Margery Kempe (ca 1373–1440) was one of the most famous female mystics of the later Middle Ages, known for her claims to experience intimate, highly emotional visions of Jesus Christ and the Virgin Mary that provoked an ecstatic state and uncontrollable weeping. In 1414, she set out on a pilgrimage that would eventually include Assisi, Rome, Compostela, and Jerusalem, among other locations. Margery later dictated her life-story to her confessor and adviser, who wrote The Book of Margery Kempe *in Middle English, the first such autobiographical work of its kind in that language. The selection below starts with Margery's departure from Venice for Jerusalem. By this point, her traveling companions, irritated by her eccentric behavior, had tired of her company.*

Source: modernized by J. Shinners, in *Medieval Popular Religion 1000-1500*, ed. J. Shinners, 2nd ed. (Peterborough, ON: Broadview Press, 2007), pp. 204–10, from *The Book of Margery Kempe*, ed. S.B. Meech and H.E. Allen, Early English Text Society, vol. 212 (Oxford: Oxford University Press, 1940), pp. 66–75.

28. Also this company [of pilgrims], which had forbidden the aforesaid creature to eat at the same table with them, hired a ship for them to sail in [to Jerusalem]. They bought containers for their wine and ordered bedding for themselves but nothing for her. Seeing their unkindness, she went to the same man they did and purchased bedding as they had done. She went to where they were and showed them what she had done, proposing that she sail with them in the ship they had hired. Then, while this creature was in contemplation, our Lord warned her mentally that she should not sail in that ship; he assigned her another ship, a galley, to sail in. She told this to some of the company and they told it to the rest of the band, who then dared not sail in the ship they had hired. So they sold the vessels they had bought for their wine and wanted to travel in the galley where she was. Though it was against her will, she departed accompanied by them, for they dared not do otherwise.

When it was time to make her bed, they had locked up her bed linens and a priest in their company took a sheet from the creature, saying it was his. She took God as her witness that it was her sheet. Then the priest swore a great oath by the book in his hand that she was as false as she could be, and scorned her, and thoroughly rebuked her. So she suffered very much tribulation until she came to Jerusalem. Before she arrived there, she said to them that she supposed they were annoyed with her: "I pray you, sirs, be in charity with me, for I am in charity with you, and forgive me that I have annoyed you along the way. And if any of you has trespassed against me in any way, may God forgive you as I do." And so they went forth into the Holy Land until they could see Jerusalem.

And when, riding on an ass, this creature saw Jerusalem, she thanked God with all her heart, praying to him for his mercy that, as he had brought her to see this earthly Jerusalem, he would grant her the grace to see the blissful city of Jerusalem above, the city of heaven. Our Lord Jesus Christ, answering her thought, granted her desire. Then, out of the joy she had and the sweetness she felt from her conversation with our Lord, she was on the point of falling off her ass, for she could not bear the sweetness and the grace God wrought in her soul. Then two German pilgrims, one of them a priest, went up to her and kept her from falling off. The priest put spices in her mouth to comfort her, thinking that she was sick. And so they helped her on the way to Jerusalem.

When she arrived there she said, "Sirs, I ask you not to be displeased if I weep terribly in this holy place where our Lord Jesus Christ lived and died." Then they went to the Temple [the church of Holy Sepulcher] in Jerusalem and were let in late in the day at evensong and stayed there until the next day at evensong. Then the [custodian Franciscan] friars lifted up a cross and led the pilgrims around from one place to another where our Lord had suffered his pains and his passion, all the men and women carrying candles in their hands. As they went about, the friars always told them what our Lord had suffered in each place. The aforesaid creature wept and sobbed copiously as though she was seeing our Lord with her own eyes suffering his passion right there. Through contemplation, in her soul she truly saw him, which caused her to suffer with him.

When they came to Mount Calvary, she fell down unable to stand or kneel, but she wallowed and writhed with her body, spreading her arms wide and crying with a loud voice as though her heart would burst asunder – for in the city of her soul she saw truly and freshly how our Lord was crucified. Before her face she heard and saw with her spiritual vision the mourning of our Lady, Saint John, Mary Magdalene, and many others who loved our Lord. She had such great compassion and such great pain to see our Lord's pain that she could not keep herself from crying and howling even if it killed her.

This was the first time that she ever cried during contemplation, and that kind of crying lasted many years afterwards no matter what anyone might do. Thus, she suffered much scorn and reproof. Her crying was so loud and so awful that it astonished people unless they had heard it before or else knew its cause. She had [these crying spells] so often that they left her quite weak physically, especially if she heard [stories] of our Lord's passion. Sometimes when she saw the crucifix, or if she saw a wounded man or beast, or if a man beat a child in front of her or hit a horse or other animal with a whip – whether in the field or in town, alone or among people – when she saw or heard it, she thought she saw our Lord being beaten or wounded like the man or the animal. When she first had her crying spells in Jerusalem she had them often, and in Rome too. After she came home to England, when she first arrived they seldom happened – once a month as it were; then, once a week; later, daily; and once she had fourteen in one day, and another day she had seven. And so God would visit her, sometimes in the church, sometimes in the street, sometimes in her room, sometimes in the field God would send them. For she never knew the time or hour when they would come....

She had such intense contemplation in her mind's eye [on Mount Calvary], it was as if Christ were hanging before her eyes in his manhood. When, through the dispensation of the high mercy of our sovereign savior Christ Jesus, it was granted this creature to behold so realistically his precious, tender body altogether rent and torn with scourges, more full of wounds than ever was a dovecote full of holes, hanging upon the cross with the crown of thorns upon his head, his blessed hands, his tender feet nailed to the hare tree, the rivers of blood flowing copiously out of every member, the grisly and grievous wound in his precious side shedding out blood and water for her love and salvation, then she fell down and cried with loud voice, wondrously turning and twisting her body on every side, spreading her arms wide as if she would have died, and could not keep from crying – these physical movements done for the fire of love that burned so fervently in her soul with pure pity and compassion.

It is no marvel if this creature cried and showed an astonishing demeanor and expression when we may see each day men and women – some through loss of their worldly goods, some for affection for their kinfolk or for worldly friendships, through too much study or earthly affection, and most of all through inordinate love and physical affection – if their friends are parted from them, they will cry and howl and wring their hands as if they had lost their wits and minds, yet they know well enough that they displease God. And if someone counsels them to cease and desist their weeping or crying, they will say that they cannot: they loved their friend so much, and he was so gentle and kind to them that they cannot forget him. How much more would they weep, cry, and howl if their most beloved friends were taken with violence before their eyes, and with all kinds of reproof brought before a judge, wrongfully condemned to death – namely, so vicious a death as our merciful Lord suffered for our sake? How would they endure it? No doubt they would both cry and howl and avenge him if they could, or else men would say they were not friends. Alas, alas, how sad that the death of a creature which has often sinned and trespassed against its maker should be so disproportionately mourned and grieved over. It is an offense to God and a hindrance to the souls on either side [of this and the next world]. The piteous death of our savior, by which we are all restored to life, is not kept in the mind of us unworthy and unkind wretches, nor will we support our Lord's own confidants whom he has endowed with love. Instead, we detract them and hinder them as much as we can.

29. When this creature with her companions came to the grave where our Lord was buried, as soon as she entered that holy place she fell down with her candle in her hand as though she would die from grief. Afterwards she got up again with great weeping and sobbing, as though she had seen our Lord buried right before her. Then she thought she saw our Lady in her soul – how she mourned and wept over her son's death – and our Lady's sorrow became her sorrow.

So, overall, wherever the friars led them in that holy place, she always wept and sobbed wondrously, especially when she came to where our Lord was nailed to the cross. There she cried and wept without measure so that she could not restrain herself. Also, when they came to the marble stone on which our Lord was laid when he was taken down from the cross, she wept there with great compassion, mindful of our Lord's passion. Afterwards, she received communion on Mount Calvary, and then she wept, she sobbed, she cried so loudly that it was a wonder to hear it. She was so full of holy thoughts, meditations, and holy contemplations on the passion of our Lord Jesus Christ and the holy words that our Lord Jesus Christ spoke to her soul that she could never afterwards express them, so exalted and holy were they that our Lord showed this creature much grace during the three weeks she was in Jerusalem.

Another day, early in the morning, they went to the great hills [around Jerusalem], and the guides described where our Lord bore the cross on his back, and where his mother met with him and how she swooned, how she fell down and he fell down too. So they went around all morning before noon until they came to Mount Sion. All the while this creature wept abundantly everywhere she went out of compassion for our Lord's Passion. At Mount Sion is the place where our Lord washed his disciples' feet a little before he gave his Commandment to his disciples. Therefore, this creature had a great desire to receive communion in that holy place where our merciful Lord Jesus Christ first sacrificed his precious body in the form of bread and gave it to his disciples. And she did, with great devotion, with copious tears, and with noisy sobbing, for in this place plenary remission [of sins] is granted, as it is in four other places in the Temple. One is Mount Calvary; another, the grave where our Lord was buried; the third is the marble stone on which his precious body was laid when it was taken off the cross; the fourth is where the holy cross was buried – and in many other places in Jerusalem.

When this creature went inside the place where the apostles received the Holy Spirit, our Lord gave her great devotion. Afterwards she went to the place where our Lord was buried. As she kneeled on her knees while hearing two masses, our Lord Jesus Christ said to her: "You do not come here, daughter, out of need but for merit and reward; for your sins were forgiven you before you came here; and therefore you come here to increase your reward and your merit. I am well pleased with you, daughter, for you stand in obedience to holy church and you obey your confessor and follow his counsel, which, through the authority of the holy church, has cleansed you of your sins and dispensed you from going to Rome or to St-James [of Compostela] unless you yourself wish it. Nevertheless, I command you in the name of Jesus, daughter, to go visit these holy places and do as I ask you, for I am above holy church and I shall go with you and keep you well."

Then our Lady spoke to her soul in this manner, saying: "Daughter, you are well blessed, for my son Jesus shall pour so much grace into you that the whole world shall be in wonder of you. Do not be ashamed, my dear, worthy daughter, to receive the gifts that my son will give you, for I tell you truthfully that they will be great gifts that he will give you. Therefore, worthy daughter, do not be ashamed of him who is your God, your Lord, and your love any more than I was when I saw him hanging on the cross, my sweet son Jesus, to cry and weep for the pain of my son Jesus Christ. Nor was Mary Magdalene ashamed to cry and weep for my son's love. Therefore, daughter, if you partake in our joy you must partake in our sorrow." This creature heard these sweet words and conversations at our Lady's grave, and much more than she could ever recount.

Afterwards she rode on an ass to Bethlehem, and when she came to the church and to the crib where our Lord was born, she had much devotion and many words and conversations in her soul, and lofty spiritual comfort with much weeping and sobbing so that her companions would not let her eat with them and she ate her meal alone by herself. But then the Gray Friars [Franciscans] who led her from place to place took her in and had her sit with them at dinner so that she would not eat alone. One of the friars asked one of her companions if she was the Englishwoman who, they had heard it said, spoke with God. When she found out about this, she knew well that what our Lord had said to her before she left England was true: "Daughter, I shall make all the world wonder at you, and many men and many women shall speak of me out of love of you and honor me in you."

30. Another time this creature's companions wanted to go to the river Jordan and would not let her go with them. Then this creature prayed to our Lord Jesus Christ that she could go with them, and he ordered that she go with them whether they wanted her to or not. And then she set out by the grace of God and did not ask their permission. When she came to the river Jordan, the weather was so hot that she thought she would burn her feet due to the heat she felt. Later she went with her companions to Mount "Quarentine," where our Lord fasted for forty days. There she asked her companions to help her up the mount, but they said no, for they could barely help themselves. Then she was very sad since she couldn't go up the hill. Soon a Saracen [Muslim], a handsome man, happened to come by, and she put a groat [a silver coin worth four pennies] in his hands, making a sign to him to help her up the mount. The Saracen quickly took her under his arm and led her up onto the high mountain where our Lord fasted for forty days. Then she was very thirsty but got no comfort from her companions. But God, through his infinite goodness, moved the Gray Friars to compassion and they comforted her when her countrymen would not acknowledge her....

Later, when this creature came down the mount, as God willed, she went to the place where Saint John the Baptist was born. Afterwards she went to Bethany where Mary and Martha lived and to the grave where Lazarus was buried and raised to life. She also went to the chapel where our blessed Lord appeared to his blessed mother before anyone else on Easter Day at morning. She stood in the same place where Mary Magdalene stood when Christ said to her, "Mary, why do you weep?" She was in many more places than are written here because she was in Jerusalem and the country thereabout for three weeks; and she had great devotion for as long as she was in that country. The friars of the Temple gave her great cheer and gave her many great relics, desiring her to stay among them longer, if she wished, due to the faith they had in her. The Saracens, also, made much of her, and conveyed and led her around the country wherever she wanted to go. She found all the people good and gracious to her, except her own countrymen.

After she left Jerusalem and went to Ramla, she wished she had turned back to Jerusalem because of the great spiritual comfort she felt when she was there and in order to acquire more pardon for herself. Then our Lord commanded her to go to Rome and then home to England. He said to her: "Daughter, as often as you say or think 'Worshipped be all the holy places in Jerusalem that Christ suffered bitter pain and passion in,' you shall have the same pardon as if you were there physically, both for yourself and for all those that you wish to give it to."

How did Margery's fellow pilgrims treat her on the journey to Jerusalem? What sort of emotional and mystical experiences did she have at the holy sites in Jerusalem, including the church of the Holy Sepulcher? How did local Christians react to her? What about local Muslims? According to her revelation after leaving Jerusalem, did Margery need to be actually present in the earthly city to enjoy its spiritual benefits?

68. THE TRIBULATIONS OF BROTHER FELIX

Whatever criticisms some Europeans leveled at pilgrimage and the cult of saints, toward the close of the Middle Ages pilgrimage to Jerusalem continued to evoke a persistent sense of pious connection to the places associated with the Bible – and a continued awareness of the dangers posed by the journey. The following account of a pilgrimage to Jerusalem was written in 1484 by a Dominican preacher from Germany named Felix Fabri, whose account offers a remarkable level of personal information and sometimes comical details about his travels.

Source: abridged by M.-A. Stouck, in *Medieval Saints: A Reader*, ed. M.-A. Stouck (Peterborough, ON: Broadview Press, 1999), pp. 335–53, from the translation by A. Stewart, *The Wanderings of Felix Fabri, Part 1* (London: The Palestine Pilgrims' Text Society, 1887–97), pp. 7–47.

At the time of the celebration of Easter, in the year of our Lord 1480, on the ninth day of the month of April ... whereon also is celebrated the feast of the dedication of the church of the Dominicans in Ulm, on that same day after dinner, as is the custom, I ascended the pulpit, and preached to the people who were present in great numbers, both to hear the sermon and to obtain indulgences. When I had finished my sermon, before the general confession made by the people on such occasions, I told them all of the pilgrimage which I was on the point of beginning, bidding them, and beseeching them, to importune God with prayers for my safe return, at the present time to sing with me in gladness the hymn of the Lord's resurrection, which the people are wont to sing, together with the hymn for pilgrims by sea....

All the people then sang after me the hymns that I had begun with loud and pleasant voices, and repeated them many times over; nor did they refrain from tears, and some broke out into sobs instead of into song. For many persons of both sexes were anxious and alarmed, fearing, even as I myself feared, that I should perish among such terrible dangers. When the singing was over, I commended them to God by bestowing upon them the general absolution, and, strengthening them by the sign of the cross, I bade them farewell, and descended from the pulpit.

Now, on the fourteenth day of April, early in the morning, after I had received the blessing which is given to those who travel, and after I had kissed and embraced my brethren, we mounted our horses, I and the reverend master Ludwig, with a servant from the city of Ulm, and rode to Memmingen, where, according to my appointment, I met the Lord Apollinaris von Stein, with his son George, and with many men-at-arms; and straightway on the morrow we prepared to depart, and the noble youth bade farewell to his father and to all his retainers, and mounted his horse not without sorrow and fear. I also rushed into the arms of my most kind and beloved spiritual father, begging his leave to depart and his paternal blessing, not without deep grief and sorrow, as was shown by the abundant tears and sobs of us both; nor was there anything to wonder at in this, for the forced parting of son from his father, and of a true man from his sincere friend, is naturally grievous. During my embraces and sobs I heard my most beloved father's last words of advice, that I was not to forget him in the Holy Land, but that, should a messenger present himself, I was to send a letter from the sea telling how I was, and to be sure to return soon. And so he sorrowfully left me, and returned with his servant to Ulm to his children, my brethren. After my father's departure, a great and almost irresistible temptation assailed me, for the delightful eagerness to see Jerusalem and the holy places, with which I had until that time been glowing, altogether died within me, and I felt a loathing for travel; and the pilgrimage, which had appeared so sweet and virtuous, now seemed wearisome, bitter, useless, empty, and sinful. I was angry with myself for having undertaken it, and all those who had dissuaded me from it I now thought to be the wisest of counselors and the truest of friends; while I considered that those who had encouraged me were enemies of my life. I had more pleasure in beholding Swabia than the land of Canaan, and Ulm appeared to me pleasanter than Jerusalem. Moreover, the fear of the sea increased within me, and I conceived so many objections to that pilgrimage that, had I not been ashamed, I should have run after Master Ludwig and reentered Ulm with him, and I should have had the greatest delight in doing so. This accursed temptation remained present with me throughout the whole voyage, and was most troublesome to me, because it took away all the delight and joy and zeal wherewith a pilgrim supports his labors and is urged to persist in his work, and caused me to be dull and stupid both in viewing places of note by sea and land, and also in writing accounts of them. What I have written was done against the grain, but I sometimes succeeded in conquering my dullness by hard work.

So young Master George and I, with one servant whom he had chosen from his father's household, set forth from Memmingen, and in a few hours he began to make my acquaintance and I began to make his, and we and our several dispositions agreed very well together, which is a great comfort for those who are making that pilgrimage together. For if a man has a comrade with whom he cannot agree, woe betide them both during their pilgrimage. So thus we entered the Alps with joy as far as Innsbruck, and after leaving that place, rode hurriedly forward, in order that we might arrive the sooner at Venice.... At Mestre we bade the land farewell, and put to sea in a barque, wherein we sailed as far as Venice to the Fondaco de' Tedeschi. At the Fondaco itself we inquired about inns for knights and pilgrims, and were conducted by a certain German to the inn of St-George, which is a large and respectable one. There we found many noblemen from various countries, all of whom were bound by the same vow as ourselves, and intended to cross the sea and visit the most Holy Sepulcher of the Lord Jesus. There were also in the other inns many pilgrims, both priests, monks, and laymen, gentle and simple, from Germany, from Gaul, and France, and especially two bishops, my lord of Orléans and my lord of Le Mans, with a very large retinue of companions and attendants, were there, awaiting the sailing of a ship; and, moreover, certain women well-stricken in years, wealthy matrons, six in number, were there together with us, desiring to cross the sea to the holy places. I was astonished at the courage of these old women, who through old age were scarcely able to support their own weight, yet forgot their own frailty, and through love for the Holy Land joined themselves to young knights and underwent the labors of strong men.

The proud nobles, however, were not pleased at this, and thought that they would not embark in the ship in which these ladies were to go, considering it a disgrace that they should go to receive the honor of knighthood in company with old women. These haughty spirits all endeavored to persuade us not to take our passage in the ship in which the old women meant to sail; but other wiser and more conscientious knights contradicted those proud men, and rejoiced in the holy penitence of these ladies, hoping that their holiness would render our voyage safer. On account of this there arose an implacable quarrel between those noblemen, which lasted until it pleased God to remove those proud men from among us. However, those devout ladies remained in our company both in going thither and in returning.

Now, Master Augustine Contarini, whose name means "Count of the Ithine," a noble Venetian, was going to take a cargo of pilgrims, and we agreed with him about the fare, and hired his galley, and received from him berths and cots – that is, places for each of us to lie in the galley – and we hoped for a quick passage, for we had waited for many days while the galley was being fitted for sea. But when everything was ready and there was nothing left to be done but set sail, as we longed to do, there came a ship which brought the bad news that the emperor of the Turks, Mahomet the

Great, was besieging the island of Rhodes, with a great fleet by sea and a fully equipped army of horse and foot by land, and that the whole of the Aegean and Carpathian and Malean seas swarmed with Turks, and that it was impossible during this year to take pilgrims across to the Holy Land. It would not be easy for me to tell with what sorrow the pilgrims heard this news, and the troubles and discord and quarrels to which they gave rise among the pilgrims would weary me to tell of.... [Eventually the pilgrims obtain permission from the Venetian authorities to set sail for the Dalmatian coast.]

Now these contrary winds rose higher and higher, and for three days and nights we lay among these rocks, and whenever we put out, we were driven back again by the force of the wind, to the great discomfort of us all. However, this discomfort saved us; for when three days afterwards a fair wind blew out of that place, and we were making for the high sea, we met a Venetian war-galley, which as it passed us asked our officers if "anything had happened to us at sea yesterday or the day before." When we answered "Nothing, except foul winds which had driven us to shelter under the mountains," they answered, "Blessed be those winds which drove you into hiding-places. For if you had been on the open sea yesterday, you would have fallen in with an armed Turkish fleet, which is sailing to Apulia to plunder the Christians there." On hearing this, we praised God, who had for this time saved us from the hands of the Turks....

We thus arrived at a place where a city stands on a mountain overlooking the sea. It is well walled, but is entirely deserted on account of the breath of a dragon, as will be afterwards explained; and next, after a tedious voyage among lofty mountains, we came to a part of the sea, where the galley remained fixed on the surface of the waters, nor could it be moved by the oars to the right nor to the left; but, as I have said, it stood stock still, because beneath it was the whirlpool called the "abyss," or opening into the earth, which there sucks up a great part of the sea, and where the waters sink down into that abyss. Wherefore the waters stand still above it, awaiting their descent into the abyss; and when the sea in that region has not much water in it, the water is whirled round, and whatever swims upon it is in danger of being drawn down. And indeed ships would be swallowed up there if their steersmen did not avoid it. So in this place we stood still, and our sailors endeavored with loud cries and much labor to row the galley away from this gulf, but their labors were in vain. However, the people of Corcyra, when they saw this – for we were within sight of the island and city of Corcyra – came to our aid from Corcyra, or Corfu, with two small galleys. They made ropes fast to our galley, brought them to their own sterns, and then by rowing their own galleys they, with great force, dragged our galley out of the jaws of the abyss, lest the deep should swallow us up. Being thus saved, we proceeded to the island of Corcyra, and after sunset entered the harbor of the city, which was full of ships of war, because, as the lords of the Venetian Senate had told us, the captain of the sea was there with an armed fleet to keep the peace at sea. So we slept until morning. At daybreak we went ashore to the city in small boats, and found it full of people, and many Turks were walking about among the Christians. After hearing mass, we Swabian and Bavarian pilgrims hired a small cottage in the suburbs, and there cooked, ate, drank and slept. This cottage was small, and built of beams of very old and very dry wood: wherefore it happened, in consequence of the enormous fire which we made up for cooking, that the place twice actually caught fire; however, we always put out the fire, so that we did not get into any trouble about it. But the second time that this happened, the neighbors, seeing that the roof was on fire, ran together with clamor and lamentation, while we mounted the roof with ladders and took away the food of the flames.

On this occasion we were in no small danger, for if the fire had gathered strength the whole place would have been burned, and the Greek inhabitants of Corcyra would have sacrificed our lives to revenge themselves for the loss of their houses; indeed, they are very unfriendly to Germans, and are easily roused to attack them. After we had eaten, we respectfully presented the letter which we had received from the Venetian Senate to the captain of the sea, begging for his advice and assistance to further our pilgrimage. He, after reading it, advised us to return to Venice with our galley; but when he perceived that this advice was grievous, he said in a sort of rage, "What folly possesses you, that you should wish to expose yourselves to such risks both of body and soul, of life and property? Behold, the sea is covered with cruel Turks, from whose hands there is no chance of your escaping. Go back to Venice, or stay in some seaport, until better news comes. But if you are utterly determined to go to the East, you must manage your passage yourselves, for I will not permit the galley in which you came to sail thither, because she belongs to Saint Mark." When we heard this, we were much disturbed, and left his presence, asking for time to take counsel. Hereupon the minds of many, especially those of the two bishops, were so wrought upon by the words of the captain that they determined to return to Venice with all their retinue. Some even of our knights were fearful and ready to go back; but others were brave and unmoved. I joined these latter, and, as far as I was able, heartened and encouraged the timid ones by preaching to them and quoting such passages of holy scripture as might raise in them hopes of divine protection. It happened on one day, when I was absent, that my lords the knights of our company were talking about the perils of our pilgrimage, and some were for going on with it, while others were timid and held back. One of them said, "You ought not to pay any heed to the words of encouragement which

Brother Felix says to you. What is life or death to him? He is a professed monk, and has no property, no friends, no position in life, nor anything else in the world, as we have. It is easier for him to die quickly by the sword of a Turk or Saracen than to grow old in his convent, dying daily." And he said much more, trying to prevent the lords from listening to me. All this was told me, and I afterwards turned the tables by putting such courage into that same knight that he could not be persuaded into turning back. The captain kept us in Corcyra for eight days, and every day told us more and more frightful news; but we Germans had all agreed together that we would not go back, but that in the name of the Lord we would go on to Jerusalem. At last, when the captain saw that we were determined to carry out our intention, he left off interfering with our pilgrimage; and we made ready to start, removing ourselves into another galley, which we had bought. When all who wished to make this voyage were together on board of this galley, and we were joyfully talking to one another as we stood on deck beside the mast, one of the elders asked that silence should be made, and thus addressed us: "My lords and brother pilgrims, we are undertaking a great, difficult, and arduous matter in making this pilgrimage by sea. And I say to you of a truth that, humanly speaking, we are acting foolishly in exposing ourselves to so great a danger against the advice and persuasion of the captain of the sea, and of everyone else. Wherefore the lords, bishops and all the most noble, powerful, dignified, and perhaps the wisest of our company have given it up, and are on their way back to their own country, following the advice which has been given them, while we are setting out in the opposite direction. Now, therefore, so that our attempt may not be a mere act of sinful foolhardiness, we must needs reform our life on board of this galley, and must more frequently invoke the protection of almighty God and his saints, that we may be able to make our way through the hosts of our enemies and their fleet."

On hearing these words, we unanimously decided that no more games of cards or dice should be played on board of the galley, that no quarrels, oaths, or blasphemies should be allowed, and that the clerks and priests should add litanies to their usual daily prayers. Indeed, before this decree was made much disorder took place in these matters, for men were gambling morning noon, and night, especially the bishop of Orléans with his suite; and withal they swore most dreadfully, and quarreled daily, for the French and we Germans were always at blows. Thus it happened that one of the followers of the bishop of Orléans struck a devout priest of our company, and incurred excommunication. For the French are proud and passionate men; and, therefore, I believe that it was by an act of divine providence that they were separated from us, and our galley cleared of them; for we should scarcely have reached Jerusalem in their company without bloodshed and the murder of some of us. We stayed one night in Corcyra, sleeping on board ship; and that same night we had a terrible fright; for when it was late and had grown dark, as we still stood round the mast gossiping, we discovered a strange boat alongside of us, wherein were Turks, spies who were trying to listen to what we were saying. We at once betook ourselves to stones, which we hurled after them as they rowed away; however the boat straightway glided away out to sea and escaped. Next morning our trumpeters blew their horns or trumpets to show that we were about to start, and we cast off the moorings of the galley, and with joy and singing turned our backs to the harbor. The other pilgrims who stayed behind stood on the quay and laughed at us, saying that we were desperate men. For it was the common talk in Corcyra that we should be taken before we came to Modon. So thus we passed out of sight of Corcyra, and went on our way in joy mixed with fear....

... Sailing along we sighted the Holy Land on the third day, and out of the joy of our hearts we sang "Te Deum Laudamus" [We praise you, O God] with loud voices, and directed our prow towards Joppa, commonly called Jaffa, and came to an anchor off the rock of Andromeda. Here the master straightway sent a slave to run to Jerusalem and announce our arrival to the father warden of Mount Sion that he might come with his brethren and with asses and their drivers to bring us to Jerusalem. So we abode in our galley for seven days, waiting for our guides, after which we were landed in small boats, and lodged in very old vaulted rooms, which were both ruinous and foul-smelling, wherein we remained for one night only; after this, we mounted the asses which had been brought for us, and thus, escorted by Saracens, we left the sea and came to the town of Ramla, wherein we abode for some days, and then entered Jerusalem, where we were taken, not to a hospice, but to a house in Millo, wherein we ate, slept, and so forth.

We did not spend more than nine days in the Holy Land, during which we went the round of all the usual holy places in a great hurry, working day and night at the accomplishment of our pilgrimage, so that we were hardly given any time for rest. Having perfunctorily visited the holy places, and after my Master George von Stein and the other nobles had received knighthood in the church of the Holy Sepulcher, our guides brought us out of the holy city along the road by which we came down to the sea, where our galley lay at anchor. None of the pilgrims remained in Jerusalem save two Englishmen, who wished to go across the desert to St-Catherine's [on Mount Sinai], with whom I would willingly have stayed had they known either the German or Latin tongue, but as I could not talk with them their company would have been valueless to me; nevertheless, in spite of all these difficulties, I would have stayed in Jerusalem with them, and would have endured the want of a common language with patience, had I not firmly determined that I would return again to Jerusalem. For from that hour when our time came to leave the holy city, I determined and vowed that I would return as speedily as possible, and I regarded this pilgrimage as merely the preamble to that which I intended to make. As a student who means to commit some passage to memory first reads it over carelessly, and then reads it again slowly and leisurely, taking sufficient time to impress it on his mind, so I did with regard to my determination; and I was far from being satisfied with what I saw, nor did I commit the things which I saw to memory, but kept them for a future pilgrimage.

[Felix and his companions set out on their return journey, experiencing more tribulations....] What miseries and hardships we had undergone since we left the harbor of Joppa in the Holy Land until we reached this place [the island of Rhodes], I am not able to tell. During those days of suffering I often wondered how any man can be so luxurious as to be troubled well nigh throughout the year by the thought of the forty days' fast of Lent and the bread-and-water fast on Good Friday.... Nay, what seems even more strange to those who have not experienced such a voyage, and more piteous to those who have, we were in such a state of want and wretchedness that even putrid, stinking water was precious, and the captain and all the ship's officers were in great anxiety lest we should run out of even such water as that. The captain, therefore, gave orders that the steward should no longer give drinking-water of this sort to the animals which were kept on board to be slaughtered for food, but that it should be kept for the human beings, because it was more cruel that they should die of thirst than the brutes. So there the sheep, goats, mules, and pigs, stood for several days without water perishing of thirst. During those days I often saw these creatures licking the planks and the spars, sucking off them the dew which had gathered in the night. And although we had an infinite expanse of waters all around us, yet sea water is not drinkable either for man or beast, for to drink that water kills a man or a beast instead of refreshing him. I do not tell you of the stale bread, the biscuit full of worms, the tainted meat, and the abominable cookery, with all of which we should have been content if we had had wholesome water in good measure, if not for the sound men, at least for the unhappy sick ones. Oftentimes I have suffered so dreadfully from thirst and have had such a longing for cool water that I have thought that, when I got back to Ulm, I would go up straightway to Blaubüren and sit down beside the lake which rises there out of the depths until I had satiated my desire. There was no lack of wine in the galley – indeed, one could easily obtain it in abundance and very good – but we took no pleasure in it without mixing it with water, because of its strength and lukewarmness. So much for this matter....

On the morrow, before we had risen, there came some of the lords of

Rhodes to us to examine the galley and to see the pilgrims. We rowed into the city with them, passing through the bodies of dead Turks cast up by the sea [from a recent naval battle], wherewith the shore was covered. When we entered the city we found it terribly ruined, full of stone cannon-balls, great and small, which the Turks had fired into it, of which there were said to be eight thousand and one scattered about the streets and lanes. The walls and towers were sadly ruinous, and we saw many other things, of which I will tell you when I come to this place again in my second pilgrimage. We remained at Rhodes four days, and spent a great deal of money, for everything was exceedingly dear because the Turks had plundered and laid waste the island. I bought two fowls for my master George for a ducat, because he was in weak health, as I myself was likewise, for I was at that time suffering from dysentery, and almost despaired of my life. At last the time came when we had to leave Rhodes, and there embarked with us on board of our galley some of the Knights of Saint John, and some who had for a long time been captives among the Turks, who had been sent to Rhodes with the Turkish army, and had deserted to that city during the siege. We also carried with us some Jews who had fought bravely during the siege. Among those who had escaped from captivity among the Turks was an Austrian nobleman, whom we found in a miserable condition, and whom my master George took under his protection and brought back to Germany. By the embarking of so many people our galley became crowded and uncomfortable, and during our voyage we were driven hither and thither by contrary winds, and suffered much want before we reached a harbor in Crete. When we arrived there we entered the city of Crete [Candia], and stayed there for a few days, after which we went on board the galley one day late in the evening, bringing our purchases with us, and intending to sail the same night. When day broke and the galley was loosed from the mooring-posts, as they were violently directing the head towards the wind, the helm or rudder struck upon the rocks and broke under water; and the ship was within a little of striking the beak-head upon the rocks which ran out from the shore, in which case the whole galley would have broken up and we should have perished.

Therefore, a loud shout was raised, and people came running from the city to help us. As the rudder was broken we could not sail, but brought back our galley into the harbor to the place where she lay before. Here a waterman made arrangements for the repair of our rudder, which he did as follows, while we looked on. He stripped to his drawers, and then taking with him a hammer, nails, and pincers, let himself down into the sea, sank down to where the rudder was broken, and there worked under water, pulling out nails and knocking in others. After a long time, when he had put everything right, he reappeared from the depths, and climbed up the side of the galley to where we stood. This we saw; but how that workman could breathe under water, and how he could strike with his hammer there, and how he could remain so long in the salt water, I cannot understand. But this much I know, that the human mind has dominion over fire and water, even as the stars have dominion over the human mind. When our rudder was mended and we were thinking of getting away, there rose a contrary wind, so that the galley could not so much as get out of the harbor; so we returned to our former lodgings in the city, and ate and drank there.

This is one of the best and richest of sea-ports, and is full of all manner of good things; the specialty of the place, however, is the Cretan wine, which we call Malvoisie, which is renowned throughout the world, and everything is cheap there. So we did not mind staying there, but enjoyed it. When about the time of vespers we were called on board the galley, some came soon and others late. I myself was one of the first on board, and stood on the poop of the galley to watch whether any strangers besides those who had joined us at Cyprus or Rhodes would come on board; and there came two Greek bishops, with many others. As for what other things I saw there I would not write them down if I wished these "wanderings" to be a grave narrative; but, as I promised my brethren in my epistle dedicatory, I often mix fun and amusement with serious matters. So while I was standing there watching those who were coming on board, I saw many of our pilgrims standing by the sea-side on the edge of the quay, with their heads dizzy, and afraid to come down into the boats, for the Cretan wine, which is sweet and pleasant to drink, makes the head dizzy when drunk in large quantities. Now, there were stone steps on the shore leading up to the city wall, down which those who wished to come on board the galley had to walk, and get into a small boat, in which they were brought alongside of the galley, and then again they had to get out of the boat and climb up some more steps into the galley. That evening many of them found it so difficult to do this that they had to be carried from the steps down the city wall into the boat, and from the boat into the galley, and right into their berths. Among the rest there came a pilgrim, who was the servant of some grandees in that city, and who was carrying his masters' baggage, together with some flasks of wine and a bag full of new bread, so that he was bowed down by his burden, besides being far gone in drink. When he came upon the steps and began to walk down them to the waterside to reach a boat there, he suddenly pitched headlong into the deep sea with all that he was carrying. At the cry which was raised by the bystanders, boatmen straightway rowed their skiffs to the place where he fell in, and, as he rose, dragged him out; but the loaves of bread and all that he was carrying floated over him, and were all utterly ruined.

There was a pilgrim, a Dalmatian priest, whom I knew very well, who also had drunk too much sweet wine, so that he had much trouble to get onboard the galley as far as the mast, where he stood talking to another Dalmatian until dark. He stood near a hatchway, through which people do not go below by night, but only in the daytime, for as soon as night comes on the ladder is taken down, so that those who sleep on that side of the ship may not be disturbed by people coming and going. So when this good pilgrim had finished his talk, and we on the lower deck were all lying in our beds gossiping, he wished to get into his berth through the nearest hatchway, and, being unsteady on his legs, he fell down through the hatchway on to the lower deck with such a crash that his fall shook the whole galley, for he was a big fat man. We all lay silent and terrified, and waited to hear who it was that had fallen. He straightway arose unhurt, and angrily began in a stammering voice, "There now! I had the ladder under my feet, and had come down three steps, when somebody pulled it from under my feet, and I fell down." To this someone answered that the ladder had been taken down an hour before, but he replied, "That is not true, because I had come down three steps, and while I was standing on the third step it was pulled away from me." On hearing this we all burst out laughing, as we knew that the ladder had been taken away an hour before, and I, being glad that my friend had not been hurt by so high and dangerous a fall, laughed most immoderately. When he heard me laughing he was furiously angry with me. "So," said he, "now I see clearly that it was you, Brother Felix, who pulled the ladder from under me. You shall assuredly not leave this galley before I have my revenge upon you!" When I tried to clear myself he became all the more angry, and cursed me, swearing that on the morrow he would take vengeance on me. However, the sleep which followed cured all these sick and dizzy men who had been the worse for Cretan wine, and on the morrow they had forgotten all about this. But if that pilgrim had suffered that fall sober, without being in liquor, he would very likely have broken his legs or his neck, for it commonly happens that in dangerous feats drunken men are more lucky, though not wiser, than others....

[After leaving Corfu, the ship encounters a storm.]

... Meanwhile the pilgrims and those who were useless at this work [of sailing the ship during the storm] prayed to God and called upon the saints. Some made their confessions as though already at the very point of death; some made great vows that they would travel from hence to Rome, to St-James [at Compostela] or to the house of the Blessed Virgin [at Loretto], if only they might escape from this death; for it is only when death is present before our eyes that we fear it. I thought of the aphorisms of Anacharsis the philosopher, who said that those who are at sea cannot be counted among either the living or the dead. Moreover, he said that they were only removed from death by the space of four fingers, four fingers being the thickness of the sides of a ship. Also, when asked which ships were the safest, he replied: "Those which lie on dry ground, and not in the sea," declaring that there was no safety at sea, because of its numerous and sudden perils. In the course of this terrible storm, lo! of a sudden there came an unhoped-for help from heaven. Amid the flashing of the lightning there appeared a light which stood fixed in the air above the prow for some time. Thence it slowly moved throughout the whole length of the galley as far as the stern, where it vanished. This light was a ray of fire about a cubit in width. As soon as the officers, the galley-slaves, and the other sailors, and such of the pilgrims as were on deck, saw this light, they all left off working, ceased their noise and shouting, and kneeling down with their hands raised to heaven, cried out in a low voice nothing except "holy, holy, holy." We who were below, not knowing what was happening, were scared at the sudden quiet and silence, and the unwonted prayer. We imagined that they had given up working in despair, and were crying "holy" because they were on the point of death, and we stood astonished, waiting to see what should be the end of this. So someone opened a door which covered the main hatchway of the galley, through which men come down from the deck into the cabin, and called to us in Italian, saying: "O, Signori pellegrini, non habeate paura que questa note non avereto fortuna," which is, being interpreted: "Pilgrims, my masters, fear not, for this night and in this storm we shall suffer no evil, for we have received help from heaven." After this, as the storm continued, the galley-slaves returned to their accustomed labors, and now they no longer howled as before, but worked with joyous shouts; for they never work without shouting. Let no man suppose that what I have told about the light is false, for it is as true as possible, and I could prove it by the oaths of more than two hundred witnesses who are alive at this day; for the arm of the Lord is not shortened that he should be unable to save those who are in distress.... At last we reached the city of Venice and broke up our company, every man going to his own home. [From Venice, Felix begins his return journey to Ulm, experiencing more dangers and hardships.]

... On the following day, which was the feast of Saint Othmar [25 October], I traveled from Memmingen to Ulm in company with a priest. On entering my convent I was gladly and kindly received, and so I betook me to my wonted labors in my cell. I may say with truth that this first pilgrimage of mine was a hundredfold more toilsome and grievous to me than my second one, and much more dangerous both by sea and by land. Our company of pilgrims during my first pilgrimage was more disorderly, for there were among them many very passionate men, and there were daily quarrels, and some thievish Picards, and some were always sick; indeed, in every way this my first journey was much more grievous, albeit my second journey was much more toilsome, more distant, more expensive, and more dangerous; yet I endured more and more deadly perils on my first journey than I did on my second. By this all men may see clearly how untrue is the common saying, that the pilgrimage by sea from Venice to the Holy Land is a mere pleasant excursion with little or no danger. O my God, what a hard and tedious excursion: with how many sufferings was it spoiled. During this excursion I saw many vigorous young noblemen perish, who once had thought in their own conceit that they could rule the waves of the sea and weigh the lofty mountains in scales; but who at last died by the just judgment of God, broken down by hard ships and lamentably humbled in spirit. May God give those who call this pilgrimage an easy excursion the power of feeling its sorrows that they may learn to have the compassion for pilgrims to the Holy Land which they deserve. It requires courage and audacity to attempt this pilgrimage. That many are prompted to it by sinful rashness and idle curiosity cannot be doubted; but to reach the holy places and to return to one's home active and well is the special gift of God. Here ends Brother Felix Fabri's first wandering to the Holy Land.

Why did Felix start to regret his pilgrimage before he set out? What sort of other Christian pilgrims did he encounter at Venice? What problems or threats did he experience because of the Turkish forces in the eastern Mediterranean? What are some of the ways in which he and his companions tried to assure the success of their journey? What trials did he and his companions experience during their return voyage? Does it seem like his account would encourage or discourage other Christians from going on pilgrimage to Jerusalem?

69. THE PILGRIMAGE OF ARNOLD VON HARFF

From 1496 to 1499, a wealthy German nobleman from Cologne named Arnold von Harff traveled widely from Germany to Egypt, Jerusalem, and Constantinople, and eventually back to Europe, visiting Compostela in Spain before returning home. He also claimed to have journeyed to central Africa (as far as the headwaters of the Nile), India, and Madagascar, although scholars doubt that he actually reached those places, which he might have known about from other travel writers. The sections below from the account of his journeys, originally written in German, describe his time in the Sinai desert and at Jerusalem. During his visit to the holy sites, Arnold paid particular attention to the number of indulgences that a pilgrim received for visiting them, illustrating how deeply ingrained and widespread this penitential practice had become in the Christian religious culture of the late Middle Ages.

Source: trans. M. Letts, in *The Pilgrimage of Arnold von Harff*, Works Issued by the Hakluyt Society, 2nd series, vol. 94 (1946; Liechtenstein: Kraus Reprints, 1967), pp. 136–48, 185–86, 192–94, 197–205; revised.

We started from Cairo the first day of the new moon in July with a large caravan, which is a company of three or four hundred people, who set out together each month at the new moon to the Red Sea, to a place called Thor, three and a half days' journey from St-Catherine's, and fetch from there the spices which arrive from Lesser India called Abyssinia. These are carried on camels through the deserts of Arabia to Cairo. With us went the embassy of the great lord from India, so that we were some five hundred strong. We traveled the first day through the wilderness of Arabia, south-east across a level sandy district called Koass, where no leaf or grass grows, and there is no water. Here we stopped for the night in the sand, and fed on what we had with us. The next day, two hours before dawn, we crossed a sandy district called Maffra. On the way some 600 Arabs descended on us with intent to rob us. These are rough, blackish, hard people. They have no houses except tents, which they carry always with them in the desert, together with their camels, asses, sheep, goats, wives and children. They have beautiful little horses, which have to lie down daily in the hot sand, and they ride with bare legs and feet in the stirrups. They carry in their hands a javelin, which is a long, hollow tube having a long iron point, and ride in this manner.

From Cairo to St-Catherine's monastery there is nothing but desert, in which no human being can live on account of the great heat of the sun. We found no village or town there, neither house nor dwelling, neither field nor garden, tree or grass, nothing but barren, sandy earth burnt by the great heat of the sun, and many arid mountains and valleys, which were dreadful to see. We saw often in the wilderness a great smoke rising, which we thought came from fire, but as we approached we saw that it was a cloud of light sand raised by the wind and driven here and there from one place to another, which in a short time became high hills. Where today there was an open way, tomorrow there would be a great hill of light sand, driven by the wind into a heap.

On the third day we proceeded through the wilderness until, at mid-day, we came to the Red Sea to a ruined house. By this there was a well, but it was salty. Here we took our wineskins or goat-skins and filled them once more with water, and rode that evening to a stony place called Hanadam, where we spent the night lying in the sand. By this time we had eaten all our biscuit, which is twice-baked bread, except what had been asked for by the wild Arabs or stolen or given to them. We had with us large bowls in which we placed meal, pouring on it the stinking water from the goat-skins, kneading it together with our hands and making cakes from it. Then we placed them on camels' dung, which we had gathered together, and lit it in the ashes and hot sand, so that the cakes were soon cooked. This was our food, and foul, stinking water from the goat-skins was our drink.

The fourth, fifth, and sixth days we continued through a stony wilderness, with the Red Sea on the left hand, and came to rest in the evening in a place where two ways part, one on the right, and the other on the left to the monastery of St-Catherine. In these three days there died many heathen, wild Arabs, and camels through suffocation by the great heat. To my grief there died also two brothers from the great heat and lack of water, whom we had to leave half-alive lying in the sand, which was most pitiful to see. For the caravan, that is the assembly of many sects of the people who travel together, elect one to be leader and head-man and obey him. He knows how to find each night a camp in the desert, where on the third, fourth and fifth days water can be obtained. If anyone is ill, or from weakness is unable to go on and prefers to die, then the company has to leave him lying alone, and press on on account of the water, which lasts only one day, otherwise all would die, as well as the camels, for lack of water. If in a caravan of 100 persons 99 die, the one left must press on each day to the water, otherwise he would die as well. We came across each day many dead persons and camels lying exposed in the sand, all suffocated by the great heat of the sun: in truth more than 50 persons and some 600 camels were lying there, which was terrible to see. One had lost his nose, mouth, or eyes from wild birds and animals, another a leg, others an arm and some had been devoured. When the wild Arabs saw them from a long way off they raced forward, as for a wager, to see who could reach them first, to see whether there was any money, pushing and pulling the bodies this way and that, but leaving them there, without pity, unburied....

When we arrived at the monastery of St-Catherine the brothers came to meet us and received us very well, and rejoiced that they could see once again Christians from our country. They told us that for the last ten years no Christian pilgrim had been there from Latin countries. The monastery lies on a high mountain, nevertheless in a kind of valley between very high rocks. When one stands in the monastery and looks upwards it seems as if the mountains round about would fall on it. It is a very small but strong monastery, surrounded by a high four-square wall, with towers, on account of the wild Arabs who threaten it daily. For this reason they have no large gates in the monastery, but only three small and low doors covered with iron plates, one in front of the other, so that one has to creep through. In this monastery the monks are from Greece. They are called *coleuri* and are clad in a long grey cloak and a black embroidered scapular in front, and follow Saint Basil's rule. They live very poorly, as all round them is desert. All the bread which they eat has to be brought on camels from Cairo, with rice and peas which they make into a mess. That is their food, and they drink water with it. They have also in front of their monastery in a garden certain sweet fruits, which they enjoy in their season. They also eat and live on manna, which is heavenly dew. This falls each year in August and September, with a dew in the high mountains round about, some six miles away from the monastery, and nowhere else on earth, so far as I have ascertained. The dew runs off the rocks and forms a heap, and resembles newly made wax: it is very sweet to the taste and melts in the mouth like sugar. These monks never taste meat, and live a poor godforsaken life, for they have no fixed income, except what the Christians, Greeks and *centuriani* give them for the love of God. The old king Louis of France used to send them each year 2,000 ducats, which King Charles keeps back. There are therefore now no more than 8 brothers, but in King Louis' time there were some 200. These brothers have all long beards and go about in this manner.

In this monastery there is a fine church, roofed with lead, and one goes up twelve steps to the church. Below it is paved with exquisite little marble-stones joined together, adorned with ancient histories. In this church there hang countless burning lamps fed with nothing but olive oil. There are also in this church 12 stone pillars, 6 on each side, in which are enclosed many relics; they are hung with the names and painted pictures of many holy martyrs, whose names are not known to us. Each month the brothers honor one of these pillars on account of the relics, so that each year one of the pillars is honored each month. They have their altars in our manner, and the high altar is dedicated to the emperor Constantine and Saint Helena, his mother, and to the right of the high altar, beneath an arch, a man's height from the ground, is a small marble coffin three spans and about three fingers long and one and a half broad, with a cover which is carved with pictures. The coffin is about two spans high. In this coffin there lies, at the top, the true head of the virgin Saint Catherine and certain limbs of her holy body laid together, which the chief guardian, with a stately procession of the brothers, lifted up and allowed us to kiss and touch with our jewels. In addition he gave us some of the cotton which lay by the holy limbs, which had a fragrant smell beyond measure. At this coffin is plenary indulgence and forgiveness of all sins, both penalty and guilt. To the right of the coffin, one goes into a chapel which is dedicated to Saint John the Baptist, wherein are many relics of 40 holy brothers. Here are seven years' indulgence and seven quarantines [a quarantine is a form of indulgence equaling 40 days of penance]. On the left of this chapel one goes into another chapel behind the high altar, called the chapel of Saint Marie de Rubro. Here one enters with uncovered head and bare feet, for where the altar stands was formerly the burning bush which was not consumed, from which God spoke to Moses and bade him take off his shoes. Here is plenary indulgence from penalty and guilt. On the left hand one goes out of this chapel into another, which is dedicated to the apostle Saint James the less. Here are seven years' indulgence and seven quarantines. Beyond this, on the left, is a chapel to Saint Antipitus. Here are seven years' indulgence and seven quarantines. Close by is a chapel in honor of Saint Herine, a virgin. Here are seven years' indulgence and as many quarantines. Item on the right hand is a chapel in honor of Saint Marine, the virgin. Here are seven years' indulgence and as many quarantines. Close by is a chapel to Saint Salvatoir, where are also seven years' indulgence and as many quarantines. Close by is a chapel in honor of our blessed Lady, where are seven years' indulgence and as many quarantines.

In this monastery is a mosque, that is, a heathen church, wherein sometimes the heathen come to pray when they make their pilgrimage in their own manner to the holy places, since Moses performed many miracles there. In this monastery, behind the high altar, is a pleasant spring, by which Moses often herded and pastured his sheep and set and planted there many rare trees, one of which still bears rare fruit. Outside the monastery, as one leaves it on the right hand to the north, is a spring by which the Jews set up the calf and prayed and danced round it, and forgot the commandment of Moses, which, when Moses descended from Mount Oreb and saw, he was wrath and cast down the tablet of the Ten Commandments against a rock, so that it broke. The rock stands hard by this spring. Not far from hence the monks have a pleasant garden in which are many rare fruits. In it is a spring which Moses cursed on account of their idolatry, so that whosoever should drink from it should die. Not far from this monastery is the brothers' churchyard. In this, as is recorded in the monastery, the brothers have been buried from the commencement of the order, and more than 9,000 are buried there....

[After traveling to various spots around St-Catherine's, Arnulf and his companions set out for Gaza.] ... we traveled through the deserts where we found neither leaf, grass, nor men dwelling there. But we saw there much wild scrub, whereon were cotton trees with great pods hanging, on which the wild Arabs support themselves, picking them in great clusters. Inside is curled up a hard thing, like a dead worm, which they extract with great care and labor, after which they prepare it and sell it in great heaps in our country, but it comes first to land at Venice. At Gazera [Gaza] we left the deserts at a customs house where we had to pay tribute, and there begins the Promised

Land. Here the Mameluks [former slaves and converts to Islam, forming the ruling dynasty in the region] left us with their army and went on the left hand to Damascus, which was a great misfortune for us, for as soon as we came to Gazera the Armareyo, who is the governor of the town, a Mameluk, seized us and imprisoned us in irons with neck, hands, and feet for three weeks, without unlocking us in this manner.

What was the real reason we were treated like this, and what we had to suffer, and the things we were forced to do, and how God helped us, would be a wonderful history, and in some points what no Christian ought to suffer, but it would take too long to write, and therefore I leave it aside. But I would advise every pilgrim or merchant, who wishes to travel in heathen parts, not to refuse to pay duty, if so advised, by Christians, Jews or heathens, since one must pay courtesy or duty at every town or village: further to beware of associating with heathen women, also with Jews who live in those parts and know our tongue well, who deceive, betray and ruin us.

When God had helped us we traveled from Gazera to Hebron, two days' journey. The first day's journey was through a beautiful, flat, fruitful land, through many villages, and the next day through small, fruitful but stony mountains. Hebron lies by a mountain, a town without walls. Here live many good Christians of the Syrians who have their own church there. There is also in this town a fine mosque or heathen church, into which I was taken in the evening. We saw in it innumerable lamps burning and went below into a crypt, also full of hanging lamps, wherein the patriarchs Abraham, Isaac, Jacob and others lie buried in costly coffins. We were taken below Hebron southwards into a little valley where there was a hole in a stony mountain, which we entered. Here Adam lived first with Eve when they were driven out of Paradise. Close by, in a valley, was a reddish field from which God is said to have created Adam....

Half a mile further to Jerusalem, we went to lodge with the observant [franciscan] friars of Mount Sion, where they have a very fine monastery. They received us honorably and well, gave us our own room by the gates on the left hand, with a bed to lie on, and offered us good food to eat and wine to drink; such as we had not seen for a year and a half, for our sleeping had been on the hot sand under the blue sky, our food cakes baked in the hot sand, and our drink stinking water from goat-skins. In this monastery I found a German observant born in Saint Tron, who went with me daily to visit the holy places, and had the descriptions clearly written down for me. He applied first to the Armareyo, who is the chief ruler of the city of Jerusalem and a Mameluk, that is a renegade Christian, sent by the sultan, in order to obtain a free pass to enter Christ's Temple and to see all the places in and outside the city as I wished and as often as necessary – for ten ducats.

We visited first the holy places in the monastery of Mount Sion and climbed a little stair in their chapel to the high altar. This is the place where our Lord Jesus ate the Last Supper with his disciples on Holy Thursday. Here is absolution with forgiveness of all sins, both penalty and guilt. On the right hand of the high altar is an altar. This is the place where our Lord Jesus, after the Last Supper, washed his disciples' feet. Here are seven years' absolution and seven quarantines. We went further outside the chapel, on the right hand, to a chapel which is now walled up, since the heathen will not suffer us Christians to visit it, as David, Solomon and the other kings of Jerusalem are buried beneath it. But we looked through a window into the chapel. This is the place where our Lord, after he had risen, appeared to his blessed mother and the disciples in the burning fire. Here is forgiveness from penalty and guilt. We continued down a small stair to a little chapel, where is the place where Jesus Christ, after he had risen, appeared to his disciples behind closed doors. Here Saint Thomas thrust his finger in the blessed side of our Lord Jesus, when he would not believe and thereby believed. Here are seven years' absolution and seven quarantines.

In the evening, at four o'clock, we were told that they would open Christ's temple for us, so we hurried from Mount Sion westward from the monastery to Christ's Temple. On the way we visited also the holy places. As we left the monastery on the right hand, below the monastery, is a small heathen mosque or church, wherein David, Solomon, and other kings of Jerusalem are buried, which no Christian may enter, but with the help of my dragoman, a Mameluk, I was taken there. The graves are lofty and finely made, and are served daily with many lights and exquisite perfumes. Not far from this mosque is the place where the first martyr Saint Stephen was buried for the second time. Close by here is the summer house where the Easter Lamb was roasted for the disciples of Christ. Here also the water was heated with which Christ washed the feet of his disciples....

In this chapel of our blessed Lady [at the site of the Holy Sepulcher], where the high altar stands, is the place where Christ appeared first to his worthy Mother after he had risen. Here are seven years' absolution and seven quarantines. On the right hand of this altar in our blessed Lady's choir, is a grated window. Inside is a piece of the pillar at which Christ our Lord was scourged. The pillar is a span and about three fingers thick, and is four-and-a-half spans high. At this place is absolution with forgiveness of all sins from penalty and guilt. On the left hand of the high altar is an altar, which is the place where the holy cross stood for a long time, after the holy virgin Saint Helena found it, and above the altar, in a window, there is a piece of the holy cross. Here are seven years' absolution and seven quarantines. In the middle of this chapel, there is, on the ground, a white marble circle. This is the place where Saint Helena sought for the three crosses which were found together, but they did not know which was the cross of our Lord Jesus until they made trial with a dead woman, who was laid on the three crosses, but when she was laid on our Lord Jesus' cross, then forthwith she awoke from the dead. At this place there are seven years' absolution and seven quarantines.

We went next out of this chapel in procession to visit the holy places, each having a lighted candle in his hand. Close by this chapel, about four paces distant on the ground, are two round circles of white marble stones placed five paces from each other. The one circle is the place where our Lord Jesus appeared after he had risen to Saint Mary Magdalene in the form of a gardener. Mary Magdalene stood on the other circle, not daring to approach nearer to him. Here are seven years' absolution and seven quarantines. We went about and came to a little chapel hewn out of the rock. In it is an altar. This is the place where our Lord Jesus was kept a prisoner while they prepared the cross for him. At this place are seven years' absolution and seven quarantines. We came to a small chapel on the left hand. By the altar is the place where the Jews cast lots for our Lord's raiment. Here are seven years' absolution and seven quarantines. We went further to a door on the left hand. Here we descended a stone staircase thirty steps to a chapel called after Saint Helena. At the end, where the altar is, Saint Helena said her prayers daily. Beside the same altar on the right is a window. Here Saint Helena waited to watch the grave-diggers who sought the holy cross, which was found there. In this chapel are seven years' absolution and seven quarantines. We went down eleven stone steps to a little cave hewn out of the rock. In it, on the right hand, is a hole in the rock 22 feet long. Here were found the holy cross, the crosses of the two malefactors, the spear, the nails, and the crown of thorns, 307 years after Christ's birth. Here is forgiveness of all sins from penalty and guilt ....

In this small chapel, in front of the Holy Sepulcher, four lamps are always burning. One creeps next through a low narrow entrance into another small chapel. In this stands the holy sepulcher on the right hand of the chapel walls, surrounded with grey marble stones, three spans high from the pavement and eight feet long. This is also the length of the chapel. This chapel is also closed round about so that no light shines there, but above the holy sepulcher hang nine ampullae [containers with oil] with oil which burn continually. In this chapel I heard mass read on the holy sepulcher, and after mass I took communion. After this there came an old knightly brother, called Hans of Prussia, who dubs those pilgrims, who desired it, to be knights. He had ready by him a golden sword and two golden spurs, and asked me if I desired to be a knight. I said yes. He asked me if I was well-born and of noble parents.

I replied that I hoped so. He told me to place one foot and then the other on the Holy Sepulcher. Then he fixed on both the golden spurs and girded the sword on my left side, saying: "Draw the sword and kneel before the Holy Sepulcher. Take the sword in the left hand and place two fingers of the right hand on it, and say after me. 'As I, a noble knight, have traveled a long and distant way, and have suffered much pain and misfortune to seek honor in the holy land of Jerusalem, and have now reached the place of martyrdom of our Lord Jesus Christ and the Holy Sepulcher, in order that my sins may be forgiven, and I may live an upright life, so I desire to become here God's knight, and promise by my faith and honor to protect the widows, orphans, churches, monasteries, and the poor, and do no man injustice in his goods, money, friendship or kin, to help to right wrongs, and so bear myself as becomes an honorable knight, so help me God and the Holy Sepulcher.'" When I had repeated this, he took the sword from my hand and struck me with it on my back, saying "Arise, knight, in honor of the Holy Sepulcher and the knight Saint George." May God in heaven provide that I and the others of my companions, who are knights, or may be created knights, may never break their vows. Amen....

This temple of Christ [the church of the Holy Sepulcher] was first built by St. Helena, the holy virgin, and there are in it seven nations of Christians:

First the Latins, Who Are Now the Observants

The observants [observant Franciscan friars] possess the Holy Sepulcher. No one can say mass at the Holy Sepulcher without permission of the observants, and they keep three lighted ampullae above the Holy Sepulcher. They also keep in this temple the chapel to our blessed Lady, in which they have always three lamps burning, and behind this chapel the two brothers have their dwelling, where they eat and drink and sleep. They have also an altar on Mount Calvary, where they have perpetually three ampullae burning before the hole in which the holy cross stood. They have also an altar on which a lamp is always burning in Saint Helena's chapel, where the holy Cross was found. They have also a lighted lamp, which hangs above the place where the sacred body of our Lord was laid on the knees of his holy Mother.

Greeks

The Greeks possess the great choir in this temple, which they tend and maintain. They possess also the place in the chapel, which was a dungeon, in which our Lord Jesus was bound and kept while the holy cross was prepared.

Here they keep always an ampulla burning. They keep also a lamp burning in Saint Helena's chapel, where lots were cast for the clothes of·our Lord Jesus.

Georgians or Jorsy

The Georgians possess the cave in which the holy cross was found, also Mount Calvary which was given to them in recent years. They possess also the chapel beneath Mount Calvary, called the chapel of our blessed Lady and St. John.

Jacobites

The Jacobites possess a chapel with an altar behind the Holy Sepulcher. They possess also the place by the door, as one enters, where they carried the holy body of Christ and placed it on the knees of our blessed Lady, when it was taken down from the holy cross. There are eight ampullae burning always, of which they must light one.

Indians

The Indians or Abyssinians possess the altar, beneath which is the column on which Christ our Lord sat in Pilate's house, when they mocked him, spat on him and crowned him. This chapel they have to keep lighted. The Abyssinians have also their own chapel and dwelling, to the left of the Holy Sepulcher, between two columns of the temple.

Syrians

The Syrians possess Saint Helena's chapel, wherein they celebrate and have their dwelling in the temple, beside the Indians, and over against the Jacobites.

Armenians

The Armenians possess a raised chapel, to which one ascends by a staircase, beside the Indians, where they celebrate and have their dwelling.

When I had well seen all the places in the temple, as described above, and visited them, we were on the next day again shut out of the temple by the heathen. As we went then ten paces eastwards in front of the temple, we came to a place on the ground, on which a stone has been set as a sign that there Christ our Lord, while carrying the holy cross, sank down unconscious on the ground. Here are seven years' absolution and seven quarantines. We continued and returned to Mount Sion by another way, and came first to an old castle which could be made very strong. This was built in former times by the Pisans when they captured the city of Jerusalem [during the First Crusade]. We went into an alley. On the left we were shown a place where Christ our Lord appeared to the three Marys after the resurrection. There are seven years' absolution and seven quarantines. Not far from there we came to a fine little church of the Jacobites. In this church is an altar, and there is the place where Saint James the Great was beheaded by order of King Herod. Here are seven years' absolution and seven quarantines.

What dangers and problems does Arnold describe during the journey from Cairo to Saint Catherine's monastery? How important do indulgences seem to the shape of his pilgrimage experience? What kind of indulgences does he describe? What seems to be Arnold's attitude toward "heathen" (Muslim) religious practices and places of worship? After his imprisonment in Gaza, what advice does he give to other possible pilgrims? Consider the "knighting" ceremony that he underwent at the church of the Holy Sepulcher: what seems to be the purpose and meaning of this ritual?

70. THOMAS MORE ON SAINTS, SHRINES, AND PILGRIMS

In many ways, Englishman Thomas More (1478–1535) was representative of the humanist thinkers of the early sixteenth century, a critical thinker who lived in the days when the Protestant Reformation had begun to reshape the Christian church in England. More, however, remained a devout Catholic, eventually suffering imprisonment and death on account of his beliefs. In his Dialogue Concerning Heresies, *written in prison in 1529, he tackles some of the criticisms being leveled by "reformers" against traditional devotional practices, including the cult of saints and pilgrimage. Attributing complaints about such forms of veneration to a young school-master called "the Messenger," More responds with a defense of relics, saints' shrines, and pilgrimage, although even he recognized that some kinds of popular devotion seemed more like common superstition than proper piety.*

Source: modernized by J. Shinners, in *Medieval Popular Religion 1000-1500*, ed. J. Shinners, 2nd ed. (Peterborough, ON: Broadview Press, 2007), pp. 217–27, from *A Dialogue Concerning Heresies*, in *The Complete Works of St. Thomas More*, ed. T.N.C. Lawler, G. Marc'hadour, and R.C. Marius, vol. 6, pt. 1 (New Haven, CT: Yale University Press, 1981), pp. 226–34.

2.10. "Sir," [the Messenger] said, "to my mind you have very nicely treated the matter that it is not in vain to pray to saints or to worship them and hold their relics in some reverence. But sir, all this misses the main abuse, for though saints may hear us and help us too, and are glad and willing to do so, and God is contented also that they and their relics and images are held in honor, yet neither he nor they can be content with the manner of the worship. First, because it takes away worship from him since we offer them the same worship in every detail that we do to God. And secondly, because it also takes away worship from them in that we offer their images the same worship that we offer them, mistaking their images for themselves. Thus, we not only make them but also their images the equals and matches of God, for which neither God, nor the good saint, nor the good man ought to be content and pleased."

"In faith," I said, "if this is so, you speak the very truth."

"What do we say then," he said, "about the harm that comes from going on pilgrimages, gadding about idly with no control, with reveling and ribaldry, gluttony, wantonness, waste, and lechery? Don't you believe that God and his holy saints would rather that they sit still at home than to go seek them this way with such worshipful service?"

"Yes surely," I said.

"What do we say then," he said, "about what I haven't yet mentioned when we do them little worship as we set every saint to his duty and assign him the craft that pleases us? Saint Eligius [a former blacksmith] we make a horse-doctor, and must let our horse run unshod and injure his hoof rather than shoe him on his feast day, which in that respect we must more religiously keep high and holy than Easter day. And because one smith is too few at a forge, we set Saint Hippolytus [martyred by horses] to help him [at the bellows]. And on Saint Stephen's day we must bleed all our horses with a knife because Saint Stephen [by legend a horse-groom] was killed with stones. Saint Apollonia [whose teeth were knocked out during her martyrdom] we make a dentist and may speak to her of nothing but sore teeth. Saint Sitha [a housemaid] women appoint to find their keys. Saint Roch we appoint to attend to the plague because he had a bubo [on his thigh]. And with him they join Saint Sebastian because he was martyred with arrows [symbolic of plague]. Some serve for the eyes only. And some for a sore breast. Saint Germain serves only for children, yet he will not once look at them unless the mothers bring with them a white loaf and a pot of good ale [as an offering]. But he is wiser than Saint Wilgefortis [reputed to rid wives of bad husbands], for she, the good soul, is served and content with oats, as they say. I cannot see why this should be so unless because she has to feed the horse for an evil husband to ride to the devil on. For that is the thing for which she is so sought – so much so that women have therefore changed her name, and instead of Saint Wilgefortis, they call her Saint Uncumber since they reckon that for a peck of oats she will not fail to un-encumber them of their husbands.

"It would be long work to rehearse for you the various ways of many prating pilgrims, but I'll tell you one or two. [Giovanni] Pontano, one of his dialogues speaks about how Saint Martin is worshiped. I've forgotten the town, but the method I cannot forget, it is so strange. His image is borne in procession about all the streets on his feast day. If it is a fair day as he passes by, then they cast rose water and pleasant-scented things upon his image. But if it happens to rain, they pour out pisspots upon his head at every door and every window. Is this not a sweet service and a worshipful devotion? And this, as I say, Pontano describes and says where it happens.

"But what I shall now tell you I dare as boldly make you sure of as if I had seen it myself. At Saint Walaric's [or Valery] here in Picardy there is a fair abbey where Saint Walaric was a monk. About a furlong or two up in the woods there is a chapel in which the saint is especially sought [to cure] the [kidney] stone, not only [by people from] those parts but also from England.

"Now there was a young gentleman who had married a merchant's widow. Having a little luxury money, which he thought was burning out the bottom of his purse, in the first year of his wedding he took his wife with him and went overseas for no other purpose than to see Flanders and France and right about for a summer in those countries. There was someone in his company who told him in passing many strange things about that pilgrimage spot. So he thought he would go somewhat out of his way either to see if it were true or to laugh at this man if he found it false, as he truly indeed thought he would. But when they came into the chapel, they found it all to be true. They found it even more foolish to behold than he had said. For just as you see wax legs or arms or other [body] parts hanging up at other pilgrimage shrines [offered in thanks for cures of those parts], in that chapel all the pilgrims' offerings hung about the walls, and they were all men's and women's private gear [genitals] made out of wax. Besides these at the end of the altar there were two round rings of silver, one much larger than the other, through which every man put his privy member, not every man through both but some through the one, some through the other. For they were not of the same size, but one larger than the other. There was also a monk standing at the altar who blessed certain threads of Venetian gold. These he gave to the pilgrims, teaching them in what way they or their friends should use the threads against the stone: they should tie it about their gear and say I cannot tell you what prayers. After the monk had described the method, the gentleman had a servant who was a married man and a merry fellow.

He thanked the monk for the thread and desired him to teach him how he should tie it about his wife's gear, which – unless the monk had some special skill in knotting – he thought would be cumbersome because her gear was somewhat short. I need not tell you that every man laughed then except the monk who gathered up his rings and threads in great anger and went his way.

"Wait a moment, I almost forgot one thing that I would not leave out for a four-pence. As this gentleman and his wife were kneeling in the chapel there came a good sober woman to him and showed him one special point used at that shrine, the surest [cure] against the [kidney] stone, which she didn't know whether he had yet been told about. If it were done, she dared bet her life that he would never have the stone in his life. It was that he should tell her the length of his gear and she would make a candle of that measurement which should then be burned in the chapel while certain prayers were said there. Against the stone this was the very last resort. When he had heard her (and he was someone who feared the stone in earnest) he went and asked his wife's advice. But she, like a good, faithful, Christian woman, had no love for such superstitions. She could put up with the other things well enough, but once she heard about burning up the candle, she knit up her brows and blessed herself: 'Beware in God's virtue what you do,' she said, 'Burn it up? Marry, God forbid! It would waste up your gear on pain of my life. I pray you beware of such witchcraft.'

"Is this kind of service and worship acceptable and pleasing to God and his saints? For people worship saints in such a way that they make them equal to God, and they worship images in such a way that they mistake them for the saints themselves. Then again, on the other hand they honor them with such superstitious ways that the pagan gods were worshiped with none worse. Finally, the worst of all is that they pray to them for unlawful things, as thieves pray to the thief that hung on the right side of Christ to speed them along in their robbery. And they have even found him a name, calling him Dismas, I think, and his companion Gysmas to rhyme with it. Do you not think that the people's dealing in this business is likely to provoke God and his saints to be displeased that the devil should have license and liberty thus to work his wonders to the delusion of our superstitious idolatry? Should these things please and content our Lord so that he should show miracles in approval of that manner of worship which we can clearly see all reason, religion, and virtue reproves?"

... When we had laughed awhile at our merry tales, I said: "In good faith, as I was about to tell you, what you said is to some extent true. For that superstitious manner of worship is evil and it is evil to endure it. And as for the story you told about Saint Martin, if it is true it is inexcusable, but it has no bearing on our discussion, for it is not worshiping but condemning and dishonoring saints. Concerning the offering of bread and ale to Saint Germain, I see nothing much amiss in it. Where you have seen it practiced I cannot tell. But I have myself seen it often and yet I don't remember that I ever saw a priest or a clerk benefit from it or once drink the ale: it is given to children or poor folk to pray for a sick child. And I would suppose it was no offence to offer up a whole ox in such fashion and distribute it among poor people. But now as for our merry matters of Saint Walaric, because the place is in France, we shall leave it to the University of Paris to defend. And we will come home here to St-Paul's [cathedral] and give one example of both – that is, the superstitious manner and the unlawful petitions – if women offer oats there to Saint Wilgefortis trusting that she shall disencumber them of their husbands. But priests cannot see until they find it there that the foolish women bring oats there, nor is it so often done nor is so much oats brought at any one time that the church may make much money from it beyond feeding the canons' horses."

"No," he said, "a whole year's offering of oats will not feed three geese and a gander together for a week."

"Well then," I said, "the priests don't support the practice out of any great avarice and they can't hear what the foolish women pray for. However, if they pray just to be disencumbered there seems to me no great harm or un-lawfulness in that. For they may be disencumbered in more ways than one. They may be disencumbered if their husbands change their cumbersome conditions, or if they themselves perhaps change their cumbersome tongues which are maybe the cause of all their encumbrance. And finally if they can't be disencumbered except by death, it may be by their own death and so their husbands are safe enough."

"No, no," he said, "you'll find them not such fools I guarantee you. They make their contracts with their bitter prayers and, as surely as if they were written, will not give away their oats for nothing."

"Well," I said, "to all these matters there is one evident, easy answer – none of them touch the effect of our matter which consists in this: whether the things we speak of such as praying to saints, going on pilgrimage, and worshiping rel-ics and images may be done for good, not whether they may be done for evil. For if they may be done for good, then although many may misuse them, that does not diminish the goodness of the thing itself. For if from the misuse of a good thing and for the evils that sometimes grow out of its abuse, we should utterly do away with the whole use of something, we should then have to make some marvelous changes in the world. In some countries it is a common custom to go hunting commonly on Good Friday in the morning. Will you break the evil custom or cast away Good Friday? There are cathedral churches into which people from the countryside come in procession on Whitsuntide, the women following the cross with many an unladylike song – such honest wives, who outside of the procession you could not pay to speak one such foul, ribald word, sing whole ribald songs for God's sake as loud as their throat can cry. Will you mend their lewd manner or put away Whitsuntide? You spoke of lewd practices at pilgrim shrines. Do you believe none occur on holy days? And why do you not then advise us to put them clean away, Sundays and all? Some grow drunk during Lent on wheat cakes and biscuits, and yet you would not, I trust, want Lent abolished. If we consider how commonly men abuse Christmas, we may think that they take it for a time of license and all manner of lewdness. Yet is Christmas to be cast away from Christian men, or are men to be admonished to amend their manners and behave more Christianly at Christmas? Let me turn to Christ's own coming and his giving us our faith and his holy Gospel and sacraments. Are there not ten men the worse therefore for everyone the better? Are not all the pagans, all the Jews, all the Turks and the Saracens, all the heretics, all the evil-living people in Christendom the worse through their own fault for the coming of Christ? I think they are. And yet would any wise man wish that Christ had not come here? Nor would it be right for God to abandon that occasion of merit and reward which good folk deserve with his help by his coming because of the harm that wretches take from it by their own sloth and malice. Nor likewise would it be at all right that we should abolish and put away all worship of saints, and reverence of holy relics, and honor of saints' images (by which good devout folk do much merit) because some folk abuse them.

"Now concerning the evil petitions, though they that ask them are, I trust, not great in number, there are not yet so many people who ask evil petitions of saints as there are who ask the same also of God himself. For whatever they will ask of any good saint they will ask of God also. And commonly among the wild Irish and some in Wales too, so men say, when they go forth in robbing they bless themselves and pray God send them good fortune that they meet with a good purse and do harm but take none. Shall we therefore find a fault with every man's prayer because thieves pray for fortune in robbery? This, as I say, makes no sense even though there were a great number of people who abused a good thing. And whereas the worst thing that you specify in our discussion is that, as you say, 'the people' commit idolatry in that you say they mistake the images for the saints themselves or the rood for Christ himself – which as I said I think no one does (for some roods have no crucified body on them, and they don't believe that the cross which they see was ever at Jerusalem, or that it was the Holy Cross itself, much less do they think that the image hanging on it is the body of Christ himself) – and although some people think this, they are not, as you put it, 'the people.' For a few foolish dames are not the people.

Furthermore, if it were as you would have it seem, and indeed the whole people were involved, still a good thing should not be put away because bad folk misuse it."

What are some of the complaints against pilgrimage and the cult of saints that More attributes to "the Messenger"? How does he respond to those arguments, in defense of pilgrimage and other forms of devotion? More wrote both sides of this "dialogue": what signs are there that he was more than willing to acknowledge some of the abuses caused by "popular" pilgrim practices but still believed that such veneration for the saints remained important and legitimate? How does this text reveal the thriving popularity of pilgrimage as the Middle Ages drew to a close, despite growing criticisms about it?

71. MARTIN LUTHER ON THE PAPACY AND PILGRIMAGE

Credited with initiating the Protestant Reformation in Europe, the German priest and theologian Martin Luther (1483–1546) leveled devastating criticisms against the Roman church and contemporary devotional practices, such as pilgrimage, indulgences, and the cult of saints. As part of his attacks on the Roman papacy, including his famous "ninety-five theses," Luther targeted pilgrimage to Rome and other places as a sign of decadence and illicit innovation in the Christian church, which had deviated from the original teachings of Jesus Christ in the Bible.

Sources: Commentary on John, trans. M.H. Bertram, in *Luther's Works*, ed. J. Pelikan, vol. 22 (St. Louis: Concordia Publishing House, 1955), pp. 254–58; The Ninety-Five Theses, trans. C.M. Jacobs, in *Luther's Works*, ed. H.J. Grimm, vol. 31 (Philadelphia: Muhlenberg Press, 1957), pp. 197–99.

Commentary on John (1514)

Although we must always expect the best from man, especially from the believers, we remember that they may err and go astray. If this truth had been observed in Christendom, we would have had neither the pope nor all the filth and stench of his anti-Christian doctrine with which the Christian church was later seduced. In the papacy one concluded: "Oh, he is a holy man and, consequently, all that he says must be true!" Take, by way of illustration, Saints Ambrose, Gregory, Augustine, and Jerome, and all the others, down to Bernard, Benedict, Dominic, and Francis. In the end all the sayings and doctrines of anyone with a reputation for holiness were collected. I need to be warned against such a practice. I must say: "I shall gladly believe that the men I have mentioned – such as Gregory, Ambrose, and Augustine – were holy men; but I do not trust myself to them. For their holiness does not make them infallible, and it does not imply that one must rely and depend on all the dicta of the fathers or approve and believe all their teachings. Rather take the touchstone of God's Word into your hands. Let this be your criterion for testing, trying, and judging all that the fathers have preached, written, and said, as well as all the precepts and human ordinances that have been promulgated. Otherwise one will be easily misled and deceived. And since this polishing stone was not applied to the pope in times past, he ran rampant and covered the church with errors. All his sayings and doctrines, yes, even the nocturnal dreams of monks and clerics, were, therefore, accepted and believed as holy and precious. This resulted in the excrescence of all those abominable and harmful errors over which we scuffled and contended and fought interminably with the popes – such as monasticism, indulgences, pilgrimages, the adoration of departed saints, masses, vigils, requiems for those in purgatory, rosaries, and other tomfoolery."...

No one will believe how great an ordeal it is and how severe a shock when a person first realizes that he must believe and teach contrary to the fathers, especially when he sees that so many excellent, intelligent, and learned men, yes, the best of them taught thus, and that the majority of the people in the world shared their views; among these were so many holy men, like saints Ambrose, Jerome, and Augustine. I, too, have often experienced this shock. But in spite of all this, that one man, my dear Lord and Savior Jesus Christ, must have greater weight with me than all the holiest people on earth put together. Yea, he must also outweigh all the angels in heaven if they teach anything at variance with the Gospel, or if they add to or detract from the doctrine of the divine Word. And then when I read the books of Saint Augustine [of Hippo] and discover that he, too, did this and that, it thoroughly appalls me. And when, over and above this, the hue and the cry is raised: "The church! The church!" this dismays one most of all. It is truly difficult to subdue one's own heart in these matters, to deviate from people who are so highly respected and who bear such a holy name – indeed, from the church herself – and no longer to have any confidence and faith in the church's teachings. I mean, of course, that church of which they say: "Lo, the church has decreed that the precepts of Saints Francis and Dominic and the orders of monks and nuns are proper, Christian, and good." This truly bewilders and dismays a person. But after all is said and done, I must say that I dare not accept whatever any man might say; for he may be a pious and God-fearing man and yet be mistaken and err. Therefore I shall not trust myself to them all, as the Lord, according to this text, did not trust himself to man either.

And in another passage, found in the Gospel of Matthew, Christ earnestly warns us to beware of false prophets who will appear and not merely declare that they are Christians, but will also "show great signs and wonders, so as to lead astray, if possible, even the elect."

Therefore we should place no reliance in any of the fathers or in their writings, but we should crawl under the wings of our brood hen, the Lord Jesus, and depend solely on him. For of him God the heavenly Father himself said: "This is my beloved Son, with whom I am well pleased; listen to him." God insists that we give ear to Christ alone, for he said neither too little nor too much.

Moses, who shines with the greatest luster in scripture, is authorized to say: "You shall not add to the word which I command you, nor take from it, but leave it unaltered as I taught it to you." And if Moses, the servant, lays claim to such honor and authority, how much more is Christ the Lord entitled to it, of whom God the Father bore witness from heaven that we should listen to him and to no other! For Christ has taught us how to know the Father and himself, how to live in our several estates, and also how to pass through the sore trials and the agonies of the hour of death, for all of which he gave us his word and sacraments. And we dare not add to or subtract from these.

But the pope acts arbitrarily, and he has the audacity to add to and to subtract from them. Thus he deprives the laity of the one kind in holy communion, contrary to the words of God, which say: "Listen to him!" Who authorized him to do this? And if it was forbidden to take away from Moses', the servant's words, why, then, should one want to curtail or mutilate the words of the Lord, Christ? Therefore, pope or no pope, I may believe that you are pious, but I will not trust you. For you detract from the divine word, and your message and doctrine are not in conformity with the faith, as Saint Paul demands. The pope also adds to the divine word, as is manifest in his indulgences, his pilgrimages, also in his claim that it is a sin to eat butter and meat on certain days. Who authorized him to add this? My Lord Christ says that I am to be untrammeled, free to eat what God grants me and what is put before me by man, if only I know the Father and believe in him.

But in the papacy they counter with the cry: "The fathers! The fathers!" You must reply: "I am ready to believe and to concede that they were pious people during their lifetime; however, whenever they talk and teach contrary to Christ, I do not believe them. How are you going to harmonize the pope's decree: 'Whoever eats meat on Friday is of the devil, accursed and damned,' with Christ's teaching to the contrary? Saint Paul says that all food should be received and used with thanksgiving to God. Does the pope's prohibition agree with the doctrine of Christ? I do not question that Ambrose and Augustine taught abstinence from meat on certain days; but since this contradicts holy scripture, I shall not comply with it or obey you."

Thus the pope also claimed that anyone who makes a pilgrimage to Rome in quest of indulgence will be saved. He forced the monks to observe their rules, to wear wool, walk barefoot, wear wooden shoes, go bareheaded and tonsured like simpletons, and girded with ropes like thieves. And any monk or nun who disobeyed was to be eternally lost. Christ, on the other hand, granted you liberty in such matters, saying: "If you do not have a gray coat, put on a black one." Christ will not have anyone restrict you with human traditions and bind your conscience. He wants you to believe only in him, to love your neighbor, to bear patiently any cross that God may send you, and to hope for eternal salvation. But all such things were taught in the papacy, and many important people were deluded and blinded into laying great stress on them and making them articles of faith. Even today many are misled by their claim that the church does not err. But you answer them thus: "Oh, yes, the church does err and can err and be mistaken. You cannot collect the church into one spot or into one compact group. The Christian church is catholic, dispersed over all the world and often found in a place where one would least expect it. Therefore Christ alone is infallible. But the Christian church is fallible"....

The Ninety-Five Theses (1517)

Look at a true penitent and you will see that he seeks revenge upon himself so ardently for his offense against God that he compels you to have mercy upon him. In fact it is even necessary to dissuade him, lest he destroy himself, as we have often read and seen it happen. Saint Jerome writes that such a thing happened to his Paula and even to himself. No punishment is enough for such individuals, so with the prodigal son they invoke heaven and earth and even God himself against themselves. David did this when he said, "Let thy sword, I beseech you, be turned against me and against my father's house."

Therefore I believe that I have spoken correctly when I say that canonical penances are imposed only upon those who are sluggards and do not wish to do better or to test the sincerity of their contrition. One can see how difficult it is even for the learned to take a middle course between hatred and love of punishments; to teach people to hate them and yet do it in such a manner that the people are persuaded to love them. But since nothing is difficult for the unlearned, there is nothing to prevent this from being easy also. But the gospel teaches us not to escape the punishments or to relax them but to seek and love them, for it teaches the spirit of freedom and the fear of God to the point of showing contempt for all punishments. But it is far more lucrative and profitable to the moneybags of the indulgence treasurers for people to fear punishments and drink in the spirit of the world and of fear in the letter of the law and in servitude. At the same time the people hear that some canonical punishments are such horrible things that they can be avoided only with great zeal, expense, pomp, and ceremonies. They are taught these matters with more zeal than they are taught to love the gospel.

The following question is raised: "What do you say, then, about those who make pilgrimages to Rome, Jerusalem, St-James, Aachen, Trier, and many other regions and places to obtain indulgences? Also what do you say about indulgences bestowed at the dedications of churches?" My answer is: those who make pilgrimages do so for many reasons, very seldom for legitimate ones.

The first reason for making pilgrimages is the most common of all, namely, the curiosity to see and hear strange and unknown things. This levity proceeds from a loathing for and boredom at the worship services, which have been neglected in the parishioners' own church. Otherwise one would find incomparably better indulgences at home than in all the other places put together. Furthermore he would be closer to Christ and the saints if he were not so foolish as to prefer sticks and stones to the poor and his neighbors whom he should serve out of love. And he would be closer to Christ also if he were to provide for his own family.

The second reason for making pilgrimages is bearable, namely, for the sake of indulgences. Since indulgences are voluntary, have not been commanded, and therefore have no merit, surely those who make pilgrimages only for the sake of indulgences merit nothing at all. Moreover, those people are to be justifiably ridiculed who neglect Christ and neighbor at home, in order to spend ten times as much money away from home without having any results and merit to show for it. Therefore he who would remain at home and consider that passage of Scripture, "Love covers a multitude of sins," as well as that other passage, "Whatever is left over give as alms, and behold everything is clean for you," would be doing far better – indeed, he would be doing the only right thing than if he were to bring home all the indulgences from Jerusalem and Rome. But there is no pleasure in being so wise, so we shall surrender "our hearts to impurity."

The third reason for making pilgrimages is a longing for affliction and labor for one's sin, which, I believe, rarely occurs, at least by itself. To satisfy that desire, a man could torture himself and labor at home, if it were labor only that he sought. Yet if he does this, it is not evil but good.

The fourth reason is an honest one namely if a man is motivated by a singular devotion for the honor of the saints, the glory of God, and his own edification, just as Saint Lucia made a pilgrimage to St-Agatha and some of the holy fathers made a pilgrimage to Rome. The result proved that they did not do this out of curiosity.

Accordingly, in such cases as these, I am glad that the vows made to go on such pilgrimages are commuted to other works. Would that they were commuted for free!

On what general grounds does Luther criticize pilgrimage? How does his attitude toward pilgrimage and other devotional practices fit with his emphasis on the overriding centrality of Christ and the Bible as the ultimate source of authority in the church? Specifically, how do his critiques of pilgrimage and indulgences form part of a larger argument against the popes of Rome and what Luther sees as their unlawful innovations in religious life? Imagine a dialogue between Thomas More (doc. 70) and Martin Luther about pilgrimage: on what points might the two men agree? On what points might they disagree?

72. MEXICO MEETS JERUSALEM: MOTOLINIA'S *HISTORY OF THE INDIANS OF NEW SPAIN*

During the sixteenth century, Franciscan missionaries began to spread Christianity among the native peoples of Mexico following the Spanish conquest of the region. In 1539, on the feast of Corpus Christi, a band of Franciscans and the Indian community at Tlaxcallan staged a number of plays, including one that imagined the Christian conquest of Jerusalem. In this drama, the Tlaxcaltecas played various roles such as the Holy Roman emperor Charles V, the pope, and the sultan of Jerusalem. As a "virtual" crusade-pilgrimage to the holy places, this imagined recovery of the Promised Land offers a fascinating display of Christian devotion toward Jerusalem from the "New World."

Source: trans. F.B. Steck, in *Motolinia's History of the Indians of New Spain* (Washington, DC: Academy of American Franciscan History, 1951), pp. 160–66.

As you know, dear father, the news reached this land a few days before Lent. The Tlaxcaltecas wanted first to see what the Spaniards and Mexicans would do. When they saw that they arranged and represented the conquest of Rhodes, the Tlaxcaltecas decided to stage the conquest of Jerusalem, a prediction which, we pray, God may fulfill in our day. To make the play more solemn, the Indians of Tlaxcala agreed to postpone it to the feast of Corpus Christi, the day which they celebrated with great enthusiasm, as I shall now relate.

In Tlaxcallan, the city which they have begun to rebuild, they set aside, down in the center of the plain, a large and pleasant plaza. Here they constructed a Jerusalem on top of some houses which they were erecting for the town council. It was on the site where the buildings were an *estado* [about six feet] in height. They leveled off the buildings, filled the shell with earth, and on this erected five towers. The principal tower stood in the center, larger than the others, while the remaining four occupied the four sides. Along the ramparts there was a parapet with numerous merlons [part of a parapet]. The towers also had many graceful merlons together with many windows and fine arches, all covered with roses and flowers. In front of Jerusalem, out on the eastern part of the plaza, the emperor was seated. To the right of Jerusalem was the royal camp where the army of Spain was to be lodged. Facing this was a place prepared for the provinces of New Spain. In the center of the plaza stood Santa Fe where the emperor and his army were to have their lodging. All these places were surrounded by walls, on the outside of which were paintings that very realistically simulated mason-work with embrasures, loopholes, and many merlons.

After the most holy sacrament had reached the plaza, accompanied by the pope, cardinals, bishops, all impersonated, these took their seat on their platform which was very nicely adorned. It was located near Jerusalem, in order that all the festivities might be enacted before the most holy sacrament. Thereupon the army of Spain began to enter the plaza and to besiege Jerusalem. Passing in front of the blessed sacrament, it crossed the plaza and occupied the camp to the right. It took considerable time for the army to enter because it comprised many men. The army was divided into three squadrons. In the vanguard, with the banner of the royal arms, came the men of the kingdom of Castile and Leon and also the men of the captain general who was Don Antonio Pimentel, count of Benavente, with the banner bearing his coat of arms. Then in battle array came Toledo, Aragon, Galicia, Granada, Bizcaya and Navarre. In the rear guard came Germany, Rome and the Italians. In point of uniforms, there was little difference among the men of the army because, not having seen European soldiers, the Indians do not know how each group dresses, and hence they are not accustomed to differentiate. This explains why all entered as Spanish soldiers with trumpets, simulating those of Spain, and with drums and fifes. All in excellent order, they marched five in a row, keeping step with the beat of the drums.

The Spanish army having passed and taken its place in the camp, immediately from the opposite side came the army of New Spain. It was divided into ten captaincies, each attired in keeping with the costume that they wear in war. They were very attractive and, if the people in Spain and Italy had seen them, the sight would have caused pleasure. They all wore their richest plumage, emblems and shields, for those who took part in the play were lords and chiefs, known as Teuhpiltín among the natives. In the vanguard marched the Indians of Tlaxcallan and Mexico. They marched in good formation and were much admired. They carried the standard with the royal coat of arms and that of their captain general who was Don Antonio de Mendoza, viceroy of New Spain. In battle array came the Huaxtecas, the Zempoaltecas, the Mixtecas, the Colhuaques, and some captaincies which were supposed to be from Peru and from the Islands of Santo Domingo and Cuba. In the rear guard came the Tarascos and the Cuauhtemaltecas. As soon as this army took its place, the army of the Spaniards took the field to give battle, marching in good order directly to Jerusalem. When the Sultan saw them coming – he was the Marques del Valle, Hernando Cortes – he commanded his army to take the field and join battle. They sallied forth in good order and it was easy to distinguish them from the others because they wore headpieces resembling those of the Moors [Muslims]. The signal "to arms" being sounded on both sides, the armies met and they fought with much shouting and noise of trumpets, drums and fifes. The victory began to fall to the Spaniards who drove back the Moors, taking some of them prisoners and leaving others lying on the field, although no one was wounded. Thereupon the army of Spain headed for its camp in good order. Soon the signal for battle was again sounded. This time the army of New Spain sallied forth, followed immediately by the army of Jerusalem. They fought for a while, likewise overcoming and encircling the Moors of the city, some of whom they led captive to their camps, leaving others as if dead on the field.

When the plight of Jerusalem became known, great assistance came from the people of Galilee, Judea, Samaria, Damascus, and all parts of Syria, who brought abundant provision and ammunition. This made those of Jerusalem happy and greatly encouraged them. To such an extent did they take heart that they immediately set out for the battlefield and made directly for the Spaniards who went out to meet them. After battling for some time the Spaniards began to retreat; whereupon the Moors fell upon them, capturing some of those who went astray and also leaving some for dead on the field. This done, the captain general dispatched a messenger to his majesty with the following letter:

"Your majesty will know how the army gathered here before Jerusalem. We immediately pitched camp on an impregnable and secure site and took the field against the city; whereupon those who were in the city sallied forth into the field. Joining battle, the army of the Spaniards, servants of your majesty, with your captains and veterans, fought like tigers and lions. They proved themselves men of great valor. The men of the kingdom of Leon seemed to excel all others. At this juncture ample assistance arrived for the army of the Moors and Jews in the shape of abundant ammunition and provision. On seeing themselves favored in this way, the defenders of Jerusalem made for the field, and we went out to meet them. It is true, some of ours fell in the encounter, such as were not very adept and had not yet crossed swords with the Moors. All the others are in high spirit, awaiting what it will please your majesty to command, so that it may be fully obeyed. Your majesty's humble servant, Don Antonio Pimentel."

Having read the letter of the captain general, the emperor replied as follows: "To my dear and much-beloved cousin, Don Antonio Pimentel, captain general of the army of Spain. I received your letter, from which I was happy to learn how resolutely you have acted. You will take great care that in the future no reinforcements enter the city. For this purpose you will place all necessary guards. Moreover, you will inform me whether your camp is well provisioned. Know also that I have been served by those knights, who will receive from me many signal favors. Commend me to the captains and veterans; and may God watch over you. Don Carlos, emperor."

Meanwhile, thanks to the reinforcements with which they had been favored, the people of Jerusalem had already set out against the army of New Spain in order to get revenge for the past defeat. Since they were angry because of what had occurred, they sought to avenge themselves. The battle having begun, they fought valiantly until the people from the Islands finally began to weaken and lose ground to such an extent that between the fallen and captured none of their men survived. Without delay the captain general dispatched a messenger to his majesty with the following letter: "Sacred caesarean catholic majesty, ever august emperor. Your majesty will know how I marched with the army against Jerusalem and pitched camp on the left side of the city. We set out against the enemy who were in camp and your vassals of New Spain acquitted themselves very well, subduing many Moors and driving them back to the gates of their city because your men fought like elephants and giants. It was then that the enemy obtained huge reinforcements of men and artillery, munitions and provisions. Immediately they set out against us and we went out to meet them. Having fought a good part of the day, the squadrons from the islands [in the Americas] grew faint and in this way brought great shame on all the army. Since they neither were adept in the use of arms nor had defensive weapons nor knew how to invoke the help of God, every one of their men fell into the hands of the enemy. All the men of the other captaincies are well. Your majesty's most humble servant, Don Antonio de Mendoza."

The emperor's reply: "Beloved kinsman and my great captain of the entire army of New Spain. Take heart like a valiant warrior and encourage all your knights and soldiers. If help has reached the city of the enemy, rest assured that our help will come from above, from heaven. In battles the outcome varies: he who conquers today is overcome tomorrow, and he who suffered defeat will be victorious on another day. I am determined to depart immediately and travel all night without sleeping so as to be in Jerusalem at daybreak. Have everything in readiness and the entire army in line; and since I will be with you so soon, be you consoled and encouraged. Write immediately to the captain general of the Spaniards that he, too, should be at his post with his army because as soon as I come – the enemy thinking I arrived fatigued – we will attack them and surround the city. I will attack from the front, your army from the left, and the army of Spain from the right, in such a way that they cannot escape from our hands. May our Lord be your protection. Don Carlos, emperor."

Thereupon, at one part of the plaza, the emperor entered and with him were the king of France and the king of Hungary, all wearing crowns. When they began entering the plaza, they went out to receive the emperor, from one side the captain general of Spain with half of his army and from the other side the captain general of New Spain. At the time, from all parts they brought trumpets and drums and discharged many skyrockets by way of artillery. The emperor was received with much rejoicing and with great pomp until he reached his lodging of Santa Fe. At this turn of events, the Moors gave signs of being in great fear, for they had all gathered in the city. When the siege began, the Moors defended themselves very well. Meanwhile, the camp-master, who was Andres de Tapia, had gone with a squadron to reconnoiter in the rear of Jerusalem, where he set fire to a place and then through the center of the plaza led a herd of sheep which he had taken. After each army again sought shelter in its camp, the Spaniards alone once more set out from their camp. When the Moors saw that the Spaniards were few in number, they sallied forth and fought them for a time and, since from Jerusalem more of their men continued to sally forth, they repelled the Spaniards and took possession of the field; they captured some Spaniards and led them into the city. When this became known to his majesty, he immediately dispatched a messenger to the pope with the following letter:

"To our esteemed holy father. Oh, my dear father! Who on earth holds so exalted a dignity as you? Your holiness will know how I have gone to the Holy Land and have encircled Jerusalem with three armies. I am with the one in person; in the other there are the Spaniards; the third comprises the Nahuales [Tlaxcaltecas]. Between my armies and the Moors a number of skirmishes and battles have taken place, in which my people have wounded and captured many of the Moors. Thereupon reinforcements arrived in the city of the Moors and Jews with abundant provision and ammunition, as your holiness will learn from the messenger. At present I am much troubled about knowing the result of my journey. I beseech your holiness to favor me with prayers and supplications to God for myself and for my armies, because I am determined either to take Jerusalem and all the other holy places or to die in the attempt; wherefore I humbly ask you to send us all your blessing. Don Carlos, emperor."

After reading this letter, the pope summoned the cardinals and, having deliberated with them, he replied as follows: "My beloved son. I received your letter which filled my heart with great joy. I have given great thanks to God for having so invigorated and strengthened you as to undertake so holy an enterprise. Know that God is protecting and helping you and the entire army. Without delay at this moment your request will be granted. I have so instructed my very dear brothers, the cardinals, the bishops and all other prelates; also the orders of Saint Francis and Saint Didacus and all the children of the church, asking them to say a prayer; and that this might be done, I immediately promulgated and granted a great jubilee for entire Christendom. The Lord be with your soul. Amen. Your loving father, the pope."

To return to our armies. When the Spaniards found themselves twice repulsed and the Moors surrounding their camp, they all knelt down, facing the most holy sacrament, and prayed for help. The pope and the cardinals did the same. While all were on their knees, an angel appeared at the corner of the camp, consoling them and saying: "God has heard your supplication and he is pleased with your decision to die for his honor and in his service for the conquest of Jerusalem, since he would not have so holy a place in possession of an enemy of the faith. But it has pleased him to visit you with such great hardships in order to test your constancy and bravery. Have no fear that the enemy will prevail over you, because for your greater safety God will send to you the apostle Santiago." All were much consoled over this and they began to exclaim: "Santiago, Santiago, patron of our Spain!" At this, Santiago entered on his horse, which was as white as snow, while he himself was attired as they are wont to represent him. And as he entered the camp of the Spaniards, they all joined him and set out against the Moors who were gathered before Jerusalem. But, being in great fear, the Moors began to flee, leaving on the field those who had fallen. They shut themselves up in the city, whereupon the Spaniards without delay began the attack, Santiago on his horse, always turning up in all parts, while the Moors did not dare show themselves at the ramparts because of the great fear they had. Then the Spaniards with their standards unfurled returned to their camp. The other army, that of the Nahuales or people of New Spain, seeing that the Spaniards had not been able to enter Jerusalem, formed their squadrons and forthwith set out against the city. But the Moors did not wait for them to arrive. Instead, they sallied forth to the encounter; and after fighting for a while, the Moors began gaining the field and driving the Nahuales back to their camp, but without capturing any of them. This done, the Moors with a great shout returned to their city.

Seeing themselves defeated, the Christians again resorted to prayer, calling upon God to help them; and the pope and the cardinals did the same. Thereupon another angel appeared over the camp of the Christians and said: "Although you are newcomers in the faith, God has been pleased to test you and allow you to be conquered, in order that you might know that without his help you can do little. But since you have humbled yourselves, God has heard your prayer and forthwith will arrive the mediator and patron of New Spain, Saint Hippolytus, on whose feast-day the Spaniards with you Tlaxcaltecas gained Mexico." Then the entire army of the Nahuales began to exclaim: "Saint Hippolytus! Saint Hippolytus!" After a while, Saint Hippolytus entered on a brown horse. After encouraging and animating the Nahuales, he set out with them towards Jerusalem; at the same time, from the other side, Santiago with the Spaniards and the emperor with his men took the front rank. Thereupon they altogether began the bombardment, so that those who were in the city, including those in the two towers, were not able to defend themselves against the balls and missiles that were discharged at them. In the rear of Jerusalem, between two towers, there stood a house of reeds, quite large, to which at the time of the attack they set fire. In all other places the bombardment continued very briskly, the Moors seeming determined rather to die than to deliver themselves to any party. Within and without, the combat went on very briskly. Large balls made of reeds were discharged together with balls of mud dried in the sun. These were filled with moistened red earth, so that the one who was struck by them seemed badly wounded and covered with blood. The same was done with some red prickly pears. The archers had fastened to their arrowheads little pockets filled with red earth, so that it seemed to draw blood whenever they struck. Thick stalks of corn were also discharged. When the attack was in fullest swing, the archangel Saint Michael appeared on the main tower. His appearance and the sound of his voice filled both the Moors and Christians with fear. They left the combat and were silent. Then the archangel said to the Moors: "If God considered your evil deeds and sins instead of his great mercy, you would already be buried in the depths of hell; the earth would have opened up and swallowed you alive. But because you showed reverence for the holy places, he wished to exercise mercy and wait for you to do penance and turn to him with all your heart. For this reason, recognize the Lord of majesty, the creator of all things; believe in his dearest son Jesus Christ and appease him with tears and true penance. Having said this, Saint Michael disappeared. Thereupon the Sultan who was in the city spoke to all the Moors, saying: "Great is the goodness and the mercy of God, because He has in this way deigned to enlighten us who are so greatly blinded in sin. The time has now come for us to recognize our error. So far we thought we were fighting with men. But now we see that we have been fighting with God and his Saints and angels. Who will be able to resist them?" Then responded his captain general, who was the *Adelantado*, Don Pedro de Alvarado, all the Moors joining him in declaring that they wished to place themselves in the hands of the emperor and that the sultan should immediately make a treaty in such a way that it pledged their lives, because the kings of Spain were kind and pious, and they wished to be baptized. Thereupon the sultan gave a sign of peace and sent a Moor to the emperor with a letter which read:

"Roman emperor, beloved of God. We have clearly seen how God has favored you and sent you help from heaven. Until I saw this, I thought of protecting my city and kingdom and of defending my vassals, and I was determined to die rather than surrender. But since the God of heaven enlightened me, I know that you alone are captain of his armies. I know that all the world must render obedience to God and to you who are his captain on earth. Into your hands, therefore, we place our lives; and we ask that you be pleased to come near our city in order that you may give us your royal word and grant us our lives, receiving us in your constant mercy as your natural vassals. Your servant, the Great Sultan of Babylon and Tetrarch of Jerusalem."

After reading this letter, the emperor immediately went to the gates of the city. These stood open and the sultan came out to meet him with a great retinue. Getting on his knees before the emperor, he rendered him obedience and tried hard to kiss his hand. But the emperor, raising him to his feet, took him by the hand and conducted him before the most holy sacrament, where the pope was stationed. Here, all giving thanks to God, the pope received the sultan with great affection. The sultan brought also many Turks, or adult Indians, who had been designedly prepared for baptism. They publicly asked the pope that they be baptized. The pope immediately directed a priest to baptize them; whereupon they were actually baptized. With this the most holy sacrament was taken away and the procession again formed and marched in order.

What roles did the Tlaxcaltecas Indians play during the staged battle for Jerusalem? For the Franciscan author of this letter, how does the recent conversion of Tlaxcaltecas seem to hold out the promise that Christians would recover the holy places of Jerusalem from the Muslims? What might this "journey" to Jerusalem have meant for the Native Americans? In this play, how is the struggle for Jerusalem ultimately resolved, and what does this drama imply about the future of the world?

INDEX OF TOPICS

Topics are listed by document number and, in some cases, by books and sections or chapters within that document. Thus, 8.10 is a reference to document 8, chapter 10 within that text; 4.3.25 is a reference to document 4, book 3, chapter 25 within that document. If the topic appears several times within a document, no book or chapter number is given. For some common topics, such as "Jesus Christ," only substantive or noteworthy appearances are included.

SOURCES

Babcock, Emily A. and August C. Krey (translators)

Excerpts from "Peter the Hermit's Pilgrimage," from *A History of Deeds Done Beyond the Sea*, vol. 1. New York: Columbia University Press, 1943. Copyright © 1943 Columbia University Press. Reprinted by permission of Columbia University Press.

Bertram, Martin H. (translator)

"Martin Luther on the Papacy and Pilgrimage," from *Luther's Works*. Edited by Jaroslav Jan Pelikan, vol. 22. St. Louis: Concordia Publishing House, 1955. Copyright © 1955 Concordia Publishing House. Reprinted by permission of Concordia Publishing House. All rights reserved.

Bieler, Ludwig (translator)

"Penance and Pilgrimage: Penitential of St. Columbus," "Old Irish Penitential," "Three Irish Canons," "Synod of the Grove of Victory" and "Penitential of Finnian" from *The Irish Penitentials, Scriptores Latini Hiberniae*. Dublin: Dublin Institute for Advanced Studies, 1963. Reprinted by permission of the School of Celtic Studies, Dublin Institute for Advanced Studies.

Brock, Sebastian (translator)

"A Christian Reaction to the Islamic Capture of Jerusalem," from *The Seventh Century in the West-Syrian Chronicles*, Translated Texts for Historians, vol. 15. Liverpool: Liverpool University Press, 1993. Copyright © 1993 by Sebastian Brock. Reprinted by permission of Liverpool University Press.

Bourke, Vernon J. (translator)

Excerpts from "Life as Pilgrimage," from *Saint Augustine: Confessions*, Fathers of the Church, vol. 21. Washington, D.C.: Catholic University Press, 1953. Reprinted by permission of The Catholic University of America Press.

Cabaniss, Allen (translator)

"Criticizing the Cult of Saints: Claudius of Turin's Complaint," from *Early Medieval Theology*. Edited by G.E. McCraken and Allen Cabaniss. *The Library of Christian Classics*, vol. 9. Philadelphia: Westminster Press, 1957. Copyright © 1957 by Allen Cabaniss.

Clark, Elizabeth A. (translator)

Excerpts from *The Life of Melania the Younger: Introduction, Translation, and Commentary*. New York: The Edwin Mellen Press, 1984. Copyright © 1984 by The Edwin Mellen Press. All rights reserved. Reprinted by permission of The Edwin Mellen Press.

Dutton, P.E. (translator)

"The Monk Bernard's Journey to Jerusalem," and excerpts from "The Translation and Miracles of Saints Marcellinus and Peter," from *Charlemagne's Courtier: The Complete Einhard*. Peterborough, ON.: Broadview Press, 1998. Reprinted by permission of University of Toronto Press.

Emerton, Ephraim (translator)

Excerpts from "Saint Boniface on Pilgrimage: Advice and Criticism," from *The Letters of Saint Boniface,* Records of Civilization: Sources and Studies, vol. 31. New York: Columbia University Press, 1940. Copyright © 1940, 2000 Columbia University Press. Reprinted by permission of Columbia University Press.

France, John (translator)

Excerpts from "Millennial Devotion and Pilgrimage to the Holy Land" and "The Destruction of the Holy Sepulcher" from *The Five Books of the Histories* by Rodulfus Glaber. Edited by John France, Neithard Bulst and Paul Reynolds. Oxford: Clarendon Press, 1989. Copyright © 1989 by John France. Reprinted by permission of Oxford University Press.

Gibb, H.A.R. (translator)

"Ibn Battuta on the Pilgrimage Sites of Mecca," from *The Travels of Ibn Battuta (A.D. 1325–1354)*. Edited by H.A.R. Gibb. Works Issued by The Hakluyt Society, Vol 110. Cambridge: Cambridge University Press, 1958. Reprinted by permission of Cambridge University Press on behalf of *The Hakluyt Society*.

Guillaume, Alfred (translator)

"The Night Journey of Muhammad," from *The Life of Muhammad: A Translation of Ishaq's Sirat Rasul Allah*. Oxford: Oxford University Press, 1955. Reprinted by permission of Oxford University Press, Pakistan.

Head, Thomas (translator)

"On the Saints and their Relics," from *Medieval Hagiography: An Anthology*. New York: Garland Publishing, Inc., 2000. Edited by Thomas Head. Copyright © 2000 by Thomas Head. Reprinted by permission of Taylor & Francis Group LLC, a division of Informa plc; "Popular Devotion and the Peace of God: Letaldus of Micy," from *The Peace of God: Social Violence and Religious Response in France around the Year 1000*. Edited by Thomas Head and Richard Landes. Ithaca: Cornell University Press, 1992. Copyright © 1992 Cornell University Press. Reprinted by permission of Cornell University Press.

Hogarth, James (translator)

"The Pilgrim's Guide to St-James at Compostella," from *The Pilgrim's Guide: A 12th-Century Guide for the Pilgrims to St. James of Compostella.* Abridged by M.A. Stouck. London: Confraternity of St. James, 1992. Reprinted by permission of the Confraternity of St. James. This and other texts are available from the bookshop at www.csj.org.uk/bookshop.

Hopkins, John F. P. (translator)

"The Pilgrimage of Mansa Musa," from *Corpus of Early Arabic Sources for West African History.* Cambridge: Cambridge University Press, 1981. Edited by John F.P. Hopkins. Reprinted by permission of Cambridge University Press.

King, P. D. (translator)

Excerpts from "Charlemagne and the Churches of Rome" and "Regulating Pilgrimage in the Carolingian Empire," from *Charlemagne: Translated Sources.* Lancaster: Kendal, 1987. Copyright © 1987 P.D. King.

Osborne, John (translator)

"The Marvels of Rome," from *Master Gregorius: The Marvels of Rome.* Toronto: Pontifical Institute of Mediaeval Studies, 1987. Reprinted by permission of the Pontifical Institute of Mediaeval Studies.

Panofsky, Erwin (translator)

"Accommodating Pilgrims at the Church of St-Denis," from *Abbot Suger on the Abbey Church of St-Denis and Its Art Treasures*, 2nd edition. Edited by Erwin Panofsky and Gerda Panofsky-Suerel. Princeton: Princeton University Press, 1946. Reprinted by permission of Princeton University Press.

Powell, James A. (translator)

"Medieval *Exempla* and Pilgrimage," from *The Exempla or Illustrative Stories from the Sermones Vulgares of Jacques de Vitry.* Edited by Thomas Frederick Crane. New York: Burt Franklin, 1971. Copyright © 1971 by James A. Powell.

Sheingorn, Pamela (translator)

Excerpts from "Pilgrims and the Miracles of Saint Faith," from *The Book of Sainte Foy.* Philadelphia: University of Pennsylvania Press, 1995. Copyright © 1995 the University of Pennsylvania Press. Reprinted by permission of the University of Pennsylvania Press.

Shinners, John (translator)

"Miracles at the Shrine of Thomas Becket" and "The Jubilee Year of 1300," from *Medieval Popular Religion 1000–1500*, 2nd Edition. Peterborough, ON.: Broadview Press, 2007. Reprinted by permission of University of Toronto Press.

Steck, Francis Borgia (translator) "Mexico Meets Jerusalem," from *Motolinia's History of the Indians of New Spain*. Washington D.C.: Academy of American Franciscan History, 1951. Reprinted by permission of the Academy of American Franciscan History.

Walsh, Patrick Gerard (translator) "Devotion in Italy," from *Letters of St. Paulinus of Nola*, volume 1. Ancient Christian Writers 35. New York: Newman Press, 1966. Reprinted by permission of Paulist Press, Inc. www.paulistpress.com.

Whalen, Brett Edward (translator) "A Miracle of Mary Magdalene," from *Le dossier Vézelien de Marie Madeleine: Invention et translation des reliques en 1265–1267*. Edited by V. Saxer. Subsidia Hagiographica, vol. 57. Brussels: Société des Bollandistes, 1975; Excerpts from "Monastic Criticisms of Crusading and Pilgrimage: Letters of Saint Anselm," from *S. Anselmi: Opera Omnia*. Edited by F.S. Schmitt. Edinburgh: Thomas Nelson & Sons, Ltd., 1940–1961. "The Breviary of Jerusalem", from the *Brevarius de Hierosolyma (forma a)*, in *Itineraria et alia geographica*, Corpus Christianorum Series Latina, vol. 175. Turnhout: Brepols, 1965. "The Discovery of the Holy Patriarchs: Relics, Ecclesiastical Politics, and Sacred History in Twelfth-Century Crusader Palestine," *Historical Reflections/Relexions Historiques* 27 (2001): 157–76. Excerpts from "The 'Saracen' Sack of Saint Peter's Basilica," from *Le Liber Pontificalis*. Edited by L. Duchesne. Bibliothèque des écoles francaises d'Athènes et de Rome, vol. 2. Paris: E. de Boccard, 1955. Reprinted by permission of Brett Edward Whalen.

Wilkinson, John, Joyce Hill and William Francis Ryan (translators) "Al-Idrisi on the Holy City of Jerusalem," from *Jerusalem Pilgrimage 1099–1185*. Edited by John Wilkinson, Joyce Hill and William Francis Ryan. London: The Hakluyt Society, 1988. Reprinted by permission of *The Hakluyt Society*.

Wright, David (translator) "Pilgrimage and Satire in *The Canterbury Tales*." Abridged by M.-A. Stouck in *Medieval Saints: A Reader*. Peterborough, ON: Broadview Press, 1999. Originally published in *The Canterbury Tales* by Geoffrey Chaucer. London: Fontana Press, 1964. Reprinted by permission of Oxford University Press.

ΞADINGS IN MEDIEVAL CIVILIZATIONS AND CULTURES
Series Editor: Paul Edward Dutton

"Readings in Medieval Civilizations and Cultures is in my opinion
the most useful series being published today."
— William C. Jordan, Princeton University